the silence of sodom

the silence of sodom

HOMOSEXUALITY IN MODERN CATHOLICISM

MARK D. JORDAN

the university of chicago press

chicago and london

The University of Chicago Press, Chicago 60637
The University of Chicago Press, Ltd., London
© 2000 by Mark D. Jordan
All rights reserved. Published 2000
Printed in the United States of America
ISBN: 0-226-41041-2 (cloth)
09 08 07 06 05 04 03 02 01 00   1 2 3 4 5

Library of Congress Cataloging-in-Publication Data

Jordan, Mark D.
    The silence of Sodom: homosexuality in modern Catholicism / Mark D. Jordan.
          p.   cm.
    Includes bibliographical references and index.
    ISBN 0-226-41041-2 (cloth : alk. paper)
    1. Homosexuality—Religious aspects—Catholic Church.   2. Catholic Church—
    Doctrines.   I. Title.
    BX1795.H66 J67 2000
    261.8'35766'08822—dc21   99-042145
                                                                          CIP

for Bill   "PRIDE—A DEEPER LOVE"

CONTENTS

Acknowledgments   ix

1. The Pope Converts: Imagination, Bureaucracy, Silence   1

CHURCH WORDS   19
2. Teaching by Threatening   21
3. Bureaucratic Morals   51

CHURCH LIVES   83
4. Living Inside   85
5. Memoirs of Priestly Sodomy   113
6. Reproducing "Father"   141
7. Clerical Camp   179

CHURCH DREAMS   209
8. Reiteration, *or* The Pleasures of Obedience   211
9. Repentance, *or* Schools for New Speech   237

Notes   263
Works Cited   285
Index   307

ACKNOWLEDGMENTS

WRITTEN AS IT WAS away from universities, this book depends more than most on the gifts of benefactors and the patience of colleagues. I wrote a first version of it while on a fellowship from the John S. Guggenheim Memorial Foundation. I thank the foundation for giving me a year in which to relearn the severe pleasures of intellectual life.

Colleagues have commented on various pieces of the book in its many stages. Among them I must thank Mark Holtz (who disagrees with me sharply), Ed Ingebretsen, Peter Jordan (whose late-night soliloquies kept me writing), Ron Lee, Doug Mitchell (who suffered my authorial neuroses equably), Kathryn Tanner, and the members of South Bend's Erasmian Brotherhood & Coffee Klatsch.

Now that the book is written, I am happy to be returning to university life at Emory, where being an openly gay man who thinks about Catholic theology is not a cause for scandal—or silence.

the pope converts

IMAGINATION, BUREAUCRACY, SILENCE

IMAGINE THIS. Overnight, God changes the hearts of a majority of officials in the Vatican. They awake in the morning convinced that the Roman Catholic church's condemnations of "homosexual acts" are both untrue and unjust. They resolve to revoke them. What would they have to revise in church doctrine or practice in order to correct the teachings about gays and lesbians?*

---

* I will often use "Catholic" to mean Roman Catholic and "the church" to mean one or another bureaucracy in the network of Roman Catholic institutions. I don't mean to suggest by my usage that the sum of Roman Catholic institutions is the true church or that other Christian institutions couldn't make an equal claim to being "catholic." I only intend to begin with our ordinary shorthand for talking about these things. By the book's end, there will be more than enough questions about both the meaning of "Catholic" and the Christianity of bureaucracies.

To give this question any force, we have to picture the Holy Spirit be-
stowing courage as well as insight. Imagine, for example, that particular
morning-after at the Congregation for the Doctrine of the Faith (CDF),
the Vatican's principal bureau for doctrinal surveillance. Each ecclesiastical
bureaucrat is aware of a profound change of heart in himself (the masculine
pronoun is appropriate). Who will be the first to broach the topic? Who
will take the risk? Imagine that it is a morning toward the end of May, say
the Monday after Pentecost, the commemoration of the outpouring of the
Holy Spirit on the first Christian community. Outside, the signs of early
summer: the sky is "almost black with its excess of blue, and the new grass
already deep, but still vivid, and the white roses tumble. . . ."[1] Inside, dry
mouths and palpitations over coffee.

———

So we must imagine a divine infusion of courage—not to say of indepen-
dence, that rarest of virtues in any bureaucracy. Let us suppose that God
has worked a change in the pope himself (here the masculine pronoun is
obligatory). It would take at least a thorough conversion in the pope to
make the doctrinal change possible, and it would take a pope not enchained
by his handlers to make it plausible. So let us imagine that the pope's heart
has been converted and then comforted with courage. He has decided to
right a wrong done to homosexuals over centuries. His advisers have persuaded him at least to go slowly—to "study" the problem before acting
on it. Rumor rushes down the clerical layers: The moral teachings about
homosexuality are to be corrected by papal command in obedience to God's
will, in faithfulness to the message of Christ. The Holy Father asks, What
is required for the thorough correction of the teachings?

———

No serious answer to the question can be simple. In fact, to change Catholic
teachings about homosexual acts would require changes under many other
headings of Catholic theology. "Conservatives" are right to suspect this,
though they are wrong to think that this is a reason for *not* correcting the
teachings. The moral teachings on this topic are just the most visible sign
of a larger failure. If the church could be so violently wrong about this for
so many centuries, there must be some deep deformity in church gover-

nance. Any correction of teachings about homosexuality will have to begin by considering topics as different as the structures of church power and the styles of moral theology, the hypocrisies of confessional practice and the screening of seminary candidates. The correction would end . . . but that is a question.

——

What is required for a thorough correction of the teachings? No one knows. Homosexuality has been silenced so successfully in the Catholic church that we do not have the kinds of evidence required for a convincing answer. A subject that Catholic theologians cannot discuss during centuries except with thunder, derision, or disgust is not a subject on which Catholic theology is ready to speak.

Some theologians have indeed begun to speak about it more freely in the last thirty years, and they have made some helpful and even bold beginnings. We now have notable first essays in lesbian and gay theology, not least because we have lesbian and gay appropriations of liberation theology, feminist theory, the writing of church history, and so on. But three decades cannot undo two millennia. Catholic theologians will have to be able to speak freely about homosexuality for many years before they can write serious moral assessments of it.

In order for them to "speak freely," many changes will be required. It is not enough for the CDF to promise that it will no longer prosecute moral theologians who dissent from its diagnosis of homosexual orientation (though just that now seems utopian fantasy). The church, in some broader sense, will have to encourage homosexual Catholics to live openly and proudly. Serious moral theology cannot be principally the framing and manipulation of quasi-legal propositions. It must begin and end in the discovery of particular lives under grace. Lesbian and gay lives will have to become audible to the church, readable within it, before their graces can be discerned and described.

Indeed, the church will need to recognize homosexual saints in order to learn God's will in same-sex love, since it is typically and properly saints that instruct Catholic communities about how to live. By "homosexual saints" I do not mean lesbians or gays who feel obligated to martyr themselves in celibacy. I mean saints with lovers. The icons that show "Harvey

Milk of San Francisco" are not just jokes, in good taste or bad. They are reminders that Catholic theology needs to watch how saints live a way of life before it can say much about it.

———

Correcting Catholic teachings on homosexuality is not only or mainly a matter of proposing amendments to specific documents. The official doctrine is more deeply embedded than that. It is more intimately connected to old arrangements of institutional power. Changing the language without reforming institutional arrangements would be useless, even if it were possible. The most important relations between Catholicism and homosexuality are not embodied in official propositions about homosexuality, nor even in official regulations for homosexual behavior. The forces at work here are not only the forces of words.

———

Imagine morning again. The Holy Spirit has indeed worked overnight in the Vatican, but microscopically. Conceive a middle-aged staff "theologian" who has spent an entire career being cautious. He awakes to find that his convictions have changed about—about *this*, of all things—living as a homosexual. Disturbed and yet compelled, he might try to broach the topic with colleagues in a roundabout way. Perhaps he would raise it more directly with a particular confidant. Or perhaps he would simply delay, hoping that his peculiar mood would pass.

On this May morning, his behavior would resemble that of many closeted gay men in the Catholic clergy. They feel compelled to play a sad game of concealed solicitation, of saying and not saying, of showing what they want only to those who surely want the same thing. Our staff theologian will be just like someone cruising from inside the closet. He may well have had that guilty experience, too.

———

Behind the fixed rhetoric of the Vatican's bureaucratic speech are comprehensive structures for creating and enforcing clerical "discipline." For centuries now, these structures have been much preoccupied with controlling the appearance and the reality of clerical sexuality, especially homosexuality. The official words about homosexual activity are anchored in an apparatus for disciplining the facts of homosexual activity in the clergy.* Whatever the original causal relations between official teachings and clerical discipline might have been, it is now certainly true that clerical discipline keeps many clergymen from speaking candidly about the possibility of changing the official teachings. It keeps some of them from even thinking about that possibility.

––––––

Clerical discipline shows itself as well in the very bureaucratic style of the modern Catholic church's moral "teachings," which is to say, its moral regulation. Whenever the Vatican does change moral teachings on a controversial point, as it did 150 years ago in the case of slavery, it insists all the more loudly that nothing has changed. Bureaucratic speech strives to maintain the illusion of unchanging control. So Vatican pronouncements work hard to convince us that nothing important ever changes in church teachings—or could change.

––––––

Imagine a final version of that Monday after Pentecost. A staff theologian awakens after a night of cruising in the city—perhaps Monte Caprino on foot, for old time's sake, or the "Capolinea" and the "Colosseo quadrato." Or perhaps he has just returned from a vacation in lay clothing on the shores of the Aegean or at a gay enclave beyond the Alps. Over the years he has enjoyed regular sexual encounters—some negotiated in gay bars, some bought on the streets, some solicited within the concealing walls of church institutions. He has always been careful to hide his employment and usually his priestly status when consorting with laypeople. Not from guilt, which he claims not to feel, but from prudence. He will narrate his encounters, deliciously, to one or another friend in an informal club of similarly active clergymen, but he professes to find the very idea of "coming out" tasteless. Yet he discovers this morning that hearts have been changed

* The notion of who constitutes Catholic "clergy" has varied tremendously over time and across different church regimes. I use it here with a clear center, but without clear boundaries. The center comprises priests who are ordained either for a diocese or in one of the religious orders. Further out from the center are various groups on the way to the priesthood and the male members of religious orders who do not seek ordination. The term "religious" contrasts any member of a religious order, ordained or not, with a member of the diocesan clergy.

around him. What has seemed so long a tidy arrangement of his private pleasures is now being called an injustice. How enthusiastically do you think he will respond to proposals for correction in official teachings?

———

The premise of my Pentecost fantasy is not entirely hypothetical. Since gay Catholics believe that God does try to guide even the Vatican bureaucracy, and since most of them also believe that the Vatican's present teachings on homosexuality are not inspired by God, they must trust God to offer during each night and during each day the grace to change the Vatican. Every morning in Rome is a morning on which the pope or his curia could be converted. If they don't convert today, that need not imply some lack in divine will. It may imply something about human stubbornness. It may also suggest the magnitude of the changes required.

———

The most important theological facts about Catholicism and homosexuality are not the bureaucratic words that Catholic authorities speak. The truly significant facts concern the homosexuality of the Catholic church itself— of members of its priesthood and its clerical culture, of its rituals and spiritual traditions. If the pope had succeeded in miraculously changing all the official words this morning, he still would not have touched the deepest connections between homosexuality and Catholicism. He would not have admitted the church's richest knowledge of the homoerotic.

———

The facts or the effects of homosexual clergy are hardly unique to the Catholic church. The current controversies over ordaining "practicing" homosexuals in the major denominations suggest how ecumenical the situation is. Nor are closeted clergymen confined to Christianity. In Apuleius's *Golden Ass,* one of the best-known ancient Latin novels, the priests of Cybele purchase a donkey, who happens to be our unlucky hero Lucius in animal form.[2] There is some suggestion that they mean to enjoy his sex immediately, but their interest turns to a "built" farmer whom they invite to their private banquet in a small town. Their well-plotted orgy is prevented by the braying of Lucius, who summons the locals. The priests are driven out of town by mockery. (Do note that these pagan priests are neither exiled to permanent silence nor burned at the stake.)

This kind of story—there are others like it in Greco-Roman antiquity—raises interesting questions about the links between sexual identity and holiness. The stories can be multiplied many times over by evidence from other cultures.[3] Is it that holy figures need somehow to be set aside from the worldly game of marrying and child-rearing, which is to say, of alliance and inheritance? Are members of sexual minorities, of a "third sex," freaky or uncanny in a way that associates them with the divine? These questions direct us to analogies for what could otherwise seem particularly Catholic arrangements. But they can also distract us from looking at the evidence right in front of us. It is often easier to think about the priests of Cybele than the priests at the parish just down the block.

———

Within any society that universally persecutes same-sex desires, those desires will be kept silent. When members of that society's religious institutions feel them, they will treat them as secrets. When they act on their desires, they will do so secretly. More elaborate priestly or clerical secrecies will be constructed when the religion itself reinforces or initiates persecution of same-sex desires. The most elaborate secrecies will be found in religious institutions that condemn same-sex desires fiercely while creating conditions under which they can flourish: the situation of modern Catholicism.

———

In what follows, I consider the multiple forms or places of male homosexuality within modern Catholicism. (The restriction to men I will explain in a moment.) It is worth doing so for a number of reasons, whatever one's views about the truth of Catholic dogma.

Throughout much of the world, first, the Catholic church remains the most powerful of Christian organizations. Even in the United States, which has never been a "Catholic country," Catholic bishops enter aggressively into public debates over homosexuality and other matters of sexual morality. They are able to do so because religious condemnation remains the most potent homophobic rhetoric. So the features of Catholic homosexuality are particularly consequential outside the church.

Second, Catholic homoeroticism has a distinguished and varied history. Catholic clerical arrangements, for example, are very old by Christian standards. They produce rich articulations of male-male desire, both because of centuries of compulsory priestly celibacy and because of the enormous development of all-male religious orders.

Third, and most importantly, the Catholic management of same-sex desire has been decisive in European and American histories of what we now call "homosexuality." This is not just a matter of moral teachings, national legislation, or international bureaucracies for enforcement and punishment. In ways that I will analyze further on, Catholicism has been one of the most homoerotic of widely available modern cultures, offering encouragement, instruction, and relatively safe haven to many homosexuals. You will not understand modern homosexuality unless you understand Catholic homosexuality, and you cannot understand Catholic homosexuality unless you begin with the clergy.

———

Other general arguments could be made for the importance of paying particular attention to homosexuality in the Catholic church. But the most telling argument for me is very particular. The Catholic tradition is my Christian tradition. It is not only the one in which I found Christianity or the one I know best by experience, but it is the tradition within which I have had to work out the central paradox for any gay Christian: many Christian churches are at once the most homophobic and the most homoerotic of institutions. They seem cunningly designed to condemn same-sex desire and to elicit it, to persecute it and to instruct it. I sometimes call this the paradox of the "Beloved Disciple": "Come recline beside me and put your head on my chest, but don't dare conceive of what we do as erotic." Perhaps it is more clearly seen as the paradox of the Catholic Jesus, the paradox created by an officially homophobic religion in which an all-male clergy sacrifices male flesh before images of God as an almost naked man. How could such a religion not be officially homophobic—and also intensely homoerotic?

———

I have said that my topic would be male homosexuality, and I should underscore that limitation. Because I am concerned with internal connections between Catholic homosexuality and its most official impositions of silence, I focus on the priesthood and the male religious orders. Women are still sufficiently disenfranchised in the Catholic church to make lesbianism a separate concern in analyses of the exercise of church power. I know by observation and from historical study that women's religious communities have provided important places in which to work out both lesbian desire and women's gifts for Christian ministry. But women's religious communities have yet to gain much power over the articulation of official moral theology or the fixing of church policy. So I shall concentrate on closeted men in the clergy and religious orders. They are at once more powerful in the church and more familiar to me.

In any case, we need to think of Catholic lesbianism and Catholic gayness separately. Categories that combine gay men with lesbians are categories created to persecute both. The false sameness implied by a category like "sodomy" or "homosexuality" is useful for dehumanizing condemnation, but not for careful analysis. If lesbians and gays must now band together in self-defense, that does not mean that they can be honestly conceived in a single theological category. I certainly don't propose such a category in this book. I work in the opposite direction, focusing on male-male desires and actions. I do so as much to mark the limits of my own experience as to contest a false generalization.

It can be objected that I am being inconsistent in my scruples. After all, similar difficulties afflict the categories that are supposed to cover the range of identities or behaviors in men who (sometimes, regularly, often) desire (to see, touch, love, marry) other men. "Modern gay man" is just as much a historically constructed category as "male homosexual" or "invert" or "Urning" or "sodomite." It can become just as conceptually confusing and just as personally confining. I reply to this objection not with a windy interruption on the subject of identity logics, but by saying: Read on to see how I try to reflect the diversity of "gay" lives.

In saying that I will concentrate on male-male desires and actions within official church words and hidden church lives, I don't mean to erase gay men's debt to women's political movements or to feminist "theory." Both the theories of modern gayness and the practices of gay community-building have long depended on the earlier labors of women, especially lesbian women. If the study of lesbianism in women's religious communities or parish life has sometimes seemed less newsworthy than gay priests, it has often been more candid and more intelligent.[4] When I restrict my view for the most part to Catholic gayness, it is not because I want to deny what women have done or said. Nor am I trying to repeat the misogynistic silencing of women. Rather, I am addressing only what I have seen and understood about male-male desire in its relation to Catholic power. I refuse to practice ventriloquism in lesbian voices.

———

Easier said than done, because modern terminology, whether Catholic or secular, has been constructed to confuse all same-sex desire or action. It has been constructed, that is, to assimilate women's experience with women to men's experience with men. Catholic moral theology, for example, now talks in general about "homosexuals" and "homosexuality," and the arguments it deploys against both are supposed to apply equally to men and women. In fact, the theological imagination of Catholicism and its institutional arrangements are preoccupied almost entirely by male-male desire.

In what follows, I will try to use more candid terminology. When I paraphrase church teachings or rehearse our everyday conceptions, I will have to talk about "homosexuals" and "homosexuality"—or "sodomites" and "sodomy." Those terms will refer to women and men. I will use "gay," by contrast, only of men, making it the strict complement of "lesbian" for women. In my usage, all gays are men, all lesbians women. When I discuss considerations or circumstances affecting both groups, I will either use both terms or else the combination "lesbigay."

I do not use a more expansive tag—like the awkward "LGBT" for lesbian, gay, bisexual, transgendered—because the desires, actions, or identities described as "bisexual" or "transgendered" do not figure in my analysis. I do not have anything to say about them. Although our political sentiments and our worshipping communities need to be inclusive, our analyses must be precise. My analysis is concerned precisely with male-male eroticism in modern Catholicism.

———

This book is constructed as three steps or stages of analysis. I could say, just as accurately, that they are three acts of literary imagination to be performed in sequence. In them, the imagination attends to very particular things—the rhetorical patterns in some recent Vatican documents, the circumstances of clerical homosexuality in America, the personal and institutional motives that keep homosexuals in the Catholic church or move them out of it. The acts of imagination attend to these particular things because they are all that we can now describe. We are not ready for mature Catholic teachings about male homoeroticism. We are in no position to recount the gay Catholic's general history (if it even makes sense to wish for such a narrative). We don't know what stable forms male-male love among Catholics will take a hundred years on. The most we can hope for is to be articulate about the things in front of us and to be cunning in trying to invent ways of talking beyond them.

———

The first section of this book is called "Church Words." It analyzes the rhetoric of the church's bureaucratic speech about sexual morality. My point is not to argue, much less demonstrate, that official Catholic documents are usually wrong when they talk about homosexuality. I don't think that the documents call for counterargument, because I don't think that they mean to authorize discussion. They demand instead a kind of media analysis, what used to be called rhetorical study. Many official texts are scripts for preventing serious speech by scrambling it. To avoid the scrambling, we must recognize some of the rhetorical devices that the documents typically use—devices of unstable terminology, incoherent principles, fallacious argument. We must then acknowledge that the documents are part of a much larger and much older program of theological rhetoric. The first part of the book isn't a history of recent moral teachings approved by the Catholic hierarchy. It is a skeptical catalog of some typical devices in those teachings and an introduction to the rhetorical program behind them.

Those who cannot bear to reread recent Vatican documents on homosexuality are welcome to skip chapter 2. And those who have already gotten beyond the rhetorical program of Catholic moral theology since Trent can spare themselves chapter 3 as well. These two chapters make for hurtful and enraging reading, but then they treat of wounding texts.

———

The book's second section is called "Church Lives." In it I try to act on the notion that the church's knowledge about male homosexuality can be found elsewhere than in its official documents. I look for that knowledge in institutional arrangements, in fragments of history, and in unspoken but widely known features of clerical culture. The failure of official Catholic teachings on homosexuality is a failure both of official speech about lives and of the official lives themselves. The failure in speech follows on the failure to admit the enormous churchly "science" of male homoeroticism, the long institutional experimentation with it. The second section looks particularly at how Catholic speech about homosexuality is blocked by the melodrama of (open) secrecy that surrounds clerical homosexuality. The effects of this melodrama are found everywhere.

———

The book's third section distinguishes two kinds of "Church Dreams." Some dreams bind us to repeat certain forms of communal suffering, while others help us find communities without that needless suffering. The first dreams are illusions; the second, hopes. The task for imagination in this section is to identify what real choices among communities are open to gay Catholics while they wait for the official church to begin articulating mature teachings about their lives. It is not just a search for a Christian community in which one can "feel comfortable." It is rather a quest for a community in which gay Catholics can speak their beliefs as creed, as prayer, as sacrament in liturgy. After all, gay Catholics are silenced most in the present church not by being asked to parrot homophobic texts or to lie about their lives. They are most of all denied adequate words and rites, truthful preaching and sacrament, to articulate their faithful lives.

———

These dreamy hopes provoke an obvious question. Can anyone live happily as a gay man within Christian faith? Edmund White puts the question as an exasperated accusation: "I never thought I'd live to see the day when gays would be begging to be let back in to the Christian church, which is clearly our enemy."[5] Unfortunately, we could speak the same accusation at most of our major institutions, which have *at best* been explicitly homophobic until the last decades. Why participate in the churches? Indeed, why participate in the universities or the publishing houses or the major newspapers?

The alternative to participation is not Bohemianism, but barbarism. Thinking about how one can be gay and a member of some Christian community is just a form of a question that every homosexual faces: How can

I make a place for myself in what has been and mostly continues to be a homophobic culture? To say this differently: For many gay Christians, thinking about church membership is the occasion for contemplating social membership or cultural identity generally. In the third part of this book, in the section on dreams, I try to present such an occasion.

———

I do not mean to suggest that questions about staying in the church should be dismissed as silly. Compelling cases can be made that identifying as a Catholic (or Christian) at this moment in American life can only be a form of collaboration with homosexuality's most dangerous enemies. I try to examine some of these cases throughout the book. But as I have already hinted, we have a great deal to learn about homosexuality from modern Catholicism, even if we never were or will not long remain Catholic. So, too, we have a lot to learn from modern homosexuality about Catholicism, perhaps especially if we are interested in continuing to conceive ourselves as somehow Catholic.

———

Who am I to write this book? Who am I to say such things? Any Catholic has been taught to practice self-examination and even self-abasement before daring to voice criticism, especially against the church. Self-examination can be an important antidote to pride or anger or vanity. It can also be an effective means for enforcing silence about Catholic homosexuality. It can function as one of a series of constraints, of double binds, that contrive to make it impossible for anyone to speak—except for the "competent authorities" in the Vatican.

If I were a former priest or member of a religious order, my criticisms would be dismissed as the bitter fruit of a failure to live up to my vows. I am neither a former priest nor a former religious, so they can be dismissed as uninformed.

If I were an accredited moral theologian teaching at a pontifical faculty, my criticisms would be dismissed as defection. I am not such a moral theologian, so they can be dismissed as the rant of an amateur.

If I were not "out," my criticisms would be dismissed as evidence of closeted gayness. I am "out," so they can be dismissed as my agenda.

These double binds are constructed to prevent anyone from talking about Catholic homosexuality except in the approved ways. The only people who are permitted to speak about it are just those who are guaranteed never to speak about it honestly. The only people who are authorized to speak about it are the silencing authorities themselves.

———

There are similar double binds of separation and inclusion. The topic of clerical homosexuality is connected immediately to a dozen enormous topics: the church's stereotyping of gender roles, its denigration of women, its preference for "conservative" political programs and regimes, its greed, and so on. But we have to start somewhere if we are to speak at all, and we have to speak within limits if we are to make sense.

There is also a more particular reason for treating male homosexuality as a separate topic within modern Catholicism: Catholicism itself treats it that way. The separation of the topic is not so much a testimony to its theological importance as to its political charge. Disputes over homosexuality are seen to be particularly threatening to the "unity" of the church. They are certainly threatening to its present political arrangements.

———

Then there is the double bind of Catholic diversity—of the historical, geographical, and cultural differences hidden within the term "Catholic." How can anyone presume to say anything general about so many different ways of life? This question can paralyze, in just the way that historical learning often does. The more you know of the evidence, the less you can speak about it in any coherent way.

In what follows, I emphasize the diversity of Catholic homosexualities even in modern times. I show why I am suspicious of narrative histories about homosexuality in Christianity, as I resist statistically based abstractions. Indeed, I have broken the text up into short sections, some no longer than an aphorism, precisely to remind the reader of how fragmentary are the speeches now available to us. But I do persist in trying to speak.

———

How to think of these fragments? They are *not* bits of colored glass for a mosaic, because they do not belong to a single picture or pattern. They are *not* photos and clippings for a scrapbook, because they do not belong to a single, collective life. If anything, they are scraps from notebooks—from diaries, reading journals, commonplace books.

The writing model I have followed is one that Walter Benjamin imagined for his never-accomplished study of the Parisian shopping arcades—which is to say, of nineteenth-century capitalism seen through the prism of the arcades. In sheaf "N" of materials for the project, Benjamin describes the method of his projected study as the art of quotation without quotation marks, of "literary montage."[6] "The first step along this path will be to carry the montage principle over into history. In this way to build up the large constructions out of the smallest, precisely fashioned structural elements. To detect the crystal of the total event in the analysis of the small, single moment" (p. 575, frag. N2, 6). The kind of insight afforded by montage is what Benjamin describes in a series of remarks headed by the word "Waking": "It's not that the past casts its light on the present. Rather an image is that in which the Then and the Now flash together into a constellation. In other words: image is dialectics at a standstill" (pp. 556–57, frag. N2a, 3).

If you change Benjamin's visual metaphors into metaphors of speech, you have something like my ideal. I am convinced that the homosexuality of modern Catholicism can't be written about except by "constellating" moral theology, church history, queer theory, the novel of manners, and utopian reveries. By gathering scraps from these kinds of texts, I hope to demonstrate both the inadequacy of official Catholic speeches about homosexuality and how challenging it will be to create more adequate ones.

———

In no way do I imagine that what I have written is comprehensive. I will have succeeded beyond my hopes if I have gathered one or two interesting samples under each of the main topics treated. If someone approaches tomorrow with a dozen, richer examples, that will be all to the good.

Better scraps of speech than silence. If we let the diversity of the evidence frighten us away from speaking at all, we surrender speech to its abusers. There are, of course, any number of prominent Catholics who are content to speak endlessly about homosexuality. They are the broadcasters of the official teachings, and they are curiously unconstrained by historical evidence or by the diversity of present experience, as we shall see. To be bound up in silence by the fear of overgeneralizing would be to allow the most aggressive programs of generalization to go forward without dissent.

———

Other contradictions bind you, my reader. Many of you who have the greatest familiarity with my topics will also have the greatest stake in denying what I say. I am not thinking in the first instance of church-employed experts in history and theology. I refer instead to closeted clergymen whose hatred of their own desire has become strict "orthodoxy"—I mean, homophobic rage.

———

This book is not a remedy for the failure of Catholic teachings on homosexuality. We are not ready for full Catholic teachings about same-sex love—or female-male love, for that matter. The book is, instead, a rudimentary vocabulary, a first dictionary, of the unexpectedly varied expressions of Catholic gayness.

———

According to an etymology that goes back in the Latin tradition at least to St. Jerome, patron of Catholic Bible translators, the place-name "Sodom" in Genesis 18–19 means "mute" or "silent beast."[7] Various explanations of this etymology are supplied by later theologians. Sodomites are rendered animal-like by their addiction to physical pleasure. Or sodomites lose rationality by acting against nature. Or the activity of sodomites is to be shrouded in silence among Christians. Sodomy is, after all, the "nameless" sin or crime—according to another misreading of the Scriptures (Ephesians 5:3). So Catholic confessors and preachers are warned against speaking about the sin with any clarity. They are not to inquire after it or preach against it for fear of inciting the laity to deeds not yet discovered. But the deepest sodomitic silence does not gag the laity. The explanations I have just been paraphrasing come from priestly texts written for priestly audiences. The same texts insist that sodomy is typically a priestly sin.

———

Over the last millennium, Catholic writers have exercised themselves in painting pictures of the sodomitic soul—of the soul of the sinner given over to the practice of sodomy. They always depict the soul from outside, from far away, because of course they have never seen it up close. They show it as a Sodom in miniature—a city of anguished secrecy, of perpetual exile, of deserved death, over which fiery clouds always rain cinders. They project every vice into this city. They compare its inhabitants with the worst of history's criminals.

If these garish pictures seem to be projections of fantasy, they still capture something real. Instead of depicting the souls of average Catholics who love members of their own sex, they show the hellishly intertwined lives of closeted inhabitants of church institutions and their pharisaical persecutors. There is indeed a silent Sodom. It is housed within the structures of churchly power. Its silence must be disturbed before there can be mature Catholic teachings on "homosexuality"—or mature criticisms of how "homosexuality" itself fails to describe gay Catholic lives. The silence of Sodom envelops a Catholic science of sodomy, of homosexuality, about which we must now speak.

church ✝ words

2

teaching by threatening

TOO MANY CONTEMPORARY discussions of Catholic homosexuality circle endlessly within the words of a few recent
documents, the oldest of which dates no further back than
1975. Historical foreshortening is typical of official moral
theology, which wants to squeeze its readers into the prevailing regulation. What matters is the current ruling. The
complexities and contradictions, the bitter disagreements
and insistent paradoxes of the tangled Catholic traditions,
are silenced. No editors of Catholic tradition are more
effective than the Vatican bureaucrats.

More is lost than theological history. The impoverished
language of the official documents hardly tries to register
the variety of homosexual lives. On the contrary, the documents turn sharply away from real lives into what can be
described most charitably as simplifications. Described less
charitably, they are caricatures. We are repeatedly told that

homosexual lives are necessarily selfish, solitary, bitter, sterile, hedonistic, and narcissistic. When it comes to homosexual life, such caricatures are dictated not only by strong programs of rhetoric, but by politically motivated institutional hypocrisies.

———

Fortunately or unfortunately, the handful of recent pronouncements on homosexuality do indeed display the most important rhetorical strategies in the contemporary repertoire of official teachings on homosexuality. They can give us what we need, so long as we read them for their rhetoric and not for their "content."

In urging that we look at the rhetoric and not the "content" or "arguments" of the official documents, I mean that we should examine how the documents are designed to move readers—to move them to opinion, passion, or action. This kind of reading resembles in some ways modern and "postmodern" critiques of ideology or authorized knowledge, as it also resembles the "suspicion" practiced so astutely by liberation theology. It resembles them, but it has older origins. I learned it first not from Nietzsche or Foucault or Freire or Gutierrez, but from the Gospels.

From my untutored reading, the Gospels seemed much concerned with distinguishing real teaching authority from its authoritarian enemies, true preaching from its aggressive imitations. When I propose to look at what official documents mean to achieve rhetorically, I don't mean to recommend anything other than what the Gospel authors show by example in many places.

———

What distinguishes "bad" theological discourse is not that it is rhetorical, but that its rhetoric works in dangerous ways. One of these is a kind of numbing repetition that impoverishes language. Another is the invocation of absolute authorities. Another, the making of violent threats. These rhetorical devices are difficult to analyze, especially when they are well constructed. Their most powerful effects prevent analysis.

To study this kind of speech, we need to step aside from its glare—or to look at it in rough reflection, as Perseus did with Medusa. We need to identify deceits about homosexuality without being deceived by them. So we cannot engage the documents "on their own terms." We cannot politely accept their categories, their rules of evidence, their patterns of argument. The categories, the rules, and the patterns enact much of the documents' forceful homophobia.

———

It will be objected that in urging a rhetorical analysis I am failing to do justice to the arguments in the official documents. I have two answers.

First, theological arguments don't work outside the rhetorical structures in which they occur. Individual arguments succeed or fail as part of larger persuasions. In looking to the rhetorical properties of the official documents, I am considering what makes the arguments within those documents possible. Rhetorical structure is not something that follows or is added to real arguments. Rhetorical structure comes before arguments: it is what gives them their force.

Second, even within the rhetorical structures of the official documents, many arguments proceed deceptively. They typically propose certain norms for human sexuality based on schematic, idealized views of both sexuality and marriage. These views are the reverse of the negative caricatures of homosexuality. For example, they restrict sexual activity to marriage because (only?) marital love is exclusive, enduring, and transcendent in its complementarity and fertility. What kind of a statement is that? Not a statement of statistical fact, certainly. It is at best the statement of a utopian norm, derived from selective and contestable readings of nature, the Scriptures, and Catholic traditions. And what commands those selective readings? A particular structure of authority. Rather than attending to the endless gyrations of the supposed arguments, I go directly to the authority projected by the rhetoric.

———

As soon as we look to the rhetoric of some official documents, we confront another obstacle. It is our own outrage. The documents about homosexuality are so carelessly offensive, so casually violent, that they provoke many readers to fury. Rage is indeed an appropriate index to the rhetorical intensity of some of the documents. Any weaker reaction would be a misreading.

———

Can someone who has not been the object of sustained, official hate speech appreciate how it feels to hear it? To hear it exempted from criticism because it is "religious"? To hear it defended not only as true and reasonable, but as the very measure of rationality? Let me propose this test. You have not felt the force of religious hate speech until you can condemn it angrily and in public precisely as hate speech. You have not taken the measure of the official rhetoric until you can sympathize with the urge to denounce its authors as "ministers of hate" and their proposals as a "witch hunt."[1]

Once you have felt that sympathy or uttered those denunciations, you must make a choice. You can either stop reading or you can force yourself to read on steadily in the service of some important purpose. My purpose in continuing to read the documents is to understand at least how the official rhetorical strategies and categorical schemes achieve their effects, not just so that we can contest them, but so that we can discover what lies behind them. Such reading requires self-control. It does not require the pretense that the documents are acceptable public speech. They are not.

———

Two official documents in particular have confined contemporary discussions of Catholic homosexuality. The first, the *Declaration regarding Certain Questions of Sexual Ethics,* was issued by the Congregation for the Doctrine of the Faith at the end of 1975. The second, the *Letter to all Catholic Bishops on the Pastoral Care of Homosexual Persons,* was released in the fall of 1986. Both the *Declaration* and the *Letter* are signed by the prefect or head of the CDF—in 1975, by Cardinal Šeper; in 1986, by Cardinal Ratzinger. Each was approved for publication by the reigning pope (Paul VI and John Paul II). The 1986 *Declaration* further claims that it was written at the pope's command (no. 2). Half a century ago, it would have been an exacting task to establish the exact degree of obligation imposed by the two documents. Nowadays the finer distinctions among official statements about morals are blurred both by the Vatican and its critics. I will presume here just that the *Declaration* and the *Letter* represent the official teaching of the Vatican and that both require serious consideration by those who want to understand the current position of the self-styled "Magisterium" or "Teaching Authority" of the Catholic church.

———

There are many, many other documents, with competing messages and various degrees of authority. Consider, as on a scale, the few paragraphs about homosexuality in the new *Catechism of the Catholic Church* approved in 1992, the private advice of the CDF that same year on opposing equal civil rights for homosexuals, and a series of fourteen articles published during 1997 in the Vatican's newspaper, the *Osservatore Romano*. Then there are innumerable statements by individual bishops or regional bishops' conferences, from Catholic associations or institutions, and from individual believers with one or another degree of authority.[2]

Indeed, one of the most striking features of recent Catholic moral teaching is its quantity. The other is the amount of tension or disagreement hidden behind apparent uniformity. These documents are hardly consistent, even with themselves. They show the extent to which homosexuality has become a disputed issue in contemporary Catholicism—or rather the extent to which "Catholicism" and "Catholic church" are equivocal terms. There is no coherent "system" of contemporary Catholicism, as there is no single Catholic church except mystically, in the eyes of faith.

My purpose is not to survey all the documents, much less to force them into some kind of grid. I am interested in looking at samples of "Catholic" speech about homosexuality in order to identify typical rhetorical devices in it. Since my first interest is with "Catholicism" as the speech of official theology and with the "Catholic church" as a set of interlocking bureaucracies, I concentrate on the most authoritative and authoritarian of the recent texts: the 1975 *Declaration* and the 1986 *Letter*. To these I will add the 1992 *Considerations* on gay civil rights, though the legal history and status of this document is confused. Of statements from outside the Vatican, I will consider in detail only one: the American bishops' letter, *Always Our Children*, issued in October 1997 and revised under pressure from the Vatican barely seven months later. In all of these documents, including the good-hearted letter of the American bishops, I try to identify typical rhetorical traps in Catholic speaking about homosexuality.

1975 *Declaration* on Sexual Ethics

The 1975 *Declaration* from the CDF is not primarily concerned with homosexuality. Its purpose is more embracing. It wants to reassert what it considers to be "natural law" arguments against a variety of sexual sins, including extramarital sex, homosexuality, and masturbation. So the document is divided into something like four parts. It begins with a justification of the need to set forth the unchanging law about sexuality in the face of modern confusions (nos. 1–5). It then offers particular comments on extramarital sex, homosexual relations, and masturbation (nos. 6–9). It next reaffirms the reality of both serious sexual sin and the virtue of chastity (nos. 10–12). Finally, the *Declaration* sets forth some rather general instructions to Catholic bishops on how to ensure proper teaching about these matters (no. 13).[3] Rhetorically, its overall pattern is lament, denunciation, exhortation, and prescription.

———

Underneath the rhetoric are what appear to be arguments about natural law. The *Declaration* sometimes claims that the teaching of the Catholic church on sexual matters derives from unchanging principles that are discoverable by human reason apart from divine revelation. The "natural wisdom of reason" can discover the requirements of human nature, at least "in the order of things proper to it" (no. 4). These requirements are not historically or culturally conditioned. Catholic sexual morality is founded upon the "nature" of the "human person," upon the "constitutive elements and essential relations of each human person," upon the "norms" or "precepts of the natural law," upon principles contained in the "divine, eternal objective and universal law" of God (nos. 3–4).

———

Anyone familiar with classical formulations of Catholic teaching on natural law will already be puzzled. Thomas Aquinas, for example, meticulously distinguishes our knowledge of natural law from our faith in the revelation of divine law. The *Declaration* seems to run these together, undoing Thomas's careful critique of the arrogance of human knowing.[4] Because the *Declaration* regularly confuses natural law with God's revelation of a divine law, because it will speak of our (natural?) capacity to know this divine law, it implies that every human being has constant and clear access to a list of basic moral principles. This may be good for denouncing those with whom you disagree, but it is definitely bad Thomism—and, I would say, a bad account of what different Catholic traditions have meant by natural law.

———

Perhaps the 1975 *Declaration* is not really interested in making traditional claims about natural law. After all, the document uses as its starting point the concept of the "human person." Those are its opening words, and so its title according to Vatican practice (*Persona humana*). The concept is also the mainstay of many of its central assertions. The "constitutive elements and essential human relations of each person . . . transcend historical conditions" (no. 3). But "human person" as a technical concept is hardly traditional Catholic theology. It is by no means the foundation of Thomas Aquinas's moral teaching—or for that matter, of the teaching of Alphonsus Liguori or any of the other approved moral "doctors." "Human person" entered the technical language of Vatican documents rather recently.[5] It gained extraordinary importance under John Paul II because "Christian" or "ethical personalism" happens to have been the doctrine advocated in his principal philosophical work, published in 1969 when he was already the archbishop of Krakow and a cardinal.[6] The timeless principles of human morals are deduced in the *Declaration* from what is really an innovation in Catholic moral teaching.

———

The *Declaration* seems to use this notion of the "human person" to argue "that certain precepts of the natural law have an absolute and unchangeable force" (no. 4). But the argument shifts quickly enough from persons to their acts. As regards "the sexual inclination [*indolis*] of man and the human reproductive power," the "natural law" precepts teach that genital acts "do not have their true significance or moral force outside of legitimate marriage" (no. 5). Any other genital activity, including any activity involving "artificial means" of contraception, is an abuse of human sex. It is not hard to predict how this teaching will apply to "homosexual relations." Both the "perpetual teaching" of the church's officials and "the moral sense of the

Christian people" refuse to excuse "the homosexual relations of some persons" (no. 8).

The document allows that there may be some reason to distinguish between curable and incurable homosexuals, between those who have a homosexual "proclivity born from bad education or damaged sexual maturity or habit or bad example" and those who are homosexuals "in perpetuity" because of "some kind of almost innate impulse" or "a vitiated constitution" (no. 8). But this distinction speaks nothing to homosexual acts. "According to the moral order of objective things homosexual couplings are acts that are deprived of their necessary and essential ordering." Again, "acts of homosexuality are disordered by their very nature, nor can they be approved in any way whatever." Those are the closing words of the *Declaration*'s paragraph on homosexuality.

———

When you get down to it, the section on homosexuality invokes not so much the "human person" or the "natural law" as the notion of an intrinsic "ordering" of acts. In context, the notion must refer to the reproductive function of genital acts, their "ordering" to reproduction. The same reasoning will shortly be applied to masturbation, which is "an intrinsically and seriously disordered act" (no. 9). Why? "The deliberate use of the sexual power outside correct conjugal intercourse essentially contradicts its end," that is, the "end" or purpose of sexual power. Human beings have genital organs for the sake of reproducing within permanent, monogamous unions. To use their "sexual power" in any other situation is to misuse it.

———

Repeating this claim a dozen different ways, the 1975 *Declaration* makes no interesting arguments. Indeed, I would suggest that the relation of principles to cases is rather the reverse of what the *Declaration*'s structure implies. The principles are in fact derived from the cases, rather than applied to them. Sex must be procreative because homosexuality must be condemned. If this reversed relation is the important one, then the *Declaration* would be centrally about homosexuality, though it devotes only one paragraph to it. In the same way, the all-too-famous papal encyclical on artificial contraception, *Humanae vitae,* may also be centrally about homosexuality, though it seems to pass over this topic.

The 1975 *Declaration* need not be careful in recounting history or making arguments because it speaks with the self-assurance of codified Law or positivistic Science. The rhetorical resemblance is no accident. *Persona humana* is indeed engaged with legal and scientific notions of homosexuality. Unfortunately, they are notions from more than one hundred years ago, from the nineteenth century's campaign to categorize and regulate sexual perversions, including the newly named "homosexuality."

It is the rhetoric of nineteenth-century Science that explains the much-discussed distinction in the document between two kinds of homosexuality. Some Catholics wanted—and want—to hail this distinction as a great advance in official teaching.[7] The Vatican was finally admitting that a homosexual disposition is not itself sinful! I don't think that the *Declaration* does that. Rather, it adopts a nineteenth-century model of the "causes" of homosexuality. The *Declaration* distinguishes curable homosexuals from incurable ones; it then asserts that the pathology in the former comes from transitory causes, in the latter from permanent ones. This is hardly groundbreaking moral thought.

Views of homosexuality as incurable pathology appear in other Vatican documents from these same years, most notably in opinions on annulments. From 1967 on, the Vatican's appellate courts for marriage cases began to hold that "perpetual" or "incurable" homosexuality produced an "incapacity" either to consent to marriage or to achieve its union of souls and bodies.[8] Something like this view was written into the 1983 *Code of Canon Law*, though in much vaguer language.[9] Medical language runs through these texts, which remind one too often of the cases in Krafft-Ebing where an anxious "homosexual" seeks a cure in order to be properly married.[10]

We should not celebrate the fact that the church is now ready to regard homosexuality as an incurable disease. It is true, of course, that some people have been able to use the nineteenth-century view of homosexuality in order to gain legal reforms or social ameliorations. It is sometimes better to be treated as a patient than as a criminal—but not always. If psychiatric

hospitals are sometimes more comfortable than prisons, prison terms usually have an end. So when the Vatican declared itself ready in 1975 to view
at least some of us as incurable, we should not have been overjoyed.[11]

———

The *Declaration* does seem to make a point of admitting or approving the
nineteenth-century categories of "sexuality" and "homosexuality." It begins, for example, by telling us, "according to the opinion of the learned
men of our time," that "sexuality" is to be counted among the most important elements of human life (no. 1). The official English translation says
this more emphatically: "According to contemporary scientific research, the
human person is so profoundly affected by sexuality that it must be considered as one of the factors which give to each individual's life the principal
traits that distinguish it." Never mind that the science isn't quite "contemporary"; the document appears to be agreeing with scientific explorations of
human sexuality. The appearance is deceptive. Whatever science appears
in the *Declaration* is completely subject to Vatican veto. For example, if scientific evidence shows how typical masturbation is in adolescent development, so much the worse for scientific evidence. "Facts do not give us a rule
by which the rightness of human acts can be judged" (no. 9). Neither do the
arguments of "contemporary psychology" or the findings of "sociology"
(no. 9). If the document takes up certain (nineteenth-century) categories
from science, it does so for its own purposes and according to its own logic.

———

This high-handed way of dealing with medicine and natural science is one
of the most disturbing features of the *Declaration*. To my mind, it effectively
undermines all of its appeals to nature and the natural. Most of the force of
Thomas Aquinas's teaching on natural law comes from his confidence that
the careful study of nature will corroborate it. For those who do not know
the Old and New Laws, Thomas argues, there is still the natural human
impulse for happiness, played out in the long experience of human societies
and so discoverable by human investigation. The 1975 *Declaration* wants to
make a similar appeal, but it tries to do so without seriously engaging the
new sciences of human sex. If it borrows older scientific or medical categories, it simply sets aside recent scientific results that don't agree with its
assertions. It selects its facts.

This arrogance toward the results obtained by human reason exactly contradicts the traditions of natural law teaching. The *Declaration* wants to appeal to the natural law traditions while disdaining the evidence that has traditionally counted in natural law arguments. When he wants to argue against male-male desire from natural law, Thomas Aquinas tries at least to incorporate the science and the history he knows from Aristotle—though he seems to misread the sources at crucial points.[12] The *Declaration* is content merely to set aside contemporary psychology and sociology while reminding us that "facts" do not teach us moral rules (no. 9). The assurance of the document's rhetoric cannot then be that of recent explanations and therapies, nor even of nineteenth-century Science and Law. Its assurance derives from nothing more than the confidence of its own assertions.

The 1986 *Letter* on Homosexual Persons

It is difficult now to remember the uproar caused by Ratzinger's release in 1986 of *Homosexualitatis problema*. Some sections of it are shocking, but reaction to the *Letter* was heightened by the sense of disappointment or betrayal—as was the case two decades before with *Humanae vitae*, the encyclical on artificial means of contraception. Many Catholics had expected a change of official teachings in regard to birth control, and so they were sharply disappointed when the prevailing doctrine was reaffirmed. So, too, some people had gotten into the wishful habit of reading the 1975 *Declaration* as the first step in a process of liberation. They were understandably stunned when Cardinal Ratzinger told them in 1986 that it was no such thing. Moreover, the 1986 *Letter* was more than a clarification of teaching. It was also an administrative order that clamped down on a variety of pastoral activities, not least by ousting lesbigay Catholic ministries such as Dignity from church property. Shock at the doctrine was doubled by shock at the administrative actions.

———

Anyone who had been listening to Cardinal Ratzinger carefully would not have been surprised. In a series of interviews published in 1985, the cardinal scoffed at the view of homosexuality as an "inalienable right." This view was, he said, a prime instance of moral "permissivism," of an "uprooting of

the human person in the depth of his nature."[13] Turning to "tensions between Magisterium and theologians," he attacked a number of theological
"trends": "Indeed, it has come to pass that bishops—on the basis of insufficient information or also because of a sense of guilt toward an 'oppressed minority'—have placed churches at the disposal of 'gays' for their
gatherings."[14] That is the gist of the *Letter* a year before its publication.
Note, by the way, that Ratzinger spoke the word "gays" in English. He
knew that his particular enemies were American activists.

———

Since I regard the 1975 *Declaration* as unconvincing and self-contradictory,
I do not read the 1986 *Letter* as a disconcerting or even unpredictable reversal of it. I do think that the rhetoric of the *Letter* is, for other reasons, more
dangerous than the rhetoric of the *Declaration*. The *Letter* fully deserves
many of the charges against it, including Mary Hunt's accusation that it is
"theological pornography."[15]

———

The 1986 *Letter* is explicitly about homosexuality—or, rather, "the problem of homosexuality," to quote its opening words. Yet the document remains vague about what exactly the problem might be. More precisely, it
doesn't specify what part of the problem is being considered, although it
announces early on that it will not be treating the whole of such a complex
matter (no. 2).[16] The answer, I think, is that the *Letter* treats homosexuality
as a political problem. It reports increasing demands within and without
the Catholic church for extending equal recognition or civil protection to
homosexuals. The "problem of homosexuality" is that more and more
people are beginning to take these demands seriously.

The *Letter*'s first rhetorical response to the problem of homosexuality is
a scolding. It reprimands Catholic bishops, priests, and laypeople who
might have been taken in by the homosexual rights movement. It admon-
ishes rather than argues. The *Letter* asserts, much more bluntly than the
1975 *Declaration*, that only the Catholic hierarchy can determine the truth
about such matters as homosexuality. Only its members have the power to
judge the results of the natural sciences and of biblical scholarship, to reveal
the inner truth of psychological needs and political struggles. But rebuke

seems, even to the *Letter* itself, an insufficient response to the ways in which homosexuality has become a political problem. So it moves from scolding to threatening, then from threatening to ordering.

———

You would not expect in such a rhetorical strategy much sophisticated argument—say, a detailed appeal to natural law. In fact, the phrase "natural law" does not appear in the 1986 *Letter*. There are a few traces of what seem to be natural law traditions, as in the claim that "Catholic teaching about morals is founded upon human reason illumined by faith" (no. 2). This expression leaves open the question whether natural reason apart from faith could conclude the evil of homosexuality. The *Letter* claims, again, that its teaching is "confirmed and augmented by elements taken from the sure advances of the human sciences" (no. 2). Not any scientific "advances," but only those that the CDF deems "sure." This means in practice not just that the Vatican's teaching reflects the fact of nature, but that the Vatican gets to decide what those facts are. Because the Vatican speaks from a theological perspective that "transcends the perspective" of the natural sciences (no. 2), it can refuse even to discuss them in any detail. It does just that: the rest of this document is silent about medical or scientific theories or discoveries in regard to homosexuality.

———

I do not want to suggest that the 1986 *Letter* signals an official retreat from natural law as an argument against homosexuality. In fact, in the new *Catechism of the Catholic Church*, approved by the pope in 1992, natural law reappears almost automatically as one of the grounds for decrying homosexuality. After asserting that Scripture and tradition have always rejected homosexual acts, the *Catechism* adds, "They are contrary to natural law" (no. 2357). Now the *Catechism* is principally a reference document for religious education; it is not a piece of sophisticated theology. Perhaps its bland tone here belongs to its educational purpose. If so, the paragraph shows that the church's central administration remains happy with simple citations of natural law. Indeed, the *Catechism* elsewhere conceives natural law as something that can be expressed in a set of permanently "valid" rules: "The natural law is immutable, permanent throughout history. The rules that express it remain substantially valid. It is a necessary foundation for the erection of moral rules and civil law" (no. 1979). One or more of those "substantially valid" rules excludes homosexual acts.

———

The central judgment of the 1986 *Letter* refutes certain misreadings of the earlier document, the 1975 *Declaration*. Some readers thought to find in the *Declaration* an allowance that the "homosexual condition" might be morally neutral or even good. They were misled. Properly understood, the *Declaration* teaches that the "peculiar propensity of the homosexual person" inclines the person "more or less strongly" to do something that must be considered "objectively evil" in the "moral order" (no. 3). So "the propensity itself is to be judged objectively disordered" (no. 3).

What complicates the relation of this judgment to the natural law is that most Catholic theologies have held that all human sexuality is "objectively disordered" as a result of Original Sin. According to Thomas Aquinas's analysis, for example, copulation between husband and wife in an approved position for the purposes of procreation still necessarily involves a number of objective disorders, not least the intensity of their sexual pleasure. For Thomas, as for Augustine before him and Alphonsus after him, all of human sexual experience is profoundly disordered. What then does it mean to say that "the peculiar propensity of the homosexual person" is "objectively disordered"?

Perhaps the *Letter*'s assertion means that such a propensity only arises as a result of our sinful condition. But if "propensity" refers to sexual desire, it would be equally true to say that all human sexual desire as we know it only arose after the Fall. Moreover, since traditional Catholic theologies deny that there were any acts of copulation before the Fall, it is rather difficult to conclude much about our original sexual desire.

Or perhaps the *Letter*'s assertion means that such a propensity goes against not just the order of grace, but the order of nature—that is, of natural animal reproduction. This would indeed be something like traditional, natural law judgments against homosexuality, but it would also introduce all the problems associated with those traditional judgments.[17] Moreover, it would question whether the *Letter* had really said what it meant to say.

In fact, I think that the confusing judgment about the "objective disorder" of the homosexual "propensity" is not a traditional theological judgment at all. It is just the conclusion of the nineteenth-century medical views already adopted in the *Declaration*. We are confronted here not with Catholic tradition, but with approved selections from Victorian medicine.[18]

The 1986 *Letter* does not provide arguments from natural law, as it does not attempt complicated replies to scriptural interpretations that run counter to its central judgment. The *Letter* simply says that the interpretations are false and that they require "particular vigilance" (no. 4). The church's reading of Scripture doesn't depend on the details of one passage or another. It rests on the "solid foundation of the constant biblical testimonies" (no. 5). These testimonies can be known without doubt because "the contemporary community of faith" is directly linked both to the ancient communities in which the Scriptures were written and to the Holy Spirit who wrote them (no. 5). Of course, it is the church hierarchy that also claims to determine who is in the "community of faith," as it is the church hierarchy that specifies the "living Tradition of the Church" according to which scriptural interpretations are regulated. So much for the lengthy scholarly arguments about what the key words of the verses most often quoted against homosexuality might actually have meant.

In the rhetoric of the *Letter*, it is enough to pretend, yet again, that the story of Sodom is about homosexuality rather than moneyed pride and inhospitality—which is how the canonical author of Ezekiel reads it (Ezekiel 16:49–50).[19] It is enough to apply these particular Levitical rules about ritual purity immediately and unproblematically to Christians, while ignoring most of the rules in the surrounding chapters.[20] It is enough to quote Romans 1 as if it were about homosexual copulations rather than about social reversals consequent on idolatry.[21] It is enough to invoke the sin lists in 1 Corinthians 6:9 and 1 Timothy 1:10 as if their meanings were specifically Christian (rather than pagan) and clearly pertinent to discussions of what we now mean by "homosexuality." For the *Letter*, all of these proof texts show the evil of homosexual "ways" or "unions." They are proof texts because the competent ecclesial authority says so—even (or especially) if modern biblical scholarship says just the opposite.

The *Letter* does not need arguments from natural law or sophisticated replies to modern scriptural exegesis. What is required is authoritative scolding—at least to a point. After that, the *Letter* offers what is meant to sound like hard-nosed political analysis, which it backs up with a hard-knuckled threat.

The *Letter* finds that some Catholics are being misled into agreeing with political positions that are "infected with views of materialism," positions that "deny the transcendent nature of the human person" (no. 8). The views are being spread by groups that pretend falsely to speak for all Catholic homosexuals (no. 9). These groups are covertly linked with non-Catholic political movements that want to change civil laws and that seek in other ways to legitimize homosexual activity and homosexuality itself (no. 9). In short, homosexuality has become a problem in the church because of the political activity of groups who are being controlled, knowingly or unknowingly, by anti-Christian outsiders.

An American reader will recognize this as the allegation of a widely shared and covert "gay agenda." In fact, the political analysis of the 1986 *Letter* much resembles the paranoid political fantasies of the American "Christian Right."[22] Paranoid delusions are evidently not confined to American religious political action committees. Neither are sweeping historical accusations about the intellectual decadence of modern times. But there are other contexts for the political worldview of the 1986 *Letter*. It quite obviously belongs with the Vatican's attacks on feminism as antinatural hedonism, on liberation theology as barely concealed Marxism, and so on. Its contemptuous portraits of liberal modernity can be found in papalist or monarchist Catholic writers of the nineteenth and twentieth centuries, but also in the European fascists of the 1920s and 1930s. In short, the political analysis of the 1986 *Letter* shows strong resemblances to a number of other political paranoias of the present century, while its emphasis on the reproductive family agrees with many other contemporary regimes for fostering reproduction in the national interest. The *Letter*'s denunciation of liberal, "materialistic" hedonism places it in frightening company. Indeed, it is important to remember that Vatican doctrine on the natural law of human sex has entered into complicated relationships of support with a number of contemporary fascisms. If the Vatican has opposed governmental efforts to restrict births, it has endorsed governmental efforts to multiply marriages and the resulting families. By 1986, you would think that the CDF would have learned some lessons from this century of political misalliances.

———

Far from resisting these associations, the *Letter* seems to play on them when it follows its assertion of a gay agenda with a brutal warning: Those who agitate for homosexual rights will be met by violence. After deploring gay bashing, the *Letter* predicts it in a remarkably convoluted sentence:

> If however the assertion is admitted [that homosexuality is not disordered] and as a result homosexual association [*commercium*] is held to be good, or if laws are proposed to teach this reasoning about how to act (to which no one can be given a right by any law whatever), then neither the Church nor society taken as a whole can have any cause to be surprised if other opinions and other aberrant ways of acting increase more and more and if irrational and violent ways gain strength. (no. 10)

In plain English: It is only to be expected that gay activism will reap its own reward in gay bashing.[23]

———

If the rhetorical function of this sentence is not to threaten gay activists or to excuse in advance those who would do violence against them, what is its purpose? More exactly, what kind of moral reasoning does it represent? It is only natural that agitation for gay rights should produce violence against gays. But this kind of violence, the *Letter* itself professes, is sinful. To threaten sinful consequences smugly seems to me to equate the processes of sin with the processes of nature. That equation would undo the *Letter*'s claims for its knowledge of nature.

———

Perhaps I credit this paragraph of the *Letter* with too much in thinking that it might conceal an argument about sin and nature. It seems such a blunt threat. Why search behind it for anything more? Threatened by the inroads of "gay activists" even within the church, dismayed by the observations of a "gay agenda," and exasperated at its declining social power in the liberal democracies, the hierarchy resorts to threats of cataclysm. This is one of the very oldest rhetorical devices in Catholicism. Indeed, it is the whole point of the church's traditional misreading of the story of Sodom.

If the sodomites are not stopped, so the old harangue goes, they will bring on the destruction of any society that tolerates them. Sodomy will produce famines and plagues, floods and earthquakes, until God's own wrath is moved against it in final conflagration. Sodomites are murderers and destroyers of humankind. If sodomy flourishes, "neither the Church nor society taken as a whole can have any cause to be surprised if other opinions and other aberrant ways of acting increase more and more and if irrational and violent ways gain strength." If the *Letter*'s threat echoes very contemporary forms of hate speech, it also repeats some of the oldest church attacks on same-sex acts. Indeed, it replicates the distancing logic by which the church could hand over or "relax" sodomites to the secular arm for public execution.

———

In order to reduce their chances of being bashed, homosexual persons are evidently not to organize, not to agitate, and not to contradict the church's official teaching. They must also stop acting out their homosexual propensities. Freely cooperating with the light and strength of divine grace, they should turn away from evil and abstain from "homosexual action" (no. 11). "Homosexual action" certainly means genital contact with a person of the same sex, but it refers to much more. Abstaining from "homosexual action" means renouncing gay life. For example, the *Letter* warns that Catholic homosexuals must not associate with one another except in organizations that frequently remind them that "the exercise of homosexuality is against the rule of morals" (no. 14). It may also require the renunciation of any strong sense of homosexual identity. "The Church . . . refuses uniquely to consider in a person the attribute [*ratio*] 'heterosexual' or 'homosexual'" (no. 16). In some situations, that statement can be a comforting reminder of human wholeness. In a society that presumes heterosexuality, in a church that stigmatizes homosexuality, it denies lesbians and gays any opportunity to experience their humanity.

The *Letter* ends with administrative directives for the bishops. The bishops are asked to communicate the official teaching clearly to all, but especially in ministries aimed at homosexual persons. Ministers working with homosexuals should be selected for their "faithfulness to the Magisterium." They must reject dissenting theological opinions (no. 17). "All patronage is to be removed from whatever organizations try to subvert the Magisterium of the Church, or treat of it ambiguously, or neglect it" (no. 17). Such organizations cannot use church property and cannot be supported liturgically. In other words, organizations like Dignity should be cut off from any form of assistance.

It is presumed in the *Letter* that none of its immediate addressees, the world's Catholic bishops, is homosexual. The *Letter* always discusses homosexuals in the third person, as outsiders to be converted or disciplined. If weaknesses are suspected in some bishops or priests, they are the weaknesses of false sentimentality or misguided compassion—not the "objective disorder" of the "homosexual propensity." Yet the *Letter* must also suppose that it is going to be read by some homosexuals. How else to explain the construction of its dark threats or its scolding exhortations? So the rhetoric of the *Letter* enacts the exclusion it prescribes. The only homosexuals who can find a place in its text are those who already accept its authoritative prescriptions. Before it excludes Dignity from church property or church liturgies, it has already excluded Dignity from church speech.

Stories are handed down about what happened to Dignity and its chapters in the wake of this decision. At the end of the last service at the University of Minnesota Catholic center, "the altar was stripped and the chalice and banners and Easter candles and other symbols of the Catholic liturgy were taken down. Carrying the ceremonial ornaments in their arms and singing, Dignity members marched out of the church and across the street to the Episcopal university center, where they had been granted approval to hold services."[24] Consoling accounts can also be given of the broader response to the 1986 *Letter*.[25] But the *Letter* stands. Indeed, it replicates itself whenever it is cited in later documents. Far from retracting it or modifying it in the light of the public outcry, the Vatican has continued to apply it to what it sees as the political threat of the gay agenda. No clearer example could be wanted than a document that surfaced almost six years after the "Halloween surprise" of 1986.

1992 *Considerations*

In June of 1992, the CDF had the Vatican's diplomatic representative in the United States, then a Pro-Nuncio, distribute an unsigned document to the American bishops through their central offices in Washington.[26] The document, in English, was titled *Some Considerations Concerning the Response to Legislative Proposals on the Non-Discrimination of Homosexual Persons.* It explains itself as identifying "principles and distinctions of a general nature" that might be useful to "the conscientious legislator, voter, or church authority."[27] But it seems to have been drafted by American consultors to the CDF in response to requests by American bishops. The original version specifically mentions American legislative proposals and seems at several points to react to their details.

The document became public when it was released to the American press on July 15, 1992, by New Ways Ministry (which had obtained a copy through undisclosed sources). Eight days later, the Vatican press office issued a revised version of the document. A prefatory note explains that the document was intended "as a background resource offering discreet assistance to those who may be confronted with the task of evaluating draft legislation" (p. 230). It is, in other words, a confidential briefing paper for American (and Italian?) bishops. It tells them how to respond to public initiatives seeking equal legal protection for lesbians and gays. Or, rather, it tells them how to oppose such initiatives.

———

Whatever their original purpose, the 1992 *Considerations* have a belligerent tone. Three introductory sections are followed by sixteen numbered paragraphs, most of them quite short. The first nine paragraphs consist of quotations without comment from the 1986 *Letter.* These include the remarks on homosexual orientation as "objective disorder" and the threat of violence against those who seek equal rights for homosexuals. The *Considerations* then apply these quotations to the issues raised by nondiscrimination legislation. The applications are chilling.

The starting point of the document, which is painful to call a "principle," is a direct inference from the 1986 *Letter.* "'Sexual orientation' does not constitute a quality comparable to race, ethnic background, etc. in respect to non-discrimination" because "homosexual orientation is an objective disorder" (no. 10). Indeed, we are told, there are a number of situations in which legislation should discriminate against homosexuals. "There are areas in which it is not unjust discrimination to take sexual orientation into account, for example, in the consignment of children to adoption or foster care, in the employment of teachers or coaches, and in military recruitment" (no. 11). Similar things are said against equal rights in housing and spousal benefits (no. 15). More generally, the rights of homosexuals "can be legitimately limited for objectively disordered external conduct," just in the way that one limits the rights of "contagious or mentally ill persons" (no. 12). In brief, "there is no right to homosexuality" (no. 13).

But what about "good" homosexuals, the Catholic homosexuals who want to lead chaste lives within the church? What happens to them? "As a rule, the majority of homosexually oriented persons who seek to lead chaste lives do not want or see no reason for their sexual orientation to become public knowledge. Hence the problem of discrimination . . . does not arise" (no. 14). Good Catholic homosexuals won't be discriminated against because no one will know that they are homosexuals. People who are "out" tend to be people who disagree with and seek to change the church's teaching. It is just fine to discriminate against them. In fact, an obedient Catholic might be glad that the civil law can be used to discriminate against those who agitate for change in the church.

What then is your average American bishop to do? He must oppose proposals for nondiscrimination legislation actively and globally. He cannot be content merely with getting exemptions from such legislation for his own institutions. "The Church has the responsibility to promote the public morality of the entire civil society on the basis of fundamental moral values, not simply to protect herself from the application of harmful laws" (no. 16).

———

Reactions to the 1992 *Considerations* were, if anything, more shocked and more outraged than in 1986. Thomas Gumbleton, auxiliary bishop of Detroit, described the memorandum as "clearly based on an ignorance of the nature of homosexuality" and "totally in conflict with gospel values."[28] Other bishops tried to distance themselves from the document by pointing to its anonymity.

I agree with the protests, of course, but I also think that the *Considerations* do just what they say they do. They apply the principles of the 1986 *Letter* to pending legislative proposals. The problem is not so much with the application as with the principles. The most prominent words in the *Considerations* are spoken in the scolding, threatening voice of the *Letter*.

———

The Vatican has done nothing to mute that voice. I think, for example, of a series of articles published during the spring of 1997 in the *Osservatore Romano* under the collective title "Christian Anthropology and Homosexuality."[29] The articles begin with a general statement of what are supposed to be principles, move next through a series of scriptural and historical summaries, and then turn to the real point: topical essays on current political controversies. In short, the fourteen articles recapitulate the entire span of concerns in the CDF documents from 1975, 1986, and 1992.

The articles do not undertake rigorous appraisals of current scholarship on homosexuality and Catholicism. The only significant work of contemporary gay writing cited is Andrew Sullivan's *Virtually Normal*, which D'Agostino uses for its characterization of the "liberationist" and "liberal" programs.[30] Nor does the series offer the "comprehensive" theological treatment of homosexuality that has been postponed from one official document to the next. It does repeat the charge that gay demands for legal equality or civil recognition of same-sex unions are part of a politically misguided and typically modern agenda. "In fact, the demands of homosexuals belong to that confusion of ideas about sexuality which is a typical aspect of modern culture."[31] "The battle that liberationists and liberals are waging against the 'traditional' (i.e., the one heterosexual) model of marriage is therefore a battle against the idea that there are objective, or—if you will—natural modes of communication, modes that the law is called on to formalize, regulate and guarantee."[32] Claims on behalf of homosexuality should be understood as political claims on behalf of a decadent modernity, which it is the duty of the church to combat politically.

Always Our Children (1997–1998)

A gentler voice certainly sounds in the American bishops' letter *Always Our Children*. Of course, it is not exactly the voice of all the American bishops. It is the voice of two committees of American bishops. The letter was drafted by the National Conference of Catholic Bishops' Committee on Marriage and Family and then approved by the Administrative Committee. It is doubtful that the letter in its original form could have passed the scrutiny of a full assembly of American bishops. Some American bishops disliked the letter enough to revise it after publication. But let me start with the gentler voice of those committees.

———

Always Our Children carries the subtitle *Pastoral Message to Parents of Homosexual Children and Suggestions for Pastoral Ministers*. The wording is precise. It is a pastoral message, neither "a treatise on homosexuality" nor "a systematic presentation of the church's moral teaching" (287a).[33] It is primarily addressed to Catholic parents "who are trying to cope with the discovery of homosexuality in a child who is an adolescent or an adult" (285b). It is secondarily addressed to pastors, who are given a list of seven pastoral suggestions (291a–b). Only at the very end, in its last 150 words, does the document speak directly to "our homosexual brothers and sisters" (291c).

———

The rhetoric of the letter mixes consolation and counsel. It supposes a Catholic parent will need consolation after discovering that his or her child is homosexual, even when that child is an adult. The Catholic parent "who is trying to cope" may feel "turmoil" in these "difficult circumstances," "in a time that may be one of the most challenging of their lives" (285b, 287a).

"You need not face this painful time alone" (287a). The document presupposes that coming out is a melodrama, that it will strike the Catholic parent in the way that a terminal diagnosis or a death might.

The bishops are no more than candid when they admit that many Catholic parents will react to the coming out of a child precisely as if it were worse than the child's death. After all, Catholic parents have been led to believe by their Catholic pastors that homosexuality is a kind of living death. But the bishops might still situate the more melodramatic reactions within a particular range, from negative to positive. As it is, the bishops never consider that a Catholic parent might be perfectly happy to learn that a daughter were lesbian or a son gay. The most positive immediate reaction they seem to allow is a reaction of "relief": "a burden has been lifted" (287b–288a). The other reactions that follow in the list are anger, mourning, fear, guilt, shame, and loneliness. Only at the end, and rather flatly, do they mention "parental protectiveness and pride."

The bishops seem to expect that most of the reactions from Catholic parents will be negative ones. Perhaps that is because the bishops know how Catholic parents have been trained to view homosexuality. It was, after all, the bishops who directed their training.

———

The letter describes the anger of a parent against "family members or friends [who] seem overly accepting and encouraging of homosexuality" (288a). It does not mention the anger of a parent against a homophobic church. The letter sympathizes with the "fear of your child contracting HIV/AIDS" (288a), but not with the desire for more HIV-prevention programs of the kind the bishops regularly oppose.[34] In pretending to describe parental reactions, the letter is instead prescribing them. Its prescriptions place blame everywhere but with the church itself.

———

The letter's rhetoric is uneasy in these and other ways. On the one hand, it wants to urge parents not to abandon children who come out. The letter is emphatic on this point. "Don't break off contact; don't reject your child" (288b). On the other hand, the letter feels constrained to reiterate the church condemnations of all homosexual activity (287a). But the anguish of decent Catholic parents is surely caused in part by the pull between parental love and church condemnation. The letter admits as much: "You experience a tension between loving your child as God's precious creation and not wanting to endorse any behavior you know the church teaches is wrong" (287a). Indeed, the letter goes further to encourage some parental condemnations: "you may need to challenge certain aspects of a lifestyle which you find objectionable" (290b).

———

Here we begin to realize how much the letter leaves out. Because it places itself rhetorically at or just after the moment of "discovering" a child's homosexuality, the letter does not have to address issues that arise over the span of homosexual lives. What, for example, is an obedient Catholic parent to do if the child decides to take a permanent lover? To have a union ceremony? To adopt children? To publish a book critical of church teaching? No mention of these questions in *Always Our Children.*

The bishops do say that Catholic parents should urge the child to stay in the Catholic church. This means that they should offer her or him a life of sexual abstinence, frequent penance, religiously informed therapy, and diocesan support groups (289a, 290b, 291a). What if the child decides against these options? What is the Catholic parent to say then? And what if the Catholic parent should want something more for the child—say, an ordinary human life with loving, intimate relationships? "Our children" remain "our children" only so long as they dwell in the melodrama of coming out—but not when they begin living as lesbian or gay adults.

———

I have already noted that lesbigay Catholics frequently find themselves in the situation of being talked about rather than spoken to. *Always Our Children* is no exception. The letter speaks of parents and children. Though the letter explicitly acknowledges that the child in question may be an adult, it talks over the heads of the "child" to the parents.

Lesbian and gay Catholics frequently find that church documents speak as if there were none of them already in the church, especially in positions of church leadership. *Always Our Children* is no exception. The letter assumes that no Catholic parent could be lesbian or gay, as it pretends that no

Catholic pastor has any personal acquaintance with gay cultures. It tells priests: "Welcome homosexual persons into the faith community." As if they weren't already there, presiding at the altar.

———

Talked about but not spoken to. Presumed to be always on the outside. When lesbian and gay Catholics are addressed at the very end of the letter, they are offered "an outstretched hand" (291c). They are urged not to "walk away from your families, from the Christian community, from all those who love you" (291c). These are moving words, but they are also costly ones. Lesbian or gay Catholics who grasp the outstretched hand will be led only to "agencies that operate in a manner consistent with Catholic teaching" (291b). They will be permitted "to lead and serve the community" only so long as they "are living chaste lives" (290a).

Practically speaking, how do these prospects differ from those offered by Cardinal Ratzinger in 1986? The voice is gentler, more compassionate, even more seductive, but the invitation is about the same.

———

Despite its gentleness, *Always Our Children* echoes the antihomosexual rhetoric of the "Christian Right." It emphasizes that it is "not intended for advocacy purposes or to serve a particular agenda," nor is it "an endorsement of what some call a 'homosexual lifestyle'" (287a). We meet here the specters of the Gay Agenda and the Gay Lifestyle, so familiar from "conservative" caricatures of homosexuals. We also meet some dishonesty. Of course the letter serves "a particular agenda." It serves the agenda of the American Catholic bishops, who are trying to figure out how to keep people in the church at a time when official condemnations of homosexuality are driving many from it.

Somewhat later, the letter advises parents not to pressure their children into entering "therapy directed toward changing a homosexual orientation. Given the present state of medical and psychological knowledge, there is no guarantee that such therapy will succeed" (289a). A more honest statement would be that informed medical and psychological opinion overwhelmingly condemns such therapies as useless or worse. The bishops can't quite bring themselves to say as much, because they are still somehow restrained by the fancies of the "Christian Right"—of their own "Right." They want to speak gently, compassionately, but also sternly and never too plainly. Their rhetorical strategy depends on being able to pacify their own superiors, the authorities in Rome.

———

The CDF itself was not pacified. In June of 1998, the NCCB Committee on Marriage and Family was moved to circulate a revised version of *Always Our Children*. Seven changes were made in the original text "to ensure the completeness and to clarify the intent of this pastoral statement." In the letter announcing the changes, Thomas O'Brien explained that they had been drafted in consultation with the NCCB Committee on Doctrine and approved by the CDF.[35] One might think that events happened the other way around: the changes were made because the CDF and its American allies weren't satisfied with some parts of the original text, which they considered "soft" on homosexuality. A similar revision was forced a decade earlier with the bishops' statement on AIDS. In 1987, the Administrative Committee of the USCC issued *The Many Faces of AIDS: A Gospel Response*, which seemed to permit some mention of condoms in safe-sex education programs. After a public rebuke by Cardinal Ratzinger and much pressure from "conservative" bishops, the full NCCB issued in 1989 a rather different document, *Called to Compassion and Responsibility: A Response to the HIV/AIDS Crisis*. Here, any advocacy of the use of condoms is strictly prohibited.[36] The forced revision of *Always Our Children* is the same kind of story, played out on somewhat larger theological issues—though perhaps not with such immediately destructive effects.

———

The Vatican-approved changes to *Always Our Children* can sometimes seem trifling. For example, in the original letter, sexual orientation is described as a "fundamental dimension" of human beings; in the revised version, it is a "deep-seated dimension" (100b).[37] There is a difference here. "Fundamental" might suggest that sexual orientation is part of one's being as a divine creation, while "deep-seated" only implies that sexual orientation is stubborn. Humanity is fundamental; Original Sin is deep-seated. Homosexuality is more like Original Sin than like humanity.

Other changes are less subtle. The original letter explains that adolescents can sometimes experiment with homoerotic behaviors as part of growing up. It counsels patience. The revised letter counsels surveillance. Parents should watch over "what the child is choosing to read or view in the media, intense friendships and other such observable characteristics and tendencies. . . . Parents must always be vigilant about their children's behavior and exercise responsible interventions when necessary" (100b).

Some of the changes, finally, reverse the document's original intent. The Vatican-approved revision adds two footnotes. Where the bishops wrote that "homosexual orientation cannot be considered sinful" just in itself, a new note reminds us, in the language of the 1986 *Letter* and the new *Catechism*, that homosexual orientation is "objectively disordered."

The second footnote is worse. The bishops had originally written, "Nothing in the Bible or in Catholic teaching can be used to justify prejudicial or discriminatory attitudes and behaviors." The new footnote adds: except "in matter where sexual orientation has a clear relevance," and then it points us to the 1992 *Considerations*. The American bishops' strong speech against discrimination has been footnoted into its opposite—a charter for discrimination.

———

The changes in *Always Our Children* were announced in the middle of so many new Vatican initiatives that they drew limited reaction. Dignity lamented the changes, as did New Ways Ministry. But most of the press focused on amendments to church canons about theological dissent and to the regulations for national conferences of bishops. That focus was entirely appropriate. The rewriting of *Always Our Children* is only one episode in a campaign to police "orthodoxy" in moral matters. In the long run, the progress of that effort matters more to lesbian and gay Catholics than the text of *Always Our Children*. It matters more, because it centrally affects the possibilities of sustained dissent from the official condemnations of "homosexual action" and the official stigmatization of "homosexual propensity."

The proof of this came a year after the changes in canon law. On July 13, 1999, the CDF announced that the founders of New Ways Ministry, Jeannine Gramick and Robert Nugent, were "permanently prohibited from any pastoral work involving homosexual persons."[38] The "ambiguities and errors" of their pastoral approach were judged to have "caused confusion among the Catholic people" and "harmed the community of the church." Replying to this condemnation, Nugent disclosed that he had been asked to sign a specific profession of faith structured according to the new legislation on dissent. "Having found no serious objections in my public presentations which were not [already] clarified and corrected . . . , the primary goal had now become an attempt . . . to elicit my internal adherence to the intrinsic evil of homosexual acts, a second-level, *definitive* doctrine considered *infallible* by a non-defining act of the ordinary and universal magisterium."[39] Dissent from the teachings of homosexuality is now silenced with blunt claims of authority. There is no need for the Vatican to answer moral counter-arguments when it can so easily impose sanctions for lack of "faith"—that is, for disobedience.

———

In the documents from 1975 on, as in its revision of *Always Our Children*, the Vatican has shifted the rhetoric toward political "debate" or campaign advertising and away from complex theological argument or convincing psychological analysis. We ought to reply to it, when we reply, as low-grade politics. But we need to be careful about replying.

Faced with the untiring repetition of official principles and their applications, with increasingly frank assertions of authority backed by cycles of self-citation, we need to ask ourselves about the functions of official speech. What purposes are served by an authoritarian and highly repetitive moral speech? This is not a question about its causes or motives. We might want to believe, for example, that the accelerating repetition in Vatican documents is a sign of the hierarchy's despair over its dwindling influence. Still, rather than imagining motives, we ought to look for rhetorical effects, for the actual operation of the official discourses.

———

One effect of the church's official discourse about homosexuality is just to keep dissidents busy rebutting them. Instead of building alternate forms of Catholic community, we spend our energy trying to explain, once again, why the latest Vatican pronouncement is unscriptural or self-contradictory or antiscientific. As Mary Hunt says, "That's the sinister genius of Roman

Catholicism: to prevent lesbians and gay people from being church, so that we are always reacting to something that we are not a part of in an integral and intimate way."[40]

Another effect is to keep reinforcing certain categories for talking about homosexuality. Repetition is a powerful way of teaching language. Authoritative repetition of certain terms or distinctions limits the possibilities for our response in another language, a new language.

Yet another effect, perhaps the most dangerous, is to convince us that the talk might actually lead to reform. So often, exchanges about homosexuality between the Vatican and Catholic dissidents are reduced to volleys of press releases. Now press releases are important tools in industrialized democracies, where public sentiment can have periodic effect by means of elections. But there are no longer any elections in the Catholic church. If massive publicity can sometimes have an effect on the church's operations through government action, that is at best an indirect threat to the centralized church bureaucracies. After all, the Vatican line now seems to be that Western Europe and English-speaking North America are too decadent for easy reconversion. Better to turn to the developing churches, where "traditional family values" still flourish and where governments can be counted on to oppress homosexuality.

The rhetorical devices of official speech about homosexuality may indicate precisely a pessimism about the usefulness of speech in controlling homosexuality. They may raise painful questions about the extent to which arguing with the Vatican is like playing a shell game—over and over again. We should respond to the rhetorical devices not with more repetitions of the arguments about objective disorders or procreation and unity, but with a more realistic analysis of the relations of doctrine to power in Catholic "teaching" on homosexuality.

3

bureaucratic morals

THERE ARE MANY ways to keep people from talking. You can punish them or gag them, but you can also drown them out by talking louder and longer. More subtly, you can corrupt any language in which they might try to say things you don't want them to say. Official Catholicism has used all of these methods, and others still, in its efforts to prevent serious speech about homosexuality.

Andrew Sullivan describes one kind of silencing: "With regard to homosexuality, I inherited no moral and religious teaching that could guide me to success or failure. In my adolescence and young adulthood, the teaching of the Church was merely a silence, an increasingly hollow denial even of the existence of homosexuals."[1] This silence then gave way, at least in the official documents and the media, to repetitive words of condemnation. (From parish pulpits, there is still a mostly embarrassed silence, for reasons to be explored in chapters 6 and 7.) But the change from silence to official speech need not be a development at all. It can be a means to achieve the same end: preventing serious discussion about same-sex love.

—

In the last chapter, I examined rhetorical devices in a handful of recent documents: belated appropriations of scientific jargon, emphatic citations of dubious scriptural readings, threats of unpreventable popular violence. These devices are parts of larger rhetorical programs. By "programs" I mean one of the most important and most nearly invisible features of moral theology: the *style* in which moral patterns or rules are taught.

I sometimes think of this feature as the tone of voice. For example, the same moral rule will function differently when spoken in the angry voice of rebuke, the hesitant voice of suggestion, or the warm voice of sincere help. The "rule" conveyed is different in each of the three voices.

We also find the reverse. A single rhetorical program can both impose silence and generate certain kinds of speech. What I will call "bureaucratic speech" is as much a way of not talking as any silence. Indeed, bureaucratic speech is more deceptive and more exhausting. Rhetorical programs that subject listeners to an endless series of official speeches can silence their audiences much more effectively than by ordering them to keep quiet.

—

Reading Vatican pronouncements about sex, and certainly trying to respond to them, requires an understanding of the rhetorical program that guides them. The "meaning" of the pronouncement is less important than its authoritative style or posture. What is said matters less than how it is said.

When disputing particular passages in official documents, we often study their contexts. We look to the surrounding words, the surface arguments and scriptural interpretations, the explicitly cited legal precedents, and so on. These elements, however, constitute the less important contexts for an official moral document. More significant is the rhetorical relationship between speaker and listener—specifically, the relationship between the authority presumed by the speaker and the docility expected in the listener. The same words, arguments, scriptural verses, and legal precedents can have entirely different meanings within different projections of moral authority.

———

A rhetorical program is most successful when it seems uncalculated and "natural," when its audience comes to expect no other kind of speech.

What do we expect of Vatican documents on sex? We expect them to be legal enactments or binding clarifications that conform to the styles of canon law. The canonical speech of the papal bureaucracy has been codified over centuries as one of self-citation. Thus many contemporary Catholics expect from official moral teachings nothing more than precise and circular regulations—not sustained efforts to persuade. Obedient or "faithful" Catholics should of course be convinced by the official texts.

This expectation is fostered quite deliberately by the Vatican's rhetoric. In the contemporary documents on homosexuality, we see a presumption that the most authoritative language for Catholic morals—the language in which this church judges Christian traditions about Christian lives—should be stipulation or regulation rather than persuasion. This presumption ignores many traditions of Latin-speaking Christianity that Roman Catholicism wants to claim as especially its own. But most astonishing is the fact that many contemporary Catholics expect nothing better: They have succumbed to a very effective rhetorical program.

———

If you do not subscribe to that program, you may want to skip ahead to the next chapter. The rest of this chapter analyzes the rhetoric in the hopes of helping out those who have succumbed to its program—who do succumb daily. So I first describe some of the rhetorical devices (chief among them the artful use of tedium) as we now experience them. I then show how the program was developed in Catholic discussions of sodomy, especially in the last few centuries. I conclude by suggesting how those discussions and the program they perfected try to limit our abilities to respond to official teaching.

If we want a name for this program, it would probably be best to call it "modern." In the same way that we distinguish "modern" philosophy or science from the medieval by imagining a boundary somewhere in the sixteenth century, so we ought to distinguish "modern" Catholicism from its predecessors. The (too) obvious boundary is the Council of Trent, the decades-long series of meetings in which Roman Catholic doctrine was fixed in response to various Protestant movements. But what happened at Trent was prepared for decades beforehand and specified for decades afterwards. My point is not to play games with historical periods (those silly fictions), but to turn attention toward important changes in Catholic moral teaching, especially in relation to sex. The official teachings we know in Vatican documents are not just Catholic moral theology. They are modern Catholic moral theology—which embodies a very particular rhetorical program indeed. Part of the meaning of this book's subtitle is to stress the curious role of homosexuality in the rhetorical programs and power structures of this "modern" Catholicism.

——————

As soon as we begin to examine the effects of rhetorical programs, the structure and procedure of the Vatican documents about sex assume a different appearance. Rhetorical features that seemed trivial or accidental suddenly appear to be central and deliberate. Consider, for example, the uses of tedium. The indescribable monotony of approved moral texts is often counted a scandal to the faith. It is also a remarkable rhetorical script. What we complain of as the "tedium" of official moral theology is a defensive rhetoric that protects the claims of authoritative speakers on obedient hearers. Tedium is, in short, part of the now prevailing rhetorical program of modern Catholic morals.

The Program of Tedium

Bernard Häring recalls that when his religious order informed him that he was being sent to study moral theology, "this was my very last choice because I found the teaching of moral theology an absolute crashing bore."[2] How could he be ordered to study something so tedious? In the hopes of making it more interesting, his superior replied. Häring did go on to make of his own moral theology something quite interesting, but that shouldn't undo his first reaction. If some Catholic moral theology has become more

interesting since the 1930s, much official moral theology about sex remains
as tedious as it then was.

How can this be? Moral theology would seem the most urgent part of
Christian teaching, not to say the most vivid. Moral theology about that
famously interesting topic, sex, should be doubly or triply fascinating. But
even a short time spent, say, with American manuals of moral theology
published before 1960 will correct this expectation. Not only do many of
the manuals try to conceal their sexual discussions by segregating them or
leaving them in the most lifeless Latin, they also repeat the same principles
and the same quarrels without any sense of limit. As Leslie Griffin writes,
with exceptional restraint: "A perceived strength of these manuals was precisely their lack of originality."[3]

To make sexual morality tedious takes work. The work is performed, I
suggest, by devices that belong to a particular rhetorical program, learned
by American Catholic writers from Vatican-endorsed European models.
Three such devices I call repetition, flattening, and the attitude of certainty.

Repetition becomes tedious, even in sex, but it is an essential ingredient in
the kind of authority that Catholic moral theology has claimed for the past
few centuries. Reiteration gives the impression of grand stability—indeed,
of immutability. Official moral theology cultivates the illusion of immutability as a way of excusing itself from the effort of arguing morals or from
the embarrassment of acknowledging how difficult that effort would be.
"We don't need to explain ourselves. We need only remind you that we are
repeating a moral truth sanctioned by the centuries—a truth given by Our
Lord to the Apostles and from them directly and only to us." Recent Vatican
documents on homosexuality make just this claim. They use it not only to
condemn the sin, but to secure the interpretation of troublesome passages
in the Scriptures and to resist new discoveries about nature. The official
English of the 1986 *Letter* assures us that "the Church's teaching today is in
organic continuity with the Scriptural perspective and with her own constant Tradition." The Latin says, "The modern teaching authority of the
Church coheres plainly and fittingly with what Holy Scripture and the constant Tradition teach" (*Homosexualitatis problema*, no. 8). History is not so
simple, but the rhetorical program must make it seem so.

Maintaining the illusion of immutability requires something more than mere repetition. It calls for destructive repetition—repetition that rewrites history or, better, abolishes it. In fact, the church's teachings about same-sex relations have changed over the centuries. Their unsettled and unsettling history must be hidden from sight to reinforce their assertion that nothing important can change. So the cycles of repetition not only try to imitate immutability, they fill up time that might be used to make inquiries into church history. "Don't look back there at those old documents. Look right here. We will show you whatever there is worth knowing in them."

Repetition not only delays the construction of counterhistories, it implies a threat in favor of its own static view of history. It reserves an artificially standardized history as an endless treasure chest of proof texts. Dissent is stifled by cultivating the illusion that ancient libraries house highly technical and perfectly consistent texts about sex that can be produced from moment to moment—and that only church officials have the leisure to retrieve or the ability decipher them.

———

Tedium is produced in moral theology about sex not only by repetition, but by what I call *flattening*. I said earlier that many official descriptions of homosexual life are caricatures. The same is true in much of sexual morality. The official rhetorical program seems to have stripped away the kinds of language that would allow anything like full moral description.

We all admit as much. I don't suppose many people have thought that they learned more about Catholic lives from a manual of moral theology than from reading Georges Bernanos or Flannery O'Connor. I take the admission one step further. If we want serious representations of Catholic gayness, we would do better to turn from the Vatican documents to writers like Pierre Klossowski, Marcel Jouhandeau, David Plante, and Patricia Nell Warren. I am not touting these novelists just because they are more pleasurable to read, though I consider pleasure an important sign of success in moral teaching. I offer them as illustrations of language that is more adequate to human reality. The novelists' portrayals of homosexual lives are truer than the fictions about homosexuality in the official texts, even when the novels are not particularly flattering. The figure of Sulpice in Bernanos's *Diary of a Country Priest* is, in many respects, a stereotype of the wheedling and falsely pious young queer.[4] But as stereotype it is both richer and more compassionate than the caricatures in the 1986 *Letter* or the 1992 *Considerations*. The official English of the *Letter* says, "The human person, made in the image and likeness of God, can hardly be adequately described by a reductionist reference to his or her sexual orientation" (*Homosexualitatis problema*, no. 16). Nor can what we misleadingly call a "sexual orientation" be well described by a "reductionist reference" to a flattened vocabulary of genital functions or disordered propensities.

———

It will be objected that unlike novels, moral theology requires "scientific" terminology and rigorous argument. This objection is not so much a self-evident truth as a claim on behalf of a particular rhetorical program. It is also an overly optimistic characterization of the official documents on homosexuality. Much of their terminology scrambles terms taken from incompatible sources. Their descriptions are not so much precisely detailed as grossly overgeneralized. In short, the rigor of argument and the accuracy of terminology in the official documents on homosexuality are themselves assertions rather than facts. The texts are advertised as terminologically precise and argumentatively rigorous. In fact, they are neither.

———

I am not suggesting that a serious theology of homosexuality should leave ordinary vocabulary unchanged. On the contrary, I will exert myself in later chapters to change our easy acceptance of the vocabulary associated with "homosexuality" itself. I also gladly concede that a technical vocabulary can become, for one who has mastered it, a deft instrument. But not all efforts to build a technical vocabulary deserve thoughtful support. The motivation behind many of those efforts can be a kind of destruction. It can be a wish to stop history, to stop life, to find a final dictionary within which the whole world can be spoken once and for all, from the vantage of eternity. The enforcement of a technical vocabulary, especially through decrees, textbooks, and other authoritarian styles, then becomes a way of prescribing rather than of describing.

———

The tedium of official moral theology is produced by repetition and flattening, but also by its attitude of *certainty*. The attitude is so familiar in official church teaching that we hardly notice it, much less take offense at it.

In one way, the attitude of certainty derives from the belief that the church must have a precise ruling on every possible issue or case. This principle is particularly dangerous when applied to sexual matters, which hardly ever have tidy answers and which often enough do not present themselves as discrete cases or issues. But the presumption that there ought to be such a ruling, such answers, has led official Catholic theology to attempt to provide them—that is, to feign having them. If human sexual life is too complicated for such an attempt, then so much the worse for life.

In another way, the attitude of certainty suffuses the style or genre of the "official document." How badly do you have to misconceive sex before you begin imagining that its important truths can be set down in a list? How certain must you be to provide the principles for resolving the "problem of homosexuality" in a few pages of propositions? We now expect official moral teaching about sex in the form of numbered paragraphs. That shows how deeply we are habituated to the attitude of certainty.

Certainty has its destructive moment in the need to conceal all the great questions of moral reasoning: What is the relation of uttered "principles" to lived "cases" after all? What is the role of virtues in finding or applying principles to cases? How do the various parts of the Christian Bible speak to our particular situations? What is the role of prayer in discerning the moral message of the Scriptures or the particular will of God? Such questions have preoccupied the most important writers in the Catholic moral traditions. They must be suppressed in an official document.

———

The constructive and destructive rhetorical processes of repetition, flattening, and certainty block serious theological speech about homosexuality. They do so by producing tedious chatter and by corrupting the language in which alternatives can be voiced.

The rhetorical processes corrupt language in one way by seeming to occupy all possible points of view, endorsing some and rejecting others. Every theological position concerning homosexuality seems already to have been considered and judged. What remains for a dissenter?

The rhetorical processes also "use up" all the available evidence. The Christian Scriptures, the natural sciences, the lessons of history, the dispositions of civil law, the life experiences of homosexuals—all of these sources have apparently already been appropriated by bureaucratic discourse, interpreted and fitted into an exhaustive account. What evidence could be used by a dissenter?

Finally, the rhetorical processes focus attention on nonexistent objects. The whole space of speech about same-sex love is filled with "intrinsic evils" and "homosexual propensities," with gay agendas and materialistic conspiracies, with feverish hedonisms and bitter loneliness. A credible objector must surely begin by talking about such things. They are, after all, the required topics of debate. How could a dissenter begin to talk of something else?

The power of nonexistent objects to block speech is nowhere clearer than in regard to the main term of discussion: "homosexuality." This designation, new in Catholic speech, behaves in it according to the rhetorical processes attached to a much older word, "sodomy." That earlier term was assigned certain roles in fixed scripts by the primary rhetorical program in Catholic moral theology's recent past. The program was called casuistry for its attention to specific moral cases (*casus*). But "casuistry" is an equivocal term, with many looser and stricter meanings. It can refer, for example, to the varieties of ancient, patristic, and medieval manners of considering moral cases. Or it can refer to the very particular manner of classifying cases and calculating judgments about them that came to dominate moral theology in the sixteenth century. Here I use "casuistry" in this second, specific sense—which I consider to be fundamentally opposed to the ancient, patristic, and medieval practices of reasoning about cases.[5] The casuists had to flatten "sodomy," to identify its repetitions and variations exactly, and to do so with quasi-legal rigor. Thus, they opened the way for the most recent documents. When we review the casuists on sodomy, we discover the church's scripts for the use of the term "homosexuality."

"The Metaphysical Essence of Sodomy"

When the nineteenth-century medicolegal term "homosexuality" was brought into official Catholic speech, it replaced the eleventh-century theological term "sodomy." "Homosexuality" took the place of "sodomy" in the way a substitute teacher takes over a class. It arrived, rushing and confused, to face an already fixed lesson plan. The category of "homosexuality" brought some of its own ideas, some of its particular legal and medical logic, but it had to fit these within a logic of definition and condemnation set in place long before it was coined.

———

"Sodomy" was a medieval invention, but its great success occurs after any plausible date for closing the Middle Ages. It is in the early modern period that we see the most elaborate bureaucracies for hunting sodomites and the fiercest negotiations between ecclesiastical and secular bureaucracies for jurisdiction over sodomites, especially in the clergy. We will visit some of these negotiations in the following chapters. Now we need to notice that it was in Catholic moral theology during and after the sixteenth-century Council of Trent that we encounter the most meticulous classifications or taxonomies of sodomy.

The simplest way to understand these taxonomies and their relations to the rhetorical program of casuistry is to trace a single textual element through a strictly limited selection of texts. Thomas Aquinas's definition of sin against nature was particularly authoritative for the casuists, but this does not mean that it was well understood. In fact, the recycling of Thomas's definition in casuistry shows clearly how a single moral formula changes meanings across different rhetorical programs of moral theology. Thomas Aquinas is cited everywhere in early modern treatments of sodomy, but his sense of that category's role in moral theology is systematically contradicted. His authority is honored chiefly by misunderstanding.

———

Same-sex acts appear in Thomas's *Summa of Theology* (1271–72) within two questions on the vice of *luxuria* (2–2.153–54).[6] It is hard to know how to translate *luxuria*, which is the key term of much Christian discourse about sex from the early theological writers through the Middle Ages. In general, *luxuria* means something like blamable self-indulgence, softness, sensuous weakness. Thomas's first question, in five articles, begins by restricting such notions. *Luxuria* is, Thomas says, properly a vice of excess in "venereal pleasures," though it is secondarily applied to a number of self-indulgent excesses such as drinking too much wine (153.1 ad 1 and ad 2). The limitation is meant to discipline lax uses of the term by Thomas's predecessors to describe a host of pleasures, from soft clothing to hot baths. According to Thomas, *luxuria* should be understood as principally concerned with venereal pleasures. It is a vice so far as it is an excess of pleasure. There is no sin in the "use of venereal things" according to proper manner and order, that is, as directed to the end of human generation (153.2 corpus). If Thomas holds that a "venereal act" is not always sinful, he argues that it often is—and, indeed, that excess in this kind of act is an important cause of other sins (153.5 corpus).

Thomas's other question proposes a division of *luxuria* into six kinds: simple fornication, adultery, incest, deflowering (*stuprum*), abduction (*raptus*), and vice against nature. The body of question 154 judges the six species of Thomas's list in the received order. The only significant addition to the taxonomy is the subdivision of the vice against nature. The subdivisions include "procuring pollution" by "lying together" (*concubitus*) with a member of another species, someone not of the proper sex, or someone of the proper sex in other than the natural way—either with an improper "instrument" or in "monstrous and bestial manners" (154.11 corpus). The question ends with an article on the relative seriousness of the various kinds of *luxuria*. The most serious is the vice against nature, the least serious simple fornication (154.12 corpus). Of vices against nature, the worst is bestiality; the least serious, solitary "uncleanness" (154.12 ad 4).

Thomas's article concerning vice against nature is one of the shortest within these two questions. It is only about a quarter of the length of the longest article, which treats the sinfulness of simple fornication (that is, of heterosexual copulation between two unmarried partners). This crude, quantitative comparison suggests that the article on vice against nature is either not particularly important or not particularly difficult for Thomas. It does not require a complex set of distinctions among the acts grouped together as "unnatural." Nor does Thomas's tone suggest that he emphasizes the horror of same-sex copulation. The language used to describe it is colorless. The only insult in the whole article is applied to improper manners of men lying with women; their positions are called "monstrous and bestial." Certainly there are difficulties lurking beneath the surface of Thomas's text, not least in the notion of the natural. But he here treats sodomy as an undetailed sin of second order. Thomas does not think it necessary to describe precisely which activities across how many moments constitute the sin against nature. He does not talk about penetration or ejaculation. What matters for Thomas in the *Summa* is not the mechanism of copulation, but the ways in which kinds of *luxuria* prevent our return to God. He is not interested in copulations, but in virtues and vices, characters, ways of life— that is, in a rhetorical program that can persuade whole human beings to seek the beatific end that they in fact desire.

In the two centuries after his death, Thomas's teaching on sins against nature was received especially within his own Dominican order and at the papal court. You can see this reception in the *Summa theologica* of the Dominican Antoninus, Archbishop of Florence. This *Summa,* completed shortly before Antoninus's death in 1459, differs already from Thomas in its exclusive concern with moral matters rather than the whole of theology. Yet Thomas is invoked as the preeminent authority in regard to sodomy. Antoninus mentions several medieval authors in his chapter "On the vice against nature,"[7] but he quotes or cites Thomas five times by name to establish key doctrines.[8] From Thomas, Antoninus derives the principle for distinguishing the species of crimes against nature. Thomas also provides the explanation of why this sin deserves especially to be called "against nature," as he further determines the relative seriousness of its kinds. But if Antoninus quotes bits of Thomas, he does not imitate Thomas's large structures for moral rhetoric. He certainly does not follow Thomas's restraint in teaching about sodomy. On the contrary, Antoninus here builds an entire "Scholastic" sermon against sodomy around a scriptural verse that he artfully subdivides into topics and then richly supplements with illustrative stories or *exempla* (668B–673C).

The scriptural text or *thema* of the sermon is a verse from Psalm 82: "Who were destroyed at Endor, who became dung for the ground." With this verse, Antoninus emphasizes the divine destruction of sodomites, as he suggests their unnatural fondness for excrement. But he also and quite deliberately likens sodomites to a political and ethnic community, to the tribe of Midian, with their "captain" and their "king" (Ps. 83:9). Sodomites have a homeland, which is forever marked with the signs of their sin. It is utterly sterile, "unnatural": its air stinks of sulphur, its produce tastes of ash (671E–672E). But while the Midianites perished at Endor, the sodomites did not die at Sodom. Antoninus finds them again in the pride of the ancient Greeks and Romans. Not only the pagan poets, but also the conquering pagan emperors were sodomites (Julius Caesar, Octavian; 668D–E). Indeed, pagan culture seems to be characterized as sodomitic. Antoninus repeats from Jerome the story that God almost refused to become incarnate in a creature or a time given over to this vice. All the sodomites had to die instantly on the night of Christ's birth (670D).

Still they reappeared—and reappear. Antoninus finds sodomitic association not only in history, but also in the present. It is an association that begins, for example, when older men, besotted by *luxuria*, persuade adolescents to sin with them, thus infecting language itself (669B, 671A). More generally, keeping company with sodomites will prove contagious to those living with them, to their whole "society" (673B). One person infected with this vice can infect a whole city. That is why God killed off the infants and the innocent in Sodom, a bloody (and ineffective) quarantine (673B). Sodomites can only be corrected when caught young and isolated from contagious contact (671E). Those who do not correct the vice in their children, relatives, and subordinates are themselves worthy of execution (673A). Unchecked, unpunished, sodomy becomes impudent: sodomites will commit their crimes in public, as if they were not sins (671E).

Now what is the relation of Antoninus's Scholastic sermon on sodomy and his citations of Thomas? Antoninus has brought back into moral theology about sodomy what Thomas deliberately ommitted—the highly colored denunciations of the global and transhistorical conspiracy of sodomites. Antoninus is recapitulating much of the older medieval tradition of invective against sodomites, as he may be echoing the recent invective of Bernardino of Siena.[9] For Thomas, the best persuasion about sodomy is a slow clarification of the proper ordering of particular sins under general vices, which are parasitic upon general virtues, which lead one to the end of human living. For Antoninus, the best persuasion about sodomy masses together into a vivid and aggressive sermon dozens of precedent texts, including those of Thomas. Antoninus quotes Thomas with respect, but he refuses the structural point of Thomas's moral teaching about sodomy.

Now Antoninus does share in other important features of Thomas's rhetorical program. Both seem convinced that the speech of moral theology must be a speech about Christian lives that addresses Christians persuasively. Both resist the demand for detailed taxonomies of acts of sodomy. In these and other respects, Thomas and Antoninus seem to agree that the rhetoric of moral theology ought to be a rhetoric of spiritual formation. This agreement marks them off from the very different rhetorical program that comes to dominate Catholic moral theology with the sixteenth century.[10]

Cardinal Cajetan's exposition of the moral part of Thomas's *Summa* was completed in 1517.[11] This text will prove decisive for those early modern moral theologians we categorize—or stigmatize—as "casuists." When Cajetan comes to comment on Thomas's article on vice against nature (q.154 a.11), he lists six "doubts"—that is, six topics in need of elaboration. He specifies the category by resolving cases.

The fourth doubt, for example, worries whether male-female copulation outside the "proper vessel," the vagina, is really the same species of sin as male-female copulation in a prohibited position. In the course of resolving this doubt, Cajetan argues that any necessarily sterile copulation is sin against nature, but he then distinguishes violating nature by copulating with the wrong person from violating nature by copulating with the right person's wrong part.[12] Copulating with the wrong person—namely, a person of your own sex—is the more egregious offense against reason and nature. Cajetan's fifth doubt concerns whether it is against nature for a man to get a woman to emit her "seed" without emitting his own. The answer is Yes, on the grounds that bringing about emission in a man or a woman under conditions that do not allow conception is just the definition of sin against nature. (For most Scholastic accounts, remember, masturbation is just as much a sin against nature as same-sex copulation.)

Cajetan writes all of this in defense of what announces itself as a literal reading of Thomas. In that sense, Thomas's authority borders every page. But Cajetan is well aware that he sometimes rewrites Thomas. In his comments on the next article, for example, he adds to the ordinary list of easily resolved topics an "arduous doubt" about how "masturbation and sodomitic vice" can be mortal sins in women. The answer that he wants to give—that he has already given—is that mature women do indeed have "seed" and can waste it just as men do. But this answer requires that Cajetan take a position on the very old dispute of woman's contribution to conception—a position that, however carefully he phrases it, fundamentally disagrees with Thomas.[13]

Revising Thomas's authority on particular points goes along with a deeper change of procedure—I mean, of rhetorical program. Cajetan appropriates Thomas's clarifying definition of sin against nature not as a way of ordering traditional theological material, but as an attempt to provide a classification that can be applied equally to all imaginable cases of the sin. Where Thomas gives order to a series of historical terminologies grouped under a controlling vice, Cajetan wants a single terminology that determines unambiguously the classification of discrete bodily acts. This change requires that Cajetan exclude not only the kind of sermon material that Antoninus offers, but also the sustained spiritual teaching that is Thomas's purpose in constructing the moral part of the *Summa*. Cajetan is beginning to detach the taxonomy of specific sexual sins from the whole of moral teaching conceived as spiritual formation.

———

I pause here to record an important lesson about Catholic moral tradition: There *is* no unified tradition. Even when the words remain the same, the contexts around them shift decisively—contexts of definition and argumentation, of purpose and procedure. Cajetan is usually described as one of the most faithful Thomists. In many ways, he is. He was immersed in Thomas's texts from an improbably early age, and he devoted himself to enormous commentaries on them. But Cajetan's model for moral teaching is fundamentally opposed to Thomas's—and not only in matters of sex. So even within the confines of mainstream "Thomism," we see important discontinuities.

But isn't it true, someone might say, that both Thomas and Cajetan condemn same-sex copulation as sinful? Yes, it is. Of course, they understand that copulation differently, argue against it on diverse principles, and treat it within opposed rhetorical programs. So what does it mean to say that they make the same theological evaluation or condemnation? Do we conceive of moral theology as nothing more than a scorecard of votes on narrowly defined acts that remain the same over time?

Exactly that view of the history of moral theology Thomas repudiated, but many readers of Cajetan embraced. It is the view of modern casuistry.

———

Cajetan was widely read by the first Jesuits not only as a commentator on Thomas, but as an authority on moral cases. So it is hardly surprising that Cajetan's explanations of Thomas on sodomy should figure prominently in the early Jesuit moralists. Where they do not appear in original editions, they are supplied later. For example, Francisco de Toledo's *Instruction to Priests* (published posthumously in 1599) defines sodomy solely by reference to Genesis 19, but the notes appended to its later editions begin by quoting Thomas.[14]

A fuller example of what happens to the category "sodomy" under the impulses of casuistry can be had in the *Disputations on the Holy Sacrament of Matrimony*, completed in 1599 by Tomás Sanchez, who belongs to the second generation of Jesuit moralists. He mentions sodomy in widely scattered contexts. There is, for example, a consideration of when exactly sodomitic clergy forfeit their clerical immunity from civil prosecution.[15] Elsewhere Sanchez reaffirms the traditional teaching that sodomitic couplings do not create affinity, that is, familial relationship.[16] But his discussions, however scattered, can still show how the rhetorical program of casuistry forces more and more exact definitions of sexual acts. Sanchez asks whether there can be sodomy among women. Yes, he says, on the authority of Thomas.[17] Sanchez adds: This kind of sodomy is to be punished with full rigor if it is done with an instrument and with the emission of female seed. It also weighs just as much as male-male copulations in divorce pleadings. But if there is little or no semination, then there is no ground for divorce.[18] This level of detail, while claiming to repeat Thomas, flattens his restraint into certainty. Thomas did not pretend to be certain about sexual acts, so he did not need to classify them meticulously. But then he did not view the speech of Catholic morals as the speech of casuistry in the modern sense.

The desire to regulate the acts of sodomy appears in dozens of related Jesuit texts, even when Thomas and Cajetan no longer figure as authorities. We can certainly see it in the most notorious book of casuistry.

Antonio de Escobar y Mendoza published his *Moral Theology of Twenty-Four Theologians of the Society of Jesus* in 1644, in the midst of a frenetic ministry. It was a revision of a confessor's manual—"a little *summa* of cases of conscience," he called it—that had already gone through multiple printings in Spanish. The Latin text had the bad luck—that is, the great literary good fortune—to be singled out for attack by a book that many still count a masterpiece: Pascal's *Provincial Letters*.[19]

Escobar y Mendoza's "little *summa*" is easy to mock. It opens, for example, with an extended allegory drawn from the Book of Revelation.[20] The seven seals are interpreted as schemes for arranging the kinds of law, the types of sin, the acts of judgment, the classes of church judgments, the virtues, the states of life, and the sacraments. The four visionary figures of ox, eagle, man, and lion become not the four Evangelists but four Jesuit theologians: Suarez, Vasquez, Molina, Valencia. The twenty-four elders who stand around the throne of the lamb are in fact all Jesuit—indeed, they are the twenty-four moral theologians mentioned in Escobar y Mendoza's title. Even for readers accustomed to the narcissism of religious orders, this might seem a bit much. It was much too much for Pascal, whose irony trembles with rage as he introduces the book.[21]

Escobar y Mendoza does provide an orderly and exact encyclopedia of Jesuit rulings. For each topic, he first runs through basic moral doctrine in catechismal form, with very brief questions and answers, usually no longer than a sentence each. Of a particular sin he might ask, for example, what it is, how many subspecies it has, which acts they include, whether those acts are always serious sins, and so on. Escobar y Mendoza then adds a section on the "praxis . . . of the theologians of the Society of Jesus." This segment resolves more subtle or disputed cases by citing one or more of the twenty-four approved Jesuits. If the case is controverted, he will, in the best casuist manner, remark on the relative probability of the various opinions, though he tends to stress Jesuit unanimity.

When it comes to sodomy, Escobar y Mendoza is principally interested in distinguishing imperfect sodomy (right sex, but wrong vessel) from perfect sodomy (wrong sex, therefore wrong vessel).[22] The question of whether women can commit "perfect" sodomy is resolved along lines fully in accord with the texts that relied explicitly on Cajetan's readings of Thomas, though these authorities do not figure in his text. The great difficulties that confronted Cardinal Cajetan have been reduced to rote formulae in Escobar y Mendoza. If there are difficulties here, they are the difficulties of prudent speech. Escobar y Mendoza suggests that there is much more to the casuistry of sodomy, but he refuses to disclose it—at least here, in this "little *summa*." Indeed, he lists only one doubtful case, namely, whether the penitent is obliged to confess his role as active or passive. The rest of the taxonomy is left in silence. This silence should be distinguished from the silence of Thomas's *Summa*, which turns from graphic descriptions to uncover more important principles. Escobar y Mendoza is not turning away from detailed cases because he considers them of secondary importance. He is turning away from them here because he considers them provocative. Thomas doesn't have a complete casuistry— or want one. Escobar y Mendoza has one and wants one, but refuses to tell us about it for fear of scandalizing.

———

By the standards of casuistry, and despite what Pascal suggests, Escobar y Mendoza is not particularly interested in finding the easiest moral rule. But he would like to determine rules that a devout Catholic can affirm without sin, rules with an acceptable degree of probability. This is the infamous calculus of moral probabilities: Which theological opinion should you follow in a case that has contradictory opinions with different degrees of authority?

· If Pascal is both merciless and unfair in exhibiting the abuses of the calculus, some recent readers have stressed its merits. After all, casuistry does bring moral theology down to earth. It deals with ordinary figures and situations. It uses a kind of moral reasoning very much like that of a prudent judge. It attempts to prevent disagreement from deverailing judgment. We might also count as a special virtue what Pascal depicts as a cynical vice, namely, the extent to which casuistry adapts moral judgments to different cultures or historical periods.[23] But the one thing that the casuistry of Escobar y Mendoza lacks is any sense that the speech of moral theology ought to be a nuanced, persuasive description of whole lives. The rhetoric of casu-istry is some combination of legal code, reference manual, and algebra workbook. For Escobar y Mendoza, the privileged language of moral theol-ogy classifies and compares authoritative rulings. It presumes that the reader is already committed to the principle of authority. Indeed, it claims that the principle of authority is paramount. The reader will be bound to act within the range of probabilities determined by the correct ordering of authorities. The best rhetoric characterizes not just the content of moral judgments, but the exact degree of their probability —which is to say, of their authority.

———

Escobar y Mendoza means to teach characteristically Jesuit solutions to cases, but his method was neither invented by the Jesuits nor confined to them. Indeed, the casuist drive toward exact definition is picked up by au-thors who claim to be recovering a purer reading of Thomas. Consider the enormous *Cursus theologiae moralis* written by the Discalced Carmelites of Salamanca between 1685 and 1715. The *Cursus* is avowedly and fiercely Thomistic, though it has already abandoned Thomas's main discovery in morals—namely, the organization of a self-limiting moral teaching that is embodied in the shape of the *Summa*. The Carmelites arrange their moral teaching, in the casuist manner, by listing commandments and related pre-cepts. In the treatise on the sixth and ninth commandments, they devote a whole section or *punctum* to sodomy. Thomas's definition is their starting point.[24] It is unfolded with logical precision: sodomy is coupling (*concubi-tus*), which distinguishes it from masturbation. It is coupling not with the proper sex, which distinguishes it from all other species of luxurious cou-pling. So the distinguishing difference of sodomy, according to the Salman-ticenses, is the gender of the partner or "supposit," as they like to say. There are questions, of course. Is a woman coupling with a woman the "true sin of sodomy"? Yes, indeed, under Thomas's definition, and it is to be pun-ished as sodomy—that is, by burning. The authorities, which include Ca-jetan and Sanchez, further concur in holding that the perfect crime of sod-omy is committed whenever one woman inseminates another, in or out of the vagina, with or without an instrument.

Can there be true sodomy when a man copulates anally with a woman, even his own wife? Here the authorities are divided. Some argue that this is true sodomy not only according to the definition, but according to the history of its punishment—for example, in the mass hanging of sodomites at Rome under Paul IV.[25] Others, and the more Thomistic, think that male-female anal intercourse is not true sodomy, but rather a crime against nature, "essentially and specifically different" from sodomy.[26] The Carmelites agree, decrying those who depart from the metaphysical notion (*ratio*) and definition of sodomy given by *Divus* Thomas: "We however, who metaphysically investigate the essences of things with the Angelic Doctor [namely, Thomas], and who think that the given definition best explains its essence, constantly say, that this crime [namely, male-female anal intercourse] is not true sodomy, but a less serious sin, even if against nature, and so it is not to be punished with the ordinary penalty of sodomy, but with a lesser one, according to the judgment of the Judge."[27]

Similar reasoning, similar grandiloquence, is mustered for the third question: whether it is important to distinguish in the confessional between active and passive sodomites, on the theory (endorsed by Sanchez) that passive sodomites are unlikely to ejaculate in the course of copulation. The Carmelites disagree. Ejaculation ("semination") in the "inappropriate vessel" is not "essentially required" by the "notion [*ratio*] and metaphysical essence of sodomy."[28] Since there can be in principle no procreative mixture of seed, simple "penetration of the vessel" is enough. Ejaculation only becomes an issue in determining the degree of sodomy, whether it is imperfect or perfect—that is, incomplete or complete. Such degrees do not have to be confessed.

The "metaphysical notion and definition of sodomy," the "notion and metaphysical essence of sodomy": I cannot imagine phrases less congenial to Thomas's moral rhetoric, to his views about human acts, the intelligibility of sin, or the hierarchy of sciences. But I also cannot imagine phrases that better capture the procedure of early modern Catholic theology in regard to this and other sexual sins. The "metaphysical notion" or "metaphysical essence" of sodomy is the necessary supposition, the necessary projection, of the desire to make sodomy a universal term of classification for discrete bodily acts. The project of casuistry demands such a classification—there must then be such a "metaphysical essence."

The Carmelites' *Cursus* was followed within a few years by a text that brought a kind of closure to the discourses of casuistry and that would determine Catholic moral theology well into our own century. The *Moral Theology* of Alphonsus Liguori was first definitively assembled in 1757. Alphonsus comes to the question of sodomy within his treatise on the sixth commandment, in a section on the species of *luxuria* consummated against nature.[29] He first repeats the received distinction between two kinds of sodomy. Imperfect sodomy is male-female copulation outside the approved "vessel." Perfect sodomy is same-sex copulation, which may be distinguished as active and passive. But we already know, even if Alphonsus did not immediately remind us, that a "great question" arises in regard to the acts that constitute sodomy. Some believe that it is copulation with the inappropriate sex; others, copulation in an inappropriate vessel. Both opinions are probable and each highlights one kind of deformity. Alphonsus himself finds the second opinion more probable and more widely approved. In his list of authorities for it, Thomas appears first. But Alphonsus's real work comes in a series of inferences from the approved definition.

First, there can be true sodomy between woman and woman, though Alphonsus admits that it is not entirely improbable to regard this as a sort of "improper sodomy, since there cannot be perfect copulation between women."[30] Second, any coupling or touching of bodies with a person of the same sex constitutes "true sodomy," no matter what parts of the body are involved. The only mitigating circumstance to be mentioned in confession is the absence of ejaculation or pollution. Third, male-female anal intercourse is "only imperfect sodomy, distinct in species from perfect [sodomy]."[31] Alphonsus then adds a question about whether oral sex is also a distinct species of sodomy. The answer: "irrumation" in the mouth of a woman (what we call fellatio, reversing the sense of active and passive) is to be regarded as "inchoate copulation." In the mouth of a man, it is sodomy.

It is very tempting to conclude this survey by noting how exactly the transformation of the theological category "sodomy" prepares for the nineteenth century's invention of the medicolegal category "homosexuality." With Alphonsus, the decisive factor in sodomy has become the sex of the partner. Any sexual contact with a person of the same sex is sodomy. Any sexual contact with a person of the other sex, no matter how "unnatural" the coupling of organs, is really a distinct species of act. It is also interesting that sodomy in the fullest sense remains for Alphonsus what men do with men—and not women with women. In this way, he reinforces the connection of sodomy to sex difference.

We could be tempted further to link the casuists' obsessive classification of sexual acts with the nineteenth century's taxonomies of perversion. Foucault describes a series of extensions by which the monastic discipline of chastity was applied to larger and larger groups—to the clergy as a whole; then to all religious, male and female; then to pious laypeople; then to laypeople simply.[32] Foucault even suggests that we can discern the birth of the modern system of sexuality in the kinds of surveillance practiced within seminaries, religious colleges, and convents since the Counter-Reformation.[33] When the recent Vatican documents introduce "homosexuality" to discussions that had been driven by the casuists' specifications of "sodomy," they are further tangling the already knotted relations between the terms. It is tempting to go back through those documents with new ears for their echoes, mixes, and distortions of the terminology.

———

I will postpone these temptations in order to focus on the rhetorical processes within casuistry, not least because of its present oblivion. The period of Catholic moral theology from the sixteenth through the mid–nineteenth centuries has become the new "Middle Ages." It is the period we tend to skip over in our narratives of Catholic moral teaching. We remember that important decisions about sexual matters were taken in the early church and then in the Middle Ages. We may somewhat recall that Catholic doctrine was fixed at the Council of Trent. We then conveniently forget the following three centuries of theological speech.

This forgetfulness is particularly dangerous to the theology of sexual acts, as the case of sodomy has shown. Certainly the categories Catholic theology uses to describe sexual acts were profoundly modified by the style of speech we call "casuistry." Again, the rhetorical processes described earlier as causes of tedium were perfected under casuistry. The uses of repetition and literalization, the degrees of certainty, the multiple voices of authority—these were practiced in hundreds of texts that we no longer bother to read, at our peril.

The casuistry of same-sex acts is so repetitive, so flattened, and so certain, its precedents are so complicated and its variations so limitless, that efforts to respond to it on its own terms are bound to concede points of principle in the effort to change details. The only effective response to casuistry is a radical critique from the outside. This was what Pascal offered in his *Provincial Letters*. Rather than argue against casuistry case by case, Pascal satirizes it, quotation by quotation. Rather than dispute its definitions and subdefinitions, its sets of maxims, and its elaborate calculus of probable judgments, Pascal exposes their political motives. Some similar strategy is required in response to the descendants of casuistry, the official Vatican documents about homosexual acts.

———

There certainly seems to be room for some contemporary satire, if only we had another Pascal. For example, the obsessive repetitions and flattenings of the official documents might seem to indicate that they are themselves a form of sexual gratification. They describe sexual acts and organs in ways that typify pornography made for men. One can even begin to imagine the pleasures derived from writing at length and in detail about acts one is prohibited from performing. In Huysmans's *A rebours*, the protagonist Des Esseintes moves from remembering the pleasures of sodomy to practicing the pleasures of reading the casuists on sodomy. His reading list includes Sanchez and Liguori.[34] As Hocquenghem says: "The laws are clearly a system of desire in which provocation and voyeurism have their place: the cop-fantasy is not the creation of the deranged brains of homosexuals, but the reality of the desiring function of the police and of justice."[35]

———

Still I suspect that the real aphrodisiac in the casuistry of sex is not pornographic depiction, but bureaucratic power. The enormous growth of moral regulation during the Counter-Reformation was accompanied not by a strengthening of moral rhetoric, but by its impoverishment. Powerful theological rhetoric is not the rhetoric of church power. To say this differently:

The rhetoric of rich moral description or sustained moral education seems just the opposite of the rhetoric of moral management—which is itself the rhetoric of a successful church bureaucracy.

———

I do not want to demonize casuistry as a single source of bureaucratic arrogance. Theological history is even more complicated than demonologies. The developments that brought the church's official rhetoric to its present pass are older and larger than casuistry. And perhaps we can learn helpful lessons about moral reasoning from casuistical procedures. We might even hope to find a few "liberal" passages in one or another casuist's remarks on same-sex relations. For example, the pioneer of homosexual rights, Karl Heinrich Ulrichs, quotes the Cistercian casuist Lobkowicz with approval.[36] My point is not to adjudicate the merits of casuistry. Rather, I question what it means for us and for our responses that important rhetorical devices from casuistry are still being used in official Catholic teaching about sex.

———

Nor do I want to "blame" the Catholic church for inventing bureaucratic morals. The modern growth of bureaucratic discourses about human action can be explained by a hundred causes, only some of which lie inside the Catholic church. Catholic moralists have willingly contributed to the speeches and the institutions of moral bureaucracy; they have also been pushed toward it by entirely secular forces.

It has been the fault of many Catholic moralists to claim that their work was not essentially modern—that they were the opponents of modernity, the mouthpieces of an ancient, unchanging Law. Bureaucratic morals have spread so misleadingly in Catholicism because they have always been classified under the name of more ancient teachings. What we call the Catholic moral tradition has been, too often, a series of substitutions underneath a claim of continuity.

———

Nearer at hand, there are historical continuities under supposed revolutions. We are supposed to have had revolutions in church teaching at and after Vatican II, and certainly in the methods of moral theology since the

1950s. Perhaps we have. But then in this as in so many revolutions, the most important thing to remember is how much has not changed. The grand styles of official moral teaching still rehearse their repetitions and flattenings, their presumptions of clarity and certainty. Those rhetorical devices continue, much as they have for centuries, to make it very difficult to construct alternative ways of speaking about same-sex desire.

———

I think that the rhetorical devices have in fact restricted Catholic responses to official teaching on homosexuality. They have fixed the rhetorical positions from which the replies could be made. Charles Curran once distinguished the contents of contemporary Catholic responses as "mediating" or "revisionist."[37] I prefer to think of them not as contents, but as roles that the official rhetorical programs assign to possible dissenters. One role is too far inside the rhetorical program, the other is too far out. Neither can respond effectively to the prevailing rhetorical program.

Responding to Bureaucracy from Inside

Not a few American Catholic writers have responded to official teaching on homosexuality in the last three decades with carefully argued alternatives. The respondents have included fully accredited teachers of Catholic theology, writing partly on the basis of standard materials in moral theology, partly from scientific and pastoral testimonies.[38] It took courage for those who were so obviously insiders to begin public criticism—courage that was tested by official retaliation.

———

The internal criticisms have other virtues than the courage of their authors. The critiques demonstrate, for example, some of the larger incoherencies that trouble official Catholic teachings on the range of sexual issues. They have tried to undo positivistic notions of natural law and schematic classifications of sexual acts or motives. They have made compelling cases for linking the official teachings with injustices based on prejudices about gender and sex. They have suggested how a reform of the teachings on homosexuality would reopen some of the oldest debates in Christian morals—say, about the normative character of Old Testament laws, the ideals of asceticism, or the deep purposes of bodily creation. They have even gone some way toward describing what a Catholic ethic of same-sex relations might be, though the descriptions are tentative and sometimes curiously hypothetical.

———

Despite their personal and doctrinal virtues, these careful critiques from inside seem to have had negligible effects on official teaching. Despite the dozens of careful histories of the misinterpretation of the biblical story of Sodom, Cardinal Ratzinger still describes it as a condemnation of homosexuality. So does the new *Catechism*.[39] And despite the dozens of careful analyses of the failures and equivocations of sloppy appeals to nature, the official documents still make those appeals with perfect equanimity. What then is the future of careful criticism from inside? What purposes could be served by yet another reading of the "clobber" passages in the Christian Bible? Or by yet another passionate denunciation of the injustice of Vatican teaching?

The intelligent and courageous efforts of internal criticism have been forced in circles by the rhetorical program of the official documents. Trying to correct the present Vatican condemnations of homosexuality by modifying the available principles is like trying to overturn casuistry by arguing cases. To speak most particularly: Since 1975, there have been many dozens of internal critiques of the principal Vatican documents on homosexuality. Some of the critiques have been more compelling than others, but none seems to have had much positive effect on the Vatican. Indeed, the Vatican's statements have only become more insistent.

———

It is understandable, then, that the official intransigence is now reflected in pessimistic judgments by some of the most courageous internal critics of the official teachings. Charles Curran, for example, writes: "the hierarchical magisterium is not going to change its teaching on homosexuality in the near future. . . . In American civil society, the hierarchical magisterium will continue to be the authoritative spokesperson for the Catholic Church even though there are dissenting voices."[40] This may be due in part to the darkening temper of the regime of John Paul II, but the deeper causes are more diffuse than the wishes of a single pope. The dissenting voices will most probably still be struggling to be heard under his immediate successors.

———

The failure of the careful internal critiques to change official teaching might lead us to look again at their rhetorical vulnerabilities. Here we need to ask not only about their effectiveness as political strategy, but about the larger consequences of engaging in such critique from the inside. It may be that careful internal critiques serve not so much to correct the prevailing concepts as to perpetuate them by exercising them. Instead of trying to find something like "indissolubility of procreative and unitive ends" in "homosexual action," for example, we might want to ask whether that indissolubility is an accurate description of human sexuality or whether any single thing corresponds to the phrase "homosexual action."

Failing to contest basic categories and principles may not only perpetuate them, it may lead us to the unhappy compromises of exhaustion. I see exhaustion in the conclusion that "homosexual relations" are "morally good but lacking something found in heterosexual marriage."[41] Of course they are lacking something found in heterosexual marriage—as they also possess something not found in heterosexual marriage. They are, in fact, a very different sort of human relationship. It is only assuming a role within the prevailing rhetorical program that leads a compassionate and intelligent critic to compare them invidiously.

———

The careful internal criticisms fail to recognize what is required for adequate Catholic speech about homosexuality. We would need, first, an adequate descriptive language for homoerotic lives in the church. We cannot have such a language until we have new forms of community—forms in which those lives can stand forth as Catholic. Once we can see them, we will begin to learn how to speak about them. Once we learn to speak about them, we may discern their life-giving possibilities. We have not even reached the moment of adequate description, because we are still trapped within the strong rhetorical programs of the official documents.

No editing or rewriting of the available formulae or rules is likely to reveal how divine grace works within same-sex relations. It is not just a matter of spinning terms and extending principles. We need to start afresh with new forms of speech.

———

Of course, one can sympathize with the desire of the critics to avoid considering such radical options. Perhaps turning the available terms by degrees and extending the available principles by inches is the only way a theologian can keep even one foot within the official discourses of Catholic moral theology. But this conclusion may lead to another. Maybe no real progress can be made on the question of homosexuality so long as one chooses to remain within the official discourses. Contesting the documents on homosexuality requires contesting the official dispositions of church power. Even if we could change official teaching on same-sex love without reforming the official methods, we should not want to do so.

———

Questions about same-sex love really are linked to fundamental considerations about methods of moral teaching and enforcement. This is not because same-sex love is the most important thing in Catholic life. It is not—though it can be painfully important to those of us who are lesbian or gay and Catholic. Nor are questions of same-sex love linked to the programs of power over morals just because any effort at reforming moral teaching will necessarily imply criticisms of the prevailing official methods. Although true, this insight is not specific enough. The links I have in mind concern rather the way condemnations of same-sex love enact hierarchical power over moral discourse and moral life.

The progress of Catholic theology about homosexuality is blocked not just by the police powers in the church, but more steadfastly by the very understanding of church power. This reinforces the posture of teaching authority in the rhetorical programs of Catholic moral theology. It might be possible to negotiate changes of teaching on some moral topics without directly engaging the basic understanding of power. It is not possible to do so with the topic of homosexuality. Homosexuality has a particular relation to the self-understanding of church power—as well as to its exercise, which is to say, its constitution. It has been the gift—and the curse—of some liberation theologies to recognize that particular relation.

Responding to Bureaucracy from Outside

"There comes a time in the collective life of every oppressed minority when passive acceptance of injustice is no longer possible." These are the opening words of Bill Johnson's "Good News of Gay Liberation," one of the first American essays in what might properly be called lesbigay theology.[42] Johnson is not Catholic, but his forceful words reflect the sentiments of a number of lesbian and gay Catholic activists at the end of the 1960s and the beginning of the 1970s. They found in liberation theology the sharpest descriptions of their theological situation—and the best hope for changing it.

———

Johnson's emblematic essay goes on to list twenty-seven demands and proposals. It is a manifesto. The genre reminds us that both lesbigay activism and liberation theology grew up in America out of the discourses of existing political efforts, whether the struggles against the Vietnam War or the liberation movements focusing on race and gender. Before there were manifestos for Christian gay liberation, there were gay manifestos simply. These general manifestos are typically explained as one consequence of the fracturing of the "New Left." When the antiracist or antiwar movements fissioned, their discourses were picked up by gay writers, many of whom had served in those movements. But to emphasize the derivative nature of "gay" liberation theory is to denigrate how perfectly it seemed to express the long suffering of lesbians and gays. Speaking against oppression had—still has—the remarkable effect of healing some of that suffering. Liberation theology is for lesbian and gay writers importantly a theology of testimony, of personal declaration.

———

The language of liberation is not now so effective in secular lesbigay politics as it was then. We hear much more about "equality" or "mainstreaming" than about "liberation." But the rhetoric of liberation remains powerful both in movements for personal actualization and in lesbigay religious groups. Certainly liberation theologies remain among the most exact instruments for analyzing the forms and functions of religious ideologies—that is, of the speeches of religious bureaucracies. So liberation theologies are among the earliest lesbigay theologies for Catholics and among the most recent.[43]

Liberation theologies written by Catholic homosexuals demonstrate more generally what I have tried to show in this chapter only by rhetorical analysis. Analyzing Catholic teaching on "homosexuality" means something more than pointing out its inconsistencies, fallacies, and misuses of evidence. It means as well contesting certain rhetorical programs in official moral theology. Such challenges require contending almost immediately with the principle of authority in moral theology. In challenging the official teaching on homosexuality, we are questioning privileged assumptions about the approved methods of moral reasoning—assumptions that resemble and perhaps reproduce larger forms of social oppression.

Liberation theologies have recognized these resemblances very astutely. They have applied a sharp-eyed suspicion not only to oppressive misuses of scriptural texts, for example, but to ideologies of oppression that have written themselves into the Scriptures themselves.[44]

———

Catholic writers on lesbigay liberation have also run risks.

First, they assume that what the church condemns is what we really are. The basic metaphor of "liberation" can suggest that what we are is already determined. We just need the freedom to exercise it. But it might be that the official conception of homosexuality does not accurately portray us. Maybe our identity as Catholic homosexuals is something to be invented, not just released.

Second, they make a sharp dichotomy between oppressors and oppressed. In the case of the rich and the poor, it makes a certain sense to draw the contrast sharply. The situation is different with regard to homosexuality. Many male homosexuals are in positions of power within the church. They are often the most violent persecutors of "out" homosexuals. We are here, among the oppressed, and also already there, among the oppressors. Indeed, the machinery of church oppression may be in many important ways just what homosexual men use to oppress other homosexual men.

Third, liberation theology writers might lead us into exile too soon, before we have had a chance to learn what we need to about the homosexuality of Catholicism. The critiques of Catholicism offered by some gay liberation theologies have been far too simple. They have stopped short. There is much more to consider in the connection between homosexuality and churchly power.

———

These risks increase when liberation theology slips too comfortably into a position outside official theology, when it becomes too simply its opposite or shadow. It then submits itself to a series of conflicts that separate it from the place of churchly power. Just at this moment, liberation theology must step closer, step back inside, and remind itself of its own complicity with the rhetorical games of church power. Because it must be both inside and outside to pursue the relationship between official speech and official power.

———

Official Catholic discourses about homosexuality are historically determined by the arrangements for power in various churchly bureaucracies—in the confessional, diocesan or inquisitorial courts, papal agencies, institutions of clerical and religious formation. Same-sex love has preoccupied a number of these agencies. The network of Catholic systems that control the production and reception of what will count as orthodox moral theology is also the network of Catholic systems that police same-sex temptation in church institutions and especially in the priesthood.

When we try to correct the official condemnations of homosexuality, we are removing one of the favorite subject matters for the exercise of the church's moral power. We need to ask, as if for the first time: Why has same-sex desire been such a favored site for the exercise of churchly power over morals? Why have the condemnations of sodomy or homosexuality excited the church's administrative energies for so long?

These questions have familiar answers. We are used to replying, for example, that this topic attracted special attention because male-male desire was perceived as a threat to good order in all-male religious institutions. Or because same-sex desire seemed to distill a pure pursuit of pleasure for pleasure's sake, contradicting Gospel charity and Gospel asceticism. Or because same-sex desire, both female and male, seemed to overturn one of the most important social allocations of power: that of gender divisions. But we cannot stop here.

Sodomy was and homosexuality is important in Catholic moral theology because it has been intimately connected to the exercise of power in the construction of priestly lives. It was one of the sites where moral regulation could be exercised purely, with a minimum of resistance. In this inner realm of churchly power, regulation could be exercised for regulation's sake.

———

It is time to enter this realm. We need to see how homosexuality is lived in it. We must, in short, begin to find forms of speech for describing the homosexuality in and of Catholicism.

church ✝ *lives*

4

living inside

THE FIRST POLEMIC against sodomy in Catholic theology
is a denunciation of the clergy. Peter Damian wrote his
Book of Gomorrah or *Gomorran Book* (*Liber Gomorrhianus*)
around 1050 in order to stop the spread of "sodomitic vice"
in the priesthood. There are networks of sodomites, he
claims, who sin together and then absolve one another in
the confessional, as there are "incestuous" families of sodomitic bishops and their priests.[1]

Peter is hardly alone in worrying that sodomy might be
a favorite sin for the clergy. The charge is frequent enough
in medieval texts to be a cliché.[2] So teaching about the silence of Sodom often assumes that an unknowable number
of the clergymen who expound upon or learn about it are
likely themselves to be silent sodomites. This makes for
anxiety about both security and credibility. Some sodomites
are already inside the citadel, overhearing plans for any

campaigns against them. But then the clerical institution will compromise its own authority if it candidly reveals how many of its own are compromised.

We can see both anxieties in Peter Damian. His principal rhetorical strategy is to urge clerical sodomites to break their own silences, to come forward and identify themselves so that they can be cured—that is, so that they can be punished. At the same time, Peter is silent about sodomy in the communities closest to him—the Italian hermitages. Moreover, while he claims that the church is overrun by sodomites, he neither names nor hints at the name of any individual sodomite in the clergy. The strategies for dealing with the concealment of clerical sodomy are themselves strategies of silence. Peter Damian calls for confessions and punishments, but the confessing is to be discreet and the punishment clandestine: deposition from office and exile for life to a remote place of penance. The official response to the chosen silence of clerical sodomy is to counter it briefly with therapeutic speech, but then lock it up forever in the silence of exile.

———

The scripts in church documents or in the rhetorical programs of moral theology are hardly the deepest reason why serious discussion of homosexuality among Catholics is so difficult. A more powerful factor is the fear of a "secret" of male homosexuality in the priesthood and religious life. Indeed, the scripts of church words cannot be understood without seeing them as one of a number of ways of trying to silence such a "secret." Church words about homosexuality are often just efforts to keep the dreaded "secret" from being spoken. If the words about homosexuality are sometimes baffling, maybe they are not meant to make sense. They are meant to silence.

———

The dreaded "secret" of clerical homosexuality is concealed by a number of devices, verbal and institutional, from the very subtle to the very crude, which continue to operate effectively. Even in a society as addicted to media disclosures as ours, the character and extent of clerical homosexuality remain secret. The "secret" is an open one in the sense that many people have anecdotal evidence about gay men in the Catholic priesthood and religious institutions. Journalists, screenwriters, and television comedians can count on a widespread belief that many members of the Catholic clergy are sexually active with other men. "Wait—maybe you didn't hear me. I'm a *Catholic priest*. Historically, that's somewhere in between chorus boy and florist."[3] But it is still surprisingly difficult to move beyond anecdote and cultural stereotype toward any clearer account of it, not least because we have no language in which to do so.

"Awful Disclosures"

The "secret" of clerical homosexuality in modern Catholicism is not a single secret at all. It is not a code of practices or a particular set of facts that can be discovered and disclosed. If there is any one "secret" of Catholic clerical homosexuality, it is the urgent anxiety that there is something unknown, something frightening, that must be kept hidden. It is the fearful effort behind the various arrangements for keeping secrets. The "secret" is the effort itself, which is designed to scramble speech about whatever kind of sex priests might be having with other men, including other priests. "'The secret is in the institution, in the phenomenon of the Church which escapes men and which leads them where they have to be led.'"[4]

If you recall the old Freudian model that links repressed homosexuality to paranoia, you could find no more curious variation on it than official Catholic paranoia about clerical homosexuality.[5]

———

We shouldn't be misled by the fearful effort, the energetic paranoia, into thinking that there is in fact a specific secret to be discovered. Clerical homosexuality can't be discovered by conventional means for revealing cultural or subcultural secrets. It can't be found, for example, in the way that Gil Herdt discovered the secret of ritual fellatio in a Melanesian culture he originally called the "Sambia" in order to protect their privacy. Herdt learned of the secret "unexpectedly" and "through the confidence of my two best informants."[6] He was then invited to witness the rites by which young boys were taught the dreadful importance and symbolic resonance of the fellatio they were about to perform, though the sexual acts themselves occurred out of his sight.

Catholic clerical homosexuality is not like the secret of the Sambia. It is neither a single set of articulated beliefs and practices nor the shared work of a single tribe. Peter Damian's fantasies aside, it is not promoted and protected by a tightly organized shadow hierarchy of sodomites. The Catholic clergy comprises a huge number of competing groups unified at most by the police powers of a set of international bureaucracies. Even individual groups lack a shared practice or explanation of same-sex desire. The typical clerical informant speaks most reliably only about his interpretations of the private, often furtive, almost always unverifiable set of his own "experiences."

––––

Our access to clerical homosexuality is also blocked in ways that Herdt's observation of the Sambians was not. If he worried about learning enough of Sambian lore to be able to retell it convincingly, he was not himself incult-urated in a system of prohibitions, deceptions, and censures surrounding the practices of Sambian men. He was not a Sambian woman, say, or a member of a rival tribe or of a regional police organization. Herdt had not only an outsider's liabilities, but an outsider's immunities.

Catholic laypeople are not so fortunate with regard to priestly homosex-uality. In public speech, we are typically treated as if we were Sambian women. We are presumed not to know; we are chided or excluded if we ask. Individual Catholic priests can be equated with the Sambian boys un-dergoing initiation. They are threatened with the clerical equivalent of death for speaking against the wishes of the hierarchy—they are threat-ened, that is, with expulsion from the group and a campaign of public hu-miliation.[7] Of course, the same threatening authority behaves altogether differently than the Sambian warriors do. However much it might deeply need and even tacitly encourage same-sex desire, it does what it can to disorganize and confuse most sexual practices.

––––

No one can know the extent of homosexual acts or desires within the Cath-olic clergy. The limitation holds as much for an outsider, like myself, as it does for the pope. Some members of the hierarchy—in the curia, among bishops and religious superiors—are certain to have better guesses at over-all rates of homosexual activity or orientation in their local organizations than I do. I know that they have richer anecdotal evidence, because I have heard some of it. But no one has anything like a complete picture. Homo-sexual clergy are often more zealous in keeping their lives secret from their superiors or colleagues than from anyone else. "I don't *want* to know gay priests in my own archdiocese," a priest told Tim Dlugos, having just em-phasized the obvious, that "some of the worst homophobes are guys in the clergy and hierarchy who are gay."[8] The reverse is also true. Many superiors these days do not want to know about the homosexual lives of their subordi-nates, for fear they would have to act on the knowledge. It is safest all around for other clergy not to know. Secrets can be best kept by compart-mentalization.

———

Compartmentalization and isolation characterize the sexual lives of most Catholic clergymen of whatever orientation, but the compartmentalization is particularly strict when it comes to homosexual relations. In the empire of closets that is the modern Catholic church, no one knows more than a few of the compartments. The church is not one big closet. It is a honey-comb of closets that no one can survey in its entirety. Consider this passage of an anonymous letter read at the 1981 meeting of the National Federation of Priests' Councils: "I'm a priest who has gone from self-hatred because I'm gay to self-acceptance and celebration of who I am. One definite prob-lem is the isolation I felt from other priests. This is surprising since so many of the clergy are gay, but it was never talked about or acknowledged and so I felt myself one of a kind and lived in a private hell."[9]

———

Self-policing compartmentalization is much more efficient than the Sambian combination of precautions and threats. First, clerical sexual activities are dispersed, so an informant cannot betray the entire group. Then, second, the official condemnations and persecutions establish "deniability." Expo-sure of any individual or group of individuals, no matter how highly placed, can be dismissed as an isolated personal failure. No matter how many witnesses are brought forward, they can be dismissed as aberrations, because "the Church herself" officially condemns homosexual acts, especially in clergymen, who are all obliged to be celibate anyway. The universal legislation of clerical celibacy becomes here too a universal pretext for denying the realities of clerical sex.

Compartmentalization and deniability are two ways of maintaining what many fear to be the "secret" of clerical homosexuality. A third method, less visible and more important, is the rhetoric of hysteria.* This rhetoric sustains secrecy by distorting any language we might use to talk about the small truths, the individual closets of clerical homosexuality.

Here we can be misled by the metaphor of the "closet." It is a metaphor of seeing and not seeing, of visibility and invisibility. We would do better with acoustic metaphors of hearing and not hearing, of speaking and silence. But it is difficult to combine all the acoustic properties into a single image. The clerical closet is not just a shield of silence that prevents those outside it from hearing. It is more like a magic spell that prevents those around it from speaking.

Sedgwick writes, "In the vicinity of the closet, even what *counts* as a speech act is problematized on a perfectly routine basis. . . . 'Closetedness' itself is a performance initiated by the speech act of a silence—not a particular silence, but a silence that accrues particularity by fits and starts, in relation to the discourse that surrounds and differentially constitutes it."[10] In the ancient discourses around the Catholic priesthood, the silence is performed not just individually or collectively, but by the language itself.

---

* "Hysteria" may be a difficult term for some readers, because it was long used in the service of misogynistic views, both medical and psychological. "Hysteria" was also applied as a diagnosis for the "effeminate"—that is, for homosexual men. But that is exactly what I mean to combat by turning the term around. The real hysteria originates not in our bodies or minds, but in the speeches of those who fix the diagnosis onto us. If the term still proves troublesome after this explanation, try substituting for it a more familiarly religious term, such as "zeal."

———

Sedgwick also quotes a passage from Foucault—one emphasized by Halperin as well:[11] "There shouldn't be a binary division between what one says and what one doesn't say. . . . There is not one silence, but many, and they are an integral part of strategies that underlie and run through discourses."[12] The silences of clerical homosexuality are an integral part of many strategies that underlie and run through the most important discourses of church authority. Because of their importance, those silences are ingeniously constructed. The greatest part of the ingenuity is spent on figuring out ways to control or corrupt the language in which anyone might "disclose" clerical homosexuality.

———

I think of this as the quandary of Maria Monk. "Maria Monk" is the supposed author of *Awful Disclosures of the Hotel Dieu Nunnery of Montreal*. This canonical work of American anti-Catholicism, first published in 1835 and frequently reprinted since, pretends to disclose what goes on in the hidden rooms of a Canadian convent. "Maria" can tell us because she has been there herself as a nun—in rooms where nuns are regularly prostituted to priests, where unwanted infants are baptized perfunctorily before being smothered, and where the uncooperative are imprisoned or killed. "Maria" escaped from the convent and made her way to New York in order to write and publish her story. When her truthfulness was vigorously challenged, "Maria" offered to lead a public tour of the hidden rooms—to show the public what was inside.[13]

For the moment, I don't care that most historians consider "Maria" a victim of delusions who was used by malicious, anti-Catholic propagandists.[14] I only mean to take her story as a parable for any inquiry into Catholic clerical homosexuality. The parable can teach several lessons. It can reinforce the lesson about compartmentalization, for example, because Maria's basic images will mislead us if we try to apply them to clerical homosexuality. There is no suite of inner rooms sheltering all the gay clergy. There are no well-established rituals or sweeping histories or even enduring networks of support. There is no *inside*. The varieties of sexual lives in the clergy are too complicated and too compartmentalized.

A second lesson has to do with what happens to a story like Maria's once it is spoken. Assume for the sake of parable that she did make her perilous way to New York in order to tell of awful crimes committed in secret. But she couldn't relate that story. Whenever she tried, it came out as anti-Catholic propaganda, as hysterical journalism. The hysteria of her story had to produce counterhysteria. Her *Awful Disclosures* were rebutted, anonymously, by the *Awful Exposure of [her] Atrocious Plot*.

The same is true when it comes to clerical homosexuality. If there is no inside, there is also no *outside*. There is no daylight world in which the facts of clerical homosexuality can be calmly examined and then perfectly judged by impartial observers. The very language we have at our disposal is already sensationalized, already hysterical, wherever we try to discuss clerical homosexuality.

———

We are unable to say even what everybody knows. Or we are unable to say precisely what everybody knows.

The last of the four species of "fags" (*locas*) that Reinaldo Arenas identifies in Castro's Cuba is the "regal fag" (one might say, the true queen).[15] "She" is, Arenas writes, "a species unique to communist countries. The regal fag is one who, because of very direct ties to the Great Leader or some extraordinary work for State Security or something similar, is powerful enough to be a fag publicly. She can lead a scandalous life and, at the same time, occupy high posts, travel, enter and leave the country, cover herself with jewels and rags and even have a private chauffeur."

The species is not confined to communism. It is a Catholic species as well, and not just among powerful prelates (whose adornments are discussed in a later chapter). But the church has taken the arrangements one step further. It has created conditions under which certain well-placed clerics can be "regal fags" publicly. But it is impossible to name them as "regal fags" without slipping into the most violent speeches of hysteria.

———

Beginning in 1970, the French writer Roger Peyrefitte began to hint at the homosexuality of Pope Paul VI, who was then still reigning.[16] Peyrefitte said, for example, that the pope had taken the papal name "Paul" because it was the name of his former lover, a young movie actor; that this man was known in Milanese clerical circles and protected by them; that the pope, while a cardinal, would go to a "discreet house" to meet young men. Paul VI was sufficiently offended by the gossip to denounce it (hysterically) as "horrible and slanderous" from the balcony of St. Peter's on Palm Sunday. Peyrefitte was besieged by reporters. Someone from *Newsweek* wanted to know whether he had seen the pope in bed with this lover. A television interviewer demanded, on camera, "a proof" of the claim. Newspapers in Latin America ran full pages of coverage: "The pope and Peyrefitte." Hysteria makes for counterhysteria, for melodrama. Peyrefitte claims to have signed depositions from two of the Swiss Guards about the "homosexual activities" of several "princes of the church." The depositions are kept in a safe outside of France.[17]

Considered from the point of view of church history, there is nothing surprising in Peyrefitte's claim (as I shall show in a later chapter). If Paul VI did have male lovers while archbishop of Milan, he would not be the first cardinal to do so. But Peyrefitte's claim could not be uttered as a simple report on an incident in church history. It was uttered as scandal and it was received as scandal. It was inevitably, hysterically changed into "horrible and slanderous things."

———

We know whatever we learn, but we will never be able to say what we know. "[T]he fact [that] the secret is always known—and, in some obscure sense, known to be known—never interferes with the incessant activity of keeping it. . . . [T]he social function of secrecy . . . is not to conceal knowledge, so much as to conceal the knowledge of the knowledge."[18] Which is to say, to prevent speaking of the knowledge.

———

In June 1995, a dozen American bishops issued a joint protest against the lack of candor in the deliberations of the NCCB. One of the topics not being discussed was the "rumors of a higher percentage of homosexual men in seminaries and the priesthood." Bishops complained to other bishops that it is impossible to talk openly even about "rumors" of homosexuality.[19]

———

We have rather more than rumors of clerical homosexuality. We are surrounded by its evidence. But because the evidence is so various and so dispersed, we can't hope to assemble a comprehensive case. Whenever we try to arrange a few of the individual pieces, we find that every single one of them can be denied or explained away. If we refuse to be reduced to silence, our insistence begins to sound hysterical.

———

To make any progress in speaking about Catholic homosexuality, we have to negotiate with the hysterical character of speech about clerical homosexuality. In our negotiations, we do best to begin in the present, describing a kind of speech that is obviously hysterical. The obvious example is in public scandals about priestly pedophilia. We next look for hysteria in a speech that seems almost entirely free of it—say, the speech of surveys. Americans are accustomed to thinking about media scandals as short bouts of mass hysteria, but we too often still regard surveys of sexual behavior as matters of hard fact. When it comes to priestly homosexuality, distorting hysteria operates in each.

Scandals of Pedophilia

However often fairness insists on distinguishing pedophilia from homosexuality, hysteria combines the two. Within and without the Catholic Church, public scandals over the abuse of boys by clergymen are taken to be the best or at least the most convincing evidence about clerical homosexuality. Indeed, one of the most serious studies of the pedophile scandals argues that a number of clerical "pedophiles" or "pederasts" were in fact "homosexual ephebophiles"—that is, gay men having sex with older teenagers.[20] "Pedophilia" points in fact to homosexuality. Certainly most laypeople think they catch a glimpse inside the closets of the Catholic clergy by means of such scandals.[21]

I have been a bystander at several scandals concerning priestly pedophilia. One of them resulted in the largest judgment to date for damages

against a Catholic diocese. It was well publicized locally and nationally—
and it disclosed almost nothing about the homosexuality of the priests in
that diocese. So it seems a good case for testing the limits of scandal in
learning about the lives of clerical homosexuals.

———

The scandal I watched was like so many others. A priest of the Catholic
diocese of Dallas, Rudolph "Rudy" Kos, was sued on behalf of eleven
young men whom he had abused over half a dozen years, in and out of the
rectory. Only ten of the plaintiffs were still alive for the trial; one, despair-
ing, had shot himself in 1992.

During the civil trial in 1997, it was established that the abuse occurred
regularly, with many boys, and blatantly.[22] Kos would lure boys with candy,
video games, cigarettes, and—later—alcohol or marijuana. He engaged in
a variety of sexual acts with some of the boys, who ranged in age from ten
up to the legal limit in Texas, which is eighteen. Many of them spent nights
in the rectory. Next morning, they would be introduced to the parish's other
priests at the breakfast table and then all would share in the mealtime
prayer. Kos pretended to adopt one sixteen-year-old in order to move him
into the rectory for several years as a steady sex partner. The arrangement
was written up in the diocesan paper as a shining example of priestly philanthropy.

———

Damages originally awarded in the case amounted to $119.6 million, of
which $18 million were punitive damages against the diocese. The jurors
found unanimously that the diocese had committed "gross negligence" and
concealed information in its handling of complaints against Kos. After
months of negotiation among the diocese, its insurers, and groups of plaintiffs, it was finally agreed that the diocese would pay $10.35 million toward
a total settlement of $30.9 million. The diocese was also left with some $4
million in legal fees.[23]

After the civil trial concluded, Rudy Kos was arrested in San Diego and
returned to Dallas on a number of criminal charges. In March 1998 he was
convicted on all but one count. The Dallas diocese took the unusual step of
asking the Vatican to nullify Kos's ordination retroactively and without

church trial on grounds that he deceived seminary officials about past sexual acts or offenses and other facts of his history.[24] The Vatican suspended Kos from priestly ministry, but did not grant the request for nullification.

————

I was a bystander. Some twenty years before his trials, Rudy Kos was a student at Holy Trinity Seminary, Dallas. In the fall of 1978, he enrolled in a class I was teaching. It was designed to force-feed seminarians the bits of "Scholastic" philosophy considered necessary for ordination. The class contained a number of "late vocations." Rudy Kos was one of these older seminarians. Indeed, he was eight years older than I was. He had worked as a nurse and explained in detail to me that he was suited for science, not philosophy. But he did learn enough of what he had to; he passed the course.

I wish I could say that Rudy Kos had the mark of Cain on him. He seemed angry and unhappy, but no more so than a number of his classmates. There were a few rumors about his past life and his homoerotic tastes, but such rumors were not all that rare about older seminarians. In any case, I was in no condition to think about such things clearly. I was too preoccupied by my own fierce combat against desires for men. Like so many others in Catholic education, I was simply incapable of helping anyone with homoerotic secrets.

————

An important witness against the diocese in the Kos civil trial was Dan Clayton, who had once been pastor of a parish in Irving to which Kos was assigned as an assistant. Clayton was so worried by boys staying overnight that he kept a log of their visits and reported them.[25] I have known of Father Clayton in recent years as a chaplain for the Dallas chapter of Dignity, and he has stood by lesbian and gay Catholics in many other ways. He testified at the trial on behalf of the plaintiffs, against his own diocese.

————

Another figure in the trial was Robert Rehkemper. I had routine dealings with Monsignor Rehkemper years earlier when he was vicar general for the diocese, the officer who kept the diocese running.

During the trial, Rehkemper was threatened several times with contempt citations by the trial judge.[26] The monsignor had some difficulty in answering direct questions. When he did answer, he typically pleaded ignorance— of Kos's activities, of the diocese's own administrative actions, of national policy recommendations about pedophilic priests. I am willing to credit some of this ignorance. I have seen how much church administration operates on the principle of willed ignorance. "Don't ask, don't tell" has been Catholic policy for centuries.

After the trial Monsignor Rehkemper gave an interview in which he blamed the victims and their parents for some or most of what happened.[27] He was asked by the bishop to step down. His punishment: a year of study in Rome.

———

The Kos case discloses the complexity of the church's habits of keeping secrets, even from itself. It is not just a matter of avoiding legal liability, though that is nowadays perhaps the most urgent motive. Pedophilia cases do threaten to bankrupt Catholic dioceses in America. But the hierarchy also wants to keep these scandals hidden because that is its universal policy in regard to clerical sexuality, especially male-male sexuality. The behavior of bishops on the witness stand is little different from their behavior in the chancery. They are not keeping secrets just from outsiders who want damages. They are keeping secrets from the "faithful," from their own priests, from one another, and from their superiors.

These customs, these habitual procedures, are the same ones that silence and scatter clerical homosexuality. In reality, pedophilia is not homosexuality, but clerical pedophilia and clerical homosexuality are handled by the same church habits—and are not infrequently coupled in the anxiety of clerical bureaucrats.

On the one hand, the story shows no solidarity between pederasts and homosexuals. Indeed, Father Clayton, a priest identified with gay causes, was one of the first to try to take action against Father Kos, the pederast. Priests I know who identify themselves as gay tend to condemn pederasts harshly and to urge prompt disciplinary action against them.

On the other hand, Kos now considers himself "gay." Since his "cure" from pedophilic desires, he claims to have lived in a "celibate" relationship with a man he calls his "lover."[28] Perhaps this is true, perhaps not. Either way, the horrible spectacle of Kos's trials is associated with anxiety over homosexuality in the priesthood.

———

If the Kos civil trial publicly exposed the defendant's sexual habits and his diocese's administrative ones, it showed almost nothing about the ordinary lives of gay priests in Dallas. This is partly because Kos's pedophilia took him out of ordinary gay culture rather than toward it. But it is also because the scandalous speeches about priestly sexuality permit no unhysterical descriptions.

The journalistic accounts, whether printed or broadcast, regularly highlighted the most sensational details. Even the very staid *Dallas Morning News* found itself recounting Kos's masturbation rituals. The stories tell us little about clerical homosexuality; indeed, they tell us much more about our prurient fascination with other people's sexual practices. The courtroom testimony was equally a caricature in one way or another—as perhaps all testimony must be in a highly publicized and lucrative case. Certainly the Catholic diocese did not enter the proceedings voluntarily, with a passionate desire to have the full truth made public. On the contrary, its speech was almost entirely the speech of denial.

Neither the journalistic accounts nor the courtroom testimony disclosed much about the ordinary forms of clerical homosexuality. Some priests in the courtroom could have spoken about their suburban dinners with other gay priests or their annual vacations in all-male resorts or their clandestine visits to Cedar Springs bars and backrooms. These priests could have described a dozen different patterns of homosexual adaptation to churchly rules and parishioners' expectations. But none of this testimony was wanted. It was not wanted by the diocese, certainly, which deliberately avoided "outing" more of its own. It was also not wanted by the plaintiffs, who had to demonize Kos and the diocesan administration. It was not wanted by journalists, whose tidy morality play would have been confused by larger considerations of the clergy and homosexuality.

People think they learn about clerical homosexuality from pedophilia scandals. In fact, the hysterical speeches of scandal, the speeches of contemporary journalism and contemporary litigation, say nothing important about it.

It is easy to recognize the hysteria in scandals over priestly pedophilia. It is much less obvious in the often tedious statistics drawn from sociologists' surveys. But there is hysteria in statistics, too—as soon as the statistics begin to speak of clerical homosexuality.

Counting Homosexuals

Battles over the "actual percentage" of homosexuals in the general population are tediously familiar. Is it "one in ten"? One in a hundred? One in five? Rather than engage in armed combat with surveys, we would do better to ask ourselves some prior questions: Do we think that homosexual identity is a digital attribute that a respondent has or doesn't have? Do we think that surveys are the appropriate instrument for discovering rather complicated truths about human sexual attitudes and practices? Consider, for example, the methodological anomalies of the recent survey of 3,432 American subjects by Laumann and his colleagues.[29] The survey was constructed with every guarantee of anonymity in a society supposedly tolerant of sexual variety. The only incontestable conclusion from an analysis of the survey's results is that some respondents lied about their sexual activities—because the numbers do not add up.

It would be astonishing if anyone were able to tell the truth about sexuality in so cramped a format as a survey. It is hard enough for people to admit to themselves what they have done under the impulse of sexual desire—or what they have desired to do, but left undone. How many men, gay or straight, stammer small talk and hurry to leave the bed, wanting to forget what happened on the way to their now cooling pleasure? How many "out" gay men construct little closets inside themselves or around selected hours of each of their weeks?

Add to these ordinary shames the particular shame of the priesthood. "I don't know if I would have explored my own gayness if I were in the priesthood. Or if I did explore it, would I have done so in a way that would have been real sleazy? I've seen that with classmates I've known in the seminary.

Having to drive a long distance to make sure they are far out of the parish, and then looking for a bar or a pick up of some kind on the road."[30]

We shouldn't expect to learn much about clerical homosexuality, then, from responses to questions in surveys. Of course, the questions don't usually get asked.

———

Many of the large-scale surveys of American priests simply missed the topic of clerical homosexuality. It may be predictable that official questionnaires should not ask about it—or should look the other way when it is mentioned. The first of the large-scale surveys of the priesthood was authorized by the American bishops in 1967 and preparations were made from then through 1969. These were the heady years just after Vatican II, as they were the years of the first stirrings of gay liberation, including Stonewall. Yet the sociological and psychological components of the survey ignore priestly homosexuality almost entirely. The section of the survey that concerns "attitudes toward sexual morality" considers views about masturbation, contraception, divorce, and abortion, but not homosexuality.[31]

We might expect this kind of silence, if not this kind of condescension, in an official survey commissioned in 1967. But things have not improved much since. A similar silence on the issue is kept in the more comprehensive survey done for the bishops under the direction of Richard Schoenherr during the 1980s.[32] "While it has been a concern for some time to many U.S. Catholics, the U.S. bishops have adamantly refused to gather information on the sexual inclinations of its priests."[33] How much of this is an official exclusion on the part of the bishops or their surveyors, how much a tacit agreement on all clerical sides not to raise embarrassing questions?

———

We see something like this agreement in collections of interviews with Catholic priests. Tim Unsworth published in 1991 his versions of interviews with fifty priests and seminarians. A number of priests remarked to him how little they know of homosexuality in their peers.[34] Unsworth himself seems to have trouble piercing the secrecy. Of the fifty clergymen included in the book, only one identifies himself as gay—and he insists on anonymity. Moreover, he is included not because he is gay, but because he is HIV positive (pp. 246–54). One in fifty is 2 percent. But Unsworth himself suggests at several points that the percentage of gay clergy is higher than the percentage in the population at large. By any calculation, that would be more than 2 percent. Indeed, Unsworth endorses the figure of 30 percent and quotes figures that range from 10 percent to 75 percent (pp. 218, 248, 269). Why is it, then, that Unsworth's interviews so grossly underrepresent gay priests? Part of the answer is that he is a straight-identified man who doesn't make any evident effort to get inside the "lavender rectories" his sole gay informant describes.

By contrast, a gay layman can find that he knows mostly gay priests. He will meet them in bars and other places for cruising, of course, but he is also likely to begin socializing with them in the older and wealthier circles of gay society. The common experience is perfectly captured in this exchange from a gay detective story: "'Are all priests gay?,' Scott asked. — 'All the ones I know are,' Neil said. 'It's an extremely closeted homophobic society. The most closeted ones being the most homophobic.'"[35]

———

Targeted surveys have succeeded somewhat better in eliciting responses and so in producing numbers. For example, in 1989 Sheila Murphy collected responses by mail from ninety-seven self-selected male clergymen between the ages of thirty-five and sixty-five, two-thirds of them members of religious orders. About 19 percent identified themselves as homosexual, another 9 percent as bisexual.[36]

A more famous study of gay priests was conducted by James Wolf beginning in 1984. While still a doctoral student in sociology at the University of Chicago, Wolf was approached by a group of gay priests who were interested in funding a national survey on the issue of homosexuality in the Catholic priesthood. Wolf tried the standard techniques for gathering information from a random sample. When it proved impossible to get a random sample of priests even to answer a confidential questionnaire through the mail, Wolf resorted to the "snowball" technique. He sent the questionnaire to gay priests, who were then asked to send it to other gay priests, and so on. In the end, he collected 101 responses from gay men still active in the priesthood.[37]

Wolf's questionnaire contained the following items (p. 186):

> Approximately what percent of Catholic priests in the U.S. do you think have a sexual orientation that is heterosexual? Homosexual?

> Approximately what percent of Catholic seminarians in the U.S. do you think have a sexual orientation that is heterosexual? Homosexual?

On average, Wolf's "network" of respondents held that 48.5 percent of priests known to them were homosexual according to some definition of homosexuality, while 55.1 percent of seminarians were (p. 60). What is most interesting is the breakdown by type of respondent. "Note that the perceived proportion of gay priests and seminarians is highest among those gay priests who have been most recently ordained. What is quite clear is that the highest percentage estimates of gay seminarians, 70.5 percent, is given by those who have most recently attended the seminary" (p. 60). Newer priests, those who have had the most recent experience of seminary and who come into the seminary from a culture where it is more permissible to be "out," estimate that more than two-thirds of seminarians currently have a "homosexual orientation." They also show the least standard deviation in the responses: their independent assessments agree more nearly with each other (roughly within a range of ± 6 percentage points).

Wolf's book also contains anonymous essays by four gay priests from among the group that originally approached him. There is much anecdotal evidence in these essays about the prevalence of gay men in the priesthood and the religious life. One number is given by "Rev. R. Edwards": "there are lots of gay priests; this fact has not been scientifically verified, but my own experience and that of many others suggests that at least half of American priests are 'gay' in one of the ways I will describe below, and I have no reason to think that the figure is lower in other countries" (p. 80).

Wolf's four testimonies constitute only a small fraction of those in print. Interviews with past or present priests, religious, and seminarians who identify themselves as gay frequently include estimates of how many there are in the clergy as a whole. Typical figures are "40" or "50" percent.[38] A religious priest from Idaho set the figure at 60 percent in private conversation; the same figure is the "educated guess" of an ex-priest in the Bay Area.[39] Sometimes no exact figure is given, but the judgment remains the same. A "high percentage" or a "large number" of priest or seminarians are said to be gay.[40] Two former Jesuit seminarians, now a male-male couple, say it most strikingly: "We know so many clergy, especially Jesuits, who are homosexual, and all in the closet."[41]

Similar reports are heard from outside North America. "Thomas, a [British] seminarian," responded to Elizabeth Stuart: "it's quite easy to be slightly camp with fellow priests because so many of us are."[42] "Father Terry," an Australian priest, thinks that 30 to 50 percent of those entering the seminary in the early 1990s were gay. "Certainly, it would be my reasonably informed opinion that the substantial majority of Australian priests ordained in the last 15 years are gay."[43] A French formation director put the figure at "20–25 percent" in 1983 on the basis of many interviews with candidates and colleagues.[44] Yet in a 1987 survey within the archdiocese of Utrecht, only 10 percent of the priests reported having homosexual tendencies.[45]

The most interesting survey on these matters is in some ways the least scientific. Using the "informal network of gay priests operative in just about every section of the country," Richard Wagner found fifty self-identified gay priests in active ministry.[46] He interviewed them about their sexual histories using an adaptation of the Kinsey protocol and then gave them a written "attitude inventory" to fill out and return by mail. Interviews and inventories were completed around 1980. Wagner's aim was not to establish the percentage of Catholic priests who had certain types of sexual experiences or desires. He wanted rather to explore the kinds of dissonance that gay priests experienced between their lives and their official roles. But there are interesting asides on the number of gay priests. One respondent said of seminary, "'There were too many like me there to feel I had to leave, so I didn't'" (49). Other respondents spoke of the relations of gayness to clerical power: "'I bumped into an auxiliary bishop at a gay hotel and saw the ordi-

nary [bishop] of a diocese at a gay bar across country'" (55). "I do mind
being propositioned by closeted priests who have found this out [namely,
his being gay]. It is most uncomfortable because some are real powerful
people and when I don't return the interest I jeopardize my own position in
the diocese" (75).

But the most startling results from Wagner's interviews may be just the
responses to the Kinsey questionnaire about sexual history. Wagner found
that forty-nine of his fifty respondents were "masturbating at a mean frequency nearly three times that reported by Kinsey," while his sample had
"nearly five times the number of respondents reporting 500 or more total
partners" (99). The respondents averaged "226.8 partners." At the time of
the interviews, the "mean frequency of same-sex contact [was] two times
per week" (26). After allowances for bragging, the distortions of surveys,
and the frenzied excesses of the years before knowledge of AIDS, these
figures still astonish.

———

Any number of objections are typically raised against these first-person reports. One objection is that the reports may be deliberate or unconscious
wish fulfillment, as if gay clergy wanted to make themselves feel better by
inflating the numbers of others in the same situation. Another is that gay
clergy tend to socialize with other gay clergy and so draw mistaken conclu-
sions about what percentage of the clergy is gay overall. Or that the esti-
mated percentages are part of a "gay agenda" within the Catholic Church.
And so on. There are replies to each of these objections, as there are yet
further objections to be made.

I would like to step around the whole debate by noticing two things.
First, it is an odd feature of debate about homosexuality that the only people
who have much experience with it, namely homosexuals, are regularly dis-
counted as unreliable because biased. Biased they may be. They are also
singularly well-informed. Second, objections to these reports don't direct us
to better reports. If the figures volunteered in the interviews are not reliable,
certainly no other figures are more reliable.

———

There are more important things to consider than percentages. We might
think about why we care so much about the numbers—why we can get so

hysterically excited about them. We can begin by noting what happens when the percentages are tied to predictions.

The most famous statistical predictions are those by A. W. Richard Sipe, a priest and psychotherapist. Sipe was concerned with priestly celibacy and sexuality in general, not just with clerical homosexuality. He gathered figures from some 1,500 persons between 1960 and 1985. One third of his group consisted of patients in psychotherapy. One third was composed of clergy who were not patients, but who were encountered in a variety of other public and private contexts. The last third comprised either sexual partners of priests or "direct observers" of priestly sexual behavior.[47]

As for the incidence of homosexuality, Sipe's interviews and reports suggest a marked increase over three decades. The "baseline" figure established in the 1960s put the number of homosexual priests, under a broad definition, at between 18 and 22 percent. Between 1978 and 1985, this figure doubled to something between 38 and 42 percent. Even more striking, the best figures for the very last segment of Sipe's reporting period, from 1982 to 1985, set the percentage of homosexual priests at half the total population (p. 107). Sipe himself concluded that in 1985 about one fifth of all American priests had "some homosexual orientation," while one tenth "involve[d] themselves in homosexual activity" (p. 133). But he also predicted, quite famously, that a continuation of recent trends would mean that by the year 2010, more than half of America's Catholic clergy would be homosexual.

It is hard to know how to consider this kind of judgment, especially since it is made in the aggregate. Everyone seems to agree both that there has been an increase in homosexual priests and that younger priests are more sexually active. Just a page before stating his summary conclusion, for example, Sipe quotes at second hand a public health officer's estimate that "one third of Catholic priests under forty-five [in urban areas?] are homosexuals, and most are sexually active" (132). One tenth of the whole priestly population sexually active? Almost one third of those under forty-five? One fifth of the whole priestly population somehow gay in orientation? One third? One half? Three quarters of those coming out of seminary in the 1980s?

———

If it is difficult to judge Sipe's predictions, it is easy to see what kind of reaction they provoke. For example, consider the responses to a piece by Richard McBrien about the increasing numbers of gay priests and seminarians.[48] Now McBrien's essay is written from a resolutely heterosexual stand-point, and it entertains ugly possibilities (for example, the relationship of clerical gayness to clerical pedophilia). Some of its points are now a bit dated: the possibility of gay marriage, for example, has a reality now that it did not have in 1987. But the essay's stated concern is to try to think about what it might mean to be in a church with a mostly gay clergy.

The editors of *Commonweal* published a number of responses to McBrien's articles, most of which attacked him either as prejudiced against gays or as prejudiced against priestly celibacy. But none of the letters really takes up McBrien's questions, except perhaps to deny their premises. Archbishop Mahony assures us that in Los Angeles "neither our seminaries nor our presbyterate is filled with homosexuals."[49] To which assurance it is hard to reply . . . without laughing. The archbishop's response is an irrational denial. It is hysterical.

———

Some writers who do think about a gay future for the American priesthood reject it. "In such a family-centered religion, the risk of gradually evolving a homosexually oriented priestly caste seems unacceptable."[50] Andrew Greeley is reported as saying, rather more candidly, that assuming that many Catholic priests are homosexual is "a moral if not a legal defamation."[51] If the first reaction seems both a little naive and a little confused, Greeley's reported reaction is perfectly hysterical.

———

I am not convinced that any amount of statistical manipulation regarding clerical homosexuality would yield more than some already evident generalities.

Everyone seems to agree that there are now more homosexuals in the Catholic priesthood and religious life than in the population at large. This is hardly surprising. The priesthood and religious life are all-male institutions that reward vows of celibacy within a religion that demands celibacy of all homosexuals. If you have to be celibate anyway, why not get rewarded for it—and do it in the company of other men with similar inclinations?

The consensus also seems to be that the percentage of reported homosexuals in the American clergy has risen sharply in the last two decades.

There are any number of plausible reasons: the exodus after Vatican II of those who could get married, the sharpening of a sense of gay identity in society at large, and the increasing social openness to discussion of homosexuality.

There is no point in fiddling with statistics to support these points. Instead, we should focus our intellectual energy on their implications.

———

If we are trying to determine how closets are constructed in the Catholic church, how they inhibit theological thinking about homosexuality, the exact percentage of gay priests is really beside the point. It doesn't much matter whether it is 5 percent or 25 percent or 50 percent. The construction and enforcement of rules of silence will operate at any of those levels, because the closet is a collaborative construction of gay and straight. The strength of the system of secrecy doesn't depend on the number of gay people who are having sex in secret. It depends on the number of those who are afraid of that secret sex, about which they may know only what their own fears or fantasies whisper. There may be just one homosexually active monsignor in a curial office of ten, but the closet around him is built by all ten together, without anyone saying a word. That is why there is no easy correlation between a higher percentage of gay clergy and better conditions of visibility. The recent increase in the perceived number of gay clergy has opened some closet doors, but it has locked others more securely.

———

The hunt for statistics also blocks serious thinking in other ways. No matter how carefully the survey categories are constructed, deriving statistics from them will require assigning responses to one category or another. This either-or thinking tends to reinforce the idea that there is a homosexual essence that one either has or hasn't got. That idea, in turn, allows many men with homoerotic desires or histories to reassure themselves that they aren't really "gay" because they don't quite fit into the definitions of the categories being used. The statistics become another pretext for not having to think about the complexities of homosexuality in relation to the complexities of church words and church lives. What exact percentage? "'Oh my dear, who can say? A hundred and ten percent.'"[52]

Discussions of homosexual activity within the Catholic clergy often emphasize a distinction between "homosocial" and "homosexual" or "homogenital" and "homophilic." The purpose of such distinctions is more than differentiating feelings or dispositions from acts. The intention is to divide an unacceptable realm of homosexuality from an acceptable realm of male bonding or comradely affection or buddies' slaps on the butt. Now this curious boundary between the homosocial and the homosexual has been set with very different degrees of clarity at different times, in different places, and for men as opposed to women.[53] The more strongly you stigmatize male homosexuality, the more important it becomes to have a separate space for the male homosocial. That is the situation in the modern Catholic clergy. It is very easy for survey respondents to take refuge in the homosocial when trying to categorize their own actions. (Recall that according to some psychoanalytic theories homosociality just is sublimated homosexuality.)[54]

But there is a larger confusion here. To assert "homosocial" against "homosexual" only begs the question, What do we mean by "homosexual"?

There are no clear, uncontested meanings for "homosexual" or "homosexuality" as applied to clergymen. A loud debate during the last two decades has established that the terms certainly don't have any fixed meaning across history. They are modern categories in the strongest sense, coined just over one hundred years ago.[55] So to ask whether a premodern priest or member of a religious order is or is not "homosexual" must provoke the prior question, How do you apply the term "homosexual" across history?

The limitation is not only historical. How do we judge today whether a priest is "homosexual"? Do we assign the identity "homosexual" when there are reported feelings, but no reported acts? When there are reported acts, but no reported feelings? When the clergyman in question denies both feelings and acts, despite evidence to the contrary?

We speakers of contemporary American English have no general criteria for calling someone "homosexual." We can strike agreements to employ the terms consistently for a time and with a certain purpose in view. But most of the time we live comfortably with the term's vagueness, adjusting ourselves to the different contexts—joking, flirting, cruising, counseling, debating, testifying. It makes little sense, then, to argue at length and in general about whether a clergyman is or is not "homosexual" without stipulating criteria for the meanings of the terms. Such criteria will be "stipulative" in the pejorative sense as well. Although they record someone's particular decision about how to use words, that decision will not fix meanings for the words in general. And it will not explain how a particular survey respondent is using them.

––––

Survey responses are in fact the easy case for definition. It becomes much harder when we are assigning the term "homosexual" against the wishes of the person and with serious consequences. It becomes much harder, in other words, when we are accusing a person of sexual acts or feelings or identities. But accusation is still the most frequent use of those terms in the Catholic church, and it raises enormous difficulties of evidence. Even if we were satisfied to translate questions of sexual identity into questions about sexual acts, and then to specify certain acts at certain frequencies, we would still have to consider the burden of proof. Before deciding whether a priest is "homosexual," do we demand the proof required for a criminal conviction? For a civil suit? For a clinical diagnosis? For an administrative decision? For a choice about beginning a long-term relationship? For selecting him as a short-term sexual partner? Then we must decide where to place the burdens of proof. On the observer who alleges such same-sex acts or desires? On the clergyman who denies them? Most of us are familiar with these and other complications of evidence in our daily lives. We seem to forget them when we enter into sociological or historical research.

In the face of these questions, I am amused to read lists of "homosexual" or "gay" saints—or to learn that Augustine was one of the hundred most influential lesbians and gays. If only our lives—or our histories—were so clear.

––––

We count so assiduously because of anxiety or fantasy, because of hysteria caused by the thought of gay clergy. Our struggles over surveys are an effect of hysteria, however muted. Certainly hysteria works to flatten the survey categories, so that we can say with clarity and conviction whether or not someone really is "a homosexual." The hysteria has worked itself into the category, making it anything but a neutral description. To be a priest and a homosexual is already to be caught up in the possibility of scandal, in the language of hysterical accusation or denial.

———

The hysteria of scandal surrounds any act of "outing" priests or religious. When you "out" clergymen, you force them to inhabit a role of melodramatic disgrace. You are a homosexual priest: you must assume this role in the unfolding public scandal. "Outing" thus becomes another means of silencing, so far as it prescribes in advance what can be said.

My own writing of this chapter and of the ones to follow risks falling into this dilemma. On the one hand, I am convinced that we need to speak about these things not only for the abstract sake of honesty, but for the real and concrete motive of resisting the effects of closeted homosexuality in church bureaucracies. On the other hand, I know that my writing not only fuels anti-Catholic bigotry, but also forces me to participate in the old inquisitorial melodrama of "outing" other gay men, even if I refuse to do so by name.

When one gay man "outs" another, he uses the violence of homophobic prejudice against one of his own. It seems most justified to do this against someone who himself espouses or advances homophobic violence. Roy Cohn spent his life targeting homosexuals. "Outing" Roy Cohn is a way of refusing him the protection of secrecy that he tried to strip away from others. It may be a satisfying act of vengeance—and perhaps a justifiable act of self-defense. But it is still an act of violence.

Sometimes, when I am very angry, I consider that I am at war with someone like Roy Cohn, and I try not to feel particularly guilty when I turn his own weapons against him. In the same spirit of warfare, I might well go to the press if I held incontrovertible evidence that a powerful and homophobic cardinal in the Vatican curia was in fact sexually active with men. I would act on impulse, in anger. I would not have Peyrefitte's patience to investigate the incriminating depositions and wait for decades. But then the best excuse I could offer myself for my actions would be that I am at the extreme moment of fighting violence with violence.

In these central chapters, I am "outing" important segments of the lives of the Catholic clergy. My motive in doing so is to make it possible to speak about homosexuality in the church. But I fully realize that my efforts can serve exactly opposite motives. Some of what I say could be used by the Catholic right wing to decry the alleged liberalization of the seminaries and religious orders. It could be used, again, to feed the anxieties of the hierarchy, encouraging them to try to get rid of openly gay priests or brothers. And, of course, it can always be used by anti-Catholics to confirm their view of the "whore of Babylon."

———

Speeches of the church, in the church, about the church, around the church. The silence that the Catholic hierarchy would like to preserve about homosexuality in general and clerical homosexuality in particular gives way, it seems, to a rush of hysterical words. But the silence enforced within and the hysteria manufactured without are not strictly opposed. Both enforced silence and hysterical speech serve to prevent serious speaking about same-sex love and Catholicism.

The Catholic church is by no means the only institution in American society that wants to prevent people from speaking seriously about lesbian and gay life. The church lends rhetorical strategies to other institutions and borrows from them. But the church is an institution with long experience in these strategies and a very high stake in their success.

———

The best response to the dilemmas of the hysteria surrounding clerical homosexuality is not to fall silent. The best response is to keep attending to the rhetoric of the swirl of hysterical speeches—and their predecessors. The conviction that same-sex desire in the clergy can't be discussed in a normal tone of voice is a very old one in the Catholic church. We can see it clearly in the discourses about "sodomy," some of which we have already sampled.

I think that the term "sodomy" was coined for theological purposes by Peter Damian in his polemic against corruption in the clergy. But even if it were invented elsewhere and by someone else, the melodrama with which Peter Damian deploys the term is typical of its medieval and early modern uses. The term makes urgent, incoherent, consequential condemnations. In this way, it is like some other terms in medieval religious discourse—most notably, "heretic," "witch," and "Jew." Indeed, it is frequently interchanged with them.

The modern hysteria around clerical homosexuality is the remainder, the residue, of those more elaborate theological melodramas. Those medieval projections of the diabolical figure of the priestly sodomite made it terribly important to know for sure, without any doubt, whether this priest was or was not polluted with the sodomitic sin. To understand how modern anxieties over clerical homosexuality block serious speech about homosexuality in the church, we need to look again at the medieval and early modern attacks on clerical sodomites. This is not the same as searching for the true history of sodomites in the clergy. We cannot have such a history—any more than we can have a dispassionate trial of a priestly pedophile or survey that finally reveals just how many priests really are homosexual. Still we can learn from our efforts to speak about history—and not least about our compulsion to find one.

5

memoirs of priestly sodomy

BEFORE THERE WAS "homosexuality" in the church, there
was "sodomy"; before "sodomy," layers of other terms: "sin
of the Sodomites," "irrational copulation," "crime against
nature," "softness," "corrupting boys," "copulating with
men." Each phrase has been used in Christian moral writing, and all have been used to describe the clergy. The terms
differ in their origins and their nuances, but they share important rhetorical features—especially the intensity of re-
crimination, the frenzy of denigration, that I have called
"hysteria." In this chapter, I draw historical analogies to
what we now call clerical "homosexuality" by looking back
at how those earlier terms, especially "sodomy," were applied to members of the clergy. The analogies are not quite
the ones we expect, as the history is not the one we might
find most useful. It turns out to be a history not of crimes or
pleasures, but of monstrous or shameful or ridiculous roles.

I concentrate on "sodomy," which is historically the most common Catholic name for male-male sex. As we have seen, the term can include other acts, like sex between women or masturbation or bestiality. But the term always refers at least to male-male copulation, and its imaginative center remains fixed there. However differently authors define it, when they imagine "sodomy," they imagine men penetrating men. So when they condemn sodomy most fiercely, they condemn it as an abandonment of masculinity. The abiding imagination is more important than the fluctuating definitions.

As terms of accusation, "sodomy" and "sodomite" carry the force of a specifically theological imagination. The imagination is hysterical. It resists efforts to justify standards of historical evidence or establish burdens of historical proof for applying the terms. The terms aren't imagined as group descriptions to be used by social historians, but rather as ways of stigmatizing sinners who have horribly polluted themselves. The terms project a sin-identity that makes the polluted into scapegoats. The hysterical accomplishment of theological imagination in "sodomy" and "sodomite" is the construction of a sin-identity that can carry out this scapegoating so well.

The scapegoating force of "sodomy" or "sodomite" is an immovable obstacle to writing any "objective" history of male-male sexuality in the Catholic clergy. Of course some historical evidence has been lost, and much of the written evidence has been subjected to censorship, as automatic as it was thorough. Yet I doubt that the evidence for homosexuality in the Catholic priesthood was ever much clearer or less partial than it is today. Even evidence that survives is distorted throughout by the hysterical character of its central concepts.

Peter Damian can serve again as a privileged example. He begins his *Gomorran Book* with a famously candid list of sexual acts. According to Peter, clerical sodomites perform what we would call masturbation, mutual masturbation, copulation between the thighs, and copulation "in the rear."[1] The acts do not constitute sodomy: They *express* it. They manifest the spiritual disease of being a sodomite. "Sodomy" is not just a name for acts; it is a diagnosis of their origin. That is why Peter Damian can avoid casuistical questions about boundaries or frequencies. He doesn't particularly care how many acts of masturbation constitute sodomy or whether ejaculation is required for copulation "in the rear." Instead, Peter treats such sexual acts according to a theological epistemology, as scraps of evidence in a spiritual mystery. The mystery is the dark sin that has taken possession of the sodomite's soul and body. Peter approaches the sin with deep suspicion. He reads through surface deceptions and denials to find sense underneath. He reads sodomitic acts, theologically, paranoically, as betraying an abominable and utterly unnatural spiritual identity from which they arise.

It is not as if we could strip away Peter's theological paranoia to reveal neutral content. No neutral criteria exist for assigning this kind of a scapegoating sin-identity. The identity is an artifact of theological epistemology, of a system of teachings about sin, spiritual deformity, discernment, rebuke, grace, expiation, and damnation. This kind of identity, this kind of artifact, can't just be incorporated into an ordinary project of social history. With "sodomy" and its cousins, for example, we can't ask whether the surviving evidence is reliable. Being a sodomite is not the kind of fact or datum, the kind of condition or disposition or event, about which it makes sense to speak of reliability. Within this theological epistemology, no evidence is simply reliable—and almost any datum can be suggestive.

————

The fantasy of reconstituting a complete and objective historical record of clerical sodomy has to be surrendered. But if we can't have a sweeping history or an orderly archive, we can have very striking memoirs of some of the roles that have been prescribed for clerical sodomites. Memoirs are notoriously unreliable about "facts," but they do tell us about the shames, fears, fantasies, and hopes enacted as ways of life. "*A Tissue of Lies?* Could there be a more persuasively apt title for a memoir?" asks Gore Vidal.[2] But those lies are the only kind of memory appropriate to the roles offered to many priestly sodomites—and taken up by them.

———

Can we hear the "real" voices of clerical sodomites behind the roles? We hear about their alleged actions. We hear their forced and stereotyped confessions. Sometimes, we hear the beginning of their resistance, before it is silenced. But we do not hear their "real" voices, because "their" voices were given to them by the theologians, who invented the identity with which they would be named and punished. How can we hear the authentic voices of priestly sodomites when we listen to them precisely as sodomites, as the creatures of theological hysteria?

We hear the dozens of voices that have been put in their mouths by different kinds of condemnations, prescriptions, and parodies. Those imposed voices are so often still the voices that determine what homosexual priests can say—or, rather, what they cannot say, what they must garble or pass over in silence. If "sodomy" and "sodomite" are not neutral identities for the social historian, much less are they neutral identities for the priests and religious asked to assume them. We must read historical texts not for clues to the "reality" of clerical sodomy, but for how clergymen were induced to play out the theological scripts written for them and through them.

———

In what follows, I consider different kinds of historical texts about sodomy in the Catholic clergy. Most of the texts are medieval or early modern, because those were the periods in which the Catholic church perfected the category "sodomy." I juxtapose texts that are supposed to be reliable or factual with other texts that are supposed to be impressionistic or literary. I sample different kinds of texts, without pretending to summarize or survey them, in order to learn how they force or induce men to play one or another version of the clerical sodomite.

———

What we learn from listening to the historical speeches about clerical sodomy is not a single narrative of acts, but episodes or scenes of rhetorical projection. The speeches can certainly teach us about persistent devices of church rhetoric, as well as about the larger institutional arrangements that confuse speech or promote silence. There are similarities or analogies between the roles historically assigned to clerical "sodomy" and modern roles given to clerical "homosexuality." But we discover these similarities or analogies only episodically, not as continuing plotlines. The only over-arching narrative that can be told in the terms of theological hysteria is the narrative of that hysteria itself.

———

The alternative to speaking the grand narrative of hysteria is just the sort of disconnected, evasive, all too interested speech we find in memoirs. Re-membering what has been said about the lives of clerical sodomites, we don't escape the hysteria. We rehearse the variations on it. We remember that prescribing speeches to clerical sodomites is a way of nullifying speech about whatever might exceed the role they are told to perform. Indeed, we learn how long church authorities have contrived ways to discuss sodomy while preventing adequate speech about it.

Denouncing Priestly Sodomites

The most infamous clerical sodomites have been popes. Their sodomy has been denounced with particular passion—and with considerable political effect. Take the case of Pope Boniface VIII (reigned 1294–1303).[3] Docu-ments assembled or manufactured by agents of the French monarchy under Philip the Fair give a number of details about Boniface's sexual activities with men. In the heat of seducing a cobbler's apprentice, Boniface is alleged to have said that sex between men was "no more a sin than rubbing your hands together."[4] At another time, two men identified as his lovers traded insults about who had really been the "pope's whore" (*meretrix papae*) and who had received which gifts from him.[5]

Now the truth of the accounts of Boniface's acts is much contested, be-cause Philip's charges are evidently partisan and extravagant. Of course they are. Papal sodomy is necessarily a partisan and extravagant charge. If the French denunciations of Boniface sound like scandalmongering, that is because the term "sodomy" must be scandalous when used against the pope. There is no way to accuse the pope of being a sodomite without be-ing scandalous.

How are we to judge the truth of the denunciations against Boniface? Do we rely on our sense of whether particular pieces of testimony seem uncontrived or "fresh" or convincingly detailed?[6] Should we rather weigh all of the French charges as a group, deciding against the charges of sodomy because other charges against Boniface seem "ludicrous"?[7] To evaluate the charges of sodomy with such criteria is to ignore the most obvious point: Highly charged rhetoric is politically useful. We need to consider not the truth of papal sodomy, but its usefulness. The same rule is true for every lesser case of clerical sodomy.

Charges of sodomy have been used often enough in political or legal struggles between the powers of Christendom, in the church or outside it. Christian kings or princes famously tarred with the sodomitic brush include William Rufus, Richard Lion Heart, Richard II, and James I of England, as well as Philip I and Henry III of France. Pope John XII (955–64) was accused by one chronicler of various debaucheries, including sex with men and boys. Paul II (1464–71) was ridiculed with feminine epithets for his love of ecclesiastical costume and beautiful young men. His successor, Sixtus IV (1471–84), created his lover (and nephew) a cardinal at the age seventeen. Perhaps for that reason he was reputed to have given permission to the College of Cardinals to practice sodomy in times of summer heat. Julius II (1503–13), better known to his contemporaries for his military ferocity than his artistic patronage, was accused of sodomy precisely because of his military prowess, since sodomy was also a military vice. Leo X (1513–21), the pope who excommunicated Luther, surrounded himself with beautiful pages, among whom he picked and chose with refined taste. Julius III (1550–55), who participated in and then reconvened the reforming Council of Trent, is also reported to have elevated a favorite boy, one Innocent, to the College of Cardinals. Paul III (1534–49) was often called a sodomite, but perhaps in a looser sense, since he was simultaneously accused of making two of his sons into cardinals.[8] One son, Pierluigi (Pietro Aloisio), was denounced for raping Cosimo Gheri, bishop of Favena.[9]

Dozens of lesser medieval prelates were also accused by one or another party of sodomitic relations, among them Archbishop Ralph of Tours. Ralph is supposed to have gotten his lover John appointed bishop of Orléans by Philip I, who also boasted of enjoying the man.[10] And so on.

A complaint of sodomy in high places has long been a useful weapon for Christians.[11] Indeed, in inventing the category of "sodomy," Christian theology created a new technology for Christian political warfare.

———

We see how lethal the technology can be in the denunciations that led to the extermination of the Knights Templar. These denunciations were also inspired and managed by Philip the Fair, though they reached well beyond the borders of France. It is as if Philip and his agents appreciated exactly the difficulties of defending against such a hysterical charge as sodomy. What other allegation of secret behavior could so excite popular hatred while giving ample legal grounds for deposition from clerical office and seizure of clerical property? The French monarchy achieved what Peter Damian only hoped in deploying the abstract category.

The diffuse list of charges compiled by Philip's agents includes a number that relate to same-sex activity within the Knights.[12] Others were added in the course of interrogations. The Templar ceremony of reception was alleged to require kissing of the anus or penis. Members of the order were supposed to have been told that they should copulate with one another rather than with women or outsiders, that this activity was perfectly moral, that it was authorized by the Scriptures, and so on. Today the soberest readings of the evidence conclude that none of these hysterical allegations was fully coherent. But their rhetoric was enough to influence the imagination—and not only of credulous medievals. They have attracted early modern polemicists, modern historians, and contemporary novelists as sophisticated as Lawrence Durrell and Pierre Klossowski. Images of clerical sodomy have such power because they enact a logic of transgression so completely. How better could a priestly community of permanently unmarried men invert its mission than by becoming a school for sodomy? By a logic of imaginative opposition, in a narrative of perfect sin, what else could the sex of the holiest be except the most unholy sex of Sodom?

Sodomy charges are politically useful within the church in part because it is so difficult to deny them and so consequential not to dispute them.

They are socially plausible because they agree with experiences in other all-male institutions and perhaps more generally with boyhood memories or fantasies. But they have such rhetorical effect on the Christian imagination because they are the ultimate priestly defilement. This is not because same-sex acts are intrinsically defiling. It is because the category of sodomy was constructed so that every other sin could be loaded on top until the weight became crushing.

———

We often say that charges of sodomy against popes or prelates or monk-warriors are not believable because they are outrageous. We should see rather that they are so often believed because they are outrageous. The category of "sodomy" was designed to record a sense of superb outrage.

So long as we think that there is some neutral historical basis for medieval or modern uses of "sodomy," we miss the rhetorical coloring of the term—the grandeur of its denunciation when aimed at a pope or princely abbot or even a parish priest. Demands for an objective history of clerical sodomy will only forestall a rhetorical analysis of the uses of sodomy charges within the clergy. Those uses construct not only the accusations, but the denials. They determine not just the expectations of the accusers, but the self-descriptions of the accused. For a pope or prelate to deny charges of sodomy, he must join the rhetorical program of sodomy. If he denies the adequacy of the category or minimizes its hysteria, he convicts himself of the sin. Only a sodomite could consider sodomy something less than an occasion for hysteria.

Prosecuting Priestly Sodomites

Hysteria cannot be sustained at the highest pitch. It must be moderated in order to last. The survival of hysteria about priestly sodomy can be ensured by moderating it into legislation and routinizing it through the church police or their secular rivals and accomplices.

———

Various kinds of church law record quite frankly their horror at sodomy or sexual "crimes against nature," especially in the clergy. So far as they legislate it, they also bring it within reach of ordinary enforcement. Clerical sodomy is not just an extraordinary denunciation to be used against popes and prelates or members of powerful religious orders. It is more generally available. The rhetoric of Peter Damian's broadside or of the French manifestos against Boniface VIII make it seem that clerical sodomy is an unexampled crime requiring urgent punishment. And church legislation hints that the crime is a recurring feature of priestly life.

———

The rhetorical challenge for a church law against priestly sodomy is to sustain some sense of hysteria, of urgency, while invoking a long line of precedents. Many Christian laws denounce the varieties of male-male sex by aligning the present with earlier crises. Many church laws not only invoke scriptural condemnations of male-male sex, such as Leviticus 18 and 21 or Romans 1, but they retell the terrible destruction of Sodom. The laws recall the old precedents and stories as if they were prophecies of the present moment, in which the crime cries out to heaven once again.

The sense of urgency is both qualified and sustained by that "once again." The sins occur regularly enough in the clergy to require fairly precise rulings. Such legislation is found in the actions of church councils, in the rules of religious orders, in confessional handbooks or other penitential collections. Medieval books of penance frankly distinguish punishments for bishops, priests, deacons, subdeacons, clerks in minor orders, and monks who are "sodomites" or who fornicate "against nature." This is true for the early penitentials and for their high medieval summaries or codifications.[13] From the High Middle Ages into the early modern period, there are conciliar enactments against clerical sodomites—say, Lateran Council III, canon 11, from 1179—and papal sentences against them—say, Pius V (1566–72), *Cum primum* and *Horrendum*. Commentary on the special problem of clerical sodomites is also attached to the great compilations of canon law.[14]

Church law repeats the texts of the hysterical denunciations of clerical sodomy, then, but it standardizes the crime both by enacting specific legislation against it and by creating bureaucracies to police it.

———

Many trials from medieval and early modern church courts show a complicated interplay between official hysteria and administrative prudence. The chief dictate of the latter is to keep the crime quiet. This means containing it within the system of clerical control.

To speak simplistically, and in theory, clerical sodomy ought to have been the concern of ecclesiastical courts of one sort or another—bishops' consistories, archdeacons' courts, "officialities," and so on.[15] In messy fact cases of clerical sodomy ended up before a variety of tribunals, and not just in such politically charged instances as Philip's attack on the Templars. Sodomy in general and clerical sodomy in particular were points of conflict between ecclesiastical and civil courts in the later Middle Ages. The church wanted to protect its own from civil intervention, and so it insisted on its prerogative to try clerical cases. But it also sought the help of secular authorities, not least when it decided to execute a clerical sodomite. A late case shows the cooperation clearly enough. In 1570, a canon of the shrine of Loreto was named as a sexual partner by a choirboy.[16] The boy's testimony was confirmed by multiple interrogations and by torture. The canon confessed to some of the sexual acts, though he denied others—to no avail. He was defrocked and then handed over to the secular arm according to the recent papal decree, *Horrendum illud scelus* (1568). He was beheaded.

The secular arm was not always so cooperative. Civil authorities resisted the church's claim of privilege or complained of it bitterly. In fifteenth-century Venice, civil authorities professed themselves scandalized by clerical sodomites and much concerned that they would not be punished in ecclesiastical courts.[17] Similar sentiments are reported as those of the "common man" in the same century at Lucerne.[18] In Florence, parishioners took matters into their own hands by chasing off a parish priest after he was spied in the church's garden with another man and an adolescent.[19] And the ineptitude of the ecclesiastical courts in dealing with clerical sodomy is one of the reasons given by Henry VIII's Long Parliament for bringing sodomy into civil law and thus under the jurisdiction of English civil courts.[20]

As more municipalities passed antisodomy legislation, more priests or religious were caught up by secular surveillance. This could happen at second hand, say in criminal proceedings against laypeople who implicated priests or religious as sexual partners.[21] It could also happen directly, as in Florence, where a number of clerical suspects were denounced to the city's authorities.

If some civil courts tried to find ways around clerical immunity, others shied away from this final confrontation with church power—even if it meant freeing the accused clerics. So, in Florence, none of the denounced clerics was convicted by a secular jury, and the civil authorities did little more than complain of churchly inaction.[22]

Clerical sodomy is a point of tense negotiation between church and civil bureaucracies. The civil side of the conflict is rather better documented than the clerical side. Clerical cases seem to have been handled informally, "discreetly," quietly. Indeed, they may not have been brought to formal trial with any regularity. The few studies that have been done suggest, for example, that religious orders rarely prosecuted their members for sodomy. Avoiding scandal seems to have been more important than prosecuting offenders.[23] Cases we do discover in the archives are often cases with aggravating circumstances, such as violence or public outcry. A Capuchin was burned publicly in Paris in 1783 for killing a boy who resisted being raped.[24]

When medieval church courts did prosecute clerical sodomites, they often punished them less severely than their secular counterparts. Civil courts could and did impose capital punishment, by burning alive or by starvation. Church courts punished by deposition or exile and severe penance. Persons convicted of sodomy were better off if they could plead clerical privilege and stand before a church court. A carefully reconstructed case from 1475 in Basel makes the point.[25] Johannes Stocker, chaplain of the cathedral, was tried in secret before a church court for sodomy with a choirboy. He made the confession and signed it willingly, writing in his own hand that he was both "priest and sodomite." Better priest and sodomite than just sodomite. Johannes was punished with permanent exile to the south. Not so many years earlier, laymen convicted of sodomy in Basel had been burned, and the bishop seems to have been persuaded that the mob at a public trial might well have forced Johannes's execution. Even when it punished, the church tended to treat sodomy more lightly than civil courts, and clerical sodomy more lightly than lay sodomy. The discrepancy was noted by medieval authors, some of whom tried to explain it as an example of the church's mercy.[26] But mercy cannot account for the stricter punishment in church law of lay sodomy.[27]

It is tempting to view this as simple hypocrisy for the benefit of clerical pleasure—or at least as the hypocritical insistence on avoiding scandal in the clergy at the expense of truth. It can seem dark cynicism about moral preaching: Let the preachers' fulminations about sodomy be applied by the laity to the laity. The clergy will handle things differently among themselves. These and other motives may well explain some or much of the discrepancy between church and civil proceedings. But consider at least two other reactions to the theological hysteria around the category of the clerical sodomite.

First, clerical sodomy is punished lightly by church courts as a form of denial. The courts cannot admit that it is what it is. If sodomy is as horrible a vice as the theologians make out, then sodomy in the clergy must be unspeakably horrible. If a city of ancient unbelievers was destroyed by God for this sin, what punishment will be required when the same sin reappears in God's own priests? Ecclesiastical courts don't study such questions at length. They prefer to put them out of sight.

Second, lighter punishments by the church can counter hysteria by reminding theologians that there is another side to the incoherent, oscillating category of sodomy. If sodomy is the great sin against nature, it is also a sin of the flesh. If it cries out to heaven for punishment, it must also remain generally secret, contained, fearful of public consequences. The leniency of church courts need not be only self-interest or self-protection. It can be pragmatic resistance to the higher hysteria surrounding clerical sodomy. But resistance seems easiest outside of speech. As soon as the church courts have to talk about clerical sodomy, they tend to repeat the official, exaggerated speeches about it. Indeed, they work hard to force the defendants themselves to repeat the prescribed speeches.

———

Many of the trial records, ecclesiastical and civil, are written up according to standard protocols—with expectations of particular acts or rituals in sodomy and certain characters in sodomites. There are judicial clichés for same-sex behavior just as there are theological clichés for it—or literary and humorous ones.

The protocols determine not only the form of confession or recantation, but also the narrative of the case. They seem to me to determine both the testimony's style and its content even in apparently trivial matters. The choirboy who testified against Johannes Stocker reported that the priest had claimed that if all the sodomites in the city were burned at the stake, "not even fifty men would survive in Basel."[28] This report can be distrusted because it is a piece of seduction. It is given in testimony by a young man who must exonerate himself. For that matter, the unknown scribe who recorded it may have had expectations and motives of his own. But I think it should be distrusted most because it resembles too closely the official portraits of the sodomite. "Not even fifty men would survive in Basel" is, after all, an allusion to the story of Sodom. Before God destroyed the city, Abraham had negotiated with the Lord to spare it. "'Suppose there are fifty righteous within the city; will you then sweep away the place and not forgive it for the fifty righteous who are in it?'" (Genesis 18:24). Did Johannes Stocker really make the remark about fifty men in Basel to the choirboy? If so, he was already placing himself within the theological narrative of Sodom and its sinners.

———

The task in many sodomy prosecutions is not only to convict the clergyman, but to convince him to assume the appropriate identity. We can see this in the outright refusals to record the self-descriptions or self-justifications when they deviate from what is required. In a Florence case, for example, the scribe refused to record the self-justification of a convicted sodomite. This Agostino was condemned to death not least for saying "he did not believe this crime was so serious." The record then deliberately breaks off. The "many other detestable and unpleasant things" he said "are thought best to leave in silence."[29]

No room can be left for speech outside what is prescribed. No identity can be asserted that differs from the theological dictates. Above all, it is the accused who must be persuaded or coerced into agreeing to this restriction.

———

The subtleties of eliciting, that is, of actively imposing an identity can be appreciated in the copious records of the most famous of church courts

charged with prosecuting clerics: the various international and national bureaucracies that constituted the "Inquisition." The records have served for
some decades now in the academic study of sexual prescriptions and practices. The early inquisitorial registers of Jacques Fournier gave Michael
Goodich the trial of the subdeacon Arnold the Catalan, which he published
as the main exhibit for his account of medieval "homosexuality" in the year
before Boswell's *Christianity, Social Tolerance, Homosexuality*.[30] This case is
as a drop in the ocean of later records from the various branches of the
Spanish inquisition.

The Spanish inquisitors were reluctant to include sodomy among the
crimes they investigated, even after it had been assigned to the papal inquisition in 1451. But in 1524 a case involving a prominent layman from Saragossa moved the *Suprema* of the secretariat of Aragon to ask the pope to
add sodomy to its jurisdiction.[31] Pope Clement VII agreed, empowering the
Aragonese to seek out sodomites in the laity and the clergy. For some decades the inquisitors availed themselves of the new prerogative rarely. They
acted on it energetically from about 1560 on, adding sodomy to the crimes
enumerated in the annual reading of the Edict of Faith.[32] By the end of the
century, sodomites made up at least 10 percent of the Aragonese inquisition's docket wherever they were prosecuted, and its various regional
branches conducted nearly 1,000 sodomy trials between 1570 and 1630.

Clergymen of various kinds appear frequently in these records. Indeed,
clerical sodomy was cited as a reason for including the crime in the charge
of inquisitors, and convicted clerical sodomites were often among the first
executed when such cases were taken on.[33] Before some tribunals, clergymen constituted almost one fifth of the sodomy cases.[34] They would have
appeared in larger numbers if inquisitors had pursued all of the clergymen
denounced to them.[35] In Seville, where sodomy prosecutions were left to
civil authority, a Jesuit active as prison chaplain between 1578 and 1616
noted the high incidence of sodomy in the religious orders and the diocesan
priesthood. He reports the view that Jesuits rarely sin with women because
they can so easily find partners among their students or novices.[36]

———

We can be struck by familiar patterns. In the overwhelming majority of
cases at Valencia, for example, the priest or religious is accused of commit-

ting acts with younger partners—that is, with adolescents.[37] Some are novices or servants within the house; others, "trade" picked up on the street with the promise of payment. One Minim friar, Pedro Pizarro, dubbed "La Pizarra," maintained a well-supplied "playroom" on the monastery grounds in Valencia until his arrest in 1572. He would invite boys into the monastery on the pretext of doing paid work, ply them with food and wine, then couple with them in various combinations, often with the assistance of other friars. Before hitting on this arrangement "La Pizarra" had, while in Sevilla, purchased the services of boys in an obliging brothel (pp. 176–77).

A number of local novice masters are denounced to the inquisition for abusing their charges, and one priest is accused of murdering boys in the religious house so that they could not inform against him—a charge he continued to deny even when he confessed to having sexual relations with eleven young men (pp. 177–80).

———

The Aragonese inquisition did not find it so easy to prosecute sodomite priests. Members of religious orders were often protected by their superiors, who claimed preemptive jurisdiction. Religious houses could move against any one of their own who attempted to act as informers or witnesses before the inquisition.[38] Moreover, since the inquisitors were bound by the original papal decree to follow civil procedure in prosecutions of sodomy, their ordinarily secret witnesses were now exposed to cross-examination. One friar succeeded in convincing the judges by cross-examination that the charges against him were merely a plot by some of his jealous brothers in religion.[39] We might expect the same in other cases, having seen how useful a charge sodomy is in church warfare. There are reports of civil cases, too, in which clerics are punished privately or released to their superiors.[40] No court was anxious to prosecute clerical sodomites as a matter of steady policy. They did so either when pushed by momentary zeal or when confronted with particularly notorious cases.

———

The quantity and detail of the inquisitorial records can tempt us into believing that here at least we are dealing with just the facts of clerical behavior. We need to remind ourselves that for the Aragonese inquisition too "sodomite" remains an elicited, imposed sin-identity. Indeed, prosecutions of clerical sodomites are often tangled with prosecutions of other such identities—especially of the "New Christians" suspected of still being Jews or Muslims. We do not use inquisitorial records as neutral depictions of those classes. Why should we do so in the case of the sodomite?

When we analyze trials of heretics or witches, for example, we most often read the testimonies and confessions as artifacts of the system of terror used to produce them.[41] We often interpret them, in short, as projections of inquisitorial fantasy or as the bloody products of torture. We ought to do the same with clerical sodomy. The quantity of inquisitorial records about clerical sodomy does not discharge the theological hysteria surrounding it. It merely controls the hysteria in order to sustain it.

We should think about the importance of self-incrimination in this connection. The inquisitors strive zealously to extract "sincere" confessions from the accused clergymen. There are a number of pastoral reasons for this. The accused will begin to be a penitent only if he admits his sins, admits that they are sins, and feels contrition for having committed them. But the interest in confession reveals as well the need for the accused to assume the sodomitic identity. It is bad for the accused to deny having committed the sin, but it is worse for him to deny that same-sex acts are sinful. It is worse still for the accused to deny the rhetorical hysteria surrounding clerical sodomy—to deny, for example, that these acts arise from a deeply deformed and historically specific sinfulness. It is bad for a priest to commit acts of sodomy, but it is much worse for a priest who commits such acts to deny that there is such a thing as being a sodomite.

———

The inquisitor must persuade the clerical sodomite—he must cajole, bully, torture the clerical sodomite—to admit to a name. The sodomite must convict himself by speaking it. So the sodomite must be talked into self-disclosure, not least by the threatening lie that he has already been recognized. The inquisitors' lists of sodomy's effects are in fact tacit pleas that sodomites should identify themselves by manifesting precisely these effects. The statements of "effects" are invitations to play a role.

If some dialogues between inquisitor and clerical sodomite resemble strategies we moderns use in dealing with criminals or patients, others enact more complicated relationships of impotence and repentance. The identity of the clerical sodomite is based on a past he is abandoning. The past becomes audible only if he has forsaken it, only if he has repented of its sins. Otherwise there is no confession—and no identification as sodomite. So the past is told not as a story about a series of acts, but as descriptions of a series of punishments—private floggings or tortures, transfer to a remote house of penance, removal from clerical office, execution by the secular arm. The accused is securely within the sodomitic identity only when he has renounced being a sodomite. He assumes the identity by repenting of its sins.

What is equally important and characteristic is that the very act of repentance is not within the power of the clerical sodomite. It comes from God. So the sodomitic identity is confirmed only in an act of repentance beyond the power of the individual sodomite to perform. It is an identity not only of repentance, but of impotence. It is a borrowed performance.

———

It is also a performance that ends in silence. We should remember that the speeches of church legislation and church prosecution were mostly private speeches, even secret speeches. They were not meant to be read by secularized scholars—nor, indeed, by pious laypeople. The proceedings of the church courts, the subtleties of church law, the admonitions of the penitentials were typically restricted to those inside. The rhetorical tensions and contradictions they manifest were held in place by powerful institutional protections that have since disappeared. When these discourses about priestly sodomy are translated into the public speech of modern scholarship, we tend to forget more than their hysteria. We forget their presumed secrecy.

———

Faced with now publicized court records, our memory can seize on the tawdry devices of clerical desire. "The monotonous evocation of similar situations throughout so many dossiers demonstrates to the point of tedium that a whole homosexual, religious population contributed to maintaining a true network of boy-prostitution, with the entire system of complicities, compromises, and corruption that such activity requires."[42] Or we can remember the violence against the accused. But we should not forget the hysterical roles that even the most routinized prosecution for clerical sodomy imposes on the bodies of those it names.

Ridiculing Sodomites

Many rules have been instituted to prevent mockery of the Catholic clergy. Many rules have been needed. Mockery goes on, not least because clergymen so often mock one another. Some accusations are surprisingly constant across centuries: ambition, greed, vanity, gluttony, drunkenness, and promiscuity. Under the heading of promiscuity are repeated sallies against priestly sodomy. Indeed, it would be an impossible labor to catalog the appearances of the sodomitic priest or monk in European literature.

I say "literature" quite deliberately. These figures appear not only in the slighter genres of popular satire or broadside, but in the most famous of canonical works. One of the few persons identified by Dante among the sodomites in hell is an archbishop of Florence.[43] One of the first stories in Boccaccio's *Decameron* tells of the God-fearing Abraham's travel to Rome. "The Jew began carefully to observe the behavior of the Pope, the cardinals, and the other prelates and courtiers; and from what he heard and saw for himself—he was a very perceptive man—from the highest to the lowest of them, they all shamelessly participated in the sin of lust, not only the natural kind of lust but also the sodomitic variety, without the least bit of remorse or shame. And this they did to the extent that the influence of whores and young boys was of no little importance in obtaining great favors."[44] Better known to English readers is Chaucer's Pardoner, the "geldyng."[45] As Boccaccio's Filostrato remarks, "The vicious and disgusting life the clerics lead provides an easy and wicked target for anyone who so desires to speak against it, attack it, or reproach it."[46]

If the clerical sodomite is an easy target, that makes him a frequent one in more popular genres. Comic writers of the Italian Renaissance present a number of sodomites in orders.[47] Indeed, they regularly connect him with that other venerable stereotype, the pedophilic teacher.[48] Antonio Rocco, a friar, wrote a detailed fantasy of pederasty and pedagogy in his *L'Alcibiade fanciullo a scola* (published around 1650), but chose to set the story in Greek antiquity.[49] Priest-sodomites recur as well in the wittier formulations of national stereotypes. For example, the humanist scholar Joseph Scaliger is reported to have said that in Spain, the priests were sodomites; in France, the noblemen; in Italy, everybody.[50]

The comic stereotypes are not always untroubled. In Boccaccio himself, sodomitic clergymen are depicted with particular disgust, and the overwhelming number of stories tell of sex between priests or monks and nuns or laywomen. The high medieval French *fabliaux*, otherwise noted for graphic sexual humor, are similarly silent. Many clergymen appear in the *fabliaux*, but they all chase women. The single mention of clerical sodomy comes in a threat: a knight threatens a particularly greedy priest with male-male rape for his inhospitality. The priest, who may prefer anal intercourse with women, exclaims that no bribe would be enough for him to assume their role.[51] In André the Chaplain's *Art of Courtly Love*, advice is given for clergymen who will be lovers, but the advice assumes that they will want women.[52] Rabelais' Friar John advises that even the shadow of a monastery's bell tower can impregnate women, and his utopian Abbey of Thélème is a spa for heterosexual athletes.[53] In *Lazarillo de Tormes*, a Mercedarian priest's advances against a young man are covered by a disgusted silence.[54]

These widely scattered examples suggest that the comic stereotype of the sodomitic clergyman was not easy to handle. Both volatile and disgusting, it could be introduced only with care in satires or literary fictions. If "sodomite" could be used as a crowning insult in certain displays of wit, it was also still simply a term of slander.

———

I would suggest, in fact, that before the Reformation the sharpest satires on clerical sodomy are found within clerical literature, where they would seem to be at once most pointed and most dangerous. Nothing makes for good jokes like sharp anxieties. One witty letter, for example, pretends to describe the summer life of the court of Pope Innocent III in the year 1202.[55] Part of the letter's explicit satire rests on the contrast between chaplains swimming like fish in the lake and the more pompous postures of the "Third Solomon," whose every hand-washing has to be moralized.[56] Part of its implicit satire rests on the contrast between the author's homoerotic banter with the recipient and Innocent's quite real legislative and administrative power over sexual sins. The gossipy narrative is an in-joke, a complicated code of references closed to the brutish multitude clamoring around the clerical encampment above the lake.

———

Much clerical satire is razor-sharp in this way. In his *Trifles*, the twelfth-century priest and poet Walter Map repeats a familiar joke about St. Bernard, the second founder of the Cistercian monastic order.[57] Two Cistercian monks are talking piously about an incident in which Bernard tried to bring a young man back from the dead by stretching out on top of the corpse. Bernard did not succeed. Another clergyman, an anti-Cistercian, interrupts the pious story with feigned astonishment. He had often heard of monks throwing themselves on top of boys, but usually both the monk and the boy got up afterward.

There are humorous counterstrokes as well. Boswell prints a poem from the twelfth or thirteenth century in which married priests complain that they are being persecuted by a hierarchy filled with sodomites. Enforced celibacy is sodomitic policy.[58] It is hard to know whether this anonymous poem is an earnest, stumbling accusation written by a married priest—or a condescending parody written by a sodomitic one. Other accusations are easier to take literally. So, for example, an anonymous annotator retitles Alan of Lille's subtle *Complaint of Nature* as a straightforward treatise "against a sodomitic prelate."[59]

———

Clerical satires are echoed almost verbatim in the literature of religious reform. What the poets and pundits satirize, religious reformers castigate. Those who campaign for the morality of diocesan clergy regularly denounce same-sex relations between its members, and founders or restorers of religious communities take steps to prevent such relations. We have already looked several times to the most famous example—Peter Damian's *Gomorran Book*. Similar accusations appear throughout the medieval literature of clerical reform. Thirteenth-century pastoral reformers single out clerics and the cloistered as particularly prone to sodomy.[60] The popular fifteenth-century preacher Bernardino of Sienna mentions sodomitic prelates and theologians in his vernacular sermons.[61] In his Latin treatise on sodomy, he considers the case of the preacher who is himself "infected with this sin."[62] Founders or restorers of religious community show similar preoccupations in their rules and counsels: religious are to sleep separately and securely clothed; adults are to be separated from young oblates; special precautions are to be taken when traveling.

———

These accusations pass from medieval reformers to the Reformation itself and then into the vast literature of Protestant polemic. In some passages it is no more than the extension of late medieval anticlericalism; in others, it reflects distinctively Protestant concerns with the regulation of public or household morality.[63] Reformation polemics made the figure of the priest-sodomite a fixed and familiar one. If Luther often used Sodom as a general figure of corruption, he sometimes linked it quite pointedly with the question of monastic chastity.[64] Later polemicists could be less restrained. They often presumed that Catholic clergymen and members of religious orders would be sodomites, as they argued that sodomy followed inevitably from the unnatural arrangements of mandatory celibacy and all-male communities. It was with particular relish that they trumpeted the sodomy of celebrated Catholic Counter-Reformers such as Giovanni della Casa.[65]

In England, sodomy recurs as a fixed attribute of the treasonous and heretical Papist.[66] The pope, the Antichrist, is the Great Sodomite, Lord over a "cistern full of sodomy." His deviant doctrine is taught especially by the Jesuits, who use their Continental colleges to inculcate it in students returning to England. At home, the monasteries ruined by Henry VIII offer visible proof of the divine judgment on the sodomy of monks. In the Netherlands, one Calvinist theologian likened Rome to "an abominable bordello of sodomitic love," while another proclaimed that enforced celibacy had produced "a hundred thousand sodomites."[67] The charges were reversed by Catholics. If Roman polemicists could not convincingly portray the whole class of (married) Protestant pastors as sodomites, they certainly executed individual portraits of Reformers in that style.[68]

———

These polemical charges are repeated in a different register by Enlightenment writers. Catholic controls over speech after the Counter-Reformation meant that early modern Catholic writers were considerably more circumspect than their medieval predecessors. But the candor of Catholic countries found another outlet in political and pornographic tracts.

Voltaire's *Candide,* for example, tells how Cunegonde's brother was recruited into the Jesuits because of his beauty. "'You know, my dear Candide, that I was very pretty, and I became more so: so that the Reverend Father Croust, Superior of the House, felt towards me the most tender friendship; he gave me the novice's habit; some time afterwards I was sent to Rome.'"[69] The pretty Jesuit, now grown, is later discovered in a Turkish steam bath with one of the Sultan's elite pages. "'I didn't know it was a capital crime for a Christian to be found completely naked with a young Muslim.'"[70] In Mirabeau's pornographic novels, any number of young men fall victim to priests of different orders—including one who goes on to become grand inquisitor of Toledo.[71] More fully and more vividly, a popular French novel describes the erotic adventures of Dom Buggerer (*Dom Bougre*), "porter of the Charterhouse of Paris."[72] This pornographic tale recounts speeches by priests in defense of sodomy, as well as a sort of portrait gallery of famous sodomites, including popes and (yet again) Jesuits. In connection with its publication, the police arrested one Charles Nourry, a tonsured sacristan.

More familiar to modern American readers, but also less interesting, are the tedious copulatory combinations in the Marquis de Sade. Clerical figures are frequently associated by Sade with sodomitic activities, but the activities are run through so maniacally, so mechanically, that the figure of the clerical sodomite seems to lose specificity. In *The 120 Days of Sodom,* for example, the "Bishop of X***" is introduced as "an idolater of active and passive sodomy, but eminently of the latter" and "a faithful sectary of sodomy," who "has an absolute contempt for all other kinds of pleasure."[73] But in Sade's monastery of libertines, everybody does everybody—and everything, with tedious predictability.

———

Many of the Reformation charges were repeated, with local coloring, in American attacks on the Catholic priesthood and religious life during the nineteenth century. But charges of sodomy are curiously muted. American ears were more tender or the subject of sodomy more forbidden. If anti-

Catholicism is Puritan pornography, it is considerably less pornographic than what imaginative writers produce in Catholic countries.

Maria Monk's *Awful Disclosures* do not concern themselves much with clerical homosexuality. She is too busy dealing with heterosexual sins. So too with many other anti-Catholic tracts. Priests (especially Jesuits) are forever debauching young women, in and out of the confessional, but mentions of same-sex crimes are rare.[74] What sometimes seem references to same-sex crime are in fact heterosexual—as in a passage often cited from Nicholas Clemangis. He describes the clergy as "the dregs and offscourings of mankind, and as persons who abandoned themselves to the most loathsome vices."[75] But the examples supplied by those who quote him are always heterosexual, as are the most frequent arguments against clerical celibacy.[76] Father Chiniquy writes that "every one of these monastic institutions is a new Sodom," but he means that "you will hear from the very lips of the nuns that the monks are more free with them than husbands are with their legitimate wives."[77] Only rarely do we read a passage like this: "A third prelate, the relation of one Cardinal, and confidential agent in the affairs of another, was taken by some gendarmes, at the moment he was about to commit the most detestable of vices, under the colonnade of a palace."[78] Or this: "only enough evidence was brought forward to convict the brothers of the unnatural and horrible crime these teachers committed against their pupils."[79] Fewer passages still name what they describe: "Fornication, adultery, incest, and sodomy are in the list of [the popes'] crimes."[80]

In a more recent example, the ex-Franciscan Emmett McLoughlin published in 1962 the third of his broadsides against the Catholic church in America. It contains some breathy accounts of the shocking sins of Catholic priests, including homosexuality and pedophilia.[81] To show that he deplores these things along with his reader, McLoughlin quotes sympathetically the complaint of one Ohio priest against his superiors: "Being subject to the will and whim of a number of queers has driven me crazy" (p. 148). These stereotypes are common in the more extreme Fundamentalist and Pentecostal sects.[82] They have flourished in recent writing about priestly pedophiles. The clerical sodomite, rebaptized as the pedophile, still sells—in newspapers, newsmagazines, and TV programs. He even finds his way into what are supposed to be more serious accounts of priestly crime, where the old speeches about him are sometimes recycled as documentary history.[83]

———

The polemical stereotypes are not history, but that does not mean that they are irrelevant. They contribute to the construction of the modern identity of the Catholic priest who wants to act on his desire for men and boys. He wants to do what has always already been denounced as the most horrible and yet most predictable crime of the Catholic clergy. He desires what has been the object of centuries of church condemnation, legislation, prosecution, control. In short, he is asked to step into an identity that has been loudly overdetermined by competing denunciations.

The ambiguities of historical evidence don't matter to that identity. What matters are not the "facts," not the "social reality," but the accusations and the imaginative constructions. The identity is constructed from fantasy rather than fact. What we need to learn from polemic, as from all of the hysterical speeches about priestly sodomy, is their continued significance in the roles that clerical sodomites must play.

The same is true for the more genial speeches of satire. The laughter directed at the clerical sodomite is not quite the laughter directed at the married cuckold or the monk who chases serving-girls. The priest-sodomite is comical in his filthiness or his humiliating machinations or his ridiculous vanity. Comedy offers him only roles of deserved degradation, not those of robust, good-humored pleasure. Imagine a contemporary priest who remembers something of these satires of churchly sodomy. Any act he might perform, any words he might say, have been ridiculed over centuries. Whenever he acts, he will find himself stepping into multiple humiliations.

Hysterical Lessons

Remembering the old speeches about priestly sodomy, we learn, first, about hatred and fear, ridicule and shame. For centuries now, writers with diverse positions in Christian cultures have assumed that many priests and monks were sexually attracted to men or boys and sexually active with them. They have also assumed that clerical desire and clerical copulation were especially characterized by secrecy. Indeed, the single most common motif in these writings, whether humorous or zealous, is that clergymen busy themselves keeping sexual secrets. Medieval satirists laugh that so much more trouble goes into concealing copulation than saving souls. Contemporary polemicists shout that the whole Catholic church in America is a great secret machine for keeping horrible things out of sight. They agree that the identity of the clerical sodomite or homosexual is an identity of shame.

———

By linking these rhetorical clichés, I don't mean to imply that there is some simple continuity in church institutions. The "Catholic priesthood" does not pass through the centuries as an unchanging substance—nor does the "Catholic church," except to the eyes of some varieties of faith. By any ordinary standards of analysis and interpretation, the Catholic church in America is not the same institution as the Latin-speaking churches before the Council of Trent. It is not the same church as the Roman Catholic church in America of a hundred years ago. Its de facto teachings are different, as are the ways of life it endorses and the kinds of people it comprises. I do not mean to fall back into the myth of Catholic immutability, but I do stress the repetition of certain rhetorical roles across succeeding Catholic cultures. We learn from the repetition to be alert for survivals of the fantastic attributes of the priestly "sodomite" behind the priestly "homosexual." These attributes belong to roles, and the roles continue to create expectations both within and without the priesthood.

———

Of course, and in the end, the more hysterical efforts to prescribe identities can be curiously self-defeating. The very intensity of their hysteria subtracts the identities from everyday life.

Alan Bray describes this as a problem of recognition: in Renaissance England, there is a "discrepancy between this society's extreme hostility to homosexuality . . . in the abstract and its reluctance to recognize it in most concrete situations."[84] We have already seen something like this "reluctance" in medieval and early modern cases of clerical sodomy. It was the striking contradiction between rabid denunciation and inconsistent, often lenient disposition. Bray suggests that the explanation for England is partly pragmatism: "There was a fundamental incompatibility between English society's uncompromising rejection of homosexuality and the hard facts it had somehow to come to terms with" (79). The incompatibility was handled, though not resolved, by separation, by keeping "the contact between the myths and symbols of homosexuality and homosexuality itself to a minimum" (79).

———

Bray's analysis cannot be transferred directly to the contradictions surrounding clerical sodomy, where the causal connections are more tangled and better concealed. Hysterical speech against clerical sodomy is produced and enforced by the same institutions that house and perhaps induce that sodomy. But I do think that Bray's analysis cautions us against taking hysterical speech too simply on its own terms—especially if we turn the analysis around.

There is a gap between ordinary copulations happening in the next room and the global melodramas of the Great Sin of Priestly Sodomy. The gap is another way in which theological discourses render ordinary copulations invisible. So long as we remain under the influence of the discourses of the Great Sin, their hysteria will prevent us from seeing what is happening right around us. Indeed, that is one of their functions. Hysterical depictions of the clerical sodomite prevent us from seeing real acts of clerical sodomy by making it seem much too melodramatic to be performed next door. Hysterical condemnations render clerical sodomy invisible by making it unrecognizable.

Think of this as the opposite of "coming out." When ordinary people declare themselves as homosexuals to their family and friends and fellow workers, they typically make it more difficult for the people around them to demonize homosexuality. The homosexual is no longer a shadowy goblin but rather someone you encounter every day. In fact, homosexuality becomes boring. Exposing the ordinariness of homosexual copulation makes it very difficult to give credit to the extravagant hysteria of homophobic discourse. So the hysterical speech against homosexuality depends on its not being applied often and in ordinary situations. Otherwise, it loses its hysterical force.

The categories of Great Sin, of Priestly Sodomy or Homosexuality, cannot be allowed to lose their hysterical force. So they cannot be applied in ordinary situations. If some ordinary situations seem to be Priestly Sodomy or Homosexuality, they must be something else. Or nothing at all.

———

We can prevent the disappearance of male-male sex within the contemporary priesthood and religious life only by resisting hysteria. We resist by looking to the particular acts and dispositions of individual priests and religious who populate our ordinary worlds. We resist by refusing to construct grand dramas around the identities of clerical sodomy and looking instead to what is right around us, precisely because it seems so mundane.

In a preface to a book that offers some sharp-eyed descriptions of clerical luxury, along with much else, Thorstein Veblen wrote this: "the data employed to illustrate or enforce the argument have by preference been drawn from everyday life, by direct observation or through common notoriety, rather than from more recondite sources at a farther remove. It is hoped that no one will find his sense of literary or scientific fitness offended by this recourse to homely facts. . . ."[85]

We resist the hysteria of surveys and scandals, of grand sodomitic histories, by looking at "homely facts" about same-sex desire or activity. These include open secrets that "everyone knows" but no one contemplates. They include obvious analogies between clerical life as we see it and the newly visible structures of gay communities. "Homely facts," not hysterical roles. "Homely facts," not eternal identities.

6

reproducing "father"

ACCORDING TO TRADITIONAL understandings, priests and
religious are "called." Some speak of their being called "in
the womb," from before birth. But Roman Catholic clergymen are never just born. They have to be trained or (in the
current image) "formed." The procedures of formation in
recent centuries have placed rather more emphasis on the
work to be done by human institutions than on the work
already done by God—especially in dealing with sex.

———

For the last four centuries, the increasingly centralized institutions of formation have been preoccupied with instilling
and enforcing celibacy. At the same time, as they isolated
groups of young men from secular influence under an imitation of monastic life, the institutions have created intensely
homoerotic conditions. The "seminary" or "seedbed" was

invented to enforce priestly discipline in the Counter-Reformation. But its enclosure meant, inevitably, that the erotic temptations of the medieval religious houses were now offered to most candidates for the diocesan priesthood as well.

———

Remarks about Catholic seminaries in America need to be made and understood with a significant qualification: "Seminarian" can refer to someone as young as fourteen or (these days) as old as fifty-five or sixty, to someone studying junior high algebra or the recent revisions of marriage law, and to someone living in a rural outpost or downtown Chicago. Seminaries differ from one another as sharply as seminarians, and not only in age or location. Indeed, it may be now that the important differences in policies about homosexuality are settled practically by whether the seminarian or seminary counts as "conservative" or "liberal." American Catholic institutions tend to be badly polarized, and nothing polarizes quite like the issues of sexual morality.

———

American seminaries and houses of religious formation have also undergone dizzying changes over the last forty years—and in no single direction. Many have simply disappeared for want of applicants. Those that remain have often remade themselves several times over in response to contradictory influences. If it is now amazing to recall the rigidity of seminaries in the 1950s, it is equally odd to remember some of the wilder experiments during the 1960s and 1970s. I have heard dozens of stories about the whims of autocratic rectors in seminaries that were built to resemble Venetian palaces and run rather like them. But I also remember seminaries in the early 1970s where seminarians would bring their girlfriends or (more rarely) boyfriends to evening meals presided over by the rector. Or seminary "rec" rooms that resembled particularly fey piano bars. "By [1973] . . . odd stories would have begun to circulate: the [minor seminary] was, some feared, turning into a floating fairy boat."[1] "Both lay and clerical observers reported the open flaunting of behavior reminiscent of and consonant with that of a gay bar."[2] Which bars the seminarians would also frequent. Around 1980 I was in a large American abbey to use the library. Friday evening, as I was chatting with the monk-librarian in gilded sunset light, I noticed half a dozen young men, wearing khakis and polo shirts of various shades. They were walking arm in arm down the hill. "Oh," he said, "that's the young monks going into town for the bar." Later, around 1994 and in another house, there was a disturbance in the refectory when two novices discovered that they were both sleeping with the novice master, apparently on alternate nights. In the same years, elsewhere, "conservatives" were reimposing codes of strict regulation in an effort to reclaim the "golden years" of the 1950s.

———

The diversity cannot be denied or reduced. It is particularly unhelpful to respond to it with one or another hysterical lament over how seminary discipline has been vitiated in the last four decades. These laments, these "conservative" narratives, assert that many or most seminaries now corrupt the faith of centuries. Why? Because their faculties have been seized by frustrated, envious, embittered gangs of feminists, laxists, and overt or covert homosexuals. So, the lament continues, they give rise to "a large homosexual culture," expressed in the "unchecked effeminate, scandalous behavior of some seminarians" and leading to "the negative reputation of the seminary" and the deplorable "kinds of role models the seminary [tacitly approves] in recommending these men for orders."[3]

This kind of lament lies about many things, but its worst lie may be the pretense that homosexuality flourished in seminaries only after Vatican II and as a result of liberal shifts. This is to confuse what happens with what is admitted, and to substitute cause for effect. Clerical homoeroticism was a feature of seminaries long before Vatican II, and what is said by professors of theology matters much less than what is tacitly permitted or required by the habits of church administration. Here, as in so much of sexual life, we tend to react melodramatically when things are named after having been kept silent. We rush about constructing explanations for changed facts when what we need are explanations for changed words.

———

Certain "liberal" narratives must be avoided as well, especially those that tell of a complete revolution after the Vatican Council. According to these stories, old evils were thrown out and the church entered upon a process of astonishing transformation until one or another reaction set in under the Machiavellian direction of a particular enemy of freedom, most often Paul VI in his dotage or John Paul II from the moment of his election.

What has happened after the council is much more complicated, and it may be too recent to be thoughtfully described. There were both superficial and deeper changes during the late sixties and early seventies. But deep clerical structures were left intact—because the deep logic of compulsory celibacy was left intact. We deceive ourselves if we believe that everything would have been modernized or liberated or redeemed after the council except for the intervention of counterrevolutionary forces. Priestly institutions are too big, too old, and too carefully constructed to be completely changed in the space of a few years. So the "conservative" reaction was not a shocking return so much as a predictable reappearance.

I will not reduce the astonishing diversity of American seminaries to an average or a stereotype. I certainly won't search for explanations of why things "declined" so suddenly. And I won't generalize from impressions of the American scene to situations elsewhere. Seminaries and religious houses were very different in central Mexico, where I grew up, and in western European countries, where I have lived. Many reports suggest that other conditions now prevail in parts of Africa, where complex cultural attitudes toward male homosexuality collude with programs to "restore church discipline." Or in Asia, where the cultural constructions of male homosexuality and the fervors of growing Catholicism are different yet again.

Certain patterns in American clerical formation are obviously connected to the regulation and concealment of male homosexuality. Some of the features I will talk about seem to me to have striking analogies with pieces of historical evidence from Europe and North America. I will underscore these by introducing older texts on seminary law or spiritual direction. Other features that were very important in church history seem unimportant in the contemporary American clergy.

So, for example, the difference between diocesan priests and members of religious orders seems much less significant now than it was in earlier periods. So too are the differences among religious orders, many of which are increasingly indistinguishable from one another. Their members often cannot say why they belong to one order rather than another except because of some accident of biography. Priests in the American provinces of some religious orders are also increasingly comparable to priests in the dioceses. Indeed, many of the orders' priests serve in parishes, while many diocesan priests serve in ministries historically reserved to the orders—higher education, health care, and so on. Even the ancient distinction between monks and other clergymen is hard to see in many cases. Often "monks" are just parish priests or schoolteachers or chaplains, while some diocesan priests live lives of extraordinary solitude and withdrawal from the secular world.

———

In what follows I juxtapose observations of diocesan seminaries with those of religious houses of formation. My aim is only to assemble a collage. The pattern will be arranged to demonstrate links to other, more recognizable gay cultures. We can now picture clerical gayness more clearly because we have detailed analogies to guide us. For the first time in much more than a millennium, public and well-developed homoerotic subcultures exist in the West. We are particularly familiar with how contemporary American men build gay communities. So when we come to the distorted and fragmentary evidence of American clerical gayness, we bring patterns for comparison.

Being Called and Being Chosen

In Tibetan monasteries, the reincarnation of an important lama was discovered by a sophisticated art prescribing many tests and requiring many signs. Something almost as complicated used to be true in the Catholic mythology of "discerning a vocation" to the priesthood or religious life. Tales of particularly dramatic or prolonged discernments were traded with zeal, and most pious young men spent at least some months of their adolescence listening inside themselves for the telltale murmuring of a divine voice. If there may be such a thing as situational homosexuality, there is certainly the situational vocation. Catholic boys were regularly put in just the right situations.

Once vocations were encouraged or elicited out in the world, they had to be tested "inside" dioceses and the religious orders. Sequences of tests were established for determining the authenticity and durability of vocations. After all, seminaries and religious orders were not collapsing institutions begging for applications, as they are too often now. They flourished, picking and choosing among those who sought a way of life higher than the married state, who were more serious and more pious and more God-fearing than worldlings. The processes of selection were so many gates on the way to privilege. Failing to pass through one of those gates was failure indeed.

"He noticed the black handkerchief which served his mother for a hat. She was sitting motionless, with her back to him. . . . She was less resigned than her husband to the idea of no longer being the mother of a priest, in whose house she had always hoped to spend an inexpensive old age, an object of respect to all her neighbors."[4]

From a sociologist's interviews about events in the late sixties in Los Angeles: "[I]n response to his religious calling and with the encouragement of his family, he moved to northern California and became a brother in a Catholic monastery. . . . The monastic life however did not suit Miguel. . . . His mother was very unhappy over his leaving the monastery. His father said little but was also not pleased."[5] Shortly after his return to Los Angeles from the monastery, Miguel "came out."

The tests of vocation and their rationale have changed many times in recent decades, not least because of declining interest in the privilege they were meant to protect. Hardly any feature of Catholic life except for the liturgy has been changed as frequently or as abruptly as programs of vocational formation. Still, certain important features survive. One of these is the preoccupation with the requirement of celibacy. In popular imagination, and in some clerical self-understandings, nothing is more distinctive of the Catholic clergy than celibacy—not even obedience. Weakness in chastity outweighs many other merits and alone constitutes grounds for dismissal from formation.[6] I wonder about the converse: How often has "strength in chastity" been judged solely sufficient for ordination in the presence of many other vices—say, greed or ambition or cruelty?

———

Tests for chastity were applied over many years. Under the old regime of minor seminaries, candidates for priesthood and religious life could be captured for the system in their early teens. The period of junior high or high school studies and even the first years in college were then a long examination of the gift of celibacy, which presupposed but greatly outshone the ordinary virtue of unmarried chastity. All Catholic boys were supposed to be chaste—that is, not to have ejaculations except unwillingly and while asleep. But young candidates for the priesthood or religious life were supposed to be *really* chaste, as a sign that they had the gift of celibacy.

———

Testing celibacy and verifying chastity required isolation in one way or another. Either the minor seminary had to be remote or its walls very high. Bishops and rectors would pride themselves on how little their students knew of what was happening out in the world. Mail was routinely censored, access to magazines or television or movies controlled. "While automobiles raced down Michigan Boulevard, while masses of people in the Loop were engaged in business, while a haze of smoke hung over Chicago, a quiet but momentous event was taking place in the little chapel off of Rush Street. There, a group of young men were meditating on a beautiful picture, a young priest ascending the altar for the first time. Ah, the nobility on that pale young face! The thrill in the glad voice intoning its first 'Gloria in Excelsis Deo!'"[7]

———

Once inside a minor seminary, the candidates were officially presumed to be as protected as could be from carnal temptations. The acknowledged dangers were outside—from women, especially, or from perverts who lurked in the parks and train stations and dim bars of corrupt cities. In this supposed safety, the discipline of celibacy was to be instilled while they were still young, well before the time for entering theological studies in the major seminary and beginning the string of ordinations that would culminate in ordination to the priesthood. The nearer theological studies and priestly ordination, the less tolerance for sins against chastity.

———

For many decades, there were fairly specific rules about the kinds of test to be applied. Consider, for example, the *experimentum* or formal trial before entry into major seminary. "In theological studies the habit of chastity should be fixed. If the young man has not kept himself immune from grave external sins, for at least one year before entering into theological studies, he should be eliminated from the path of the Priesthood. . . ."[8] The standard for success in the test was "negative": One "grave external sin" *without* another person was enough for dismissal.[9] To translate: A single act of solitary masturbation was grounds for dismissal if the candidate had been a frequent masturbator. If he had not masturbated for a long time, he might be subjected to another year's experiment after his single lapse.

The rule for "grave external sins" with another person was much stronger. "At any time, without delays and without granting further tests, there should be excluded anyone who, after his entry into the seminary, has committed even one single sin with a person of the opposite sex or with a companion."[10] Of course, the rule was not applied rigorously. Indeed, there seems to have been de facto indulgence for slips right up to ordination.[11]

———

When it comes to judging the actions of younger boys, those in minor seminary, the official documents show some hesitation. If repeated masturbation is reason enough for dismissing a seminarian in college, sex play with another boy may perhaps be forgiven in junior high school. "This case seems to admit of mitigation in the first years of secondary school, in which a boy doesn't always realize the gravity of the act."[12] "If after his entry into a minor seminary, a student should sin gravely against the Sixth Commandment with a person of the same or the other sex, or give grave scandal in the matter of chastity, he is to be dismissed at once . . . , *unless* it is the case of a boy of excellent qualities who was seduced and who is truly penitent, or when the sin in question was an objectively imperfect act. . . ."[13] Which exceptions seems to mean: If your best student allows himself to be "se-

duced" and then regrets it, or if the act in question didn't result in ejaculation, you can exercise "prudent" discretion.

———

Sometimes judgments of prudence reversed established moral teaching.
Lack of sexual experience was widely held to be the best predictor and safeguard of celibacy. What they didn't know couldn't tempt them. But this
opinion sometimes yielded the inference that sex with other boys or men
was less dangerous than sex with girls or women. "Limited homosexual
experience in a candidate's background could be better tolerated than an
experience of heterosexual intercourse. . . . 'Once they get a taste of that, it
is very tough to keep the discipline.'"[14]

———

Over against amended rules about actions and the play of prudence stood
the more stringent demand to scrutinize characters. Pius XI pronounced
that young men "with a proclivity to sensuality" were "neither born for the
priesthood nor capable of it."[15] He was reaffirming the traditional suspicion
that candidates would arrive with latent defects that would render them
sooner or later incapable of priestly celibacy. They might go for years without any "external" sin, leading seminary lives of perfect chastity and effu-
sive zeal. But once they stepped outside the protective walls, their hidden
sins would emerge. They would then bring ruin on themselves and great
scandal to the church.

So vocation directors and seminary staff were asked to make predictions
based on character, beginning in one's early teens. If it was important to
gather information about what had been done, it was also necessary to discover what might be done. Purity had not only to be kept in boyhood past,
but in approaching manhood.

———

Particular suspicion was cast on those who seemed to be drawn to sins
"against nature." Technically, the phrase could cover any genital activity
outside of heterosexual intercourse in an approved position and without
artificial contraception. In ordinary use, sins "against nature" meant acts
with a partner of the same sex. After many years of struggle against these

tendencies in thought and action, a candidate could still hold little hope that he would be suitable for the priesthood. He would always carry a dark impurity, a psycho-physiological fate. He would always be too sensitive or sensual or imaginative or tender, would always burn with a forbidden flame.[16] Better to divert him from priestly formation as early as possible.

Certainly such candidates were to be weeded out when they reached college years and drew near to theological study. It is necessary "to evaluate new students accurately, at the moment of admission, so that there do not enter into the seminary corrupt boys and young men, or those physically and morally defective, or those abnormal in any way." Seminary rectors must "expel inexorably and promptly boys and young men who are scandalous, sensual, sentimental."[17]

"Those who are affected by the wicked inclination to homosexual vice or pederasty are to be prohibited from religious vows and ordination, since common life and priestly ministry would be a grave danger to them."[18]

———

Better, wiser, safer to identify such young men much earlier. But how could one judge a proclivity to "sensuality" in a twelve-year-old who has been raised in a strict Catholic home, who has never kissed girls, who has probably never dated them? One had to look at external signs that might betray his latent perversion, his secret. Diagnostic characteristics mentioned in the older documents include—beyond sensuality—sentimentality, sensitivity, excitability, a strong imagination, a taste for solitude, and a dislike for physical education. In short, the stereotype of the pansy or sissy.

———

Only real boys need apply to seminary. "The American seminary is a unique institution chiefly because the American boy is a unique institution. . . . [T]he boys . . . are American in every sense of the word. They love joking and kidding. They are sports enthusiasts, who talk with vigor and conviction about the seasonal game. Will the Giants win the pennant? Are the Red Sox an improved club? Seminarians, like all people in the United States, enjoy eating hot dogs smothered in mustard and get a kick out of popping popcorn. Mother looks somewhat relieved to know that you are not living with a tribe of mummies."[19]

Still, the all-American boys in Chicago's minor seminary wrote love poems to a teenage Jesus: "Guard me by night and protect me by day / Show me the path that I may not stray / From Thy side and fall by the way. / Youth of Youths, Amo Te!"[20]

———

Most of the minor seminaries were dismantled in America in the 1960s and 1970s. This was precipitated not so much by a change of theory as by a sharp decline in numbers, the leading edge of what has since become a general catastrophe. There just weren't enough vocations anymore—and certainly not enough young vocations. With the minor seminaries went the luxury of long years for evaluating chastity. Attention shifted abruptly to the college years and to the theological seminary itself. What had once been the finale of a long trial became for many the moment of arrival. Indeed, more and more men were accepted into the seminaries who had not only never heard of a minor seminary, but who were much older than the typical student of theology in earlier decades.

———

As "late" vocations increased, as more older men were gratefully, if not desperately, accepted, there lingered the prejudice that it was risky to let "impure" wolves in among the innocent lambs. Sometimes the prejudice was borne out. I know cases in which older seminarians who had been "out in the world" were charged with raping younger seminarians. Some infamous clerical pedophiles, including Rudy Kos, have indeed been "late" vocations. But more important for the seminary system than cases of sexual violence or even the scandals of pedophilia has been the change in the timetable for testing and reinforcing a call to celibacy. The seminary system as such presupposes that vocations are fostered best when they are identified early and then kept apart. A number of causes have rendered that presupposition impossible in the American church. The timing of a celibate vocation had to be reconceived, and, with it, the testing. It would no longer be possible to watch over and protect the budding vocation in the seedbed of a secluded junior high school or even a college. Other ways had to be found.

———

The need for new methods of discerning celibate vocations seems to have reinforced a growing dependence in the American church on psychological theories and professional consultations. Psychological testing had been used on candidates for the priesthood and religious life since the 1940s, but it gained ground on more traditional practices of spiritual discernment in the 1960s. This was not necessarily a good thing. The shadow side of the new ideal of mature celibacy was the hope that new tests would predict its success. Indeed, some vocation directors seem to have hoped that the expert knowledge of "mental health professionals" would provide quick diagnoses of latent defects in candidates. In place of years of minor seminary, a battery of psychological tests. Psychological testing was a quicker and perhaps surer way to the old goal of protecting the reputation of the priesthood from sexual scandal, especially the scandal of homosexuality.

———

The hope that psychological analysis might uncover hidden homosexuals is particularly clear in the first large-scale psychological profile of American priests, which was undertaken in the late 1960s. The index in the volume of psychological studies contains a single entry for "homosexuality." It points to a long discussion of how to recognize the "maldeveloped": "For example, the maldeveloped person might engage in homosexual acts and still be able to maintain a very smooth public presence. He isolates deviant behavior through these intellectual defenses and does not face his own inconsistencies. It takes a close look, however, to properly identify some of these men."[21]

———

The psychiatrist or psychologist now appears alongside the confessor as the detective of "latent" homosexuality. Indeed, he or (more rarely) she often replaces the confessor. "The psychiatrist—not the spiritual director—is ordinarily the competent person to make the judgment" whether the candidate actually has the "illness" of the "homosexual tendency."[22] Only a "clinician," it seems, can prevent some homosexual clergymen from deluding themselves and others about their hidden tendencies.[23] So "the psychiatrist also shares in the responsibility of the spiritual director to dissuade doubtful candidates from advancing to Holy Orders or from remaining in religious life."[24]

Similar hopes of uncovering homosexuals by science are reflected in practical manuals. One guidebook from 1964 considers screening candidates with both interview-driven, thematic apperception tests (like the Rorschach) and multiple-answer "inventories" (like the MMPI). It admits frankly that interviewers "are not well agreed . . . as to which signs or behavior patterns are to be designated as abnormal. Nor are they sufficiently explicit in distinguishing between merely covert attitudes toward sex and overt sexual deviation."[25] As for the MMPI: its scale for sexual adjustment "is the one of the original scales which has least validity." Why? Because it tends to identify "artistic interests" with "effeminacy," so that college-educated men in general "score badly."

Nothing explicit is said about identifying or eliminating homosexual candidates. The guidebook just assumes that a "wholesome and healthy attitude toward sex" is a well-balanced heterosexual attitude. The risk for "young males" is of "swerving from the balance between a healthy respect for the opposite sex and too great an interest and curiosity about the female role in society and homemaking."

Anxiety over effeminacy figures in many of the psychological studies of American seminarians and candidates for religious life. A 1968 inventory of students in theology found that diocesan and religious seminarians exceeded a general population of undergraduate students in both "Estheticism" and "Masculinity-Femininity." "The Religious seminarians in particular had somewhat strong esthetic and social inclinations and admitted sensitivity and emotionality, attitudes identified in this inventory with more feminine views."[26]

A few years later, another survey is willing to explain away the "aesthetic" scores as reflecting the "avocational interests" of religious life, "especially in contrast to the scientific and technical occupations."[27] But another scale has been introduced in this later survey, that of "heterosexual disinterest." It is supposed to measure "lack of interest in marriage, girls, uneasiness with them, no experience with dating or 'being in love'" (40). The lower scores here may reflect "idealism," but they may also reflect "a difficulty in sexual identification" (47). Indeed, one of the items most sharply distinguishing high school seminarians from the general population is agreement with the statement, "The male body sometimes attracts me." With progress from seminary high school through college to theological studies, the "heterosexual disinterest" scores align more closely with the general population, but the "aesthete pattern" diverges more sharply. The authors hypothesize: "At an earlier age, more masculine avocational interests are espoused, but direct heterosexual interests suppressed; at maturity, the situation is reversed." Or is it that an older seminary student has learned that direct expressions of desire are much less acceptable than "aesthetic" sentiments?[28] "Heterosexual disinterest" and "the aesthete pattern" appear in surveys of seminarians conducted as late as the 1980s.[29]

While surveys of seminarians were still trying to calculate "heterosexual disinterest" and "aestheticism," American society at large was beginning to grapple with the notion of a proudly avowed gay identity. The presupposition in many of the psychological discussions of seminary homosexuality had been that it was an "illness," "a serious obstacle to a healthy life." Writers supposedly motivated by psychotherapeutic concerns for homosexual candidates often repeated the worst homophobic clichés. Homogenital relations "neither go beyond themselves nor incorporate permanent commitment."[30] "In general, it seems that continence is more difficult to obtain with a homosexual than with a heterosexual because of the incompleteness of sexual evolution represented by homosexuality."[31] So imagine the shock of finding gay pride knocking at the seminary gates.

How to keep it out? All Catholic seminarians and novices are supposed to be sexually inactive, as we have seen, and so the evil of homosexual *acts* cannot be used as an argument against admitting gay-identified candidates. When the CDF entertained the moral distinction between homosexual orientation and homosexual acts in its 1975 declaration, it created a real quandary for vocation directors. When Cardinal Ratzinger insisted that the orientation itself, without any acts, was "objectively disordered," he seemingly resolved that quandary: vocation directors could again employ the old reasons for refusing to admit candidates who identify themselves as gay. However scrupulous homosexual candidates were about not using their genitals, their very characters would render them unfit for ordination or community life. Of course, the application of Cardinal Ratzinger's theory has never been consistent. "Because of worries about homosexuality and pedophilia, most dioceses and religious orders now require extensive personality and psychological testing for their recruits, and some have even resorted to penile response tests."[32]

———

Reports from diocesan seminaries about gay candidates are confused and confusing. The American bishops have discussed the issue, but only in closed session.[33] Publicly, some bishops perform denial. Archbishop Mahony of Los Angeles, writing in 1987, assured readers of *Commonweal* that the screening processes in Los Angeles, "both at the entry level and throughout the man's years of formation, have proven most adequate to identify and dissuade the homosexual from entering or progressing through our seminary system."[34] Note that the archbishop is talking about homosexuals simply, not "practicing" homosexuals. In this, he repeats "conservative" criticism of policies designed to admit celibate homosexuals into diocesan seminaries. For example, Bishop John D'Arcy, then of Boston, argued that it would be impossible to distinguish practicing from nonpracticing homosexuals. Both would come flooding into the seminaries, and then those "who are active and totally without personal control will immediately begin to act out homosexually in the seminary with serious harm to sound formation, and eventually to the life of the Church."[35]

———

Specific directives from the Vatican have contained similar views. In 1985, for example, Cardinal Baum argued that men either with a history of homosexual practice or with a homosexual orientation should not be admitted to seminary. Those who suffer homosexual "temptations" could be admitted, so long as the "behavioral impulse, inclination, or appetite" appeared, not as orientation, but as a "temptation."[36]

More recent Vatican statements have remained curiously mixed. On the one hand, the pope and his deputies now regularly speak of "psychosexual maturity" as a prerequisite for mature celibacy.[37] On the other hand, "maturity" seems to exclude even the disposition to homosexuality.

———

Policies and practices in religious orders also vary confusingly. In a survey conducted during the early 1980s, almost two thirds of the men's communities stated that they would consider openly homosexual candidates, while less than a fifth said that they would refuse consideration.[38] Only 36 percent of male and female religious agreed that "declaring a homosexual orientation" would prevent someone "from being admitted to my congregation."[39]

Some religious orders have indeed made strong statements of acceptance. In the late 1970s, the Long Island/New England District of the Christian Brothers held that "criteria for admission do not include the question of sexual preference. If a candidate is acceptable, the question of sexual preference would have no bearing on his application."[40] Regional bodies of a few other orders have issued similarly affirming guidelines.[41]

———

During recent decades, individual spiritual writers have also tried to develop a counterideal of celibacy. In place of sexual purity as lack of dangerous affect, they have described celibacy as earned acceptance of one's own sexuality—including homosexuality. This counterideal further suggests a harmony or synchronicity between the stages of coming out and the stages of growth into celibacy.[42] Homosexual orientation is no longer a bar to the happy practice of celibacy, and its rejection might say more about the community than the candidate.[43]

Descriptions of the new ideal seem to me beautiful in the way that utopian writing often is.[44] Certainly the policy proposals based on them are utopian. They misunderstand the basic logic of the seminary as an arrangement for education.

"Very different is the case of the man who has already dealt with these 'coming out' issues outside the seminary, perhaps even in the promiscuous gay subculture, and who has 'come to his senses' (Luke 15:17), and who decides to embrace celibacy and priesthood as a more genuine, a more fulfilling way of life. Far from being treated with suspicion, such a man should be welcomed to the seminary and supported in his vocation."[45] To accept this congenial suggestion is to undo the logic of the Catholic seminary. There is in fact a stubborn contradiction between the human timetable or life cycle implied in seminary training for celibacy and common notions of gay "coming out." The more proper analogy in gay culture to seminary training in celibacy is not "coming out," but staying in.

———

The contradiction goes something like this. Societal oppression leads homosexuals to repress, delay, and deny the appropriation of their own sexual identities. They often discover their sexuality late. But mature celibacy requires both acceptance of one's sexual identity and a proven history of chaste living. You have to have enough time to get through the acting out of "coming out" and then to clean up your record. "If active sexual activity has marked a person's life right up to the moment of application to the seminary or novitiate, this person is presently not a good candidate for acceptance."[46] In some seminaries, indeed, homosexuals are required to have "cleaner" records than heterosexual candidates.

The contradictions between seminary testing and "coming out" have not gone away just because people are coming out earlier.[47] The young men who are "coming out" in high school or the first years of college are often the "gayest"—the most politically radical or most marginal or most obvious. They are also often those who find their ways early on into an urban gay enclave and its networks of support or of pleasure. In short, they are unlikely candidates for diocesan seminaries or religious novitiates.

———

Homosexuals are unique among American minorities in not typically finding role models in their families or neighborhoods or churches. They have to look elsewhere, in gay enclaves, in order to find their heroes and their history. But gay enclaves are generally thought to be enclaves of sexual activity. "It would certainly be unfitting and imprudent for priests and religious sisters and brothers to deliberately place themselves in situations where this commitment [to chastity] is compromised: for example, in cruising or frequenting gay bars and baths." Is it any wonder, then, "that certain priests and Religious have never had the opportunity to manage the various [stages of coming out] . . . and they are somehow searching for the meaning of their sexuality in imprudent ways. These persons must be sensitively cared for and directed but it is never legitimate to *approve* of such behavior."[48]

———

"Coming out" is not something that can be accomplished by anyone at eighteen or nineteen in a homophobic society. So far as "coming out" means correcting the social presumption that everyone is heterosexual, it is never done. As a young man, you can of course appropriate and act on and even declare your sexual orientation to anyone who will listen. But you cannot, I think, truly appreciate what has already been done to you by the ambient homophobia. Your "coming out" has only begun. A Catholic seminary or novitiate, no matter how accepting, is perhaps not the likeliest place to continue it.

Conservative authors seem to admit this when they suggest that the candidate be sent away for a while. "One should perhaps invite the subject to take on life situations that confront him with a certain solitude and a certain number of frustrations. It would then be possible to verify how his affective equilibrium resists situations of little gratification."[49] As if the candidate should be sent out to live as a chaste Catholic in a gay neighborhood, and without any mention of when exactly he is to come back.

———

Even if one manages to reconcile the contradictory logics of "coming out" and being able to prove a call to celibacy, there is the problem of acceptance by the religious community. The very self-assurance of a gay candidate might make him more unacceptable to his future brothers. "Is it not possible, for example, to reach a conclusion that a homosexual candidate is healthy and acceptable, but the community into which he or she would move is not able or willing to receive such a person?"[50] "[T]here are institutes which are seriously unqualified to provide a fit environment for a homosexual candidates, regardless of how qualified he or she is to join."[51]

———

There is no way to sum the statements of policy for diocesan seminaries and religious congregations. They are, in any case, not usually candid about practice. Clear answers about either policy or practice are harder and harder to get as the Vatican tightens its regulatory control. Some religious orders and apparently some dioceses are still willing to accept self-identified gay candidates, so long as the candidates are committed to celibacy and so long as they are willing to be discreet about their homosexuality. Many fewer are willing to state this as a matter of policy. Most formation programs are officially much less encouraging of gay candidates, often rejecting them outright. I should say, rejecting *openly* gay candidates outright, because the numbers of gay seminarians doesn't seem to be diminishing. On the contrary.

———

Old attractions are still exerted under the more homophobic policies. "Aesthetic," "sensitive," and even "effeminate" young men are still admitted to seminaries, are still ordained. Indeed, and this should be particularly disconcerting for "conservatives," there seems to be some connection between closeted homosexuality and antimodern tastes in theology, discipline, and liturgy.[52] The increasing conservatism reported in recent seminary classes is perfectly consistent with their containing fewer open homosexuals and many more hidden ones.

———

"Why do so many gay boys grow up to be priests?"[53] Because they are promised an exchange of their anguished identity as outsiders for a respected and powerful identity as an insider. Because they want to remain in the beautiful, queer space of the liturgy. Because they are drawn to public celebration of suffering that redeems. Because they want to live in as gay a world as the Catholic church offers.

———

Pious young men struggling with homoerotic desires are still attracted to seminaries, and seminaries are still attracted to such young men. There has been much public and private fretting in the last two decades that "too many" gay men are entering the priesthood and religious life. No one seems to worry that this might imply criticism of God. After all, clerical vocations are supposed to be divine callings.

———

"It scarcely occurred to him that his religion could establish any quarrel with his sexual habits. Indeed, in some curious way the emotion which fed both arose deeply from the same source, and some vague awareness of this kept him from a more minute reflection."[54]

———

Catholic policies about admission to clerical life are ultimately applied by clerics. Laypeople may serve as personnel consultants or psychological assessors, but the final decisions about Catholic priests are still typically made by priests. Many of these priests have homoerotic desires. These desires, admitted or suppressed, affect decisions about candidates in formation. Gay men are assigned to implement policies designed to screen out or cure gayness.

The consequences fall out in a dozen directions. Sometimes closeted gay priests persecute "out" gay seminarians from resentment or suppressed desire or fear of disclosure. "Before his ordination he had prayer for spiritual armour, and had received a coat of self-satisfaction which had so far held out against all assaults of man or woman."[55] Sometimes they support them with a sense of regret over their own lost opportunities. At other times a very attractive candidate, straight or gay, triggers directors or whole communities into a crisis of action or decision or violent denial.[56]

While candidates for the clergy can be drawn by the tacit analogies between religious formation and coming out, formation officers are caught by analogies between priestly formation and a basic conundrum of gay "culture": Gay communities must reproduce themselves outside of procreative family structures. A celibate clergy faces exactly the same situation. How is the next generation of priests to be raised? The survival of the celibate clergy depends on raising young men outside and even despite their families. So too does the survival of a gay tradition.

———

Seminary admission decisions are occasions not only for acts of survival, of cultural reproduction, but of cultural repetition. Seminaries are and have been finishing schools for a certain kind of homoerotic identity. Efforts to weed out gay candidates, to cure them or teach them concealment, repeat the oldest conditions for producing homoerotic identity in Christian Europe. A Catholic seminary, especially a conservative seminary, is one of the few places left in modern society for building baroque closets. This is not so much the work of the effeminate candidate as it is of homoerotic clerical cultures trying to compete against the ideals of "coming out." Seminary education is often enough training in how to be homoerotic the old-fashioned way.

Teaching Purity

In the long system of formation that ran from entry into minor seminary all the way to priestly ordination, the testing of a vocation to celibacy was accompanied by the teaching of purity. The instruction took many forms, from the most formal to the most informal. Together they constituted what I can only call a curriculum of ignorant shame.

The curriculum was meant to produce feelings that sexual activity was a pollution that rendered one too dirty to be a priest. Even to speak about it brought a measure of risk. Some forms of sex, notably male-male sex, were so intrinsically polluting that they could hardly be spoken about at all except by circumlocution. The challenge was to construct a system for teaching seminarians purity without explaining to them what you were doing or what the opposite of purity might be.

———

From the title page of *The Major Seminarian* (1948), these psalm verses, in Latin: "Who may go up to the mountain of the Lord, or who may stand in His holy place? One who has innocent hands and a clean heart, who does not give his soul to vanity."[57]

———

Lessons in clerical purity were often lessons in misogyny. Many seminary handbooks repeated the most misogynistic passages from the Church Fathers. The patristic sentiments were reinforced by the voice of modern experience. "If it is dangerous for any priest to have frequent contact with women, especially if they are young, it is most dangerous and almost always fatal for seminarians who are still in formation and at a highly flammable age."[58]

Admonition was reinforced by detailed practical counsel. Seminarians were warned to stay away from girls, especially during summer vacation. They were also cautioned against tutoring young girls, directing girls' choirs, or even spending too much time at the pastor's house if his young sisters were frequent visitors.[59]

It was not enough to avoid conversation with girls and women. One had to avoid looking at them. This is the old doctrine of "custody of the eyes." Certain of its precautions are understandable, if a little nervous. In 1949 the Sacred Congregation for Seminaries solemnly warned seminarians from going to summer beach resorts because of the danger of "nudism."[60] But understandable precautions were only part of a more comprehensive instruction. The teaching was taken over from ancient monastic doctrine and applied to diocesan seminarians. It prohibited looking not just at scantily clad women or their lascivious portraits, but at fully clothed women in the conduct of ordinary business, as if the mere sight of them were infectious.

From Rodriguez, once required daily reading for Jesuits in formation: "The holy Abbot Ephrem says that three things are great helps to virtue, to chastity particularly—temperance, silence, and custody of the eyes. And though you keep the first two, yet if you do not guard your eyes, your chastity cannot be depended on; because as, when aqueducts are broken, the water is spilled and lost, so is chastity lost when looks and glances are scattered and thrown about here and there."[61] Rodriguez then praises St. Hugh of Grenoble for not having looked at a woman's face during fifty years of active ministry, "except one ugly old crone that was a servant in his house." St. Aloysius Gonzaga, patron of chastity, is praised elsewhere for having averted his gaze from his mother's face.

Unfortunately, custody of the eyes had to be exercised not only with women, but with one's classmates in seminary. Common showers and changing rooms were causes of concern, though the more bizarre precautions may not have been as common in America as, for example, in Spain. There I was shown a well-crafted wooden paddle that novices had formerly used to tuck in their shirts: No hands below the belt. It goes without saying that this Spanish house's showers were curtained off from one another and that special trunks had to be worn while showering.

———

"At four o'clock every afternoon we showered. The Prefect of Discipline would come through in his habit, reading his breviary, sidestepping puddles. 'Eight minutes, gents,' he would say. 'Custody of the eyes, gents.'"[62]

———

Custody of the eyes stood in tension with the use of physical exercise as therapy against libido. The gym provided physical release of sexual energy—but it also presented temptations. The risks were taken because hard physical exercise burned sexual frustration so efficiently. For example, one text advises young monks to exercise immediately after awakening in order to avoid erections during matins.[63] The same principle seems to lie behind many of the frenzied games and even the wearying manual labor.

———

Seminary masturbation was something of a theoretical quandary. In traditional moral theology, masturbation is an unnatural act and hence more serious than heterosexual intercourse. But in seminary life masturbation was much more frequent than heterosexual intercourse—and more excusable. It could happen more quickly and alone, inside the walls, without long planning or the violation of other seminary rules, say, about enclosure.[64] Masturbation could follow on the rush of desire from an erotic dream in the drowsy half-sleep of early morning. It could become confused with that other object of expert concern, the nocturnal emission.

———

The diagnosis of nocturnal emissions depended precisely on assessing how much consent had been involved, how much lingering over the images, how much "morbid delight" in them. The act could be excused, for example, if it were strictly involuntary so far as the waking mind was concerned. Of course, frequency of spontaneous erections or nocturnal emissions served as an index of spiritual progress. Cassian had summarized the old monastic traditions according to which complete freedom from emissions and then from erections was a sign of highest chastity. His scale of perfection was repeated in the spiritual handbooks for novices.[65]

––––––

Scrupulous attention to particular impurities, that is, to overt sexual acts, went right along with a blindness toward the erotic implications of other acts. Many of the rituals of seminary hazing, for example, seem to an outsider remarkably "impure." Recall "pantsing" or "depantsing"—or "detrunking" if in the swimming pool; "mooning"; shower chases and wrestling; the rite of "reddening" a classmate's stomach—or ass—with slaps or spankings. It's not odd that the repertoire of prep school "high spirits" should appear in a closed community of young men. It is peculiar that they were so often described as infractions against good order rather than as problems of sexual purity.

––––––

Indeed, the extraordinary thing about all of this older instruction in purity is that it was exactly half a teaching, half a speech. An elaborate instruction was given about dangers that were never specified. Certainly the "sex ed" offered, especially during adolescence, was enigmatic and anti-erotic.

––––––

A more effective "sex ed" was given by seminary sarcasm. The conversation of religious communities is notoriously cruel, and so the manuals of religious life were filled with warnings against gossip. Cruelty was not repressed, was indeed cultivated, when it could be used against sex, sexuality, or those suspected of sexual rebellion. A friend remembers the most effective lesson in minor seminary as a denunciation one day, by a particularly severe dean of discipline, of "ninny-boys" or "sissies."

Ridicule is still used today, and sometimes encouraged, when it comes to openly gay seminarians or novices. "In the realm of community the [survey] responses pointed to a lack of knowledge, biased attitudes, and prejudicial behaviors of members. . . . This was expressed in an uninviting and nonsupportive environment; the community's own discomfort with sexuality; a releasing of latent homosexuality in others; fear of becoming a haven for homosexuals; poking fun at, joking about, and making judgmental statements on homosexuality; and an overall lack of education on homosexuality."[66]

"Clerical conversation often hones in on characters that are different and it is the easiest label to call someone gay or lesbian—and by God it sticks."[67]

———

Seminary teaching on purity was just another hysterical speech. It warned, cajoled, threatened, satirized, but it did not describe. The thing itself was often left in the dark, like the monster in a horror film. The result was to create an anxious tension around sexual topics that had to be left in ignorance.

———

The tense silence about sex was perhaps nowhere more noticeable than after dismissals. When someone was sent away for failing to demonstrate a vocation to celibacy, little or nothing was said. Seminarians just disappeared. The assigned place in choir closed up. The room or dorm bed was cleaned and someone else was moved into it—or no one, if there were too few candidates. The seriousness of the sexual fall was underscored precisely by saying nothing about it. It was too awful or ugly or threatening to be spoken.

"I recall only two incidents in thirteen years of seminary. Once a major seminarian touched another in a vulgar way; he was dismissed. On another occasion when someone left the community I was told only one word: homosexuality. I knew better than to pursue the matter."[68]

"Homosexuality was a taboo subject [in seminary]. It was dealt with only by the phenomenon of people (by the pair) disappearing mysteriously and without official commentary from the seminary-scape."[69]

———

American Catholic seminaries and religious houses of formation prized sexual purity. They instilled, in various degrees, a sense of shame about sexual temptations. So they tended both to attract and to retain young men who were already threatened by sex. In homophobic societies, young men who begin to experience homosexual desires typically find them very threatening indeed. A seminary's way of marking off sex as defiling and dangerous matches all too well the processes of internalized homophobia.

———

So too does the seminary's emphasis on the "special" character of the vocation. Seminarians lived in isolated circumstances, took distinctive vows, deserved deference because they were specially called by God. They were required to be sexually pure because they were set apart for service to God. Many gay men confess that they feel "different"—not so much special as abject—because of their sexual feelings. The mechanisms of clerical formation created a sexual minority of men who are subtracted from the ordinary world of marriage. So too do the mechanisms for forming gay identity. But the church prized the sexual minority of clerical celibates. It ridiculed and punished the sexual minority of gay men. Of course a young man struggling with homoerotic feelings would find it easy to see seminary as a way of redeeming his shameful desire. As a priest, he would never have to marry. He would be encouraged to view women as alien. He would be helped to put a heavy lid on all sexual thoughts by considering them as polluting. In short, he would be set apart by his sexual characteristics. What a perfect match: Having a vocation is a way to come out without having to say any risky words.

———

The curricula of shame have been reformed in the last decades, at least in most houses of formation. It is unusual to find the kind of explicit disgust for women that used to characterize much of the talk about purity. Many of the Vatican documents call, on the contrary, for a full and well-balanced curriculum of studies in sexuality, both theological and scientific. But then and now the emphasis on purity is backed by mechanisms of enforcement. The teaching of purity is only the articulation of a prior and most powerful system of surveillance, which recreates the most familiar conditions for homoerotic life in American history.

Celestial Surveillance

When I first began to teach seminary students, they were required to spy on one another. Much of the system of spying seemed to be concerned with how the seminarians behaved when they hiked up the hill from the seminary buildings to the college campus, where most of their academic classes were held. They could never be on campus alone. Indeed, they were always at least to be paired. Nor were they allowed to eat in the college cafeteria or sit down there at a table with women. They had to wear clerical garb so that they could not blend in with the lay students. Most of all, and whether they were up on the college campus or down the hill, they were obliged to watch one another and to report any infractions of discipline immediately.

———

When the system was first described to me, I was reminded of one of those ideal, eighteenth-century prisons in which every cell could be observed from a central vantage point. Long before video cameras, the penal ideal was perfect surveillance. The same was true of this seminary regime. Every seminarian was to be watched as much as practicable.

Now this ideal was rather old-fashioned in America by the mid-1970s. I was lucky or unlucky enough to run across one of the few survivors. But similar ideals have been widespread during the last four centuries of Catholic life. They have reasserted themselves since the 1970s in a number of places, and they have taken on some ingenious new forms. Their importance for the present inquiry is that much of their obsessive character is specifically sexual. If the ideal of perfect surveillance encompasses all behavior, its particular concern is with sex.

———

Regular and quite specific reports were compiled by formation officers or teams on seminarians and members of religious orders still in formation. They were typically gathered confidentially and without any chance for the candidate to respond. The candidate knew the results when a decision was made.

Some questionnaires used for the reports particularly emphasized sexual matters, though the topics were indicated in the approved code words. Pastors in a candidate's home parish were asked in the 1930s, for example, to inquire whether he was given to reading books or newspapers contrary to "good customs," whether he had been familiar with persons of either sex of "dubious reputation," whether he had been seen in suspicious places or heard to say improper things, and whether his family showed any physical or psychological abnormalities, especially any "proclivity" to sexual pleasure that might suggest "atavism" in the candidate himself.[70]

More recent questionnaires can be more specific, and seminary staff members are urged not to shy away from the most pointed interrogations. "Are night-time or daytime erotic fantasies (notably masturbatory fantasies) always or very predominately homosexual?"[71]

———

The obsession with sexual surveillance deforms aspects of seminary life that don't seem to have anything particularly to do with sex—for instance, the sense of personal privacy and the possibility of relaxed friendship. What is more important, the surveillance creates conditions for secret sexuality, which is the hallmark of many homosexual identities. The obsession with surveillance replicates the environment in which closeted homosexual activity flourishes. The seminary can have the excitement of a public bathroom in a busy park. It can become, in sum, a "queer space."[72]

———

Men who attended the same seminary during the same years will disagree sharply about how much emphasis it placed on preventing homosexual contacts. Some of this has to do with individual sensitivity or susceptibility to the sexual energies in institutional arrangements. Some of it depends on the different experiences of gay and straight seminarians. One of the students I taught in those early years seems to have passed through the system of spying unperturbed. He found it funny, especially because he was spending so much time reminiscing about his high school girlfriends. He left the seminary after a few years and enjoyed life as a straight man-about-town before he eventually married. Another student from those years, who now identifies himself as gay and who remained in the seminary much longer, suffered the surveillance as a kind of daily invasion. But both men agree that the seminary had a lot of rules aimed at desexualizing daily contacts.

Where to look in seminary arrangements for anxiety over homoerotic temptations? One place is in the so-called house rules, the detailed regulations by which candidates are bound. These rules are not easy for an outsider to find. Some of the older ones are preserved in publicly accessible archives. Others have been saved or remembered by those who lived them. Some contemporary ones can be had for the asking. But it is usually much harder to get a copy of a diocesan seminary's house rules than it is to obtain the adjacent Catholic college's student handbook.

The house rules that can be read or reconstructed from testimony are alternately charming and chilling. Many rules prevent seminarians from being alone with another student—never in each other's rooms or in secluded parts of the seminary grounds: ". . . one of our great commandments was, Thou Shalt Not Enter Another Seminarian's Room."[73] After certain hours, two men cannot be together even in public spaces like hallways. Indeed, the close-order drill of the daily schedule is not only a way to exhaust sexual energy, it also ensures that the candidates will be visible, will be at certain places at certain times. The timetable becomes an instrument of surveillance.

One of the effects of this comprehensive, celestial surveillance is to sexualize the most routine transactions. Seminary becomes something like a "gay ghetto" in which the shortest errand is an occasion for cruising and being cruised. Or to draw the analogy more precisely: Systems of clerical surveillance recapitulate and distill the experience of growing up gay in a homophobic church. A seminary is a big Catholic family in which all the children are suspected of being gay—and watched accordingly. "To grow up homosexual is to live with secrets and within secrets. In no other place are those secrets more closely guarded than within the family home."[74]

In order to put them under surveillance, seminaries bring together young men from different regions. For many of them, it is their first time away from home. It may also be their first time in an enclosed, all-male environment. So seminary is often the first place where young gay men can encounter a significant number of other young gay men. Catholic seminaries have long done what the World War II draft is credited with doing for American gays generally: seminaries teach young gay men that there are other young gay men.

———

Catholic seminaries become for many gay men places of sexual self-discovery. Some of this is just the coincidence of adolescence and the old regime of seminary formation. If young men are spending their years of adolescence in seminaries, then some of them will have their first sexual experiences and their epiphanies of sexual identity in seminary. But some of it has to do with the conditions of seminary life.

It is frequently admitted that the "homosocial" setting of seminaries generates "homoerotic ideation."[75] The seminary reverses the psychological context of the world outside, where the full array of social pressures and the bombardment of heterosexist images can lead homosexual boys to think for a time that they really do study straight pornography for the women. In the reversed world of the seminary, it is not unusual for men who will later identify as heterosexual to have same-sex infatuations and homosexual dreams or fantasies. Their experimentation often excludes homosexual seminarians, for whom the stakes may feel higher. "I now know that there were guys having sex with each other in the seminary, all of whom again turned out later to be heterosexual and got married. But I was not involved."[76]

———

I have in mind another kind of homosociality in the seminary, the sociality of a community in which there is an unusually large percentage of homosexuals. Seminary can be a site of sexual discovery because it is, in its own curious way, a little gay enclave. Young men who will later identify as gay often have their first sense of that identity—and often their first sexual experience—while in seminary. For them it can figure not as a passing "situation," but as a disclosure of self. Seminary can provide the first place in which a young gay man feels able to fall in love.[77]

———

Testimonies are not hard to find. "I was very popular there [in seminary] because there were a lot of young gay men in the Servites."[78] "After graduation I made up my mind that I was going on to the [Xaverian] novitiate. From that time on, with the exception of a few 'trysts' with two or three other young brothers prior to age twenty-one, I was celibate until I was twenty-nine."[79] Of course, any sexually active space will draw predators. The first sexual experiences with other seminarians are not always happy.[80]

Particular Friendships

"A seminarian is not long in the minor seminary before he learns that the peculiar institution known as a particular friendship is held in high disfavor by the faculty. The reasons for this disfavor will doubtless be obscure and unintelligible to him for quite some time, and understandably so."[81]

———

The anxieties over homosexuality in formation crystallized around the threat posed by "special friendships" between seminarians or novices. So too do the conventions of silence, because it was rarely clear why so much stress should be placed on them.

The usual explanation was that brotherly love or harmonious community life required you to be equally friendly with everyone. "Take advantage of the many opportunities which recreations offer to cultivate sociability and to practice fraternal charity. Associate freely with all your fellow-students, and avoid being habitually with the same ones."[82] "A particular friendship in a seminary is destructive of community life and, therefore, of fraternal charity."[83] But they were also stigmatized as being merely "natural," hence open to unspecified degradation. To enter into a particular friendship was to place your foot on a slippery slope. "Their real reasons for seeing each other so often can then become the sound of a voice, a handsome countenance, a jovial personality, witty conversation, flattering compliments. Nourished and encouraged by endearing remarks, the affair can continue to roll down the hill."[84] Toward what? Nothing more is said; nothing more need be said.

———

A suspicion of merely natural friendships is an old feature of religious life. The Desert Fathers warned against it, and their warnings pass through various spiritual writers into the manuals for young religious and diocesan clergy. "St. Basil in his Monastic Constitutions says that religious ought to have great union and charity one with another, but in such sort that there be no particular friendships nor affections whereby two or three band themselves together to keep up such affections, for this would not be charity, but division and sedition, even though such friendship seemed just and holy."[85] How far these warnings were, in the "Fathers," a code for homoerotic relations is disputed. What seems sure is that they have functioned as a code in many American seminaries and novitiates or scholasticates. "We know well that in the not-too-distant past the strong emphasis forbidding 'particular friendships' prevailed as a safeguard against gay and lesbian relationships within communities."[86] But the code was almost too good, because it seems to have been unintelligible to many seminarians who later identified themselves as gay.

A former Dominican: "All the statements in the seminary about not having particular friendships I interpreted as not getting too close to somebody emotionally, because if he leaves it will affect me. I was naïve about what was going on in the seminary. There were gay relationships developing there. All of a sudden two people would leave at the same time; overnight they were gone."[87]

A former seminarian for the Oblates of Mary Immaculate: "There was discussion in the seminary about homosexuality, although I didn't know what they were talking about. . . . Then there was the constant discussion about particular friendships. Any time you made friends with anyone it was frowned upon. . . . If you were ever seen more than three days in a row talking to the same guy, you would be called in and told that you were forming a particular friendship."[88]

In other cases, when the condemnation of particular friendships was invoked to separate and even segregate two young men, they may have understood all too well that it was indeed "the code phrase at that time [in the 1950s] for homosexual relationships."[89]

The code was perfectly intelligible to seminary authorities, who regularly fulminated about particular friendships.[90] They imagined clearly enough the transit from friendship to sexual passion. So they acted against them. "Watch carefully to insure that there are no equivocal conversations, gestures or allusions; that no sentimental or sensual friendships are established. Suppress any attempt of the kind with timely and severe measures."[91]

Anxieties over particular friendships put enormous pressure on the possibility for candid affection among seminarians. They sometimes corrupted the ideal of friendship. Perhaps this was not entirely accidental. It may indeed be a tacit recognition of the erotic ambiguities latent in traditional practices of Christian friendship.

These ambiguities have recently been explored from various angles by gay historians. For example, John Boswell has claimed, notoriously and I think unconvincingly, that the Byzantine liturgical rite of "brother-making" was used in both the Eastern and Western churches as a de facto rite of same-sex marriage. Although I am not persuaded by his main claim, I do think that Boswell was right to say that we need to pay much more attention to the discipline of friendship in monastic and clerical Christianity.

The ambiguities of religious friendship have also been dissected in disputes over the "gayness" or "homosexuality" of historical figures. Consider, for example, the ongoing debate over the homosexuality of the twelfth-century abbot, Aelred of Rievaulx, one of the principal spiritual writers of the Cistercian movement. Aelred enters the history of homosexuality in part because of biographical facts, in part because of certain themes in his theological writings. Aelred himself describes the passionate attachments he felt for other men, and he confesses that he was particularly afflicted with sexual temptations. His biographer conceded when challenged that Aelred was sexually active as a young man and perhaps even notoriously so.

Moreover, Aelred's writing includes many passages that strike modern readers as homoerotic. His treatise *On Jesus at the Age of Twelve* encourages quite graphically the practice of devotion to the body of the young savior. In other writings, Aelred fixes equally strong affect on the body of the cruci- fied Jesus. Of course, and at the same time, in many passages Aelred explic- itly condemns as serious and degrading sin any genital contact between members of the same sex.

———

To say that these texts are about friendship between men rather than about homosexual attraction is to beg the question, what exactly is the difference between the two? We can't say that the difference is whether or not the two men "feel sexual attraction" to each other, since that term is no clearer. We obviously can't say that the difference is whether genital contact actually occurred: We usually don't know, while we do know that self-identifying gay men can share strong erotic attractions that are never physically con- summated.

The anxiety around these questions, the difficulty of segregating homo- erotic passion from intense fraternal charity, makes it easier for religious institutions to avoid the question altogether by command: No particular friendships. Everyone loves everyone equally—and purely.

———

With particular friendships as with so much of the rest of the regulation of clerical sexuality, an emphatic prohibition neither changes histories nor quashes unspoken recognitions provoked by them. The lives of the saints read during so many refectory dinners proclaim the heroic "brotherly love" of a number of paired saints, such as Cosmas and Damian. The lives of the founders of religious orders are filled with extraordinary examples of tender affection, expressed not least in care for the founder's body, before and after death. You can sit in refectory and hear these as the proper sublimations or transfigurations of sinful feelings. You can hear them as exhortations to chaste comradeship in place of carnal copulation. Or you can hear them— some young men do hear them—as suggestions, expansions, enrichments of homoerotic feelings.

So too with the whole project of seminary education in chastity. The lessons about purity, the imposition of surveillance, the punishment of particular friendships have an odd way of reversing themselves into so many confessions of the power and durability of male-male love. That kind of love is too often connected to the privileged moment of seminary teaching: the activity of spiritual direction.

The Use and Abuse of Seminarians

The most intimate of approved relationships in seminary life is that between a regular confessor and his penitent, between a spiritual director and those who are entrusted to him.

Some gay men testify that they were helped in their coming out by good spiritual direction. "While, in some ways, I had gone to the seminary to escape my sexuality, paradoxically, in the seminary I was forced to confront who I was."[92] Others remember spiritual direction that at least did not get in the way of their coming to terms with themselves through community life.[93]

Many writers look forward from such positive relations to a time when heterosexism will be eliminated from spiritual direction.[94]

––––––

The other side of mentoring, of spiritual fatherhood, is sexual abuse. Seminarians and novices are targets for sexual abuse from their superiors. Sipe reports that 100 of the priests in his survey were sexually harassed while in seminary.[95] Pennington writes: "Many a young man has related to me how a trusted counselor or vocation director has tried to engage him in genital activity."[96] Anecdotes about similar, if less structured relations of mentoring are very common. "What confused the situation was that there were older men in the [Jesuit novitiate] community who made passes. There were very vibrant sexual things going on. Within my first few weeks there someone made a pass at me."[97] "My first sexual experience was with someone in the Order ['a religious teaching order'], a person who taught me when I was in high school."[98]

––––––

The sexual harassment of seminarians is sometimes blatant. A college friend of mine tells the following story: He was sent to Rome to study for a con-

gregation that specializes in the care of troubled priests, including pedophiles. Shortly after his arrival, he was propositioned by his director. He
refused. A few months later, he began a fairly visible sexual relationship
with an African-American seminarian at one of the other houses of formation. My friend was dismissed from the order and sent home for sins
against chastity.

———

"Sexual abuse" itself is by no means an unambiguous category—as it is by
no means a simple phrase.[99] It can be very hard to know how to apply it in
cases where the "victim" disputes such an interpretation. Consider the
story told by Hendrickson. For more than five years, from the time he was
fifteen, he participated in an odd ritual with his spiritual director. "I would
go in, sit in a chair beside his desk, talk for a short while, await his nod,
unzipper my trousers, take out my penis, rub it while I allowed impure
thoughts to flow through my brain, and, at the point where I felt myself
fully large and close to emission, say, 'Father, I'm ready now.' He would
then reach over and hand me a black wooden crucifix."[100] One hand on the
crucifix, the other on his penis, Hendrickson would proceed to recite the
various reasons why he wanted to conquer sexual temptation.

Now Hendrickson is sure that his director did not relish this as an erotic
opportunity. "I never once saw or felt him studying me with what seemed
like the least erotic urge or lustful desire" (169). Years later, when he confronted his director with what had happened so often between them, the
priest "said the act had come about in an era following the Kinsey Report,
when some new approaches to guidance were being tried in pastoral circles" (174). Not just with Hendrickson: the same ritual had been carried
out with other boys, though not with all. Those who were not involved in
it accused him of either lying or being insane when he tried to describe
it (172).

Many people familiar with clerical sexual abuse would find Hendrickson's sense of confusion and even complicity typical. They would find the
priest's excuses all too familiar—and unconvincing. I find just as important
the utter incredulity of other seminarians who were not "going to the green
chair." Compartmentalization and secrecy are essential to this kind of relationship. That is one reason why two seminarians going through the same

seminary program in the same years can have such different experiences of what was taught—and what was done—in it.

———

I might dismiss Hendrickson's story as an anomaly except that I know of other cases in which sex was solicited or demanded as part of spiritual direction. One spiritual director, for example, would use "massage" in order to give lessons in the "intimacy" that his male students had failed to learn at home. "Massage" escalated quickly enough into copulation. But when confronted with multiple complaints about these activities, he denied, in public and in private, that he had done anything wrong. The same priest still refuses to identify himself as gay, and he continues to denounce effeminacy in seminaries and religious orders.

———

Doing things without naming them—or naming them as something else, something spiritual. The sexual abuse of seminarians by their spiritual directors or formation superiors recapitulates the project of seminary education with regard to homosexuality. Homosexuality itself cannot be spoken, admitted, described. So whatever happens cannot be homosexuality.

This education in silence may indeed be the best preparation for later life as a homosexual priest or religious in the church at large.

7

clerical camp

SOME CATHOLIC PRIESTS participate expertly in one or another of the American gay marketplaces. They can pick the appropriate seasonal outfit for a dance club or a Levi's/leatherette bar. They can find their way to backrooms, bathhouses, or somewhat leafier places for public sex.[1] Some priests also read gay newsmagazines, listen to gay folk songs, or read gay novels. But all Catholic priests in America, gay or not, participate in one culture deeply colored by gay tastes and gay fantasies: the predominant clerical culture itself.

———

I need to remind you, especially here, of the important exclusion I made at the beginning in focusing on the Catholic clergy—that is, on men. Modern Catholicism embraces any number of cultures. Some are national or linguistic, others

socioeconomic or aesthetic, and others still organized around different constructions of gender. By looking to the "predominant clerical culture," I
don't mean to deny or erase the variety of cultures within the church, as I
don't mean to suggest that the only Catholic cultures are male-produced or
male-dominated. Instead, I describe what is most characteristic of clerical
culture—that is, of the cultural products of what is normatively an all-
male system.

Women have contributed enormously to Catholic cultures and even to
clerical culture. But in its fantasy of an all-male hierarchy, clerical culture
ignores those contributions. This chapter analyzes that fantasy, in part to
show how quickly the "all-male" tips over into the "effeminate"—at least,
according to the fantasy's stereotyped terms.

American clergymen are divided by all the social differences that separate other Americans—ethnic, educational, economic, chronological, geographical. Alongside these differences, despite them, are social roles shared
by Catholic clergymen. Some of the shared roles are generated by common
experiences of clerical discipline, especially celibacy. As official celibates,
the clergy are householders without wives. They take on a number of domestic roles typically assigned to women. (I mean roles and not chores,
since the chores are often still performed by hired laywomen.) Other shared
roles come with common liturgical duties. As presiders over liturgy, and in
many cases as sole producers of it, priests are actors in public rituals that
confuse gender roles. In these and other ways, the Catholic clerical style
comprises elements stereotypically associated with gay identities—that is,
so far as all gay men are reputed to be effeminate.

This does not mean that all Catholic priests are "really" gay—or that
all gay men are effeminate and that the "feminine" ought to have a lower
status than the "masculine." I am describing a system of stereotypes, not a
set of facts. So far as it traffics in these stereotypes, modern Catholic culture
requires that all priests, straight or gay, adopt some "effeminate" roles.
These roles are otherwise derided as belonging to sissies, faggots, pansies—that is, to gay men. If heterosexist cultures expect all people to behave in public as if they were straight, modern Catholic culture expects all
priests to act publicly in some ways ordinarily stereotyped as gay. It also
insists that no one mention this curious equation of clichés.

———

It is easy to imagine why closeted gay priests want to resist public consideration of Catholic homosexuality. It is also easy to discover some of their larger arrangements for resistance. They block public consideration by enforcing silence about it or by chattering over it in endless condemnation. But it is much harder to imagine how the very gayness of clerical culture would be an obstacle to speaking seriously about Catholic homosexuality.

The problem is that clerical gayness remains familiar as something clerical, not as something gay. We think of it as a separate set of practices and sensibilities. The habits of priests are set aside in the magical box of "Religion." Whatever is in that magical box cannot be analyzed. We do not think about clerical style in relation to gay culture because we do not think about it at all. If we did, we certainly wouldn't compare it to something so secular. But we may need to do exactly that in order to be able to speak about homosexuality in Catholicism—and not only in stereotypes.

We can interpret many aspects of clerical life, from ritual to rectory routines, as expressions of a gay sensibility. Perhaps we can then reclaim these expressions, however distorted, as forms of lived Catholic homosexuality—and not just any homosexuality, but the homosexuality of the Catholic ruling class.

———

The name I will appropriate for much of what is or is reputedly gay in the predominant clerical culture is the imprecise and essential term "camp." Though gay men agree on its outstanding exemplars, camp escapes exact definition. Attempts to define it, even when they are helpful, are typically more tantalizing than satisfying. For example, Jack Babuscio identifies four features in camp: irony, aestheticism, theatricality, and sharp humor.[2] He then restricts these features by allowing them to be camp only where they "express, or are created by, a gay sensibility." And "gay sensibility" means?

In applying "camp" to clerical culture, we should reconceive it as a series of effects rather than as a set of conscious motives. We have to understand irony and sharp humor as products of situations or systems, with or without the conscious consent of those acting in them. Aestheticism and theatricality can be present underneath their explicit denial, just as they can exist alongside bad taste and ugly mediocrity. Clerical camp is produced not by deliberate parody with caustic intent, but by a set of roles and styles that present themselves as perfectly "normal." For every Catholic priest who takes malicious delight in subverting official homophobia by camping it up at the altar, there are ten or a hundred who perform a kind of camp just by doing what they were taught in seminary. Instead of describing small groups of self-consciously gay clerics who transfer camp manners from gay life to church life, "clerical camp" is most useful for categorizing all the rest of the priests who don't think they are doing anything odd when they dress up in silks on Sunday morning to promenade, sing, act, and host a meal.[3]

———

Daniel Harris analyzes camp in relation to the (vanishing) gay worship of movie stars and popular singers. It is the moment, inevitable in such worship, when reverence becomes ridicule, when the rush of pursuit swivels around as mocking familiarity. "Gay diva worship is a cult that requires the blind faith of credulous fans who are content to kowtow and genuflect and never to even think of peeking behind the curtain. Camp is what happens when the curtain is lifted."[4] By understanding camp in this way, Harris is able to give it a role in his narrative of decline. But hasn't he tailored the definition to fit the narrative?

In Catholic clerical culture, camp does not signify a moment of inevitable decline. It is not the transit from reverence to ridicule so much as the simultaneity, the inseparability, of reverence and ridicule. Clerical camp is lifting the curtain once again to giggle—and then dropping it solemnly back into place.

———

Wayne Koestenbaum does not try to define camp—wisely, I think. He describes it as an experience, the experience of the "camp glow" or "camp rush."[5] Camp is here a "style of resistance and self-protection, a way of identifying with other queer people across invisibility and disgrace" (85). Its essential operation is to "fill degraded artifacts to the brim with meanings," "making a private airlift of lost cultural matter, fragments held hostage by everyone else's indifference" (117). The private retrieval of what the straight world has discarded: make that an emblem of inner transfiguration. "Gay culture has perfected the art of mimicking a diva—of pretending, inside, to be divine—to help the stigmatized self imagine it is received, believed, and adored" (133).

Clerical culture takes any number of degraded artifacts—childless men, overwrought decorative objects, bread wafers—and fills them with the most important possible meanings. But it does all of this institutionally, prescriptively, by system. Its camp is the camp of required routine.

Perhaps as its symbols and rituals become more degraded culturally, more trivialized, what is camp in Catholicism becomes more visible.

———

Whether you define camp or narrate it, whether you search for its causes or amplify its effects, you will find striking similarities to Catholic clerical culture. Almost any notion of camp will do, no matter how incomplete or suspect. Consider, for example, a few elements from Susan Sontag's often contested description.[6] Sontag writes: "Camp taste has an affinity for certain arts rather than others. Clothes, furniture, all the elements of visual décor, for instance, make up a large part of Camp." They also make up most of the realm of liturgical art, that is, of priestly patronage. "Many examples of Camp are things which, from a 'serious' point of view, are either bad art or kitsch." Say, church statuary, holy cards, Christmas-light halos, the lyrics of many hymns. "All Camp objects, and persons, contain a large element of artifice." For example, statues and cloths made out of precious metals, daylight colored by windows, perfumed smoke, and legally specified fake flowers. "As a taste in persons, Camp responds particularly to the markedly attenuated and to the strongly exaggerated. The androgyne is certainly one of the great images of Camp sensibility." Consider officially celibate men dressed in brocade who perform stylized domestic ritual. "Camp sees everything in quotation marks." The Mass is a repetition or memorial of an ancient event, narrated by rote, framed by prescribed quotations from authoritative texts.

The field of objects and styles Sontag associates with camp epitomizes the public activity of the Catholic priest.

———

"Barren as Shakers and, interestingly, as concerned with the small effect, homosexuals have made a covenant against nature. Homosexual survival lay in artifice, in plumage, in lampshades, sonnets, musical comedy, couture, syntax, religious ceremony, opera, lacquer, irony."[7] Rodriguez means, but does not say, male homosexuals. Being an "old Catholic," he knows Shakers hardly as well as his own priests.

———

The last person to ask me detailed questions about the iconography of the Immaculate Heart of Mary was a shaved-head, gay bartender. He wanted to get the design of a new tattoo exactly right. At another club, some blocks nearer downtown, the dance floor is dominated by a towering figure of a hooded monk. On the club's strictly Goth nights, which are called "The Church," the crowd sports pieces of a dozen kinds of vestments and antique liturgical jewelry. Historically these borrowings might derive from the inversions of Catholicism associated with the occult. But by now they are not so much desecrations as imitations or quotations. They borrow, with not a little respect, an old and intricate language of symbols, objects, and gestures that are already exaggerated, melodramatic, even grotesque. Images of Catholic devotion pass so easily into secular camp because they are already camp.[8]

———

How can camp remain campy when a whole field of cultural activity appropriates its devices? Perhaps we should distinguish technically accomplished and deliberate "high" camp from a sort of "broad" or even "systemic" camp. High camp in the Catholic Church is that brilliant and self-mocking clerical humor that much resembles Fellini's ecclesiastical fashion show in *Roma*. By contrast, broad Catholic camp needs no technical cunning, no brilliant parody, no self-consciousness at all. The only emphasis required for broad clerical camp is just the denial that it represents anything out of the ordinary, especially in regard to secular expectations of gender. The gender reversals or inversions that distinguish the Catholic priest are thus framed by denials of an effeminacy tacitly identified with male homoeroticism.

———

I think of the doublespeak of slapstick drag. Here, the aim is not to "pass" as feminine. It is to stress how ridiculous one looks in a feminine role—

and how effortlessly one can still perform it. The performers don't shave their beards. They wear traffic cones for breasts and rip off fluorescent wigs at the beginning of the act rather than the end. In the minutes between, they also manage perfectly "feminine" gestures or a passionate investment in lip-synching. "I regard this as a joke—and I perform it with utter seriousness." "I detest pansies—now watch me do drag."

Similar doublespeak occurs in many priestly performances. It is the inevitable and inescapable camp of the clerical role, which is both tacitly and tensely marked off from ordinary masculine roles. "I am not doing anything unusual—and yet no other man could get away with doing this." "I condemn homosexuality—now watch me do the most public drag."

Clerical culture acts out camp by stretching the prevailing gender roles and then denying that it has done any such thing.

———

Broad or systemic camp is misconceived when we regard it as the activity of "subculture." There are, as we have seen, groups or networks of self-consciously gay priests and religious brothers. We can indeed talk about these men with some plausibility as a gay "subculture" in the Catholic church. But there are many other ways in which homoerotic desire or the fear of it shoot through the life of the church, especially its public worship. Instead of a subculture, this kind of homoeroticism is a gay "paraculture." It is not a small, separate component. It conditions or even characterizes the whole.

———

Hocquenghem paraphrases Adler: "Homosexuality haunts the 'normal world.'"[9] Homosexuality is a ghost or ghost-image.[10] It shadows or mirrors or inverts or mocks the straight world. It is the night to every day—and is sometimes as invisible as night under high noon.

Gay "invisibility" is neither just repression nor protective camouflage. It signifies the way identities linked to sexuality have operated. Our invisibility is a constant temptation to assimilate, a constant invitation to collaborate softly. Many of the monuments of the dominant secular culture, many of its canonical works, many of its styles, are the products of gay artistry. If this artistry is tacitly ignored or maliciously ridiculed, it is nonetheless real. During long centuries when women and various ethnic minorities were excluded, some homoerotic males could gain access to the machinery of cultural production. The cost to them was one or another code of silence, of painful "passing." When we think of those we claim for predecessors as a "subculture," we forget that they were always present in the dominant culture of even the most homophobic regimes. They were culturally active even when they were most violently silenced. They were not a subculture, then, nor even an alternative culture, but a "paraculture," a universal irony inside the dominant culture.

———

Homoerotic desires and perceptions are present throughout the dominant clerical culture of the Catholic church, more strongly and more centrally than in secular cultures. The expectations we impose on the Catholic priest, especially the combination of celibacy and ritual, bend his public gender— make him "queer" in several senses. We then specify that the priest be officially homophobic. This makes his gender-bending an odd and bitter camp. Because that role is just what we have been taught to assign to priests, we don't speak of it as camp. We no longer recognize its queerness, in part because we wouldn't know what a "straight" clerical culture would look like.

Traits elsewhere stigmatized in men—effeminacy, artifice, "aestheticism"—are permitted in Catholic priests and even encouraged. From the vantage of the men's locker room, fervent religious worship has always been a matter for women and pansies.[11] "Effeminacy" is not an attribute of a subset of priests. It characterizes the highly visible actions required of all priests. These queer actions become camp not just through deliberate exaggeration, but because they are punctuated by loud assertions that there is absolutely nothing queer about them.

———

How would you "queer" Catholic liturgy? How could you make it any campier than it already is? To make 1950s American "womanhood" camp, you change the sex of the performer and move the show from a Midwest Main Street to a converted urban warehouse. To make the Catholic Mass camp, you certainly don't have to change the sex of the performer, or the

clothing, or much of the script, and you may not even have to move it—
church decoration being what it sometimes is.

Liturgical Drag

Eve Sedgwick writes: "Catholicism in particular is famous for giving count-
less gay and proto-gay children the shock of the possibility of adults who
don't marry, of men in dresses, of passionate theatre, of introspective investment, of lives filled with what could, ideally without diminution, be called
the work of fetish."[12] We have already heard similar testimony from Catholic boys drawn by the eroticized beauty of liturgy: "Mass was the ballet of
my youth."[13] The Anglican protagonist of "The Priest and the Acolyte"
explains: "I had to choose a profession. I became a priest. The whole aesthetic tendency of my soul was intensely attracted by the wonderful mysteries of Christianity, the artistic beauty of our services."[14]

———

The last two centuries have demonstrated a well-known correlation between ritualism and "effeminacy" in Roman Catholicism and Anglicanism
(to implicate no other denominations).[15] The correlation is too often explained with the most simpleminded stereotypes. Gay men are supposed to
love color and good music, so of course they are attracted to liturgy. David
Hilliard quotes a sociological study of British homosexuality from 1960: "'it
is not difficult to understand that the services with impressive ceremony
and large choirs are more likely to appeal to homosexuals.'" It is not difficult
to understand because stereotype replaces thinking.

Hilliard adds two confirming passages of fiction set in the nineteenth
century.[16] Many other passages suggest more interesting ways to regard the
connections of homosexuality with liturgy.

———

Dorian Gray, that platonic form of the urban gay male, "had a special passion . . . for ecclesiastical vestments, as indeed he had for everything connected with the service of the Church. In the long cedar chests that lined

the west gallery of his house he had stored away many rare and beautiful specimens of what is really the raiment of the Bride of Christ."[17]

Des Esseintes, the protagonist of Huysmans' *À rebours* (*Against the Grain* or *Against Nature*) and one of Dorian's inspirations, decorates his retreat at Fontenay with choice vestments. The ceiling tondo shows angels from the fabric of a cope "embroidered by the weavers' confraternity in Cologne"; the curtains are made of priests' stoles; and the fireplace screen is cut from the "sumptuous stuff of a Florentine dalmatic."[18] Later Des Esseintes will suffer the onrush of memories from his Jesuit school, remembered seductions yielding to sensory hallucinations and liturgical flashbacks. "The chants learned among the Jesuits reappeared, establishing just by themselves the boarding school, the chapel, where they had echoed, their hallucinations striking olfactory and visual organs again, veiling them in incense smoke and shadows lit by glimmerings from the stained-glass windows, all under high arches."[19] The memories of seduction are inseparable from an excessive sensitivity to high liturgy. No wonder Charles Ryder, newly arrived at Oxford, is warned so succinctly by his cousin: "Beware of Anglo-Catholics—they're all sodomites with unpleasant accents."[20]

———

For Dorian Gray and Des Esseintes, if not for Charles Ryder's informant, liturgical collecting is among other things an advanced snobbery. It marks them off from their more pedestrian surroundings. For Dorian, high liturgy is flirtation with Popery. For Des Esseintes, it is a medievalist's repudiation of the dreary town that surrounds him—that he means to blot out.

Modern homosexual identities do in fact prescribe a kind of "artsiness" that would be drawn to strong liturgy, but that "artsiness" needs to be analyzed in turn as a kind of resistance or rejection of bourgeois reality. The theatrical world of a great church can offer escape from the conflicts or disappointments of "the world." Taking up a minority or reforming cause within the church, such as the "Liturgical Movement," can become a sort of political affiliation, even a substitute for the more arduous and dangerous cause of homosexual organization.[21]

———

Other motives link sexual deviance with liturgy. The Catholic liturgy is a performance that affords new pleasures in gender dissembling, in the exploration of male beauty and the male body. It is a performance that solicits passionate attention, even ecstatic participation. The liturgy creates its own divas, on both sides of the communion rail. It is a show that makes for ardent gay fans.

There is a type of gay man in the Catholic Church—and not only in the Catholic church—known derisively as the "Liturgy Queen." Since I was one, I claim the prerogative of pinning on the insult as a badge of honor. So I define the Liturgy Queen as a fierce fan of "good liturgy."

———

Liturgy Queens need not be members of the clergy, but they are typically found in the vicinity of the altar—or at least in the choir loft. They are sacristans, altar servers, lay readers, choir directors, and organists. Most have put in time on liturgy committees, though often unhappily. A liturgy committee is a place, after all, where the fantasy of the liturgy meets the reality of weekend "Mass." Whatever they do, wherever they are, however they serve, Liturgy Queens are distinguished by a passionate engagement with the minutest questions of liturgical practice, about which they are often obsessively well-informed.

———

"Homophobic, to call the queen a queen, . . . a prissy librarian, a fussy knowledge-monger, a fact policeman: homophobic and inevitable, to equate homosexuality with detail and trivia and superficiality (as opposed to heart and depth and substance), and then to forbid the queen from enjoying his facts and surfaces, to forbid the queen from marshaling his details like armor."[22] The Liturgy Queen's favorite facts concern the public ritual of a brutally homophobic organization. The homophobia implicit in my caricature—even in my use of the notion of camp—must be understood as a reply to the homophobia of the church whose cult the Liturgy Queen adores. We caricature ourselves as Liturgy Queens because we seek the protection, the collaborative distraction, of erudite adoration.

———

The Liturgy Queen is a version of the adoring gay fan—which is to say, a worshipper of details about divas. The divas in liturgy are both the legendary performers and the learned arbiters of taste. Liturgical performance might seem to be too local and ephemeral to promote legends, but it has its divas, its great houses, and its unforgettable moments as much as grand opera. The performers are praised and compared in the ceaseless gossip of the "coffee hour," the planning meeting, the clerical dinner, the monastery "rec" room, the regional workshop, and the summer institute. It is not just a matter of how he preached or chanted, but how he moved, held his hands, handled the censer. What choice did he make among the available vestments? Which tropes or optional texts from among those specified for the day? Did he let the choirmaster arrange the music—and, if so, was it really the prudent thing to do?

Unforgettable liturgical performances are burnished into anecdotes and perhaps even recorded. "The novice slipped a bell rope off its catch and pulled. About forty monks gathered at the far end of the nave, with what looked like the *schola cantorum* in the middle of the nave. The bell rang again. Artificial light sprang on about the altar. A hymn in English. In twin lines, the vested priests paced forth, kissed the altar, and streamed into the chancel." That was a liturgy for All Saints Day 1973 at Melleray Abbey near Cappoquin in Ireland. I quote the description from the journal I kept when I was twenty-one and a visitor there. Nothing extraordinary about that journal. So many pious young Catholics kept them that we could fill libraries.

———

More famous, more literate, and more consequential writing is done by the other diva in Catholic worship, the liturgist. The liturgist is now most often a professor, but he has also been an antiquarian, a musician, an artist. He may even be an important church official. The popes' masters of ceremonies have written many volumes, at least since the fifteenth century.[23] If some of these writings seem to be historical records, they are more often intended as expressions of authoritative taste. "Martinucci, Master of Apostolic Ceremonies: *Manuale Sacrarum Caeremoniarum*, Rome, 1871. —The name and the title of the author are a high recommendation of the work."[24] As of so many others.

The diva-liturgist need not have high ecclesiastical position, but he must have evident erudition, fluency, and the assured, precise, personal voice of the connoisseur. "The reader will find, in this chapter, principles opposed to many preconceived ideas, ideas that are willingly admitted, indeed savored in certain quarters."[25]

————

Liturgy Queens are fierce gay fans who take as their divas the legendary liturgical performers and the authoritative connoisseur-critics. But the main object of their devotion is the liturgy itself. In the same way that Opera Queens will talk about voice expressing wedded word and music in the perfect realization of opera, so Liturgy Queens pursue that sublime combination of elements, that *Gesamtkunstwerk,* that liturgy should be. The pursuit is endlessly absorbing. If some gay men have spent years in passionate quests for bootleg tapes of Maria Callas or publicity stills of Maria Montez, others have exhausted themselves over the vexed question of the "neo-Gothic" chasuble.

————

The chasuble is the outermost robe that a priest wears when celebrating a Latin-rite Mass. The chasuble that American Catholics see nowadays at most Masses is a full, flowing garment that reaches down to the knees or even the ankles. But chasubles were not always so—and there lies the melodrama.

The Latin chasuble started out as a variation on an ancient Roman cloak. It resembled full-sized ponchos (without the hoods). During the Middle Ages, as more and more ornate fabrics were used, chasubles of this fullness became too heavy for fluid movement. So the chasubles were cut down— first on the sides, to free the arms, and then everywhere, until the chasuble became two panels of fabric held together by shoulder-straps. One Roman version of this chasuble, which can be seen on statues of modern saints who were priests, had a square back and a front panel shaped like the body of a violin—though sometimes front and back are both "fiddle-shaped."

Then came the last century's Liturgical Movement, that shifting alliance of liturgical criticism, liturgical history, medieval studies, musicology, medievalism, Pre-Raphaelitism, dandyism. It brought, among many more important changes, a certain distaste for the skimpy Roman chasuble. Churches of various kinds—diocesan, monastic, religious—began to return to the Gothic or Semi-Gothic or Revival or Oval chasuble. They did so without securing the Vatican's permission. In 1925, the Sacred Congregation of Rites reminded everyone that such chasubles were illegal. It quoted a letter of its own from 1863: "no change should be made [in chasubles] without consulting the Holy See, as the Sovereign Pontiffs have more than once announced in their Constitutions, wisely declaring that such changes, being contrary to the approved practice of the church, can often cause disturbance and produce astonishment in the minds of the faithful."[26]

Disturbance and astonishment were caused immediately by this decree in the minds of liturgists and "lovers of sacred art." The legality of the "ample chasuble" became a hotly disputed question, provoking immediate commentary in major theological and liturgical journals. Books followed, accumulating complex arguments on both sides of the question. For example, the Benedictine Roulin argued that "the approved practice of the church" must, in liturgical matters, be interpreted according to local traditions.[27] Many local traditions had used the neo-Gothic chasuble for centuries—and had returned to it decades ago. Again, there had always been regional variation in modern-style chasubles, including those manufactured or used at Rome. Moreover, ample chasubles seemed to be presupposed by a number of liturgical rubrics. Finally, decisively, it was a matter of beauty even more than of historical precision. "Under the impulse of a powerful liturgical and aesthetic sense, we have come to slightly different forms, to chasubles which are certainly of their own time, but which share plainly in the 'spirit' and the meaning of all the great old chasubles."[28]

The canonists and the more legally minded liturgists were not persuaded. It didn't matter that something like the Gothic chasuble had been widely worn in the Middle Ages. The rule for liturgical fashion is set by what is *now* being worn in Rome—unless specific permission has been granted to wear something old-fashioned.[29] Nabuco could advance six classes of argument in favor of the ample chasuble, including the fact that the pope himself had said Mass in one fully five years after the decree.[30] This argument and all the others in the six classes are refuted by Sadlowski.[31] Sadlowski concludes: A modern, Roman-style chasuble cut to the dimensions he recommends "can be ample, graceful, dignified, as the laws of sacred art demand, and still be in accordance with the received usage of the church in Rome."[32]

The controversy is an old one—and by now well settled. Neo-Gothic chasubles have long since won out. I rehearse the controversy to show the passion expended over decades in regard to liturgical fashion. The Liturgy Queen seeks out such esoteric and exacting knowledge of these artifices in the way other gay fans do. The Liturgy Queen collects liturgical memorabilia as avidly as others collect old interviews with Hollywood stars. He will hunt down amateur chant recordings, visit out-of-the way sacristies, buy up reproductions of famous paintings of liturgical scenes, and dream of being able to afford historical vestments. He aspires to be like Dorian Gray and Des Esseintes.

Liturgy Queens show themselves to be true gay fans—yearning for transfiguration through fierce attention to what is different from daily life. There is something in what Daniel Harris says: "At the very heart of gay diva worship is not the diva herself but the almost universal homosexual experience of ostracism and insecurity, which ultimately led to what might be called the aestheticism of maladjustment, the gay man's exploitation of cinematic visions of Hollywood grandeur to elevate himself above his antagonistic surroundings and simultaneously express membership in a secret society of upper-class aesthetes."[33] We could say, less cruelly: Being a gay fan of liturgy offers a beautiful fantasy in a homophobic church.

The intensity of personal investment may explain why the Liturgy Queen's knowledge is defended with desperate passion. There is nothing like a liturgical controversy to rend communities.

Many explanations are given of the ferocity with which Christian communities fight over small liturgical changes: that ritual matters more to parishioners than doctrine; that liturgical texts are deeply bound up in childhood memories and family customs; that liturgical issues serve as ready substitutes for more threatening, less articulate issues. I would add that liturgical quarrels are sometimes so bitter because they are quarrels over cherished fantasies. For Liturgy Queens, in particular, someone who wants to change the liturgy also attacks the fantasy on which an escape from unhappiness depends. But because Liturgy Queens support different sides of most controverted questions, disputes over liturgy come to resemble long-running wars among the fans of rival divas.

Style Wars

Curiously enough, one of the weapons in liturgical style wars has been the charge of "effeminacy." Since the late nineteenth century, the partisans of the Liturgical Movement have struggled against "bad art": mass-produced, heavily ornamented, sentimentally "realistic" works. "Good art," on the other hand, included handcrafted, unembellished, rigorously unsentimental and "antirealist" works. What is more interesting, "bad art" was gendered feminine, "good art" masculine. In 1863, a congress in Belgium declared itself against "sensual and spineless representations which are a perversion of good taste and emasculate piety."[34] Compare this very practical Irish pastor in 1926: "Let sham and frippery and showy colourings live in the drink saloons, the theatres and circus wagon, but in the house of God let there be solemn simplicity, chaste colouring, nothing flaunting, out of place, glaring, tawdry."[35] Or Roulin in 1930 on liturgical linen: "The simplicity of the fabric is beautiful, and much more beautiful than the fussiness, the loveliness, the complication, the tangle represented by the majority of little decorations put onto so many altar cloths and linen vestments."[36] A monsignor in San Francisco quotes the insistence that saints are not "smooth-faced, characterless, doll-like, languid, feebly sentimental individuals."[37] As a prominent American liturgist declared in 1958: "What is required are well-made, genuine things: things that are simple, manly, solid, chaste, honest, unsentimental, noble, hieratic."[38]

It might be tempting to read these attacks on effeminate art as a quarrel between straight and gay sensibilities, except that the ideal of the unornamented, functional, visibly structured artifact is itself, as McDannell suggests, an image of male beauty. "Like a man's body, the [modern church] should be smooth, powerful, and strong."[39] Indeed, though McDannell does not say it, the "smooth, powerful, strong" male body belongs to a very recognizable gay aesthetic, the "muscle boy" ideal. So that the quarrel between the Liturgical Movement and the "art of Saint Sulpice" can also be interpreted as a dispute between two recognizably homoerotic sensibilities.

———

There are gay bars with chandeliers, red velvet drapes, paintings in gilded frames, faux classical sculpture, and large pianos. Conservatively dressed men gather in them to sing Broadway hits. Then there are gay bars with bare lightbulbs, black walls, pornographic posters, sections of chain-link fence, and freestanding subwoofers pounding out dance music. They are all gay bars, but the inhabitants of the latter sometimes refer to the patrons of the former as "faggots" or "queens."

When a partisan of folk masses and rough-hewn worker-saints accuses a devotee of alabaster angels, draped tapestries, and the cult of the Infant Jesus of "effeminacy," this too can be a quarrel among Liturgy Queens.

———

Let me construct the analogy more exactly by making its terms more specific. In the wake of Vatican II, horrific battles were waged about the church remodeling required to turn the altars around to face the congregations. The results in some cases resembled a victory of iconoclasm—or the Puritan stripping of English churches. In other cases, churches resembling border-town curio shops were restored to something like their eucharistic function. Translating the Mass into English had equally mixed results. If many of its texts were banal or worse, the structure of the liturgical action was at least visible.

The loud quarrels that continue to swirl around these changes have been presented as an aesthetic choice between Mystery, Tradition, Conservatism and Honesty, Innovation, Liberalism. You could favor complexity, ornament, and elegance or simplicity, bare passion, and informality. Figured this way, the liturgical styles wars following Vatican II paralleled the quarrels between the assimilationist "homophile" movement and radical "gay liberation." Both can be understood as competitions between gay styles.

———

Recall Parker Tyler's *Screening the Sexes* (1972), professedly a book on film but actually a meditation on gay styles. Tyler's stated purpose was "to expand that limited idea (the pleasure of making and rearing children) with an idea of sexual behavior that achieves magnitude through variety of form, hence variety of sensation and emotion."[40] "Variety of sensation and emotion" is definitely not the goal of gay liberation, for which Tyler has only disdain. Nor is the visibility he wants for homoeroticism the same as the visibility of free love in the streets. The vulgarity of "gay-power newspapers" and "street demonstrations" should be explained as "self-advertising," "group hysteria," and "the modern obsession (still underestimated) for basking at whatever price in publicity's many spotlights."[41] Here is Tyler's essential contrast: the "vogue," "now-now-now," "corny," "grotesque," "low," "out" visibility of gay liberation as against the "high" and "esoteric."[42] This is, again, the contrast between advertisement and art, between the "happy porno violence" of "untrammeled sexual expression" and a taste for the "aesthetic and historical" (49–50).

Tyler supposes a set of contrasts between camp and grotesque, between the free/imaginative and the mechanical/literal, between the poetic and the aggressive. The street demonstration of the liberationists is "a lot like the circus parade, whose only purpose is to titillate appetite and to advertise the joys to come at the *real* performance" (321). The demonstration belongs, in other words, to the disvalued sphere of vulgar advertising, aggressive titillation, and pornography. The visibility sought by gay liberation is the visibility of the homosexual exhibitionist who can think of no better way of being seen than by standing in a park and dropping his (doubtless flamboyant) pants.

The important thing to remember is that Parker Tyler's critique of low gay style is not the accusation of a "straight" homophobe. Neither is it just the fussy admonition "Be tasteful!" or the nervously self-restrained "Higher Sodomy" of Edwardian Cambridge.[43] Tyler's critique is advice from a gay man that gay lives will be more honest, more interesting, and more erotic if they refuse to be "vogue," "now-now-now," "corny," "grotesque," "low," and "out." Tyler's appeal to the "aesthetic and historical" is made on behalf of a more intense and more sexual gayness.

All of Tyler's arguments can be rewritten as liturgical commentary merely by identifying him as a "traditionalist" or "preconciliarist" and his adversaries as "modernists" or "postconciliarists." I infer from this editorial experiment that our nastiest liturgical quarrels resemble contemporary quarrels among gay men about styles of gay visibility. I wonder, more ten-tatively, how far liturgical quarrels are precisely the *same* quarrels as those others.

———

There are further analogies. In many ways, for example, the liturgists' long-ing for the styles of the earliest church is just a way of getting close to the Greeks. What "Hellenism" once did for Oxford undergraduates, imag-inative reconstructions of the earliest Christian worship do for liturgists. Where should we look for the standards of liturgical vestments, Roulin asks? "To the origins of Christianity, in those ancient times which partici-pated in the sense of beauty that the Romans had as heirs in part of the Greeks, the uncontested masters in fact of the natural, cultivated, and re-flective style, intimate and profound."[44] He goes on to praise the newest vestments, which exhale "the perfume of Christian antiquity," that pristine Christian period when "the faithful lived by charity, in an artistic and deli-cate ambience. We can only gain by contact with their brotherhood, with their spirit and their simple tastes."[45] The description of the fashion sense of the earliest Christians could have been written by a Hellenizing lover of boyish beauty. Indeed, something very much like it was—by Walter Pater, in the fourth part of *Marius the Epicurean*. From the first description of "the Church in Cecilia's House": "a taste, indeed, chiefly evidenced in the selec-tion and juxtaposition of the material it had to deal with, consisting almost exclusively of the remains of older art, here arranged and harmonized, with effects . . . so delicate as to seem really derivative from some finer intelli-gence in these matters than lay within the resources of the ancient world." From the first description of Cecilia herself: "With certain antique severity in the gathering of the long mantle . . . to the mind of Marius her temperate beauty brought reminiscences of the serious and virile character of the best female statuary of Greece."[46] Note the "virile."

———

These analogies are enough for my purpose, which is only to show struc-tural similarities between liturgical controversies and gay style wars. Re-semblances do not imply that every liturgist is gay or that the authors quoted took men for lovers. I am talking about rhetorical positions, not copulatory ones. But many speeches of liturgical passion belong, as speeches, to the world of gay rhetoric.

So does their vehemence. "Gays are not always nice to each other. . . . Anger (among its many uses) is a form of flirtation." Indeed, in church circles it seems the most approved form. "Battling divas offer lessons in the art of anger: how to fight an oppressive order by inventing a resilient self."[47] There is also this simpler fact: The rage that comes with being a gay Catholic must be expended somehow.

The Excesses of Eunuchs

An official portrait of Cardinal Spellman poses him wearing full regalia in his "Throne Room" (or perhaps his living room).[48] He is decked out in layers of lace and watered silk, with an ermine mantle and train. But gaudier still are the curtains behind him: gold-brocade outer curtains over lace sheers. In a television documentary, ABC's Robert Considine discussed these curtains with the ruggedly handsome Monsignor Patrick V. Ahern, one of "two associates and close friends" who shared the cardinal's mansion with him.

> AHERN. [The mansion] remains completely unchanged from what it
>   was when Cardinal Spellman first came here in 1939. Everything
>   is just the same except the new curtains.
> CONSIDINE. You don't see lace curtains like these much these days.
> AHERN. Everybody admires them, especially the ladies.[49]

No wonder the posing cardinal looks so pleased with himself. Free, free at last, to appear in drag before his own amazing curtains—about which no one dare mutter a disapproving word. This kind of portrait can be published on the front page of Catholic newspapers and hung on the wall in chancery offices, rectories, and homes of wealthy benefactors.

"'She ["Nellie Spellbound," that is, Cardinal Spellman] was very upset when the pope ordered the cardinals to shorten their trains from ten yards to two.'"[50]

The cardinal's portrait shows how well Catholics have been taught to indulge their ecclesiastical superiors. The portrait assaults not just our ordinary gender expectations, but our ordinary sense of what constitutes appropriate display. Indeed, I am at the moment less interested in Spellman's well-known tastes for drag or young men than in his execrable taste in drapes.[51] When Nixon attempted to make the uniform for White House guards a little grander, he was ridiculed until the uniforms disappeared. But here is Cardinal Spellman, in New York of the 1950s, in front of those curtains: an emblem of our tolerance for the excesses of clerical taste.

There is an essay to be written on the gay iconography in ecclesiastical portraiture—and not only in regard to vestments. For example, the portraits from the same centenary of Cardinal Spellman and his longtime patron, Pius XII, are *tableaux vivants* of power and tenderness, discipline and desire—all done up in the costliest dresses.

———

Many clerical pomps are excused in Catholic conversation by the argument that they help maintain church dignity. The greater glory of God somehow requires commodity fetishism. The habits are also sometimes justified as a kind of compensation. Father drives an expensive car, wears Gucci shoes, buys tailored suits on his summer trips to Italy . . . well, Father has had to give up a lot to be celibate. If many diocesan priests nowadays live on quite restricted budgets, others—friends of the rich and powerful—still use the priesthood as an excuse for excess. The "feminine" excess is forgiven or expected because they are officially "unsexed." As modern eunuchs, they are permitted to take on the stereotypes of women. They are allowed to worry about embroidery and the cut of garments, in chasubles as in suits.

"In our culture a man in a cassock is wearing a skirt."[52] When it comes to clothes, we assign Catholic priests to a mixed or third gender. We have been taught to indulge them as if they were the stereotyped trophy wife of the distant suburbs. They have the "right" to shop at boutiques, to buy gourmet cookware, to collect bibelots, to cultivate expensive hobbies. Complaints about the luxuries in one diocesan seminary were answered with the argument that "the boys have to get used to the kind of life they'll be living when they get their own rectories."

———

Other bizarreries of clerical taste are a kind of ultra-Montanism, a form of obeisance to Rome. Some priests still try to model themselves after the fashions of the Eternal City. They go there on vacation. They order their clerical outfits there—or, if a number of them are promoted to monsignor together, they fly the best Roman tailors to America to cut their new robes. During the drearier months at home, they gather over a three-martini lunch at an Italian restaurant to reminisce.

———

The analogies between this kind of clerical life and one older style of gay refinement are too obvious. Think of those apartments with shag carpet, white baby-grand pianos, framed Broadway posters or autographed programs, some Lalique in mirrored displays, Mardi Gras masks or oil portraits of Mother. Make it a little less gaudy, a little less artsy, and you have the sense, the smell, of wealthy rectories. In the same way that priests are excused for their little indulgences, some gay men of a certain era were excused for buying too many cashmere sweaters—after all, they don't have families and they can't have children.

Note that the cliché has continued much longer in Catholic circles than in gay ones. In this way too, modern Catholicism is a cabinet of abandoned cultural collectibles.

———

More interesting than the resemblances of certain clerical excesses or excuses with other gay identities is our continued silence about them. There is a tacit exchange of identities, with their privileges and limitations but without their names. The derision directed at gay aestheticism or consumerism is deflected or refracted when it comes to the (gay) aestheticism or consumerism of powerful members of the clergy. Cardinal Spellman is allowed his excesses, but they are considered only the excesses of an official eunuch, not the neuroses of a faggot.

———

The exchange of identities has interesting consequences for clerical shopping. There is another study to be done, for example, of the rhetoric in ads directed to clergymen. Vestments are not sold using the same language as business suits—though the buyers could be men of the same age and income bracket. An advertisement for the line, "Expressions in Wool": "An exclusive collection, where the media of fabric, design and colours are given a harmonious expression of religious conviction."[53]

———

If wealthy gay men are stereotypically art collectors, successful Catholic clergymen are still in the unusual position of commissioning artists and musicians. They are patrons of the arts in the real and not the euphemistic sense.

Their authority has long rankled some lay liturgists. The Liturgical Arts Society, which was founded by laypeople in the late 1920s, regularly beat the drum for more consultative arrangements. "The pages of [its journal] *Liturgical Art* . . . were filled with anecdotal observations of the ways in which local clergymen had impeded the progress of liturgical and artistic renewal in the life of the Church."[54] One of the society's leaders was more blunt in private: "if, perchance, I found myself the Prime Minister of a country, I would forbid the clergy to have anything to do with the building and decorating of churches."[55] Reasons for the unhappy state of affairs were explored and remedies were offered, beginning with better education in the seminaries. But what was not explored—what was not spoken—was the role of protected gay camp in this patronage.

———

The complex influences of clerical camp on Catholic art can be glimpsed by looking to controversies that directly affect members of the Liturgical Arts Society—and every other Catholic. These concern religious representation, especially in sculpture and painting. Clerical control over religious art means clerical control over images of two very important bodies, one male and one female: Jesus and Mary. So far as the clerical aesthetic is a camp aesthetic, the representation of the gender of these two bodies should be particularly problematic.

———

Canon law has long required that the art in churches should not allow for doctrinal error.[56] More difficult are questions of style and taste. Pius XII provoked considerable debate when he spoke in 1947 against some forms of "modern art" that "seem to be a distortion and perversion of true art and which at times openly shock Christian taste, modesty and devotion, and shamefully offend true religious sense." The controversy intensified five years later when the Holy Office, under the same pope, issued its "Instruction on Sacred Art." But these general incidents conceal more than they reveal.[57] What we need to see is more particular—and perhaps more shocking.

———

A poorly articulated danger is felt concerning Catholic representations of holy figures. In one of its modern forms, the danger is described as "the repugnancy of feminizing" Jesus.[58] Jesus shouldn't be made to look like a seductive girl. On the other hand, Jesus shouldn't be shown too explicitly as a man. Indeed, naked representations of Christ crucified or raised from the dead are too much for modern Catholic sensibilities.

———

It almost seems too much for us even to talk about them. Leo Steinberg's groundbreaking book on the sexuality of Christ in Renaissance art stresses the theological seriousness of the paintings it treats in order to steer far away from scandal.[59] One might say that he realizes the difficulty of speaking unhysterically about Christ's sexuality—even though Christ's full humanity is one of the most central and most public doctrines of Christianity. Indeed, and as he insists, Steinberg must account not only for the prominence given Christ's genitals in Renaissance paintings, but for our own ability to study those paintings for centuries without noticing the genitals.

———

Some things must be said here, even at the risk of provoking hysteria. Otherwise we will stop short of the most powerful questions about homosexuality in Catholicism. The first concerns representation. In modern Catholic art, since Christ is not usually "feminine," he must be sexless. This representation is often controlled by clergymen who are themselves often conceived as sexless—or at least officially so. We might see this as connecting Christ's gender with priestly gender. But in our society, a man who is represented as sexless risks falling into that other category of half-men, namely, gay men. Gay men are still "faggots" because they fail to be real men. In this way, clerically controlled representations of Jesus risk aligning him with stigmatized figures of gender inversion. They risk camping Jesus as gay.

Looking at some artistic representations of Jesus almost naked without any hint of genitals, I wonder if there could be more striking examples of habitual camp. Jesus has everything a man has, except the one thing that makes him a man. His gender has been artistically reconceived as decoration, as a kind of performance, as drag. The art of eunuchs, indeed.

If the metaphors of "camp," "drag," and "eunuchs" seem too scandalous to approach the body of Christ, I can rephrase the point without them.

Hanging over every liturgical quarrel, sometimes quite literally, is the almost naked body of a man that makes up the representation of most modern, Catholic crucifixes. This nude man signifies a great risk for Christian art, the risk that it should become as fully homoerotic as some statues of Greek gods now seem to us. Given the fixation on Jesus' body in Catholic art, and on that body as growing, suffering, dead, and resurrected, an impartial observer might wonder how Catholic art could avoid becoming intensely homoerotic. Many have worried aloud that one or another style of representing Jesus might be too effeminate. Might the unspoken worry have been whether the most "manly" representations of Jesus, the best and highest portrayals of his body, wouldn't be most at risk of soliciting and even enacting homoerotic desires?

Historically, we have dismissed this kind of consideration outright for two reasons. First, Christianity is vehemently opposed to homosexuality, hence Christian art cannot be homoerotic. Second, faithful Christians cannot be homosexuals, so the main audience for Christian art contains no one who might react to it homoerotically.

We can now recognize the faulty logic behind these two arguments. First, the Catholic opposition to homosexuality seems to be essentially connected with efforts to silence homosexual speeches *within* the church. Second, there is every reason to believe that the Catholic clergy contains many men with homosexual inclinations. The class in the church that patronizes and defines religious art shares a culture deeply colored by homoerotic desires. How then can we avoid careful examination of the homoerotic element in Catholic representations of Jesus? We cannot. Yet Steinberg himself, who has done more than anyone to recover the art of Christ's sexuality, seems deliberately to rule out homoerotic motives or reactions.[60]

Trexler writes: "Unlike the reproductive organs of many other divinities, the penis and testicles of Jesus Christ have only recently been suspected of having much meaning."[61] Or is it that representations of them have all along been suspected of having *too much* meaning—and certainly not as "reproductive organs"?

———

The question of whether Jesus should ever be depicted naked has been asked often enough in relation to Catholic art. It has provoked curious answers, most notably the insistence that we should not permit naked crucifixes even though we know them to be historically accurate.[62] The question becomes more interesting and more urgent if we base it on the presumption that male homosexuality has long affected Catholic clerical cultures.

———

Worries about the "feminization" or "effeminacy" of Christ in Catholic art may displace more scandalous worries. Whenever we begin to feel the erotic energy around Christ's body, we screen it with the "mystical" language of the bridegroom or the misogynistic language of feminization. What we cannot quite say is that there are other ways for men to be sexually attractive to men than by being transmuted into women. If we have begun to think about "Jesus as mother" in Catholic literature and art, we have not at all begun to consider the adult Jesus as "companion" or the younger Jesus as ephebe. We find it easier to change Jesus' sex than to place it within homoerotic contexts.

———

Our inability to sustain questions about the homoerotic quality of art sponsored by Catholic clergymen does not eliminate that feature. It does make it available to silent uses—and, I suggest, to the most habitual and grotesque sorts of camping.

———

Imagine this anthropological report. A group of men kneel in a room for long periods to contemplate a figure. Their focus is a mostly naked man who wears only a cloth to cover his conspicuously absent genitals. His nude and curiously unsexed body is represented to the audience as the central object of love. They regard its every detail as overcharged with affective significance. A number of the kneeling men are homoerotically inclined, though they are pledged not to engage in any voluntary use of their genitals. And they have this rule: They can never ask whether there is any connection between that representation of the naked man and their own erotic inclinations.

———

Test questions: How might one of those kneeling, homosexual men describe his predicament? Might he find it ironic and even sharply humorous? Might he sometimes think of it melodramatically? Might he try to make the view of that almost naked figure more tolerable by aestheticizing his own reactions to it? Such questions suggest the possibility that clerical art in the Catholic church is forced into camp as a way of defusing or concealing certain possibilities that are inseparable from central dogmas.

———

Male homosexuality must always be particularly threatening to men in a religion of the God who assumed a male body. It threatens to resexualize our relationship with Christ, hence our life in God. Instead of pretending that this threat doesn't exist, instead of denying the correlation between gayness and priestly vocation, we ought to take it up as a challenge. Can we have a religion of an incarnate God in which sex takes its appropriate role, being neither denounced nor fetishized?

Gay Catholics must reconcile this question with their love for Christ. It may be just here that they have most to contribute to understanding fundamental truths of the faith.

The Word Took Flesh

Clerical camp shows itself in religious art both by excess and by avoidance. Most of all, it has to step around certain implications of the bodily aspect of Christ. For modern clerical taste, his body has to be veiled and desexed before it can be represented. Something similar has happened in modern liturgical language: We are hardly comfortable with hymns to the beauty of Christ's bodily parts or detailed sermons on the import of his circumcision. Yet the most immediate presence of Christ's body is neither in artistic representation nor in liturgical poetry. It is in eucharistic transubstantiation. Here priests cannot avoid Christ's body, since it is their office to invoke it, break it, and feed it to their congregations.

The central act of Catholic worship presupposes immediate bodily contact of many kinds. A priest holds a piece of bread and speaks over it in such a way that it becomes the body of Christ. He holds onto the bread while it becomes body, and then he feeds this body to the faithful.

This is a remarkably direct and primitive understanding of union with God. Not surprisingly, it has attracted a number of psychoanalytic interpretations, in which communion becomes, for example, patricidal cannibalism or communal fellatio.[63] I will not consider those interpretations here. I want to focus instead on the gender of the (male) priest who holds the bread while it is transformed into God's (male) body.

————

The priest who holds the body of Christ is supposed to be an unmarried man who cultivates sexual purity. He is allowed or encouraged to take on certain stereotypically female attributes, such as fancy costume, (ritualized) domestic service, specific luxury goods, and a competence in beautiful furnishings. More cynically, but no less generally, he is suspected of being "womanish" sexually—that is, of wanting sex with other men. The Catholic priest is, in this system of cultural stereotypes, doubly demoted from masculinity. He behaves in some ways like a woman and he is probably queer. So the man deputized to make and serve the body of God, to hold it, is unmanned. His sexual purity is sexual stigma. He is free from sex because he is linked with transgressions against sex.

We should ask, much more than we have, why we construct the gender of the Catholic priest in just this way.

A friend suggests that we should understand the construction as a kind of exchange. Gay men are brought into the priesthood with the understanding that they can live out their gayness in various ways. They are not permitted to copulate with other men, of course, but in exchange for renouncing sex they are given the power to make a man's body with their own breath and hands. The gender of the priesthood is constructed around this tacit approval of the one Catholic way to be gay.

If this explanation seems too bizarre, it is worth considering not just the implications of transubstantiation, but the vehement insistence that only men can perform it.

———

I think about the curiously gendered body of the Catholic priest in another way, in its liturgical impersonation of Jesus just at the moment he made bread into his own body. Celebrating the Eucharist is an impersonation of a very complex relation of words, acts, identities, and bodies. Liturgical vestments conceal the celebrant's body, dislocate it with respect not only to gender, but to historical time. The priest at the altar is Jesus at table in Jerusalem so many centuries away. "To crosscut rapidly between yesterday and today is an effect that, in different circumstances, we recognize as camp." The words spoken by the priest are now and then, in the present and of the past. It is a kind of "sonic drag."[64] The congregation watching participates with its own practiced repetitions, with its own complex imitations. "The delight we take in the unanimity of our response, in our virtually reflexive recognition of the source of the allusions. This esoteric knowledge contributes to the elitist pleasure of a coterie sealed off from the rest of the uninitiated American public."[65]

For traditional piety, the true Celebrant of every Eucharist is Jesus himself. The Liturgy Queen pursues not the liturgical expert, but Jesus himself. And the priest at the altar possesses no longer just his own dangerous and despised body, but the body of Jesus. He possesses it by making it, and he possesses it by impersonating it. The priest holding the consecrated wafer has become Jesus holding his own consumable and divine body. For God to do this may be a supreme symbol of divine generosity, of the willingness to be broken in order to be shared. For a man to do it is a symbol of the most physical elevation. The priest as Jesus makes his body perfect and then passes it around to be eaten.

––––––

Jouhandeau compares the "sincerity" of a hustler having sex with his client to the intensity of a priest without faith who celebrates Mass: "[The hustler's] least attitudes, his simplest gestures, his expression, his voice, obey an innate discipline, obey the function to which he has given himself—just as priests who have lost faith celebrate the Mass with an emotion, a respect which perhaps redoubles in them the regret, the remorse at no longer believing in what they do."[66] Or might we imagine that these hustlers and priests, afterward or meanwhile, watch themselves with fascination at their own camp?

––––––

A gay priest, who is in some way always breaking faith, might react to his cultic closeness to God in a number of ways. He might revel in the mixed and half-hidden messages of his role. He might sometimes feel transfigured by God's touch. He might amplify the most flamboyant aspects of his performance—or sheath his queerness in perfect reserve. He might joke bitterly or rage at the hypocrisy of the institutional arrangements that place him at the altar. A gay priest ordained by a homophobic community to invoke the male body of its God—that is an endless source of irony, aestheticism, theatricality, and sharp humor. Camp is not so much a feature of Catholic clerical culture as its basic predicament.

church ✝ *dreams*

reiteration, or *the pleasures of obedience*

MANY GAY MEN FEEL, with reason, that Catholic institutions have been throughout history havens for people like themselves. Gay men feel this both when they read church history and when they examine the shape of Catholic institutions today. They feel it more immediately from their own lives.

These sentiments have something of the nostalgia of survivors. Many gay Catholics look on the old institutions as an ark that enabled people like themselves to survive howling storms. However bad life in the ark was, it was better than drowning. The sentiments of gratitude rest on a kind of argument. Historically Catholicism has created all-male institutions that attracted and even tacitly tolerated high percentages of men who desired men. Those institutions have offered more than protection: they have provided possibilities. They have given men the opportunity to live outside the confining norms of secular masculinity. They have permitted them to be different—to be neither farmers nor warriors, neither fathers nor husbands. The most traditional Catholic institutions, the priesthood and the religious orders, have asserted the possibility of a different—that is, a queer—masculinity.

————

The survivors' nostalgia and its felt arguments move some gay men to stay with the Catholic church. As motives, these sentiments can be captivating in the way daydreams are, but for that reason they are not yet sufficiently self-conscious. They conceal the more powerful motives that trap gay men in Catholic systems that simultaneously solicit and repress them. Many gay Catholics who think that they stay with the church out of nostalgia or argument are really kept in place by a system of pleasures, the pleasures of masculine authority. This means more than the "passive" satisfactions in following orders or submitting to punishment or—more subtly—in collaborating with those who want to manufacture an identity for you. It also includes the "active" satisfactions of seducing others to submit to your authority, to the authority that dominates you. Note the quotation marks around "passive" and "active." The homoerotic pleasures of churchly authority can be as mixed, as dialectically related, as the pleasures of any gay copulation.

————

At the turn of this millennium, the Catholic church is in many respects a voluntary tyranny. There are fewer and fewer legal obligations to be Catholic. Leaving the church or disagreeing with it is no longer punishable by most states—however much it is punished in Catholic social circles, Catholic institutions, or Catholic families. But the legal fact that most adult Catholics are "free" to choose whether they stay can conceal more cunning compulsions. Consider, for example, the ways in which one's erotic identity depends on "staying in church."

Gay men who remain within the institutional church are for the most part voluntary subjects of its authority. They need to remind themselves of this. They should ask not only what reasons they have for staying, but what erotic inducements the church uses to make them want to stay. The success of the church's claims for obedience from gay men depends on soliciting their investment of pleasures in its structures. Some gay men remain in the church because they have restricted themselves to the supply of pleasure in religious domination.

———

In what follows, I describe some of the homoerotic pleasures solicited by the mechanisms of Catholic authority. These are not unusual or perverted effects of modern Catholic power but rather the most typical and "normal" examples. I am not talking about how eighteenth-century pornographers or contemporary dominatrices parody Catholic forms. I discuss instead what happens in the most "orthodox" and "approved" expressions of what is supposed to be the virtue of obedience. Precisely for that reason the descriptions here may seem outrageous. I can only invite objectors to look around them—or, better, to look within.

Ecclesiastical Bondage

In the last few centuries, Catholic life has been ravaged by the requirements of absolute obedience. Whether seen from inside or outside, the distinguishing mark of modern Catholicism has often seemed obedience and nothing more. The theological virtues are no longer faith, hope, and charity, but submission, submission, submission.

The obedience demanded is total in several senses. It is both external and internal, an obedience in behaviors or actions and in beliefs or thoughts. It is also unlimited. The theological possibility of conscience has been eclipsed by the administrative reality of "Magisterial" prescription. The Magisterium—that is, the papal bureaucracy—asserts its right to interpret every document or phenomenon that might be used to contest or even balance it. The Scriptures, the great creeds, the theological traditions, the codes of canon law, the liturgy, the phenomena of miraculous appearances, the meanings of private revelations—all these are "authentically" interpreted only by the pope's officers. The claim for authority envelops all of church life. Someone searching for the pleasures of obedience will be hard pressed to find a more complete system of them.

———

We have already noticed the rhetorical effects and devices of this kind of authority in Catholic intellectual life. In ways already cataloged, the church bureaucracies have increasingly conceived the task of theology in sexual matters as providing reasons for whatever regulations the bureaucracies want to enforce. Even the forms or genres of serious moral writing have been discarded in favor of edict, regulation, and memorandum.

The contemporary American Catholic who seeks direction will be overwhelmed by the abundance of Vatican documents and statements from the American bishops, which flow off the presses and across the Internet more quickly than they can be read, much less comprehended. If you have the taste, you can spend your every waking hour reading official instructions about one aspect or another of what you should believe and do.

———

The intellectual satisfactions of submitting to such an active and embracing system of authority are not difficult to recognize. Intellectual submission can bring feelings of comprehensiveness, certainty, and superiority. It can sweep you up into the vast, shining army of Those Who Know Truth, an army with divisions in every (Catholic) country and every (Catholic) century. What is the minute, misshapen fact of a half-ashamed "gay agenda" in the face of that splendid army?

Intellectual submission can also keep you occupied, if not entertained. The Catholic system is so complicated, so detailed, so various, and so contradictory. You can wander off for years into one room or another: Neo-Thomism, Gregorian chant, the modern Catholic Novel, *plateresco* churches of colonial Latin America, titles and apparitions of the Blessed Virgin, the disciplines of bodily mortification. What are the boring facts of homoerotic desire in the face of those inexhaustible libraries?

———

Still the keenest pleasure of intellectual submission must be the submission itself, the dissolution, the letting go. From the outside, Catholicism is often praised for vindicating the right of reason in theology, especially moral theology. From inside the overwhelming tendency of modern Catholicism, its great gravity, pulls intellect to "sacrifice" itself before authority. Whether it is St. Ignatius's "Rules for Thinking with the Church" or the fantastic exuberance of papal authority in theories like those of Joseph de Maistre, the emphasis in Catholicism since the Reformation has been on how grandly and improbably the intelligent believer could defy her or his own rationality in submitting to the church.

The more powerful the rationality, the more delicious the submission. Nietzsche describes the faith of Pascal as "a continuing suicide of reason," "of a tough, long-lived, worm-like reason, that can't be killed all at once with a single blow."[1] Nietzsche is astute to single this out as a distinctively Catholic pleasure—the protracted, the deliciously painful self-mutilation of a magnificent mind undoing itself in obedience.

———

The ideal of intellectual sacrifice is less colorful today, in part because the intellects drawn to Catholicism are less magnificent. But it can still exercise its attractions. Mary Gordon has written, in a review of Richard Gilman: "no bookish 27-year-old in our day would be in the least tempted by the Church of Rome."[2] Oh, but some are. Not the poets, novelists, and philosophers, perhaps, but the young lawyers, polemicists, and politicians. Not Jacques Maritain and Simone Weil, not Newman or Hopkins or Merton, but William F. Buckley Jr. They are attracted still by a power that can dictate totally. The Vatican reciprocates their needy advances by insisting on the importance of certain moral doctrines precisely because they are so improbable. What better way to test loyalty than to demand adherence to the incredible?

———

The adherence required is lovingly described and fetishistically differentiated. In 1998, Pope John Paul II amended the code of canon law to make it easier to prosecute and punish dissenters. In the Apostolic Letter announcing the change, the pope reminded readers of the Vatican's latest typology of intellectual obedience, which had first been fixed in 1989 when the CDF decided that the Nicene Creed was insufficient for its purposes.[3] The pope explains that there are three mental acts: "firm faith," "firmly accept[ing] and hold[ing]," and "religious submission of will and intellect." The objects of these acts are demarcated. "Firmly accepting and holding," for example, is required with regard to "everything definitively proposed by the Church regarding teaching on faith and morals." "Religious submissions of will and intellect" is required with regard to "teachings which either the Roman Pontiff or the college of Bishops enunciate when they exercise their authentic Magisterium, even if they do not intend to proclaim these teachings by a definitive act." You submit to whatever they teach, even if it doesn't satisfy the canonical requirements for infallibility.

In an explanatory note published alongside the papal decree, the CDF provides examples for propositions in each category. Among teachings to be firmly accepted and held as true in virtue of infallibility, Cardinal Ratzinger mentions "the teaching on the illicitness of prostitution and fornication." Traditionally, fornication is the least serious of sexual sins. If fornication is included in this category, same-sex copulation must be included *a fortiori*. "Whoever denies these truths would be in a position of rejecting a truth of Catholic doctrine and would therefore no longer be in full communion with the Catholic Church."[4] Gay Catholics are required to firmly accept and hold, on pain of separation from the church, the church's condemnations of same-sex copulation. They are required to "adhere with religious submission of will and intellect" to the various other things the pope and his teaching agencies have said against homosexuals. Now that is submission, and not only of the intellect.

———

"Religious submission of will and intellect." "Submission" here is a translation of the old Roman word *obsequium*. The historian Tacitus uses it to describe the numbing obedience demanded by the succession of emperors.[5] We are reminded that analogies between the church and the Roman legions are very old, as are comparisons of Christian life to military service. These parallels ought to make us wonder whether churchly obedience doesn't also generate something like the military's homoerotic allure. It is a commonplace belief in American church life that Catholics make good soldiers, good cops, and good government agents. After all, they are used to living in an organization that makes a fetish of masculine obedience, of the "submission of will and intellect."

Church authority demands submission of both women and men. It is exercised if anything more unthinkingly and more thoroughly over women.

But the hierarchy is most anxious about the loyalty of its own clergy: the submission of men to men. Freudian writers associate this kind of obedience with the severe rites of boys' puberty. As Sipe says: "The power structure of the Roman Catholic hierarchy can be seen psychically only in the context of encapsulating, solidifying, and protecting this [adolescent] stage of development; in this sense, it can rightly and *only* be called homosexual."[6] Clerical power is, in this sense, originally and essentially "homosexual"— same-sex—power. But the system of pleasures it constructs to solicit voluntary submission is often homosexual in the more ordinary sense. It is a system of older (closeted) gay men soliciting the submission of "will and intellect" from younger (closeted) gay men.

———

"Religious submission of will and intellect." We pass from intellectual obedience to the bending of volition and affect, to obedience in actions and feelings. The pleasures to be had from this kind of compliance are not only the cool pleasures of self-denial, but the hot pleasures of shame.

From the *Leatherman's Handbook:* "For a great many M[asochist]s, humiliation is the keyword. This may be a form of verbal abuse, or it may manifest itself in various physical forms. . . . But universal to them all, at least when they take the position of bottomman, is the need to be completely dominated—physically and/or emotionally mastered."[7]

———

Gay men who submit to the church can find shame in many forms. The most ordinary is that of repeatedly failing to sustain the submission of will and intellect. Then there are the guilty pleasures of backsliding, of hooking up with someone at a bar, slipping into a busy toilet stall, walking down the wrong path of the park. *Boys in the Band* ends with Michael going to church after the betrayals, revelations, and mysteries of an utterly queer birthday party. "The bedroom is *ocupado,* and I don't want to go to sleep anyway until I try to walk off the booze. If I went to sleep like this, when I wake up they'd have to put me in a padded cell—not that that's where I don't belong. [*A beat*] And . . . and . . . there's a midnight mass at St. Malachy's that all the show people go to. I think I'll walk over there and catch it."[8] A midnight Mass—and just maybe the hearing of confessions.

Those who deliberately dissent from official teaching, privately or publicly, can participate in the scheme of shameful pleasures in a different way. Gay Catholics who deny Vatican teaching on homosexuality typically find themselves subjected to personal attack. If someone challenges the church's teaching on homosexuality, it must be because he or she is inflamed with hidden incontinence, with unrestrained and disfiguring homosexual desires. So that the very act of dissent is meant to enkindle, at the margin of consciousness, the old shame, the old trembling before Father as he calls you hurtful names in public. When a Catholic man claims a homosexual identity, he puts on a coat of shame that the church fathers cut for him.

No institution berates dissenting gay men as variously, as ingeniously, as allusively as the Catholic church. It does so to ensure that our dissent will be quarantined. But it also wants to remind us of the pleasures we could have back inside the church if only we would shut up. Accept the public shame—or come home and accept the better fitting, the more durable bonds of private shame. Return to the twilight rooms of private punishments and their approved pleasures, their approved identities.

———

Gay priests and religious are formed in the pleasures of submission to male authority. Who can be astonished, then, that sexually active gay clerics and ex-clerics seem so often to prefer the leather or S&M "subcultures"? Nor is it shocking that priestly cassocks or monastic robes figure so prominently in some S&M rituals. Pornographers throughout the modern period have represented the practices of pain as the practices of clerical choice. Even "straight" clerics are reputed masochists in the lore of the brothel. "It is a cliché of eighteenth-century pornography that ecclesiastics [in a Catholic country] can only become erect when slapped on the behind with 'a handful of steel rods [*une poignée de verges*].'"[9] The pun on "rods" is fully intended.

———

American Catholics need to remember, because it is so easy for them to forget, that Catholic spiritual traditions have long required practices of physical self-punishment—what we diagnose as "masochism" in any other setting. It was only in the mid-1960s that many American religious houses abandoned such "disciplines" as weekly whippings or the wearing of devices intended to pinch, chafe, or cut the skin. Many of these customs were justified not just as a general asceticism, but specifically and explicitly as guarantees of celibacy.

———

These clerical practices were part of an American cult of pain preached by the Catholic clergy—which we would also like to forget. "It isn't suffering that's the tragedy, only wasted suffering." The accumulation of human pain is "a vast storehouse of spiritual power," "a subtle but true coin that may be exchanged for spiritual goods for ourselves."[10]

The pleasures of pain: we touch here on something more than the sociology of organizations. Fundamental Christian doctrines lend themselves implicitly to a cult of pain as a display of male obedience. The story of Christ's Passion is, after all, the story of a son who is handed over to torture for his father's purposes. I do not believe that the Gospels are essentially about sadomasochistic domination.[11] I do see that central features of Christian teaching are all too vulnerable to erotic exploitation by human authorities.

———

Recall Cardinal Ratzinger's advice: "What then should a homosexual person who wishes to follow the Lord do? To speak briefly, these persons are called to complete the will of God in their life, joining all the pains [*or* punishments] and difficulties that they might experience because of their condition to our Lord's sacrifice of the cross."[12] What could be more orthodox? What could be more open to institutional abuse?

We like to distinguish authentic spiritual teachings from their aberrations. But how can the authentic spiritual teaching of obedience "unto death" be distinguished from its institutional aberrations?

———

Human maturity seems to come only through certain experiences of suffering. Catholic believers can admit that difficult truth, even if they cannot understand it. Still the "religious submission" demanded by the church seems excessive. Mortal life brings enough inevitable suffering. Why exercise ourselves in imposing so much more?

The extravagant demands of churchly obedience are often explained by appeals to institutional unity and efficiency, the "good of the whole," "the needs of the community." They are "explained," in other words, by the kinds of arguments we use in justifying political or military authority. But in Catholicism such arguments are only secondary. The highest justification for Catholic claims to authority is just the strange logic that expects God's crucifixion.

Catholic believers can neither admit nor understand this. As Kierkegaard explains, hearing "divine" voices that tell you to sacrifice your child is usually taken as evidence of insanity, not sanctity.[13] Yet Abraham is our father in faith. The claims of Catholic authority reach beyond any ordinary reasoning to assert a logic of inevitable sacrifice. They surround the structures of administrative power with the spectacle of the bodily sacrifice of God-in-male-flesh. The logic that transmutes the most severe submission into the most exalted domination is not one of the common good, but of a suffering man's body.

———

The Son who is faithful to the point of death will be glorified by the Father. Within the structures of Catholic power, this means young men who submit to the totalized authority of older men will inherit the older men's power. This power is totalized as "orthodoxy." By means of "orthodoxy," abject submission will be "redeemed" as untrammeled power. One of the principal expressions of orthodoxy is the obedience of young male bodies to the sexual prescriptions of older men. It is the exchange of young male bodies for older male power. How could that exchange not be a homoerotic transaction—a version of what the Greeks meant by "pederasty"?

The Catholic Dandy

There are many Roy Cohns in the Catholic Church. I mean, there are many gay men who hide behind the mask of a politically aggressive "conservatism." Indeed, so many closeted homosexuals spout the rhetoric of religious homophobia that it is very tempting simply to adopt the familiar rule: The more shrill a man's condemnation of homosexuality, the more likely it is that the condemnation is a confession. With "conservative" homophobes, we see another set of pleasures in authority: the pleasures of inflicting it.

—

Although I have used the term "conservative," I don't think it is accurate. Nor is it generally helpful to think of Christian life under the duality of "liberal" and "conservative." The issues are different—and more important—than those political labels suggest. But the people I describe do call themselves "conservative." They also call themselves "faithful," "ortho-dox," "true," and "right-thinking." These names are not simple descriptions, of course. They are battle cries.

I prefer to think of many "conservatives" rather as Catholic "dandies," at least in one sense of that term. "A dandy is a Clothes-wearing Man, a Man whose trade, office, and existence consists in the wearing of Clothes."[14] It is true that young Catholic "conservatives" are usually overdressed, their dark suits and blazers studded with the pins or embroidered heraldry of politico-religious loyalties. But they are clotheshorses in a more important way. They wear their orthodoxy with a fastidious attention to its least de-tails precisely because it is an inherited costume. "All his bon-mots turn upon a single circumstance, the exaggerating of the merest trifles into mat-ters of importance, or treating everything else with the utmost *nonchalance* and indifference, as if whatever pretended to pass beyond those limits was a *bore,* and disturbed the serene air of high life."[15] For Catholic dandies, there is no hierarchy of the truths of faith. Orthodoxy treats the slightest, most improbable utterance of church authority as terribly important. The only hierarchy is that of the authorities.

—

Beau Brummell, the original English dandy, inhabited a world in which ap-parently trivial details mattered enormously, much more than ordinary no-tions of courtesy or kindness. The details were so important that it would have been tasteless to conceive of justifying or explaining them. They were universal standards obvious to everyone—that is, to gentlemen, or rather Brummell himself. Or Brummell and his long-suffering valet, who was ex-pected to remember what the dandy himself hadn't the patience to register.

For the Catholic dandy, the details are the tics of church power and their

ideological echoes. These details are paramount—more important than ordinary notions of charity and forbidding any justification. The pope's authority is like the universal canons of taste. It cannot be questioned without
forfeiting one's social standing.

———

Resemblances between the Catholic dandy and other gay devotees—such
as the Liturgy Queen—are not coincidental. Certainly Catholic dandies
dwell in an atmosphere of palpable sexual tension. The odd behaviors they
display in regard to sex pass without comment because Catholic dandyism
depends on not acknowledging certain evident realities, especially those of
a sexual nature. The culture of Catholic dandyism is most of all accustomed
to abuses of power and denials of sexuality.

———

Recall Huysmans on "quarrels" between church parties that "lead to uncompromising hatreds."[16] If anything characterizes the dandies' culture of
authority, it is the violence of attacks on those who disagree. The violence
generates narcotic pleasures—pleasures strong enough to sustain a variety
of repressions.

———

Each May, I receive florid ordination announcements from the most conservative seminaries and religious houses. I read them as so many announcements of gay weddings.

The story of the dandy's romance goes something like this. A well-
behaved young man discovers his sexuality. He may fall in love with another man—or find himself having a sexual experience with him. Or perhaps he begins just to have homoerotic "feelings." The ensuing guilt tears
at him. So the young man finds the most conservative institution he can—
an extreme religious house or an isolated seminary. The institution is typically presided over by charming and tyrannical older men, who are also
beautiful or "actively" homosexual or both. These older men describe the
dream of a victorious church in which there are no more enemies—no
more feminists or Marxists, but especially no more homosexuals. Behind
the local leaders, there is the grander dream of the "Holy Father" in Rome.

Both the local "Father" and the remote "Father" promise the young man the keys of a kingdom *without homosexuals* in exchange for his obedience in everything, but especially in trifles. They will teach him privileged sciences and deputize him to perform great mysteries. They will reward him with a heterosexual future, the future of religious repetition.

If he stays, the young gay man becomes a dandy in the service of the Taste—that is, the "Truth"—of these powerful men. He no longer suffers the guilt of gay desire. He no longer sees it as a threat. After all, the whole of his life has been transformed into homoerotic submission. He gets to repeat, over and over again, his delicious release into the power of the "Fathers."

———

In Klossowski's *Suspended Vocation*, the spiritual director La Montagne is a converted member of the "race" of Sodom.[17] He exchanges his pederasty for an efficient pedagogy, adopting the model of the Boy Scouts to the church's purposes. The church is pleased to have this "political science" brought over from the sodomites, as it is glad for his seductive persuasiveness, now in the service of its own teachings. Of course, La Montagne still collects ancient or Renaissance sculptures, "adolescent gods and ephebes."

Klossowski's fictional portrait is a likeness of many conservative institutions, which are both scout camps and collections of ephebes to be gazed at.

———

There are nonclerical versions of this dandified dream. They require the young gay man to demonstrate his submission to the norms of Catholic heterosexuality. Sometimes he will do this by teaching natural family planning or publicly denouncing gay rights. Sometimes, more sadly, he will demonstrate his orthodoxy by marrying early and having children. In some "conservative" circles, infants have become the most respected currency of orthodoxy.

Those who know something of the early years of Christianity will find it ironic that many people should now regard bodily fertility as the essence of Catholic orthodoxy. Those familiar with the modern political uses of reproduction, of "bio-power," will be less amused. Management of human reproduction—which is to say, management of human sexuality—is one of the most disquieting aims of modern states, especially totalitarian ones. The growing concern of the Catholic hierarchy with regulating reproduction is not a quaint survival of olden times. It is another instance of Catholic power's assimilation to very modern forms of state power. Or, to speak more precisely, it illustrates how Catholic authorities have found yet another way to systematize power. Catholic bureaucracies are the great omnivores of power. Having helped produce the bureaucracies of contemporary bio-power, the church now learns from them.

————

Whether clerical or lay, gay romances with "conservatism" offer a range of pleasures. There is the preening pleasure of seeing yourself as the protégé of the mighty; the smug pleasure of telling others, often and loudly, that you are right; the salacious pleasure of being able to talk endlessly about stigmatized acts—which are all the more fascinating for being stigmatized. But the chief pleasure, I would think, is that of dwelling in the charged space of Catholic dandyism itself—that space of tense "chastity," of barely sublimated sexual anger, of endlessly deferred desire.

————

These romances of gay submission offer pleasures, but they do not often have happy endings. The damage done to the men caught up in them is terrible to see. It is not surprising, then, that gay men who are drilled so fiercely in a crushing orthodoxy end by revenging themselves on gayness. They pass indeed from accepting suffering to inflicting it, from bottom to top. They become managers in the system of authority's pleasures.

————

Catholic "conservatism" is not all the work of gay men, but much of it is. In my experience, the most violent homophobic rhetoric is almost always delivered by gay men. This is the ironic truth underlying the "conservative" accusation that gay activists are attempting to hijack the churches. The most successful gay activists in the Catholic church are closeted, homophobic members of the clergy—the priestly dandies. They have indeed hijacked the central administration of the church. They use their political power to solicit obedience from other gay men to the church's scheme of authoritarian pleasures.

———

In speaking of pleasures, I do not mean to hide the real damage done—and not only to those who flirt with or submit to the structures of Catholic authority. Catholic dandies have harmed more than just themselves or their fellow soldiers. Their fierce rhetoric encourages wider violence against homosexuals. Their intransigent opposition to open gayness within the church perpetuates life-threatening conditions of despair, especially for lesbian and gay youth. Their attacks on safer-sex education programs contribute to the spread of AIDS. All of this is familiar. The Catholic church has become, in many areas, one of the most powerful opponents of civil protections for homosexuals. In the same way that it allies itself internationally with fundamentalist Islamic regimes against women's groups, so it collaborates locally with some of the most virulent secular homophobes to block attempts at reform.

Resisting Repetition

In modern Catholicism, obedience is demanded by structures that foster so dysfunctional a form of homosexuality. Every time we look at the hierarchy, we can't help but see closeted gay men who are consumed by their unhappiness. Obeying them, we risk endorsing the form of homosexual self-hatred that they so vigorously enact. This much is obvious in "conservative" groups. With a little more practice, it is easy to see it as intrinsic to modern Catholic power, even when it is wielded benignly.

———

What is a gay Catholic to do in the face of the church's demands for obedience? Many gay Catholics have been moved to dissent piecemeal. They disagree with the teaching on homosexuality, or on that issue and others related to it, but they don't know how to formulate that dissent either as a comprehensive critique of churchly practice or as a theologically justified alternative. This is not surprising. They receive no help in these tasks from their teachers in the faith.

———

There has been precious little official encouragement since the Protestant Reformation for developing a Catholic theology of responsible dissent. In recent years, there has been none. Many popes of the last two centuries have done their best to identify total obedience with Catholic believing. They have done everything to divert attention from whatever theological grounds there might be for dissent within Catholic traditions.

———

Fortunately, Catholic traditions are older than two centuries, older than the Catholicisms elaborated and imposed in response to the Reformation. Many elements in those pre-Reformation traditions actually point away from tyranny and emphasize freedom of intellect and the authority of conscience. From these doctrines, some Catholic theologians have tried to construct a theology of responsible dissent. They have stressed quite rightly that old traditions oblige Catholics to speak out against the teaching of falsehood or the practice of gross injustice in the church. They also require each worshipper to testify to God's action in his or her life.

The obligation to speak the truth given by God to an individual believer is not exclusively or primarily for the sake of that individual. The individual conscience must also offer a means of correcting abuses in the church.

The obligation does not address only points of doctrine. The most urgent responsibility concerns judgments about how well or badly the church meets the spiritual needs of its people. Catholics must accuse the church hierarchy when it fails, consistently and stubbornly, to feed the flock. That is the principle on which great saints have accused powerful popes. It is the principle that governs the situation of homosexuals in the present church. If prolonged and prayerful deliberation makes it clear that the church is not providing the faithful what church doctrine says it must, then there must be an outcry.

———

Here is a powerful analogy between the present condition of Catholic homosexuals and that of all Catholic laypeople. The worldwide shortage of priests is already depriving Catholics of access to the sacraments. The situation is going to worsen quickly. Richard Schoenherr, formerly the American bishops' chief sociologist, states the matter bluntly: The church must choose "between its sacramental tradition and its commitment to an exclusively male celibate priesthood."[18]

Lesbian and gay Catholics already find themselves deprived of the sacraments by official teaching—and, I have argued, by the deep logic of the "male celibate priesthood."

———

The longer the sacraments are withheld, the more inadequate merely speaking out seems. For Catholic Christians, the practice of the faith requires regular participation in the celebration of the Eucharist. It demands membership, in a very strong sense, within a community that revolves around the sacraments. So if a Catholic Christian is consistently denied access to the sacraments by a church organization, the person must decide to go elsewhere. Life without the sacraments is not Catholic life. When you speak out against members of the hierarchy for failing to provide sacraments and they ignore you; when the same hierarchy teaches that you should not come forward to receive the sacraments without repenting of any full expression of your sexuality; when you may be actively denied access to the Eucharist for identifying yourself as lesbian or gay—then, precisely as a Catholic, you need to deliberate about going to another eucharistic table. You must, in short, ask whether you shouldn't leave the Catholic church in order to live as a Catholic.

———

Many Catholic homosexuals find it painful to raise this question. There are good theological reasons for their distress, which I will explore concretely in the next chapter when it comes to considering what eucharistic tables are available. There are also good biographical reasons. Like anyone else, Catholics are held to their religious traditions by uncountable links of personal memory, family history, ethnic identity, by affection and social role. But some of the pain provoked by the thought of leaving the church has different psychological origins. Some of it comes from a lack of confidence that homosexuality could be divinely created. Some of it, again, derives from thinking that sexuality couldn't be so important after all—couldn't be worth fighting over.

Theological uncertainties also keep us from thinking clearly about leaving. I would describe many of these as confusions between schism and heresy or between schism and loss of faith. The papacy has been asserting for many centuries now that its authority is a central article of faith, but it is entirely possible to deny this claim on traditional, Catholic grounds. Separation from the Vatican is not simply equivalent to a loss of faith. It is possible to be a schismatic Catholic. Indeed, under certain circumstances Catholics can be required as Catholics to break from Rome.

———

It is not easy to define those circumstances. Nor do I think that they can be described abstractly. But a gay believer will never get to the point of examining circumstances unless he can disengage himself from the pleasures of authority. So long as he traffics in the delights that Catholic authority offers, his homoeroticism will remain largely *its* homoeroticism—which is the homoeroticism of concealed suffering.

———

I have tried to describe some of authority's pleasures and to suggest where one might look for others. A slow and unflinching examination of how they attach us to the authority of the church is an essential spiritual task for Catholic gay men. But I have yet to describe what I consider the most intense pleasure, the one that holds us in place most securely within the system of authority and that many carry with them right through their dissent.

The Pleasures of Repeating Identity

Many times in conversation with other lesbian or gay Catholics, with laypeople or clergymen, I have reached the point when someone asks, "Why do you remain a Catholic?" The question can be spoken in exasperation or anger, tenderly or sadly, as provocation or as pity.

I find the question most poignant when asked of gay priests or religious who torment themselves with what they consider their ugly hypocrisy. I have heard them answer the question in many different ways. Some plead economic necessity or family pressure. Others say that they couldn't think of giving up pastoral ministry or the spiritual consolations in celebrating the Mass. Only a few times have I heard someone offer what I consider the most insightful reply: "Because I don't know who I would be without the church."

The final and most powerful inhibition that prevents gay Catholics from speaking out is the threat that they will lose their identity. Not just their identity as Catholics, but their identity as a certain kind of gay man. I can only explain this odd claim by drawing analogies to something we have approached several times already: the debate in gay studies over the modern origin of the "homosexual" identity.

In the first volume of his *History of Sexuality,* Michel Foucault claims that the category "homosexual" was invented in the nineteenth century as part of a much larger legal and medical system intent on regulating human sexuality. Now Foucault's claim is regularly misunderstood. It is taken to mean, for example, that there were no males before the nineteenth century who preferred to copulate with males rather than females; that there were no earlier homoerotic habits or institutions or artworks or discourses; and so on. The passage is thus regularly taken to be "refuted" by citing examples of such preferences, habits, institutions, artworks, and discourses—say, the kinds of evidence we considered for clerical sodomy. And then Foucault is damned for being a bad scholar, or a philosopher rather than a historian, or a bad philosopher, or a self-loathing homosexual, or, in the characteristic idiom of Camille Paglia, "a glib game-player who took very little research a very long way."[19]

Foucault is saying none of the things his accusers attribute to him. He means that a certain model for conceiving and explaining same-sex desires or actions was constructed a little over a hundred years ago, and that this model is embedded in the equally recent term "homosexual." Foucault refuses to think that the notion of "homosexual" is neutral, as he refuses to concede that a fixed homosexual "identity" runs through history—or undergirds our present. Instead of fixed identities, we have identities that are produced at certain times for certain purposes, the purposes of different kinds of power. "But this word 'power' risks inducing many misunderstandings. Misunderstandings about its identity, its form, its unity."[20]

Foucault corrects these misunderstandings about the identity of power in some famous pages that describe it instead as dispersed, fluid, multiply conditioned relations. "Power (*pouvoir*) is not an institution, and it is not a structure, and it is not a certain capacity (*puissance*) with which some are endowed: it is the name that one gives to a complex strategic situation in a given society."[21] If "power" is not an identity, much less is "homosexuality"—which is, after all, only one of the circuits through which power flows, around which power is condensed, in its transit through "sexuality." Homosexuality is not for Foucault a fixed identity that stands unchanged through history. It is a historically conditioned role, character, personage, even a form of celebrity. And on Foucault's own account, this kind of identity owes much to the Catholic church. We have by now seen enough to agree with him.

———

Homosexuality is not a fixed identity. It is an artifact produced in the nineteenth century by refashioning older Catholic materials. This would suggest that we need to be concerned not just with the homosexuality of Catholicism, but with the Catholicism of homosexuality. Let me explain by continuing for a bit longer with Foucault.

———

Foucault's denial of a fixed homosexual identity continues to provoke very strong reactions within gay discourses. These can be divided into personal, tactical, and strategic responses.

First, the personal reaction is to counter Foucault's claim with a testimony: "I experience myself as a homosexual" or "I choose to identify myself as a homosexual." This affirmation is linked with one of the most powerful antihomophobic rhetorics, "coming out." "Coming out" is discovering a secret about yourself that you then share with the world in a potent declaration of identity and solidarity.[22] Foucault knew this, of course, and yet he still wanted to deny that homosexuality was a secret about oneself, a hidden identity to be discovered and then displayed. "We don't have to discover that we are homosexuals," he would say. "We have to create a gay life."[23]

Foucault's gentle—or ironic—proposal of an alternate way to conceive the task of gay liberation should not conceal his judgment on this type of testimony. Sexual identities are made precisely to shape people's experience, to encourage them to declare the identity. Of course we modern homosexuals describe ourselves and our experiences through the category "homosexual." How else is the category supposed to work? The outraged testimony in favor of homosexual identity does not discount Foucault's argument. It confirms it.

———

Second, the tactical objection to Foucault's denial of identity is to maintain that we can effect political changes only by assuming a fixed "homosexual" identity. The most current and supposedly most effective arguments in favor of "equal rights" for homosexuals begin from the premise that we are made this way and can't become otherwise. This is, in fact, the kind of medicolegal view that the church itself has endorsed since 1975, and it seems to many the best ground for reforming arguments within the church.

Now Foucault was vividly aware of the need for effective political action: "It is important . . . to have the possibility—and the right—to choose your own sexuality. Human rights regarding sexuality are important and are still not respected in many places."[24] But Foucault wanted also to remind us of the price we pay in arguing for rights from this standpoint. It forces us into the prevailing regime of sexualities, of sexual management, in the hopes that we can negotiate a better deal for ourselves. We take on the nineteenth-century perversion in order to reverse its valuation, changing pathology to pride. But we are still submitting ourselves to the regulatory scheme of identities according to which our sexuality defines us.

———

Third, the strategic reaction is to say that Foucault's denial of identity gives homophobes what they want—namely, the abolition of homosexuals. We not only deconstruct our identities in the present, we relinquish our claim to have existed all along, to have our own history. Far from being mere academic exercises, historiographical projects are terribly important politically and culturally. If we can't have a history of our kind, our people, our nation, our tribe, then we can't make privileged or prioritized claims for rapid redress, for an emergency extension of rights. If we lack our own national or ethnic history, then we simply do not exist within many of the discourses of modern politics.

I do think that Foucault's resistance to the notion of homosexual identity is a refusal to be useful to some projects of gay historiography. Foucault certainly knew the real stakes of identity politics, as he knew the real political value of histories. And even in a more familiarly academic way he spoke often enough in favor of historical studies—say, of John Boswell's *Christianity, Social Tolerance, Homosexuality*.[25] In interviews, he was even willing to talk about a unitary "gay consciousness" that undergoes transformations through the centuries.[26] But Foucault did repudiate the historical continuity of identities—as of most other objects of traditional historical narrative. Foucault denies history writers—including lesbian and gay writers of church history—their heroes and villains (the homosexual, the oppressor) as well as their progressive or apocalyptic plots (of dark repression and shining reform). No simple stories; no clear morals; no prospect of utopia.

Foucault disallows these kinds of gay histories not least with respect to the Catholic church. He offers instead minutely detailed descriptions of ever-mutating discourses—that is, ever-mutating strategic arrangements—in which not even the main actors remain on stage for more than a while. What was the history of homosexuality before the projection of that identity in the discourses of the nineteenth century? It was . . . nothing. It was certainly not the history of something else just like homosexuality, but with a different name. Nor was it the history of the anticipations or forerunners to homosexuality. Before homosexuality were strategic arrangements that cannot be spoken as "homosexuality" except sloppily or tendentiously or imperialistically.

Does this mean that Foucault is destroying the lives or the communities of men who love men? Only if you think that those lives and communities were created along with the nineteenth-century category of the homosexual. Only if you believe that "homosexuality" offers the sole reason for those lives and those communities.

Official Catholic documents have now adopted the categories of "homosexuality" and the "homosexual person." They are playing catch-up with the regulatory inventions of the nineteenth century. Some gay Catholics have been encouraged by this, as we have seen. Better to be a "homosexual" than a "sodomite," certainly, especially if the church allows that the "homosexual condition" might not be something for which we are to blame personally—though it is, of course, still an objective disorder.

Other Catholics, dissenting Catholics, have pointed out how little the church has actually changed its teaching on homoeroticism. They have gone on to contest the church's official descriptions of homosexuality and homosexual life, to dispute its uses of Scripture or theological tradition, and to deplore its remarks on violence against homosexuals. But they haven't wondered enough about the category of "homosexuality" itself—or their own ease in assuming the identity that the church now provides for them.

The oldest function of Catholic power in relation to homoeroticism is to posit a fixed kind of personal identity behind desires and actions. Whether the person is called "sodomite" or "homosexual," whether the person's sin is "nameless" or "against nature," whether the person's punishment is burning or exile or excommunication, the church has extensive experience in manufacturing and managing homoerotic identities. Perhaps the time has come to confront that kind of church business.

———

I suspect that the steadiest pleasure the Catholic church offers gay men is that of a fixed identity. Our fear of its loss hinders us from considering whether to leave the church. We cannot do so until we can imagine not only finding another church home or another eucharistic table, but another way of conceiving ourselves, our desires, and our loves. We don't need just another home or a healthier set of pleasures. We need another name. We need to be rebaptized.

———

Hocquenghem once wrote: "There is no homosexuality without an avowal. This fact is of infinite consequence, it is consubstantial with the thing: the intimate connections, the profound complicities that homosexuality has to the medico-psychiatric network which once took it to the baptismal fonts. . . ."[27] Every lesbian or gay Catholic is baptized twice, once with a Christian name, once with the name "homosexual." We are carried to the fonts when we are brought into the church, and then again when we announce—or are discovered to be—homosexuals. Why is it that the second baptism seems so much more important than the first? How is it, in a Christian church, that being called a "homosexual" seems to have so many more consequences than being called by your Christian name?

———

"Homosexual" is not just a name we are given. It is a name we put on, take in, speak inwardly. When we are telling our stories to one another, we often ask, "When did you come out to yourself? And then when did you start telling other people?" Coming out to yourself means naming yourself "homosexual." It means accepting that name as something you will say to yourself about yourself.

"In the name of Kertbeny, Krafft-Ebing, and Havelock Ellis, I baptize myself 'homosexual.'" That is not a sacramental formula, though it would almost seem so according to the church today.

———

Just here we discover one of the most striking connections between the category of "homosexuality" and modern Catholicism. For many "straight" Catholics in America, being baptized Catholic means forever being subjected to another kingdom of authorities, with painful or stigmatizing consequences. It is an invisible mark placed on the psyche at some point before memory. It is an inherited liability for subjection. "Once a Catholic, always a Catholic." Growing up Catholic is remembered as growing up in a kind of bondage.

To the extent that homosexual Catholics begin to free themselves from viewing their sexual orientation as submission, as a second baptism, they will need a new understanding of their Catholic identities. They will find themselves trying to conceive both of a homosexuality in which suffering subjection is not the only role and of a Catholicism in which the abuse of masculine authority is not the essential article of faith.

Or else they must conclude that Catholicism is irredeemably a homosocial system for the management of sexually defined identities. That would make for a melancholy end.

———

I want to turn from the sad, recurring dreams of masculine obedience to another kind of dream, which may have to appear at first as utopian fantasy. It is a dream of what must be, interchangeably, gay Catholicism and Catholic gayness.

I turn from dreams of repetition to dreams of new ways of speaking because I do not regard the dialectic of identity as closed. However tightly we are bound to the Catholic church, we must still have the freedom to leave it if that is necessary for faithful speech.

So too with homosexuality, which is now curiously tangled with Catholicism, which both approves it and reflects it. The name given to us at our baptism into "homosexuality" need not be our final name. It need not be the last word.

9

repentance, or schools for new speech

A COLLECTION OF liturgies for lesbians and gays offers the "Rite for the Invocation of Divine Judgment," an artful revision by James Lancaster of an old Roman rite of solemn excommunication.[1] Here the rite is used by lesbians and gays to call down God's judgment on those who have persecuted them. Among its imprecations: "May your spiteful words be swallowed up in insensible noise, never to harm or incite violence against our people." "Let your writings be gibberish to all who read them."

The rite would be celebrated most fittingly on the steps of St. Peter's—a Roman ceremony for rebuking Roman sins. The rite would remind us of the centuries in which Roman authorities have indeed scrambled homoerotic speaking with their official speeches and their bureaucratic pleasures. It would then register the decision by many to break off communion with Rome, to share Christian fellowship elsewhere.

————

It is no secret that many lesbian and gay Americans are leaving the Catholic Church, even as others struggle to protect public or private places for themselves within it. Some who leave go to other Christian denominations, some to other religious traditions, some to one or another secular system. The departures have not all been solitary. Groups of lesbians and gays who have left communion with Rome in one way or another often join other communions. Nor is it just a matter of numbers. The exodus of lesbians or gay Catholics resembles the exodus from the priesthood in one respect: it is often the most active and best informed members of a parish or religious congregation who leave.

————

Feminists and lesbians have led the way in this as in many other aspects of church life. They framed the question of separation from patriarchal structures and responded to it early on. The power of their answers has been shown both in the alternate forms of community, such as WomenChurch, and in the new forms of speech and worship created for those communities. If gay men have borrowed much feminist and lesbian theory, they have been less eager to create new forms of Christian community. Indeed, they have been more reluctant to leave the "traditional" churches in the first place.[2] As I have argued, they are held in place more tightly by the systems of male obedience.

————

Division within the church is a serious matter. Its familiarity shouldn't blind us to its damage. Christians proclaim mutual love as the second moment of Christ's central commandment: Love God and your neighbor as yourself. They proclaim this, but they cannot even bring themselves to sit down together around the Christian table.

Still there are times when it is not only permitted but required to show publicly that a falsely "Christian" unity has already been broken—that church members have already been cut off from the table or cast out of the assembly. The question for many lesbigay Catholics is whether now is such a time in church history.

———

Modern Roman Catholicism has made institutional concord an idol. The beauties of Christian unity—of peace, helpfulness, mutual affection, shared contemplation—have been steadily replaced by the disciplines of bureaucratic control. The words "Christian unity" no longer refer in Catholic practice to communal beauties. They proclaim instead the success of bureaucracies. The question for many gay Catholics is whether Christian unity wouldn't be better served by freedom from those bureaucracies.

———

The question is only confused by brandishing the charge of schism. As a category, "schism" is by now almost entirely misleading. It is important to remember, first, that the unity of the Christian church is already scattered by the diversity of denominations. Then, second, the Catholic church itself can no longer claim to be "one body." Many theologico-political parties within modern Catholicism would certainly have counted as heresies in the early church. Third, in a century that has been dominated by violent totalitarianisms, it is hard to voice claims for strong institutional unity without implying a program of repression.

Perhaps we long ago lost the capacity for anything like what was originally meant by Catholic unity. No one can now claim to possess that oneness, least of all the official bureaucracies.

———

Assume that there can be responsible freedom in breaking communion with Rome. Where does the lesbian or gay Catholic go?

This question cannot be tacked onto previous theological descriptions and analyses. In the same way that church words must be differentiated from church lives, so church lives must be contrasted with church dreams—with the possibilities for future churches. These possibilities offer hope, but remain dreams until they are enacted. Church words and church lives grow out of the forms of Christian community. What new words, what new lives would become possible for Catholics if the church had a new form, if it were ordered differently, if there were other kinds of Catholic community? Such dreaming is required of those who think about leaving the church.

———

Analyzing the possibilities for reform within the church or dissecting its alleged theological limits is not the most important exercise for imagination. Rather, imagination should be used to aid choice: What could the future of the Catholic church be under God's providence? Might divine providence point outside its present boundaries? The believer needs to imagine both a Catholic church of the future and a future without the present Catholic church.

———

Within the past ten years, choices have multiplied for those who consider leaving the bureaucracies. A homosexual Catholic who wishes to be publicly queer and publicly involved in a Christian community has at least the following possibilities:

—To remain in a "liberal" Catholic parish or parishlike community

—To take part in the liturgies of one of the approved diocesan lesbian and gay "outreach" programs

—To join a predominantly gay dissenting group, such as Dignity, or one of the reforming or radical Catholic movements

—To enter an Anglican or Protestant denomination in which the official views or the local congregation affirm Christian "homosexuality"

—To join one of the predominantly lesbian and gay denominations (say, the Metropolitan Community Churches)

—To establish a new lesbian and gay community based on Catholic principles

———

I have listed these possibilities separately, but they are often mixed in practice. Many lesbian and gay Catholics I know attend regular parish masses, liturgies sponsored by Dignity, and services or group meetings at an MCC congregation. Some of them do all three on a single Sunday. My point is not to present an exhaustive scheme for categorizing choices. I mean only to recall the range of communities that promise support for lesbigay Catholic life.

———

Once the range of possibilities is glimpsed, the difficult task of discernment begins. Where do I belong? is not a question that can be answered in general. Indeed, so far as the believer is concerned, it cannot be answered outside of a prayerful encounter with God. The discovery of the providentially intended church community is as deeply personal a discernment as one can imagine. The answer is not to be calculated by anyone else. It is to be perceived and perhaps invented—even if that means building something remarkably new.

———

There is actually a series of discernments or of motives for it. Lesbigay Catholics often start to look for a new home because they need a community in which they can feel safe from assault, especially directed from the pulpit or the altar. They then look for communities in which they might find support for their relationships, their families, their times of grief or joy. But finally they look for a community in which they can learn to speak the new languages of their possible lives, their possible selves.

———

Instead of proposing general arguments as a substitute for individual discernment, I offer some preliminary descriptions of community types. Since this kind of deliberation must always be concrete, I take up four embodiments of the options listed above: the choices to stay in a Catholic parish, to join a dissenting group like Dignity, to join a congregation of the MCC, and to establish a new kind of Catholic community. I consider all of these in relation to one issue only: overcoming the silence that Catholicism has imposed on homosexuality. My descriptions are correspondingly limited and even schematic.

———

Because I am most concerned with exploring the situation of a lesbian or gay person who has so far lived Christianity through the Catholic church, I will not consider the choice to leave Catholicism for another "mainstream" Christian denomination. This is not because I consider that Catholics have nothing to learn from the other denominations. On the contrary, and despite negative publicity about particular controversies, many of the mainstream Anglican or Protestant groups have made notable progress in reforming their teachings on homosexuality and in recognizing homosexual lives as fully Christian. A group like the United Church of Christ, for example, not only has a long tradition of lesbian and gay ministry, but has undertaken congregationwide discussion of same-sex unions. Many other denominations offer active programs for "affirming" or "reconciling" or "open" congregations.

So lesbigay Catholics can learn—should learn—from recent efforts in Anglican and Protestant groups. But I do not want to discuss at length the choice by a Catholic to join one of those groups, because that often entails a resolution to leave behind Catholic issues and to take on a new identity. It is like learning to speak a "foreign" language. The language may be akin to your mother tongue, but it is not the same. I focus instead on the possibilities for the speech of gay Catholicism—and about its implications for both gayness and Catholicism.

―――――

For similar reasons, I will not sketch possibilities altogether outside Christianity. They are in any case perhaps more familiar in lesbian and gay cultures than the Christian possibilities.

Lesbigay cultures often display strong animosities toward Christianity. How could they do otherwise? Not only do many lesbians and gays carry scars from "Christian" childhoods, they are buffeted on any given day by "Christian" campaigns against their basic liberties or their lives. The Christian Bible regularly appears in our political debates as the most powerful support for homophobia. We expect signs that say "God Hates Fags" with citations to scriptural verse. We remember court opinions in which the "Judeo-Christian ethic" or a set of scriptural passages function as the "evidence" for denials of our civil rights. So of course the Christian Bible can seem a book of hate and the Christian churches our most dangerous enemies.

I feel that myself on many days. Still I persist in exploring the engagement of homosexuality with Catholicism—and not just because of my religious convictions. Gay men, in particular, will not understand central features in their own identities unless they anatomize the connections between homosexuality and the oldest Christian institutions. These constructions are best understood not on paper, but in community.

Fitting In

Richard Rodriguez describes the life of one gay Catholic: "A neighbor of mine—retired navy officer. He smokes too much, drinks. Homosexual. He hangs out at gay bars, where he drinks with his buddies. But I met him once at a hospital. It turns out he visits the sick, takes Communion to them. . . . And every Sunday he drives several old women to Mass. There he sits, toward the back of the church—the head usher. His job is to assign a heterosexual couple to take up the bread and the wine at the offertory. He is what the Church will not accept officially. And yet, literally, he is the Church. He is the only smile of welcome parishioners meet. His are the hands dispensing the Body of Christ."[3]

This story could be matched by a hundred others I know and by tens of thousands that I don't. Today many Catholic parishes are animated by the lives of openly lesbian and gay parishioners to a degree that would have been difficult to imagine even twenty years ago—and not only in the officially queer urban neighborhoods.

———

I am often asked whether I think that an "out" homosexual who is not celibate can still be a Catholic. I reply that the question can be translated in at least two ways.

First: Can such a person receive Communion and even be an active member of an American Catholic parish? The answer depends on the parish. Obviously there are any number of Catholic parishes where same-sex couples take Communion together and participate as a couple in some moments of parish life. It's a matter of finding that kind of parish.

Second: Would the pope or most bishops approve full membership of an "out," noncelibate homosexual in a Catholic parish? Obviously not. As we have seen at painful length, official speech about sexually active homosexuals is perfectly clear at least about this: they are habitual sinners who cannot receive Communion unless they repent—and who should be discriminated against in certain situations precisely because of their homosexuality. These are not just abstract teachings. Prominent bishops do refuse to give Communion to politically active or publicly declared homosexuals.

Being a gay Catholic in a regular parish demands that you live between those two translations of the question.

———

Living between those translations means not being able to have many sacramental needs met by the parish. I know Catholic priests who will bless same-sex unions, but not in public (public blessings result in suspension). The same goes for baptizing the adopted children of same-sex couples. I heard of a male-male couple that was turned down by some two dozen priests before the local chapter of Dignity was able to arrange a baptism. And I have been to Catholic funerals where the surviving partner of a lesbian or gay couple was given a prominent place and even named from the pulpit, but without ever admitting the nature of her or his relationship with the deceased. Is this pastoral care?

Even when an individual priest bends as much as he can, the text of the Roman liturgy does not. It fails to recognize same-sex unions or bereavements, much less the lesbian and gay need to "come out" or to be healed from homophobic assault. Gays and lesbians can be active and even prominent members of regular Catholic parishes, but they will not hear their particular needs or difficulties spoken in the missal or sacramentary.

———

Then there is the matter of collaboration—with its wartime overtones. When a gay man or lesbian participates in the life of a Catholic parish, donates time and money to it, he or she must answer to the charge of actively supporting an institution that persecutes homosexuals.

The charge is serious, but also confusing. If we become too scrupulous about cooperating with homophobic structures, we will have to secede from most of American society. What government or corporation or cultural institution has not been actively homophobic in the quite recent past? Unless we intend to withdraw altogether, we have to negotiate our participation in historically homophobic structures.

This answer may seem a dodge. After all, participating in the Catholic church is not just another case of having to tolerate the prevailing homophobia. First, membership in it is voluntary, not obligatory. You must be a citizen of some country, but you don't have to belong to any Christian church, much less the Catholic church. Second, it seems that religious communities ought to be answerable to higher moral standards, not lower ones. For Christian believers, the churches are held precisely to gospel standards. Churches can't be justified by arguing that they are no worse than other social institutions. Then, third, the Catholic church is not only historically homophobic. It is actively and acutely homophobic in the present. In a number of countries, it represents the most powerful voice in favor of the repression and persecution of lesbians and gays.

———

What responses can be made to the charge of collaboration? Some lesbian and gay Catholics would contend that the Catholic church is not a moral unity. If they participate in the activities of their local parishes, if they make local contributions, that has nothing to do with Rome.

At its best, this attitude represents a spiritual freedom from the arrogance of church authorities. But it also signifies a detachment from the history of Christian believing. I have friends who, in trying to find a church home, decided that they could only begin by forgetting the history of every denomination they visited. But such forgetting is neither safe nor satisfying for lesbigay Catholics. Neither is ignoring the power of church bureaucracies. The task is not to forget history, but to redeem it.

———

Other homosexual Catholics who remain in regular parishes fall back on the claim so commonly heard from gay priests and religious: Staying is the best way to change things.

The familiarity of this claim doesn't guarantee its truth. It may simply be mistaken. Remaining within officially Catholic structures may not be in fact the most efficient way to change them. We might effect reforms much more quickly by shaking the dust of Catholic parishes from our feet and leaving them behind.

The claim on behalf of staying may also be spiritually misleading. It may simply be another form of queer Catholic masochism. No temptation is more potent for Catholics than to suffer injustice in the church because suffering must somehow show a profit. American Catholics have been taught to suffer superbly for religious causes. Their "education" makes it easy to equate what is spiritually right with what brings most suffering.

Finally, the claim that we will reform the church by staying within it may simply be incoherent. It is not at all clear what "reform" means.

———

Imagine that by some miracle you were admitted to a secret interview with a papal emissary to discuss the specific reforms sought by you and other Catholic homosexuals. Would you consider it sufficient to soften official Catholic teaching on homosexuality? For example, would it be enough to say that copulation between confirmed or incurable homosexuals in a permanent, monogamous relationship is only a lesser—that is, a venial—sin? That it might in some circumstances hardly be a sin at all?

Would that really be enough for you? Wouldn't you want some honesty—say about all the damage done down through the centuries? A papal apology "for centuries of moral cowardice"?[4] John Paul II undertook a series of apologies on the eve of the millennium. Homosexuals were not included.

Wouldn't you also want some larger justice on issues of sex and gender? A reconsideration of the cruel principles of Catholic sexual morality for heterosexuals? Justice for women on a dozen major points?

The difficulty in offering a concise answer to the papal emissary, in narrowing down the list of changes, shows that any simple wish for a "reform" of teachings is incoherent. The questions raised in this book suggest that the Catholic condemnation of homosexual acts belongs to the issues that are central to Catholic moral teaching and its modern institutions. What is a "reform" that doesn't address those issues or institutions?

———

We shouldn't seek a loosening of the Catholic strictures on homosexuality at the price of a more general tightening of control over our sexual identities. We shouldn't be willing to give up our dissent in exchange for more comprehensive regulations of who we are. If we do that, we let the Catholic bureaucracies manage us not by condemnation, but by comprehensive supervision.

One issue here is "mainstreaming" or "assimilation." Sometimes homosexual Catholics (or homosexual Americans) are told that they would be acceptable in the church (or the country) if only they would behave respectably. The meaning of "respectability" varies. It can carry class overtones— or political or racial ones. Be more like parishioners in a wealthy Midwest suburb! (At least, be like what those suburbanites would like to seem to be!) Or be more like chaste religious brothers! Be more like heterosexuals! These exhortations are so many stipulations that we will only be let inside if we conform to the tastes or vanities of those in power. The stipulations ought to be even less acceptable in the church than they are in civil society.

Other prescriptions or expectations are more subtle and more destructive than "assimilation." These direct us to take on our role as "Catholic homosexuals." We recognize what is wrong with the prescriptions when they are stated as baldly as in the official documents: Be more like the silent, suffering, solitary homosexuals of old! Be more fixated on the damage done to you by your sexuality! Be more eager to be nailed to your cross!

These exhortations are evidently lethal. But other exhortations, "changed" and even "reformed," can also damage. Imagine a doctrine that permits monogamous homosexual relations as the expression of a second-class and incurably defective sexuality. God's providence allows for homosexual copulation even though the fullness of human intimacy can only be achieved between married man and woman. Hear the new exhortations: Be more comfortable in being defective! Be more fully identified with the anomaly that has made your sexuality second-class! We should not be grateful for that kind of "reform." We should not accept it.

———

Homosexual Catholics are driven to consider alternative religious communities because their demand for a nonhomophobic Catholicism is itself a mandate for a new community. When we insist that the church disavow its homophobia, that it speak candidly about the role of homoeroticism in its clergy, its liturgy, its forms of community, that it apologize for the evils it has done during centuries, we have already asked for a radical change in its structures of power. We cannot demand candor about homosexuality in Catholicism without asking for a very different kind of church. To do justice to Catholic homosexuals will disrupt the Catholic church as we know it. So when we ask for "reform," we have already left the present form of the Catholic church.

Joining the Rebels

Andrew Holleran remembers things this way: "The attempt of gay men to merge their Catholicism with homosexuality has always seemed to me touching but doomed. I used to walk past the church on Sixteenth Street in New York where I knew Dignity—an organization for gay Catholics—was meeting, but I never went in. I felt sorry for the men inside, sympathetic to their attempt, and superior to what seemed to me their naiveté. Don't even try, I thought, as I walked past, on the way from the gym to the bath (my new church), you're just kidding yourselves. There can be no commerce between, no conflation of, these two things. Fellatio has nothing to do with Holy Communion. Better to frankly admit that you have changed gods, and are now worshipping Priapus, not Christ."[5]

Holleran is remembering a time when chapters of Dignity were allowed to meet in Catholic churches—a time before Cardinal Ratzinger's 1986 *Letter* ordered their expulsion. Dignity had a history before that. Its present predicament was determined as much by its past as by anything Cardinal Ratzinger did to it.

————

Let me describe the predicament as a puzzle. In late 1968 and early 1969, two organizations were founded in Southern California that would attract large numbers of lesbigay Catholics and ex-Catholics. Today, one of these organizations comprises more than three hundred congregations in eighteen countries with a total membership exceeding thirty thousand people. In some American cities, such as Los Angeles itself, the largest number of new members for this organization consists of people who were raised Catholic. The second organization, which confined itself to the United States and Canada, has fewer than a third as many congregations and only about 15 percent of the membership (if that). Early years of growth have been followed by declining or stagnant numbers, and some of its members worry that it will soon cease to exist. The first organization is known as the

Metropolitan Community Churches (MCC), the second as Dignity. Puzzle: What differences between these two organizations, founded in the same place at the same time, account for their disparate fates?

The obvious answer to this question is that MCC declared itself from the very beginning an independent, cross-denominational Christian body. It recruited its own clergy, bought or built its own churches, and tried to offer a full liturgical and community life. Dignity, by contrast, was and is an organization in uneasy dependence on the Roman Catholic hierarchy. It has begged and borrowed priests, rented or cajoled space, and offered at best a partial set of sacraments and liturgies. In some places and times, it has been nothing more than a monthly or bimonthly therapy group for lesbigay Catholics whose sacramental life was carried on elsewhere.

Dignity has limited itself in this way in order to preserve its sense of Catholic identity. Its actions are also consistent with its history—though Dignity tends to forget that history.

———

Dignity began as a support group run by an Augustinian priest, Pat Nidorf. Nidorf placed ads for "Catholic Gays" in a San Diego "underground" newspaper in 1969.[6] Frustrated by the lack of response, he advertised in the *Los Angeles Free Press* and *The Advocate*. Response increased sharply. Some people who had been attending the new MCC began driving to San Diego for the meetings. After alternating between San Diego and Los Angeles, Nidorf eventually held all meetings in L.A., where most of his membership lived. A layman was appointed as "General Chairman" and the group moved out of private homes into a church auditorium. In early 1971, a letter went to the archdiocese asking for recognition. The response was predictable: Timothy Manning, then a co-adjutor (or deputy) to the archbishop, rebuked Nidorf for working in the diocese, judged the principles of Dignity "untenable," and ordered him to stop working with the group. In response, Dignity became a lay-led group, and it began a campaign of national outreach. A first national meeting was held in Los Angeles in 1973, with a dozen recognized chapters and another dozen in formation.[7]

What were the principles of Dignity that the bishop found "untenable"? Almost a year before meeting with him, the organization had adopted its "Statement of Position and Purpose," based in part on recently published articles by John McNeill. It claims, among other things, that "homosexuality is a natural variation on the use of sex. It implies no sickness or immorality. Those with such sexual orientation have a natural right to use their power of sex in a way that is both responsible and fulfilling." The document also asserts, to my mind more provocatively, "We believe that gay Catholics are members of Christ's mystical body, numbered among the people of God. . . . We believe that gays can express their sexuality in a manner that is consonant with Christ's teaching."[8]

Most early members of Dignity in L.A. did not perceive this statement as a charter for separation from the church. Meetings were held on Saturdays rather than Sundays and members were encouraged to be active in their home parishes. Dignity Masses were celebrated only rarely, and then to mark special occasions. But some members had grown up in more political organizations (Mattachine, Catholic Worker) and were at least familiar with models for "oppression" and "liberation." The political rhetoric carried over into the national organization. In 1975, for example, Dignity approached the American bishops asking for the appointment of a committee to address "the oppression of the gay Catholic."[9] Some members were also willing to use civil disobedience or other forms of street activism. When Brian McNaught was outed in 1975 as gay and as president of Dignity's Detroit chapter, his regular column was canceled by the diocesan newspaper.[10] He went on a hunger strike. He was then fired from his job as staff writer—but under the glare of national publicity. Twenty-four days later, two auxiliary bishops delivered a letter undertaking as a serious obligation "'to root out structures and attitudes that discriminate against the homosexual as a person'" (p. 77).

———

Dignity was polarized from the first—even before the Vatican entered the discourse with the 1975 *Declaration*. To some, Dignity functioned as a support group for lesbigay Catholics whose sacramental and liturgical life was lived in their parishes. For others, Dignity represented a catalyst for radical reforms in the Catholic church. The tension was present before 1975. In the period between 1975 and the 1986 *Letter*, it became, if anything, stronger. Those same years saw the first waves of deaths to AIDS. Along with every other gay organization, Dignity began to lose members—and leaders. So that when the 1986 *Letter* arrived, it found an organization long divided over principle and consumed by grief and the need to care for its dying.

Dignity's expulsion from Catholic property following the *Letter* was more damaging as symbol than as practical reality. Other places to meet could be found quickly enough. It was not so easy to retain a sense of legitimacy. Rome had spoken: Dignity was no longer a pastoral ministry of the church. It was a rebel group with no official right to call itself Catholic. In that situation, all of the tensions over identity already latent within the group erupted.

———

A number of chapters split, officially or unofficially. A novelist describes the situation this way: "The Faith group [i.e., the Dignity chapter] splintered in three. The largest, retaining the Faith name . . . kept close ties to the national organization, which declared . . . that being gay was okay. The other groups named themselves Hope and Charity. The Hope group . . . was still trying to work within the current church structure. The Charity group, smallest of the splinters, had something to do with the Council of Trent and Latin masses."[11]

The satire can be translated into more general, if less pungent, terms. After 1986, their options limited, members of Dignity veered in three different directions. Some stayed with the national organization, which became a kind of temporary government-in-exile. Others submitted to the official Vatican line and resumed their places in regular parishes or joined an officially approved "diocesan outreach program." Yet other members perceived an opportunity to seek out "conservative" protest groups of one sort or another. Some gay Catholics are Liturgy Queens before all else. Men of this kind had never been particularly happy with Dignity's left-leaning politics or its liturgical experiments, say, with gender-inclusive language. So they went in search of florid vestments and liturgies in unknown languages, gay solidarity be damned.

Even today, Dignity chapters show these tensions. Some members want Dignity to become fully a church in exile, ordaining its own priests and creating its own liturgies until Rome is reformed or the Lord returns in glory, whichever comes first. Other members want a place where a "real" mass will be read out of the missal by a "real" priest who knows, but never says, that the men and women in the room happen to be homosexuals. Yet others come to Dignity because they want to be priests and couldn't elsewhere, or because they want to see something of Catholicism without getting too close, or because it provides "a daylight cruise-bar with wheezy organ music" (to quote one friend, now an Episcopalian).

It is the genius—or the downfall—of Dignity since 1986 that it doesn't force its membership one way or the other. Indeed, it doesn't force much of anything, either personally or theologically. Most of all, it doesn't force one to decide between being Catholic and leading one or another of the urban gay lifestyles. Perhaps that is why Dignity chapters function so often as a waiting room for people who are trying to sort through questions about Catholicism and homosexuality. For those who quit the church as young men in order to be gay, it provides a gay space with what is (usually) a recognizably Catholic liturgy. For those who stayed in the church but now need to negotiate a gay identity, it provides a Catholic space in which there are a lot of gay men.

———

The problems with Dignity as a waiting room arise not for the people passing through, but for those who try to stay. Most chapters are not able to offer the spiritual support or the sacramental sustenance of a regular Catholic parish. If the national organization has opened a registry for committed relationships, many members are still fearful of doing anything that will take them too far away from the official church. If some members want active programs of confrontation or evangelization, others want a quiet Mass that won't get anyone into trouble. And then there is the persistent question of "finding a priest"—who may or may not be in good standing, who may or may not preach on appropriate topics, who may or may not be pastorally available outside the liturgy.

———

The sense of Dignity as waiting room accompanies the idea that Dignity remains a sliver of church, a "special interest" congregation. This is a problem for many "straight" parishes, which can be sharply segregated along class and race lines. But it is even more problematic in Dignity, which has historically been mostly male,[12] mostly middle class, and mostly Caucasian. There are not enough women, not enough children, not enough people of color. It feels too much like a fragment of a community. And it too often conceives of itself as a fragment, as a party in exile, waiting to be called back home.

———

The most positive way to view Dignity's predicament is as the seed of a new form of Catholic religious community. Many religious orders have had haphazard beginnings, and some have been actively opposed for a time by members of the hierarchy. Perhaps Dignity will survive its present confusion to flourish as a new form of apostolic life within a rejuvenated Catholicism. But for the moment it lives on the edge of its seat, waiting to be invited onto the next flight to Rome. Rather than remaining in that waiting room, however familiar it seems, lesbian or gay Catholics may decide to search for a more balanced and independent community.

A Church for People Like Us

The Universal Fellowship of Metropolitan Community Churches also originated in Los Angeles at the end of the 1960s, as I said in posing my puzzle. The first service was held on October 6, 1968, in the living room of a former Pentecostalist pastor, Troy Perry.[13] For lesbian and gay Christians, that date must be as much a milestone as the street fights around Stonewall eight months later. The MCC is a Christian denomination in which lesbian and gay lives are at the center of worship and teaching.

———

Many affecting and heartbreaking stories describe the denomination's growth from that living room to an international association of more than three hundred congregations. Troy Perry himself appears to have been tireless in generating publicity on behalf of homosexual rights. Early films show him striding around picket lines in an almost Anglican cassock, delivering speeches on gay liberation with a southern preacher's rolling cadences: the gospel of gay liberation in the language of King James.

Something of Perry's energy and willingness to improvise has carried forward into the fellowship. Its churches are remarkably diverse. They vary from groups of a dozen to an institution that regularly bills itself as "the world's largest" lesbigay church, comprising several thousand members.

———

MCC congregations of all sizes have drawn and continue to draw ex-Catholics—or half-Catholics, since not a few go to the MCC service and then to a regular parish. Indeed, MCC churches have struggled to be a sort of ecumenical movement in miniature. This is true in several senses. The fellowship has tried patiently to make peace with national and international ecumenical groups. Nancy Wilson, who was active in many of those efforts, has written a chilling account of the hypocrisy and bad faith of many of the leaders of Christian ecumenism.[14] But MCC churches are ecumenical in a more concrete sense. The "converts" who come to them from other churches bring traditions with them, and the MCC tries to take it all in. On a given morning you can hear something like a mixture of Catholic and Episcopal liturgy, with Baptist preaching, Methodist hymns, and Pentecostalist moments of inspiration.

———

I admire this. But any Catholic who believes that a lesbigay church far from Rome can be the New Jerusalem will find shocks in the reality of MCC congregations. The fellowship has suffered factionalism from early on. Disciplinary problems in the clergy were remedied at the cost of establishing more rules and a larger bureaucracy. Struggles continue concerning the roles of women and people of color. With the usual rivalries between ambitious pastors has come the desire to assume grand titles and to build magnificent churches. To Catholic eyes, this looks like a disheartening repetition of the follies of church history. We've done this once already—and very badly. Couldn't we learn from our mistakes?

———

Lesbigay churches do end up resembling churches in the "mainstream." Changing church doctrine about homosexuality does not, in itself, achieve a universal reign of justice. But this is a lesson that lesbian and gay communities are learning more generally. The utopian hopes of the early gay liber-ationists have not been realized. Queer politics, queer media, and queer capitalism very much resemble their straight counterparts. So perhaps it is not surprising that large lesbigay churches of mostly Protestant extraction should resemble nothing so much as other large Protestant churches.

———

These resemblances can be disheartening or consoling, but I suspect that they are not the most important lesson to learn from the history of the MCC. Rather, its experience highlights the difficulty in keeping theological questions open long enough to consider them carefully. If a change in Christian teaching on homosexuality really does require a fundamental re-evaluation of the gospel and its expressions, then a central task for any lesbigay church will be to avoid settling things too soon.

———

Here I want to be as fair as I can, and not only because I admire many MCC leaders and church members. MCC congregations have served as emer-gency rooms. They have had to work in ongoing crisis, ministering to lesbi-ans and gays who often arrive in despair, needing to be healed from the abuse of the mainstream churches, needing sometimes just to be kept alive. MCC congregations have responded compassionately to these crises, de-spite considerable opposition and very real dangers. There has not been much time to spare for theological reflection.

They have also lacked sufficient resources. No young denomination could be expected to match the liturgical or intellectual accumulations of the older Christian groups. Any lesbigay church must take liturgical materials, theological formulations, trained personnel, and institutional arrangements from older churches. It depends on the mainstream churches not only for degrees, libraries, and endowments to buy leisure for study, but also for historical experiences, complex languages, and accomplished artworks. I take all of this for granted. I even expect that lesbigay churches will end up accepting a number of the vices of the older churches, because those vices walk through the front door.

What I cannot accept is the assumption that lesbigay churches can teach or live "just like" other churches except in regard to homosexuality. The assumption does not make sense.

Given Troy Perry's Pentecostalist background, MCC congregations began by emphasizing personal inspiration over doctrinal elaboration. This predilection seems to have become ingenious policy. The fellowship tries to avoid the kind of doctrinal disputes that Christians have long used as pretexts for civil war. Its doctrinal statements are minimal and, indeed, quite traditional. MCC theological practice tends to avoid questions in fundamental or systematic theology to concentrate on the defense of lesbigay believers or the perplexities of social ethics.

The practice is prudent. It has held the fellowship together fairly well despite the disparate backgrounds of its members. It has also addressed the most urgent questions. But it is not clear that this cautious avoidance of foundational questions will continue to serve so well. It may now have become urgent for lesbian and gay believers to focus on the ancient and contentious claims of Christian belief.

MCC has had the disadvantage of being first. Because it had to invent a lesbigay church quickly, from the ground up, it had to settle a number of issues all at once. The relative success of those agreements may now block thinking—institutional success is always a mixed blessing in Christian life.

Faced with the challenge of a more radical transformation, the "homosexual Catholic" may decide to turn from the MCC back to Catholic traditions, in the hope of building a new community from them.

Queer Catholicism

Why seek out new institutional forms for lesbigay Catholicism at all? Why not turn our backs on Catholicism and its hateful homophobia? Let me translate these objections into another kind of question: Why try to protect or encourage queer Catholic lives? Here "queer" means not only consciously lesbian and gay, but also consciously resistant to the bureaucracies of modern Catholic power.

I rehearse the sequence of answers I have been suggesting. First, these queer Catholic lives have been our lives.

Second, queer and Catholic is what the Christian church has been for much of its history. Given the importance of the Christian church in world culture, that conjunction has been historically decisive in many ways.

Third, the modern western identity of the "homosexual" was constructed at least in part out of Catholic materials. We cannot understand it or undo it without involving Catholicism.

Finally, queer Catholicism may offer us not only new forms of religious life, but new forms of queer life.

———

The search for a queer Catholicism can be conceived in many ways. One is to ask how it would be organized. But church history suggests that organization is discovered before it is deduced or theorized. The great religious orders arose by imitation of a founder's life. The form of that life was then articulated—and often betrayed—as a rule or constitution. Still the founder's life came first. We will have to wait on the founders before we know what the institutional forms will be.

———

An easier way to search for a queer Catholicism is to define what tasks it will confront.

For example, it must show an intimate relation between "homosexuality" and holiness—that is, human fullness. This task requires something more than arguing that there are or have been holy homosexuals. We must consider how far the identity of the "homosexual" satisfies the demands of holiness. Finding or founding a Catholic community in which "homosexuals" are sanctified requires something more than resisting homophobic authority or affirming ourselves to one another. It demands a reconsideration and perhaps a reversal of the construction of the "homosexual." The most important constitutional question is not about our communities, but about ourselves.

———

Catholic theology has proven remarkably fertile in generating homoerotic identities. They have been officially sin-identities, identities of condemnation. In recent dissent, they have been transposed into identities of pride or protest. But these reversals ignore a fundamental feature: The "homosexual" was constructed as a damaged or incomplete identity. To be a homosexual was not only to be pathological or undeveloped or marginalized, it was to be imprisoned by one's "sexuality." The identity was conceived precisely as lacking human fullness, as a deficiency, as a permanent human poverty.

We should be bolder. We should deploy Catholic theology to help us reconstruct the identity altogether. We don't want queer Catholicism so that we can gain acceptance as "homosexuals." We want queer Catholicism so that we can be queerer than "homosexuals" were ever supposed to be.

———

Once again, I describe this best as looking for a new way of speaking. Monasteries were traditionally "schools of charity." I conceive of the communities of queer Catholicism as schools for new speech.

They will certainly be schools in which we are free to speak. So much of our short, public life has been taken up with the relief of hearing our suffering, our needs, our loves spoken aloud. It is understandable that one of the recurring images of lesbigay theology is of hearing God call our names. But we should be careful that we hear the name correctly. Most of the names we have been called have been imposed from outside. We may not yet have a proper name. We may not yet know what to say about ourselves. It is not only the pope who should be at a loss for words about us.

———

Feminist theology has already marked out a parallel path. It has struggled seriously not only with misogynistic hate speech, but with the deep gendering of language. It has also experimented with the relations between theological speech and community-building.

Some of this work has begun in queer theology, though mostly outside of Catholic circles. We need more of it. We must imagine theological languages as both the cause and effect of communities in which full cycles of queer speech will be elaborated—the speech of liturgy, private prayer, and proclamation, but also the speech of inquiry and contemplation. We then must write speeches that will hasten the founding of new communities. Some discourses may be "scholarly," but others—perhaps most—will be "literary." We need more utopian novels about Catholic queers, as we need more liturgies of poetic power.

———

We must also fight against speeches that prevent the founding of such communities. This includes, of course, the homophobic denunciations of the official "Magisterium" and the well-meaning "compromises" offered by some of our friends. But much of our own chatter is also culpable. The flood of writing about homosexuality and Christianity in the last two decades has brought many benefits, but also an unexpected disappointment. It sometimes seems as if the same few books are being written over and over again. I attribute some of this repetition to the excitement of a new field. Writers keep discovering important truths for themselves—say, about specific biblical passages or about the history of Christian teaching or even about the facts of homosexual lives. But they have also begun to talk in circles.

How much of this is due to a naive expectation that we will convince our opponents? We seem to be waiting for official church bodies to agree with our arguments. But the quarrel over homosexuality is not a quarrel to be settled by arguments, because the passions it provokes are not amenable to rational persuasion. Other means are needed.

Waiting on the official church bodies not only wastes life, it encourages us to repeat the dismal history of chatter in moral theology. When we convince ourselves that we can represent our lives adequately and persuasively in the ordinary styles of theological argument, we trivialize ourselves. We ought to be engaged not in endless disputes with official theologies, but in reconceiving their terms. Before we can begin an argumentative theology of homoerotic life, we need what traditions have called a "negative" theology of it. We must criticize and perhaps surrender our central terms, our favorite metaphors, and our paradigms for argument.

It would indeed be nice to have a standard moral theology in which we were not being attacked, but our aim ought to be higher. We should see the theological controversy over homosexuality for what it is: a privileged opportunity to rethink the genres of moral theology altogether. Our lives can challenge not just the principle that sex has to be procreative, but the assumption that moral theology has to be founded upon such principles.

———

Guy Hocquenghem once wrote, in a utopian moment: "Our homosexuality is not a revolutionary value that must be extended to the whole world, but a permanent situation of putting into question."[15] We might want to hope that a queer Catholic theology would view its objects and itself as permanent questioning. It could thus be a reminder of the modesty, the ingenuity, the skepticism, and the linguistic discipline that all Christian thinking is supposed to exhibit so far as it professes the venerable ideals of negative theology.

———

The first act in a negative theology of "homosexuality" should be a repentance by gay Catholics. The "invisibility" of our sexual orientation, the possibility of keeping it as an open secret, has tempted us with silent collaboration for centuries. Many men we would call "gay" have collaborated in the making and disseminating of official Catholic condemnations of male-male love. Many silent sodomites burned sodomites who started to speak. Many closeted homosexuals in the hierarchy now condemn open homosexuals in the pews. When the American bishops threw Dignity off church property, a number of them should have had the honesty to follow.

In the long line of Catholic theologians who have denounced male-male love, it would be statistically freakish if not one of them desired men more than women. Augustine, the compilers of the penitentials, Peter Damian, Alan of Lille, Peter the Chanter, Albert the Great, Thomas Aquinas, Bernardino of Siena, Antoninus of Florence, Cardinal Cajetan, Tomás Sanchez, the "Salmanticenses," Alphonus Liguori, Cardinal Ratzinger—who of them has been a silent sodomite? We may never know, and still we can do some penance for them.

———

For ourselves too, so far as we have collaborated in their handiwork for perpetuating the identities. We gay Catholics ought to repent of having been "sodomites" and "homosexuals." We ought to regret not the full pursuit of lives in which we love men, but our agreement to put on the identities made for us. We should feel contrition for having pretended to have a sexual identity, when what we had were desires, memories, and loves. To be good "homosexuals" is, for Catholic men, to conspire with our old persecutors in a sin against our selves. The "homosexual" is only the "sodomite" in approved drag.

———

Learning to speak about ourselves differently means learning a new language for both our erotic lives and our sacramental ones. There are official church descriptions of what it is to be a homosexual or a Catholic. The descriptions are linked by a hundred histories, but not least in stressing that living either identity properly means submitting to a bureaucracy of "care," that is, of control. To contest the official descriptions publicly, you need to remove yourself from that bureaucracy's reach. To find another way of articulating your erotic and sacramental life, you need to be in a community that is a school for new speech. That community cannot dismiss issues about your being Catholic any more than it can dismiss issues about your being homosexual. It must take them up as the indispensable material out of which new life will be made.

Here solitary imagination fails. You cannot imagine a new language. You can only make it in trying to speak with others.

You cannot project it all at once. You must discover little patterns, fragments of paradigms, new sounds and surprising turns in grammar. You have to drill, correcting yourself or what seemed the paradigms. You will stumble, hunt for words, tangle yourself in mid-sentence. Then you will realize that you have begun to make sense.

You cannot imagine beforehand what you will learn in the school for new speech. You can only enroll.

———

The end of the old Catholic silences about sodomy cannot be the "spiteful words" of the new condemnations.

It should not be the chatter of a well-managed homosexual identity within or without a tidily defined Catholicism.

The end of the silence of Sodom is like the beginning of a Eucharist: recollection, repentance, the undertaking to speak differently.

NOTES

CHAPTER ONE

1. James, "After-Season in Rome," p. 191.

2. Apuleius, *The Golden Ass*, 8.26, 8.29. The "fortissimus rusticanus" makes his appearance in 8.29 (Helm, *Opera*, 1:200.16).

3. For the merest sample of anthropological studies on relations between ritual role and homosexual or transgendered identities, see the essays in Herdt, *Third Sex, Third Gender*.

4. So, for example, Curb and Manahan's *Lesbian Nuns* gives a richer, better textured representation of the lives it describes than most of the anthologies about gay priests or religious, which tend to be rather more statistical or polemical.

5. White, "What Century Is This Anyway?" p. 58.

6. Benjamin, "Das *Passagenwerk*," pp. 572–74, especially frags. N1, 10; and N1A, 8. The parenthetical citations in the rest of the paragraph are also to this work.

7. Jerome, *Liber interpretationis hebraicorum nominum*, De Genesi "S" (Lagarde, p. 71, lines 18–19).

CHAPTER TWO

1. The phrases are from Monette, *Last Watch*, pp. 55 and 67, respectively.

2. Different sorts of "positive" Catholic statements through 1995 are gathered by Gramick and Nugent in *Voices of Hope.*

3. The parenthetical citations in this section refer to the paragraph numbers of the Congregation for the Doctrine of the Faith's *Persona humana.* The translations from the Latin are my own. Even the "official" or "Vatican" translations of these documents often seem to me to differ in nuance from the Latin originals.

4. This is a sign of a much more general incoherence in official appeals to natural law, which is to say, in arguments from experience in Catholic morals. For one recent instance, see Hanigan, "Sexual Orientation," pp. 69–70, with note 55. Because of the incoherence, all remarks about a continuous tradition of natural law teaching should be regarded with suspicion. The best review of theological arguments from nature is Pronk, *Against Nature?* Pronk is stronger on Protestant texts than on Catholic ones, and his reading of Thomas Aquinas, pp. 27–36, differs considerably from the one I offer.

5. In suggesting the contrary, Sullivan falls victim to the Vatican's rewriting of the history of moral theology. See his *Virtually Normal,* p. 37.

6. There is an English translation: Wojtyla, *The Acting Person.*

7. See, for example, Hanigan, "Sexual Orientation," pp. 67–68, who speaks of "very significant developments"; Pilant, "Evolution of Pastoral Thought," p. 124, who calls it a "breakthrough"; and Sullivan, *Virtually Normal,* p. 33, who finds it "remarkable" (a claim paraphrased in his *Love Undetectable,* p. 49). Smith is more accurate in stressing the continuities between the *Declaration* and Pius XI's *Casti connubii* (*AIDS, Gays,* p. 45).

8. Vernay, "L'homosexualité," especially pp. 30–39; and Grelon, "Homosexualité et pratique," pp. 12–13.

9. *Codex iuris canonicis* [1983], canon 1095, 3°. For some cases applying the new canon, see Weiss, "L'homosexualité."

10. See, for an introduction to some of these cases, Katz, *Invention of Heterosexuality,* pp. 23–28, and chapter 2 more generally.

11. For some of the pastoral implications of returning to the medical model, see Moore, *Body in Context,* pp. 195–99.

12. Jordan, *Invention of Sodomy,* pp. 149–50.

13. Ratzinger, *Ratzinger Report,* p. 85.

14. Ibid., p. 87.

15. Hunt quoted in Holtz, *Listen to the Stories,* p. 19.

16. Unless otherwise indicated, parenthetical citations in this section refer to the paragraph numbers of the Congregation for the Doctrine of the Faith's *Homosexualitatis problema.* Translations from the Latin are my own. Official English versions are available in Gramick and Furey, *The Vatican and Homosexuality,* pp. 1–10; and Siker, *Homosexuality in the Church,* pp. 39–47.

17. See the analysis of Thomas Aquinas's arguments in Jordan, *Invention of Sodomy*, pp. 143–58.

18. Norton argues against the medical origin for the term "homosexual" and its immediate predecessors (*Myth of the Modern Homosexual*, pp. 64–71). Even if he is right about the academic training of those who first coined it, he has shown nothing about their use of medical and legal rhetoric. Nor has he addressed the main issue, which concerns the early deployment of the term within medical contexts by the nineteenth century. Recall, for example, the enormously influential treatment of "homosexuality" in Krafft-Ebing's *Psychopathia sexualis* (first published 1886), the second subtitle of which is *A Medico-Legal Study for Doctors and Lawyers.* The same argument can be made from Havelock Ellis or the early Freud. Even if those who coined the term "homosexual" were not trained as forensic or clinical physicians, their term was offered and was received as a medicolegal category.

19. For an introduction to more precise readings of the story of Sodom in Genesis 18 and 19, see Boswell, *Christianity, Social Tolerance, and Homosexuality*, pp. 93–97; for the original misreadings of the story, see Jordan, *Invention of Sodomy*, pp. 30–36.

20. For an introduction to more precise readings of Leviticus 18:22 and 20:13, see Olyan, "'And with a Male.'"

21. For an introduction to more precise readings of Romans 1, see Brooten, *Love Between Women*, perhaps especially pp. 215–302.

22. For much more precise descriptions of the evolution of these views, see Herman, *Antigay Agenda*, especially chapters 2 and 3.

23. Sullivan reads this section with opposite emphasis. He skips over the threat to praise the condemnation of gay bashing as "a stunning passage of concession" (*Virtually Normal*, p. 37). I'm not sure how much of his irony is intentional.

24. Miller, *Search*, p. 232.

25. I will say more about Dignity and its history in chapter 8. For a narrative of the public reaction to the 1986 *Letter*, see Gramick, "Rome Speaks," with its bibliography; for a selection of written responses, see Gramick and Furey, *The Vatican and Homosexuality*, perhaps especially pp. 13–91; for additional anecdotes about the reaction, see Holtz, *Listen to the Voices*, throughout.

26. For the document's origins and probable legal standing, see Gramick and Nugent, *Voices of Hope*, 175–77.

27. I follow the text of the second, revised version in Gramick and Nugent, *Voices of Hope*, 229–33. Parenthetical references in the rest of this section are to this document.

28. Press statement of July 28, 1992, as in Gramick and Nugent, *Voices of Hope*, p. 187. This volume provides a selection of responses on pp. 178–227.

29. The fourteen essays in the series were published in the daily Italian edition between March 1 and April 23, 1997. Translations appeared in the weekly English edition between March 12 and June 18, 1997. I will cite the English translations, both because these are much easier to locate in American libraries and because I have not found places where the English differs from the Italian in ways pertinent to my discussion.

30. D'Agostino, "Should the Law Recognize Homosexual Unions?" p. 10, column 2.

31. Bruguès, "Elements of Pastoral Care," p. 14, column 3.

32. D'Agostino, "Should the Law Recognize Homosexual Unions?" p. 11, columns 1–2.

33. Until otherwise noted, parenthetical references are to the pages and columns in the *Origins* edition of the original version of *Always Our Children*. The first column is referred to as "a," the second as "b," and the third (when there is one) as "c." There are no section numbers in this first edition of the letter.

34. For a discussion of the American bishops' principal documents on AIDS, and for some samples of other comments, see Smith, *AIDS, Gays,* especially pp. 65–69.

35. O'Brien's covering letter of June 26, 1998, is quoted in the prefatory note for the revised version of the text, *Origins* 28:97a.

36. See the account in Smith, *AIDS, Gays,* pp. 58–86, with special attention to pp. 66–68.

37. Until otherwise noted, parenthetical references are to the pages and columns in the *Origins* edition of the revised version of *Always Our Children*. I refer to columns as before.

38. Congregation for the Doctrine of the Faith, "Notification" released July 13, 1999.

39. Nugent, "Statement" of July 14, 1999.

40. Mary Hunt quoted in Holtz, *Listen to the Voices,* p. 15.

CHAPTER THREE

1. Sullivan, *Love Undetectable,* p. 42.

2. Häring, *My Witness,* p. 19. The story is retold in Häring, *Free and Faithful,* p. 22.

3. Griffin, "American Catholic Sexual Ethics," p. 454.

4. The decisive moment and the most negative description come in Bernanos, *Diary,* pp. 120–21.

5. I disagree with the narratives—and the more positive evaluations—in Jonsen and Toulmin, *The Abuse of Casuistry;* and Keenan, "The Casuistry of John Mair," especially pp. 93–97. While Jonsen and Toulmin admit that modern Catholic casuistry is distinguished by its desire for a "systematic taxonomy of human behavior" (p. 142), they do not see that this notion of system contradicts the most important features of those older ways of thinking and writing about concrete actions.

6. I discuss these texts with more technical detail in *Invention of Sodomy,* chapter 7, from which I here paraphrase. The parenthetical references are to Thomas's *Summa theologiae* according to its standard medieval divisions into parts, questions, articles, and elements within articles.

7. Antoninus, *Summa theologica,* pars 2, titulus 5, caput 4, cols. 672E ("Bernardus"), 671A ("Raymundus"), 672D ("Nicolaus de Lyra"), and 672B ("Vincentius"). Other medieval authors are used without being named, of course.

8. Antoninus, *Summa theologica* 2.5.4, at 667D (with an extended quotation from *Summa theologiae* 2–2.152.11), 668A, 668B, 670A, 670B. The following parenthetical citations refer to this text.

9. Bernardino's *De horrendo peccato contra naturam,* in which Thomas is not named, gathers dozens of the older medieval topics and authorities on sodomy.

10. I omit much here because I do not need a more complete narrative about the reception by late medieval authors of Thomas's definition of sin against nature. That kind of narrative would have to consider why certain influential Thomists found the definition completely unremarkable. For example, John Capreolus's *Defenses of Thomas* follows the sequence of Thomas's commentary on the *Sentences* of Peter Lombard. Capreolus could very well have taken up Thomas's discussions when commenting on *Sentences* 4.41.1. He does not. He skips instead from topics in 4.36 to topics in 4.43.

11. The commentary is printed in the Leonine edition of Thomas's *Summa,* that is, in Thomas Aquinas, *Opera omnia,* volumes 4–12.

12. Thomas Aquinas, *Summa theologiae* 2–2.154.11, "Commentaria Cardinalis Caietani" section 8 (Leonine 10:246a–b).

13. Ibid., 2–2.154.12, "Commentaria Cardinalis Caietani" sections 20–21 (Leonine 10:252a–b).

14. Toledo, *Instructio sacerdotum* 5.13.7 (646–6e).

15. Sanchez, *Disputationes* 7.46.18–20 (2:169a).

16. Ibid., 7.64.13–14 (2:214a).

17. Ibid., 10.4.5 (3:338a).

18. Compare ibid., 10.4.13 (3:340a).

19. The choice of Escobar y Mendoza was not entirely Pascal's. When Arnauld

and Nicole recruited him in 1655 to write against the Jesuits, they also undertook to supply him with research material. They could find no more convenient summary of Jesuit moral doctrine than Escobar y Mendoza.

20. Escobar y Mendoza, *Liber theologiae moralis*, "Operis idea," a2ʳ–a4ʳ.

21. Pascal, *Les Provinciales*, Lettre 5, pp. 98–99.

22. Escobar y Mendoza, *Liber theologiae moralis*, pp. 139–40.

23. Pascal, *Les Provinciales*, Lettre 5, pp. 93–94, "personnes de toutes sortes de conditions et des nations si différents," and so on.

24. "Salmanticenses," *Cursus theologiae moralis* 6.7.5.1 (6:162b ¶77).

25. Ibid., (6:163b ¶81), reporting the firsthand testimony of the moralist Farinacius.

26. Ibid., (6:163b ¶82).

27. Ibid., (6:164a ¶84).

28. Ibid., (6:165a ¶87).

29. Liguori, *Theologia moralis* 3.4.2.3 no. 466 (Haringer 3/10:38).

30. Ibid., (Haringer 3/10:40).

31. Ibid., (Haringer 3/10:40–41).

32. Foucault, *Histoire de la sexualité*, 1:29.

33. Ibid., 1:142.

34. Huysmans, *À rebours*, p. 214.

35. Hocquenghem, *Le désir homosexuel*, p. 28 (*Homosexual Desire*, p. 66).

36. Ulrichs, *Riddle of "Man-Manly" Love*, 1:233–34. Lobkowicz is also cited at 1:183 in support of an inaccurate statement about Islamic approval of pederasty.

37. Curran, *Transition and Tradition*, p. 69.

38. Famous early examples include McNeill, "The Male Christian Homosexual" (1970); Curran, "Homosexuality and Moral Theology" (1971) and *Catholic Moral Theology in Dialogue* (1972), especially pp. 184–219; Baum, "Catholic Homosexuals" (1974); McNeill, *The Church and the Homosexual* (1976); Kosnik and others, *Human Sexuality* (1977), especially pp. 187–218; Keane, *Sexual Morality* (1977), pp. 71–91; Farley, "An Ethic for Same-Sex Relations," and Maguire, "The Morality of Homosexual Marriage," among others in *A Challenge to Love* (1983). I discuss the liberation theologies below. The most comprehensive survey of recent writing by Catholic academic theologians is Thurston, *Homosexuality and Roman Catholic Ethics*.

39. Congregation for the Doctrine of the Faith, *Homosexualitatis problema*, no. 6; Catholic Church, *Catechism*, no. 2357, note 140.

40. Curran, "Sexual Orientation," p. 86.

41. Ibid.

42. Johnson, "Good News," p. 91.

43. Consider, for example, Ménard, *De Sodome* (1980); and Cleaver, *Know My Name* (1996). Much of the self-understanding of Dignity in the 1970s and 1980s was also indebted to liberation theology. Liberation themes are not prominent in the first versions of McNeill's *Church and the Homosexual* (1976).

44. So, for example, Ménard, *De Sodome*, pp. 58–107; McNeill, *Freedom,* pp. 129–44; and the various rereadings of scriptural stories throughout Cleaver, *Know My Name.*

CHAPTER FOUR

1. I have analyzed Peter Damian's broadside more fully in *Invention of Sodomy,* pp. 45–66. For a response to my reading, and a careful description of Peter Damian's larger role in church politics, see Scanlon, "Unmanned Men."

2. As it is in writings on the "history of homosexuality." See, for example, Goodich, "Sodomy," pp. 427–28; Greenberg, *Construction of Homosexuality,* pp. 259, 205, 307; and Rocke, *Forbidden Friendships,* pp. 134–35. It is worth noticing how slim the selection of evidence presented for the generalization can be.

3. Rudnick, *Jeffrey,* p. 48.

4. Klossowski, *La vocation suspendue,* p. 99, from the mouth of the atheist priest-psychotherapist, Persienne.

5. On classical psychoanalytic theories and their problems, see Hocquenghem, *Le désir homosexuel,* pp. 63–64, 69–71 (*Homosexual Desire,* pp. 98–100, 104–106).

6. Herdt, *Guardians of the Flutes,* pp. xv and 11.

7. Herdt, "Fetish and Fantasy," pp. 61–62.

8. Dlugos, "A Cruel God," p. 25 (*Reader,* p. 308). Dlugos conducted the interview near Washington in 1979 with an old friend who appears in the story anonymously.

9. The letter is quoted in Nugent, "Priest, Celibate and Gay," p. 257.

10. Sedgwick, *Epistemology,* p. 3.

11. Ibid.; Halperin, *Saint Foucault,* p. 37.

12. Foucault, *Histoire de la sexualité,* 1:38–39.

13. "Maria Monk," *Awful Disclosures,* pp. 5, 326.

14. See, for example, Billington, "Maria Monk," especially pp. 286–87.

15. Arenas, *Antes que anochezca,* pp. 103–4.

16. I follow the accounts in Peyrefitte, *Propos secrets,* pp. 240–42; and Gunn and Murat, "Roger Peyrefitte," p. 412.

17. De Villiers, "Peyrefitte," p. 277.

18. Miller, *Novel,* p. 206.

19. For the text and context of the protest, see Morris, *American Catholic,* pp. 344–45.

20. Jenkins, *Pedophiles and Priests,* p. 82 and throughout. Jenkins provides a convincing sociological analysis of how journalists constructed such scandals during the last two decades. He is much less convincing, I think, in his remarks on homosexuality in the Catholic priesthood.

21. For compelling examples, see Harris, *Unholy Orders,* pp. 17 ("the clergy" as "haven for homosexuals and perverts"), 45 ("known homosexuals"), 51 ("'Queer!'"), 52 ("'You're gay too'"), and so on.

22. The civil trial of Rudy Kos was covered almost daily by the *Dallas Morning News* from early May through the end of July, 1997. When the judgment was handed down on July 24, 1997, summary stories appeared in the *Dallas Morning News,* as well as *USA Today* and the *New York Times.* The case came to trial too late for inclusion in Jenkins, *Pedophiles and Priests,* which does not mention it.

23. Housewright, "Diocese, Kos Victims Settle," p. 1A.

24. Press reports claimed that the diocese requested nullification on the basis of Kos's "sexual orientation." See, for example, Housewright and Slover, "Kos Arrested," p. 21A; Slover and Housewright, "Kos Faces," p. 37A. The diocese's press officer told me that the request was not based on Kos's "being gay," but on the fact that he lied about much of his past, including past sexual acts, some of which were criminal offenses.

25. Housewright, "Priest Sought Bishop's Help," pp. 1A, 28A.

26. Housewright, "Kos Trial Judge Warns Monsignor," pp. 37A, 39A.

27. Housewright, "Parents of Abused Boys Share Blame," pp. 1A, 34A. This is a fairly common official response in pedophilia cases. See, for example, the remarks of Bishop Colin Campbell in May 1989, as quoted in Harris, *Unholy Orders,* p. 16.

28. Egerton, "Therapy Ended Attraction to Teen Boys," pp. 1A, 17A.

29. There are two analyses of the survey results. The more "popular" version is Michael and others, *Sex in America,* while the more "scholarly" is Laumann and others, *The Social Organization of Sexuality.* For the methodological problems and statistical anomalies in the latter, see Adam, "Accounting for Sex."

30. Tom Cunningham, former Dominican, in Holtz, *Listen,* p. 81.

31. National Opinion Research Center, *Catholic Priest: Sociological Investigations,* pp. 99–118. In 1972, Greeley also published *Priests in the United States,* his summary reflections and supposedly candid comments on the survey. Greeley has one chapter on "sexuality," another on celibacy. Neither mentions homosexual clergymen. In 1989, Greeley would estimate that 25 percent of priests under 35

are homosexual, with about half of them sexually active. See Fox, *Sexuality and Catholicism*, p. 176 and note 10.

32. Schoenherr and others, *Full Pews*, which does not contain an entry for "homosexuality" in its index and which does not discuss homosexuality when considering, for example, how many priests might prefer heterosexual marriage to celibacy—and why.

33. Fox, *Sexuality and Catholicism*, p. 176.

34. For example, Unsworth, *Last Priests in America*, pp. 157, 218, 245. The parenthetical citations in the rest of this paragraph are also to this book.

35. Zubro, *Only Good Priest*, p. 32.

36. Murphy, *Delicate Dance*, pp. 26–27, on the numbers, ages, and status of respondents; and p. 133, for their sexual orientations.

37. Wolf, ed., *Gay Priests*, pp. 3, 8, 177–78, on history of survey and rate of return. Parenthetical references in this section and the next two are to this book.

38. Mary Hunt in Holtz, *Listen*, p. 28: "forty percent of the clergy"; Leo Tesconi, in *Listen*, p. 166: "My estimate is that at least fifty percent of the religious are gay."

39. Monette, *Last Watch*, p. 67; Leyland, ed., *Gay Roots*, p. 15.

40. Hilgeman, "Sycamore," p. 192; "Will, a seminarian," in Stuart, *Chosen*, p. 56.

41. Derrick A. Tynan-Connolly in Holtz, *Listen*, p. 182

42. Stuart, *Chosen*, p. 51.

43. Rosser, *Gay Catholics*, p. 119.

44. Strasser, "Homosexualité et formation," p. 122.

45. Tager, "Des prêtres," p. 41.

46. Wagner, *Gay Catholic Priests*, pp. 12–14. The parenthetical citations in the rest of this section are to the pages of this same work.

47. Sipe, *A Secret World*, p. 8. Parenthetical references in the next two paragraphs are also to this book.

48. McBrien, "Homosexuality and the Priesthood."

49. Mahony, "Prayer Brings Men," p. 494.

50. Morris, *American Catholic*, p. 407.

51. Ibid., p. 376.

52. An ex-Trappist in Monette, *Last Watch*, p. 58.

53. Sedgwick, *Between Men*, pp. 1–5 and then throughout.

54. Compare Hocquenghem, *Le désir homosexuel*, p. 75 (*Homosexual Desire*, p. 110).

55. See, for example, Halperin, *One Hundred Years*, pp. 15–18, 26–29; Katz, *Invention of Heterosexuality*, pp. 19–55; and, to the contrary, Norton, *Myth of the Modern Homosexual*, pp. 67–71.

CHAPTER FIVE

1. Peter Damian, *Liber Gomorrhianus* = *Epistola 31* (Reindel, p. 287, lines 19–21).

2. Vidal, *Palimpsest*, p. 3.

3. Coste, *Boniface VIII*, especially the summary of the evidence with respect to the charges of sodomy on pp. 899–902.

4. Ibid., p. 537.

5. Ibid., pp. 534–45.

6. For a judgment from "freshness," see ibid., pp. 899–902.

7. Boyle, "An Ambry," p. 345.

8. Basic information about each of these popes can be found, for example, in the individual entries for them in Larivière, *Homosexuels*. I have already spoken my worry about such lists of "gay" or "homosexual" figures in history.

9. Schleiner, "'That Matter,'" pp. 54–58.

10. Meticulously narrated by Boswell, *Christianity*, pp. 213–15, who wants to use them as evidence for his general claim about toleration in the twelfth century.

11. For a reflection on some other political cases outside the church, see Brundage, "The Politics of Sodomy."

12. I depend on Gilmour-Bryson, "Sodomy and the Knights Templar."

13. To cite only a few examples, Bieler, *Irish Penitentials*, pp. 60 (Gildas) and 68 (Grove of Victory); Wasserschleben, *Die Bußordnungen der abendländischen Kirche*, pp. 222 (Bede), 234 (Egbert), 598–99 (Ps-Theodore), and so on; compare Alan of Lille *Liber poenitentialis* 2.100 (Longère 2:111). The best review of this kind of homosexuality in the penitentials is now Frantzen, *Before the Closet*, pp. 149–75, with its supplementary tables, pp. 175–83. These supersede the tables in Payer, *Sex and the Penitentials*, pp. 135–39.

14. Brundage, *Law, Sex, and Christian Society*, pp. 472, note 283, and 533, note 24.

15. These courts also dealt with sexual offenses by the laity, of course. For an introduction to them, see Brundage, "Playing by the Rules," especially pp. 31–34 and the corresponding notes.

16. I follow the account in Sherr, "A Canon," which is based on an archival dossier of the case.

17. Labalme, "Sodomy and Venetian Justice," pp. 237–41; and Ruggiero, *Boundaries of Eros*, pp. 141–43.

18. Puff, "Localizing Sodomy," p. 183.

19. Rocke, *Forbidden Friendships*, 83.

20. For some details of the political context, see Smith, *Homosexual Desire*, pp. 43–44.

21. Rocke, *Forbidden Friendships*, p. 139 and table B.12 (p. 249).

22. Ibid., pp. 72, 139. See also the 1416 case of Heinrich von Rheinfelden from Cologne, Puff, "Localizing Sodomy," pp. 181–82.

23. Füser, "Der Leib ist das Grab," p. 233 (Cluniacs, thirteenth to the fifteenth centuries); Puff, "Localizing Sodomy," pp. 176–78 (generally), 188 (Dominican reaction to Heinrich von Rheinfelden).

24. Rey, "Police and Sodomy," p. 129.

25. Puff, "Localizing Sodomy," pp. 171–75 and 189–91, for the episcopal court records and a separate, contemporary account.

26. For example, the influential canonist Johannes Teutonicus, as in Brundage, *Law, Sex, and Christian Marriage*, p. 400.

27. As, for example, in the acts of the third Lateran Council (1179), conveniently translated in Boswell, *Christianity*, p. 277.

28. Puff, "Localizing Sodomy," pp. 172–73.

29. Rocke, *Forbidden Friendships*, p. 26.

30. Goodich, *The Unmentionable Vice*, pp. 89–123. Goodich translated the text from Duvernoy, *Le Régistre d'inquisition de Jacques Fournier*, 3:14–50.

31. Monter, *Frontiers of Heresy*, pp. 276–77.

32. Haliczer, *Inquisition and Society*, p. 303.

33. Monter, *Frontiers of Heresy*, pp. 284, 290.

34. Haliczer, *Inquisition and Society*, p. 304.

35. Carrasco, *Inquisición y represión sexual*, p. 174.

36. Perry, "'Nefarious sin,'" p. 79.

37. Carrasco, *Inquisición y represión sexual*, pp. 175–76. The parenthetical references in the rest of the section are to the pages of this same book.

38. Ibid., pp. 178–79.

39. Haliczer, *Inquisition and Society*, p. 304.

40. Perry, "'Nefarious Sin," pp. 79–80.

41. See, for example, Russell on inquisitorial procedure in *Witchcraft in the Middle Ages*, pp. 42–43.

42. Carrasco, *Inquisición y represión sexual*, p. 176.

43. Dante, *Inferno*, 15.112, for the sense of which see, for example, Musa, *Divine Comedy*, 2:218–19.

44. Boccaccio, *Decameron*, First Day, Second Story (Musa, pp. 34–35).

45. About whom see Dinshaw, *Chaucer's Sexual Poetics*, pp. 161–62.

46. Boccaccio, *Decameron*, First Day, Seventh Story (Musa, p. 48).

47. Rocke, *Forbidden Friendships*, p. 136 and note 107.

48. Ibid., pp. 94 (with note 35) and 104 (with note 126).

49. See the summary in Maggi, "The Discourse of Sodom."

50. Cited in Schleiner, "'That Matter,'" p. 48.

51. The story is *Le prestre et le chevalier* by Milon d'Amiens, noted in Baldwin, *Language of Sex*, pp. 46–47, 61.

52. Andreas Capellanus, *Art of Courtly Love* 1.8 (Parry pp. 141–42).

53. Rabelais, *Histories of Gargantua and Pantagruel*, book 1, chapters 45 and 52–57, respectively.

54. *Lazarillo de Tormes*, Tratado 4, as in Rico, *Novela Picaresca*, pp. 66–67. For the sense of this strikingly brief section, see Thompson and Walsh, "The Mercedarian's Shoes."

55. Hampe, "Eine Schilderung," with the text of the letter on pp. 528–35. The letter is treated as an authentic record of court life by Tillmann, *Papst Innocenz III*, pp. 234–36 (= English translation pp. 289–91); Brentano, *Rome before Avignon*, pp. 154–55; and Bolton, "*Via ascetica*," pp. 168, 177–78.

56. Hampe, "Eine Schilderung," p. 529 for the chaplains; p. 530 for the handwashing.

57. Walter Map, *De nugis curialium*, 1.24 (James, Brooke, Mynors, p. 80), on Bernard's failed miracle.

58. The poem "Nos uxorati," lines 6–8, as at Boswell, *Christianity*, p. 400. Boswell discusses a number of related texts on pp. 217–18.

59. D'Alverny, *Alain de Lille*, p. 43.

60. Jordan, *Invention of Sodomy*, pp. 102 (Paul of Hungary) and 134–35 (Albert the Great).

61. Bernardino of Siena, "Questa è la predica dello vizio della sodomia," p. 109, and "Della sodomia," p. 50.

62. Ibid., *De horrendo peccato contra naturam*, 3:280. On Bernardino's attack against sodomites, see Mormando, *Preacher's Demons*, pp. 109–63.

63. So Puff, "Localizing Sodomy," 178–81. For an exception in Reformation history writing, see Roper, *Holy Household*, 17–20, 255–58.

64. For example, only one of Luther's mentions of Sodom in *De votis monasticis* seems to me to allude to male-male sex specifically. He there quotes Ezekiel 16:49–50 and goes on to describe arrogance and luxury as threats to monastic chastity (Weimar *Werke*, 8:650–51).

65. Schleiner, "'That Matter,'" pp. 49–54.

66. Bray, *Homosexuality in Renaissance England*, pp. 19–21, 26, 29, 52.

67. Van der Meer, *Sodoms zaad in Nederland*, p. 372.

68. Schleiner, "'That Matter," pp. 63–65.

69. Voltaire, *Candide*, chapter 15 (Morize pp. 87–88).

70. Ibid., chapter 28 (Morize pp. 209–10).

71. Ragan, "The Enlightenment Confronts Homosexuality," p. 19.

72. The work is the *Histoire de Dom B . . . , portier des Chartreux* (1741), as de-

scribed in Jacob, "Materialist World of Pornography," pp. 183–87; and Ragan, "The Enlightenment Confronts Homosexuality," pp. 19–20.

73. De Sade, *120 Days*, pp. 203 and 255.

74. So, for example, Sparry, *Mysteries of Romanism*, pp. 211–14.

75. As in Mayerhoffer, *Twelve Years*, p. 244.

76. For example, Blankeney, *Manual of Romish Controversy*, pp. 87–89.

77. Chiniquy, *Fifty Years*, p. 445, in an approving reference to De Ricci.

78. "Scipio de Ricci," *Female Convents*, p. 190, narrating events around 1790 in Rome.

79. Butler, *Inner Rome*, p. 281, with regard to the trials of the "Ignoranti" near Turin.

80. Beecher, *Papal Conspiracy Exposed*, p. 167. There follows a quotation from Gieseler that speaks of "'unnatural vices'" (pp. 167–68).

81. McLoughlin, *Crime and Immorality*, pp. 144, 160–61.

82. Jenkins, *Pedophiles and Priests*, pp. 30–32.

83. Ibid., pp. 19–20, on the "history" in Burkett and Bruni, *A Gospel of Shame*.

84. Bray, *Homosexuality in Renaissance England*, p. 77. Compare Hocquenghem, *Le désir homosexuel*, p. 52 (*Homosexual Desire*, p. 88), on the "imaginary of homosexuality."

85. Veblen, *Theory of the Leisure Class*, preface, p. xxix.

CHAPTER SIX

1. Hendrickson, *Seminary*, p. 285.

2. Sipe, *Secret World*, p. 110.

3. "Papist Seminarian," "Death of a Catholic Seminary," p. 22.

4. Mauriac, *Flesh and Blood*, p. 16.

5. Carrier, "Miguel," p. 212.

6. Harvey, "Homosexuality and Vocations," pp. 44–45, following two Vatican documents from 1955 and 1961.

7. Clark, "Four Days of Heaven," p. 34.

8. Congregation for Seminaries, Letter of March 13, 1943, as in Tomassini, "Castità," p. 41.

9. Ibid.

10. Ibid. Tomassini also refers to the 1917 *Code of Canon Law* (*Codex iuris canonici*) canon 1371.

11. See the somber stories in Tomassini, "Castità," 47–49; Harvey, "Homosexuality and Vocations," 46; and Thévenot, *Homosexualités masculines*, p. 301.

12. Tomassini, "Castità," p. 42, with reference to Misani and Angioni.

13. Quoted in Harvey, "Homosexuality and Vocations," p. 45, note 3.

14. Sipe, *Secret World,* p. 105.

15. Pius XI, *Ad catholici sacerdotii,* section III, p. 40 (= *Enchiridion clericorum* no. 1388).

16. Biot and Galimard, *Guide Médical,* pp. 210–11, 213, after Valat's remarks in 1909.

17. Tomassini, "Castità," p. 34, paraphrasing Pius XII, *Menti nostrae.*

18. Quoted in Harvey, "Homosexuality and Vocations," p. 46, note 6.

19. Myers, *Seminary,* pp. 38–39.

20. Seery, "To the Statue of Youth," final stanza.

21. Kennedy and Heckler, *Catholic Priest: Psychological Investigations,* p. 60.

22. Harvey, "Homosexuality and Vocations," p. 53.

23. See Harvey's account of the intervention by "Dr. Kinane" during a retreat for "clerics with homosexual tendencies," in "Reflections," pp. 137–38. Compare Cavanagh, *Counseling the Invert,* pp. 147–48.

24. Harvey, "Homosexuality and Vocations," p. 54.

25. Herr et al., *Screening Candidates,* pp. 80–81. The other quotations in this section are also from these pages.

26. Lonsway, *Seminarians in Theology,* p. 48.

27. Potvin and Suziedelis, *Seminarians of the Sixties,* p. 47.

28. The "results" for "heterosexuality" and "aestheticism" are also singled out in the summary of research by Hoge et al., *Research on Men's Vocations,* pp. 22–23.

29. Potvin, *Seminarians of the Eighties,* pp. 14, 36–37.

30. Kraft, "Homosexuality and Religious Life," p. 372. Compare Cavanagh, *Counseling the Invert,* pp. 154–55.

31. Thévenot, *Homosexualités masculines,* p. 300.

32. Morris, *American Catholic,* p. 374.

33. Nugent, "Homosexuality and Seminary Candidates," p. 203.

34. Mahony, "Prayer Brings Men," p. 494.

35. Quoted in Nugent, "Homosexuality and Seminary Candidates," p. 208.

36. Ibid., pp. 209–10.

37. For example, John Paul II, "Seminarians' Healthy Psychosexual Development," p. 77, quoting *Pastores dabo vobis* no. 50. Compare Congregation for Catholic Education, *Directives on the Formation of Seminarians,* no. 34, quoting its own *Guide to Formation in Priestly Celibacy.*

38. Schweickert, *Who's Entering Religious Life?* p. 97

39. Nygren and Ukeritis, "Executive Summary," p. 264.

40. Quoted in Helldorfer, "Homosexual Brothers," p. 45, note 1.

41. Compare Woods, "Gay Candidates," pp. 28–29.

42. See, for example, Goergen, *Sexual Celibate*, pp. 190–96; Struzzo, "Intimate Relationships," pp. 107–9; James and Evelyn Whitehead, "Three Passages of Maturity"; and Coleman, "Homosexual Question," pp. 13–14.

43. For example, Pennington, "Vocation Discernment," throughout.

44. See, for example, Anonymous, "Sex, Sexuality, and Religious Formation," pp. 10–13.

45. Helminiak, "A Policy," p. 27.

46. Coleman, "Homosexual Question," p. 17.

47. Compare Gramick, "Surfacing the Issues," pp. 95–96.

48. Coleman, "Homosexual Question," p. 18.

49. Thévenot, *Homosexualités masculines,* p. 301.

50. Coleman, "Homosexual Question," p. 18.

51. Woods, "Gay Candidates," p. 25.

52. Nugent, "Seminary and Religious Candidates," p. 114.

53. Shekleton, "Homosexuality and the Priesthood," p. 15. I paraphrase his three main points and add one of my own.

54. Murdoch, *The Bell,* p. 99, of an Anglican priest in an experimental contemplative community.

55. Scott-Moncrieff, "Evensong and Morwe Song" (1907), of an Anglican priest, as in *Pages Passed,* edited by Mitchell and Leavitt, p. 380.

56. For example, Woods, "Gay Candidates," pp. 32–34. A "realistic" parable about violent denial is told in the "Joachim" section of Carson, *Brothers in Arms.*

57. Marcetteau, *Major Seminarian,* title page.

58. Tomassini, "Castità," pp. 36–37.

59. All mentioned in ibid., p. 37, with special reference to the Congregation's circular letter of April 28, 1949.

60. Cited in Tomassini, "Castità," p. 37.

61. Rodriguez, *Practice of Perfection* 20.1 (Rickaby 3:232).

62. Hendrickson, *Seminary,* p. 23.

63. Biot and Galimard, *Guide Médical,* p. 270.

64. See the excuses, for example, in ibid., p. 277.

65. For example, Rodriguez, *Practice of Perfection* 20.1 (Rickaby 3:229).

66. Schweickert, "God Calls," p. 241, summarizing the reactions in religious communities to openly gay or lesbian candidates.

67. "Father David" in Stuart, *Chosen,* p. 38.

68. Kelty, "The Land," p. 146.

69. "Father Simon" in Stuart, *Chosen,* p. 44.

70. Congregation for the Sacraments, *Quam ingens Ecclesiae,* section 2,

nos. 6–7 (pp. 123–24), and the points of inquiry in appendices 2 and 3 (pp. 128–29).

71. Thévenot, *Homosexualités masculines,* p. 300.

72. See the suggestive but impressionistic remarks in Betsky, *Queer Space,* pp. 42–43.

73. Hendrickson, *Seminary,* p. 98.

74. Rodriguez, *Days of Obligation,* p. 30.

75. Sipe, *Secret World,* p. 123.

76. "Father Terry" in Rosser, *Gay Catholics,* p. 115.

77. See the testimonies of "Len" in Rosser, *Gay Catholics,* pp. 49–50.

78. Toby Johnson in Holtz, *Listen,* p. 40.

79. Joe Izzo in Holtz, *Listen,* p. 60.

80. "Father Brian" in Stuart, *Chosen,* p. 34.

81. Dubay, *Seminary Rule,* p. 87.

82. Marcetteau, *Major Seminarian,* p. 110.

83. Dubay, *Seminary Rule,* p. 88.

84. Ibid.

85. Rodriguez, *Practice of Perfection* 4.20 (Rickaby 1:259).

86. Schweickert, "God Calls," p. 245. For condemnations of "particular friend-ships" in women's communities, see Curb and Manahan, *Lesbian Nuns,* pp. xxiv, xxxvii (with reference to Mary Gilligan Wong), 63, 78, 87–88, 94, 101, 106, 123, and so on throughout.

87. Tom Cunningham in Holtz, *Listen,* p. 77.

88. Jim Bussen in ibid., p. 128.

89. "Father Paul," "We Shall Not Cease," p. 136.

90. See the testimonies by "Father Paul," "We Shall Not Cease," p. 136; "Father Aelred," "Without Shame," p. 171; Hilgeman, "Sycamore," p. 190.

91. Tomassini, "Castità," p. 34.

92. "Brian" in Rosser, *Gay Catholics,* p. 144.

93. "Lawrence," "Growth in Community."

94. Kropinak, "Wooden Beam," pp. 19–20. For more recent reflections on Catholic spiritual direction of lesbigay believers both inside and outside seminary, see Empereur, *Spiritual Direction.*

95. Sipe, *Secret World,* pp. 112–13.

96. Pennington, "Vocation Discernment," p. 238.

97. Derrick A. Tynan-Connolly in Holtz, *Listen,* p. 178.

98. Tom Kaun in Holtz, *Listen,* p. 203.

99. See the cautions in Jenkins, *Pedophiles and Priests,* pp. v–vi.

100. Hendrickson, *Seminary,* p. 167.

CHAPTER SEVEN

1. For those who do not believe the evidence of their own experience without notes, here is one testimony: "At the same time, some of those [gay] priests will take advantage of every gain (and having been there I know), frequenting clubs, dancing at gay discos and picking up young men for sexual liaisons" (Lynch, "Land Beyond Tears," p. 217).

2. Babuscio, "Camp," p. 20.

3. There are other ways of describing the curious gender of the Catholic clergy than by appealing to the category of "camp." Indeed, some other descriptions do a better job of showing how clerical gender is connected with macroscopic problems of gender in the church. See, for example, Ingebretsen, "'One of the Guys.'" My point in focusing on the category of "camp" is precisely to provide a microscopic description of something that we would prefer not to see.

4. Harris, *Rise and Fall*, p. 33.

5. Koestenbaum, *Queen's Throat*, p. 117. The parenthetical references in the rest of this paragraph are to the pages of this book.

6. Sontag, "Notes on 'Camp,'" with the quoted phrases from pp. 107–9. The most trenchant—and campiest—criticism of Sontag's essay continues to be Miller, "Sontag's Urbanity."

7. Rodriguez, *Days of Obligation*, p. 32.

8. I here step around the question of the relation of "Gothic" to "camp." I am not suggesting that they are identical—or that the Gothic style is nothing more than a species of camp. My point is that for gay men the two often overlap.

9. Hocquenghem, *Le désir homosexuel*, p. 12 (*Homosexual Desire*, p. 50).

10. Compare Muñoz, "Ghosts," p. 369.

11. I paraphrase Philip Brett: "All musicians, we must remember, are faggots in the parlance of the male locker room" (Brett, "Musicality," p. 18).

12. Sedgwick, *Epistemology of the Closet*, p. 140.

13. Shekleton, "Homosexuality and the Priesthood," p. 17.

14. Bloxam, "The Priest and the Acolyte" (1894), as in Mitchell and Leavitt, *Pages Passed*, p. 271.

15. For general arguments in support of this claim, see Hilliard, "Unenglish and Unmanly"; Dellamora, *Masculine Desire*, pp. 148–49, endorsing Hilliard; Shand-Tucci, *Boston Bohemia*, 1:178–95; Hanson, *Decadence and Catholicism*, throughout, but with a particularly forceful summary on pp. 24–26.

16. Hilliard, "Unenglish and Unmanly," pp. 181, 205–6.

17. Wilde, *The Picture of Dorian Gray*, section 11, in *Works*, p. 110.

18. Huysmans, *À rebours*, pp. 94–95.

19. Ibid., p. 324.

20. Waugh, *Brideshead Revisited*, p. 22.

21. On these three motives, see Hilliard, "Unenglish and Unmanly," pp. 190, 210, 205–6, respectively.

22. Koestenbaum, *Queen's Throat*, p. 35.

23. Bishop, "Leaves," pp. 434–35.

24. Roulin, *Linges*, p. xi.

25. Ibid., p. 10.

26. I follow the English translation in Sadlowski, *Sacred Furnishings*, p. 146.

27. Roulin, *Linges*, pp. 109–11.

28. Ibid., p. 119.

29. Anson, *Churches*, p. 185, to which compare his gentle mockery of priests avid for Roman styles on pp. 193, 194, 200, 202.

30. Nabuco, "Form of Vestments," pp. 251–53.

31. Sadlowski, *Sacred Furnishings*, pp. 148–57.

32. Ibid., p. 156.

33. Harris, *Rise and Fall*, p. 10.

34. The "Assemblée générale des catholiques en Belgique," quoted in McDannell, *Material Christianity*, pp. 167–68.

35. Quigley, *Church-Making*, p. 77.

36. Roulin, *Linges*, p. 11.

37. Collins, *Church Edifice*, p. 153.

38. John Ryan quoted in McDannell, *Material Christianity*, p. 174.

39. McDannell, *Material Christianity*, p. 175.

40. Tyler, *Screening the Sexes*, p. xx. Parenthetical references in this paragraph and the next are to the pages of this book. I have discussed Tyler at greater length in "Making the Homophile Manifest," part of the argument of which I follow here.

41. Tyler, *Screening the Sexes*, p. 20. Compare the remarks on "moral crusades" (p. 20), "the new homosexual militance" (p. 49), and "militant minorities" (pp. 52, 61).

42. See, for example, the scathing criticisms of *M*A*S*H* in *Screening the Sexes*, pp. 33 and 43 and the other deprecatory phrases on pp. 188 and 194.

43. On "Higher Sodomy," see Taddeo, "Plato's Apostles."

44. Roulin, *Linges*, p. 2.

45. Ibid., p. 9.

46. Pater, *Marius*, chap. 21, pp. 227–28 and 233.

47. The quotations are from Koestenbaum, *Queen's Throat*, pp. 39 and 113.

48. The portrait was widely published in the fall of 1950 when the archdiocese

of New York celebrated its centennial. A cropped version of it can be found in the special supplement of *The Catholic News* 65, no. 10 (October 28, 1950), section 2, p. 3C.

49. Steibel, *Cardinal Spellman*, p. 9.

50. Stephen Reynolds in Kaiser, *Gay Metropolis*, p. 109. Kaiser also reports Roy Cohn's refusal to discuss his close friendship with the cardinal (p. 77).

51. On Spellman's homosexuality, see Cooney, *The American Pope*, p. 109, with note 25 (some named and many anonymous sources); Hurewitz, *Stepping Out*, p. 174 (anonymous testimony relayed by Gore Vidal); and Kaiser, *Gay Metropolis*, p. 108 (anonymous testimony). I myself was treated to anecdotes about the cardinal's trips to parties on Long Island by friends of a retired chauffeur—at a book-signing in Atlanta.

52. Psychiatrist Margaretta Bowers in 1962, quoted in Waller, "'A Man in a Cassock,'" p. 10.

53. In a glossy insert for Abbott, from the 1998 *Official Catholic Directory*.

54. White, *Art, Architecture*, p. 135.

55. Lavanoux in personal correspondence, as quoted by White, *Art, Architecture*, p. 209, note 107.

56. Collins, *Church Edifice*, p. 150; O'Connell, *Church Building*, pp. 33–34.

57. For these and related documents, with attempts to interpret them optimistically, see Henze and Filthaut, *Contemporary Church Art*, pp. 12–13 (in the preface by Lavanoux) and 35–37 (in the body); O'Connell, *Church Building*, pp. 36–41.

58. The phrase comes from E. M. Catich, as quoted in McDannell, *Material Christianity*, p. 180.

59. Steinberg, *Sexuality of Christ*, pp. 24, 36, 41, and the "apprehension" of "public controversy" in O'Malley's response, p. 213.

60. As Rambuss points out so astutely in *Closet Devotions*, pp. 44–45 and p. 138, note 6.

61. Trexler, "Gendering Jesus Crucified," p. 107. Trexler himself goes on to argue, on pp. 115–17, that unspoken avoidance of homoeroticism has been a powerful motive in representations of Christ.

62. Ibid., pp. 113–15, on the treatise of Gilio da Fabriano (published in 1563); and Perez Escohotado, *Sexo*, pp. 211–14 and 219, on the treatise of Francisco Pacheco (published posthumously in 1649).

63. Psychiatrist Margaretta Bowers in 1962, quoted in Waller, "'A Man in a Cassock,'" pp. 9–10.

64. The two quotations are from Koestenbaum, *Queen's Throat*, pp. 145 and 49.

65. Harris, *Rise and Fall*, p. 20.

66. Jouhandeau, *Journaliers*, 20:240.

CHAPTER EIGHT

1. Nietzsche, *Beyond Good and Evil*, no. 45 (Colli-Montinari 5:66.23–26).

2. Gordon, review of Gilman, p. 27.

3. John Paul II, *Ad tuendam fidem*, nos. 2–3, referring to the Profession of Faith established by the Congregation for the Doctrine of the Faith on January 9, 1989. The three degrees of submission described in the papal letter have already been applied quite explicitly to the teachings about homosexuality. In December 1998, the CDF demanded that Robert Nugent sign a compendium of recent teachings arranged according to the degrees of *Ad tuendam fidem* (Nugent, "Statement").

4. Congregation for the Doctrine of the Faith, "Nota doctrinalis" (June 29, 1998).

5. Compare Syme, *Tacitus* (2:547): "Obedience to authority ('obsequium'), once fervently extolled as duty to the Commonwealth whoever the ruler might be, began to wear thin and look shabby, not least if the despot were benevolent: that kind of despotism enfeebles the will and blunts intelligence."

6. Sipe, *Secret World*, p. 117.

7. Townsend, *Leatherman's Handbook*, pp. 183–84.

8. Crowley, *The Boys in the Band*, act 2, p. 130.

9. Norberg, "Libertine Whore," p. 232.

10. Respectively, a motto of the Catholic Union of the Sick in America and remarks from a 1953 essay by Florence Waters, as quoted in Orsi, "'Mildred,'" p. 31.

11. In *God's Gym*, Stephen Moore has shown how far they can be read in that way.

12. Congregation for the Doctrine of the Faith, *Homosexualitatis problema*, no. 12, p. 550; substantially repeated in the new *Catechism*, no. 2358.

13. Kierkegaard, *Fear and Trembling*, Problema 1, especially pp. 60–61, 66–67.

14. Carlyle, as quoted in Moers, *Dandy*, p. 31.

15. Hazlitt, *Brummelliana*, as quoted in Moers, *Dandy*, p. 20.

16. Huysmans, *À rebours*, p. 262.

17. Klossowski, *La vocation suspendue*, pp. 59–68.

18. Schoenherr, *Full Pews and Empty Altars*, p. 353.

19. Paglia, *Vamps and Tramps*, p. 99; see also the approving summary of attacks on Foucault in Norton, *The Myth of the Modern Homosexual*, pp. 6–11.

20. Foucault, *Histoire de la sexualité*, 1:121.

21. Ibid., 1:123.

22. Halperin describes quite precisely both the self-defeating dialectic of "coming out" and the possibility that it might serve as an act not of liberation, but of resistance. See Halperin, *Saint Foucault*, pp. 13, 30.

23. Foucault, "Sex, Power and the Politics of Identity," p. 163.

24. Ibid., p. 164.

25. Foucault, "Sexual Choice, Sexual Act," pp. 141–42.

26. Ibid., p. 143.

27. Hocquenghem, *Derive homosexuelle*, p. 14.

CHAPTER NINE

1. Lancaster, "Litany for Divine Intervention." The phrases quoted next are from pp. 142 and 143, respectively.

2. Comstock, *Unrepentant*, p. 67.

3. Rodriguez in Crowley, "An Ancient Catholic," p. 263.

4. Ibid., p. 264.

5. Holleran, "The Sense of Sin," p. 83.

6. I follow the chronology in Roche, *Dignity/USA 25*, especially pp. 1–13. I have supplemented that chronology with the recollections of some of the first members of the L.A. chapter, compiled by Armand Avila and Jim Kyger.

7. See the opening summary in Baum, "Catholic Homosexuals," p. 7; and the personal recollections in McNeill, *Both Feet*, pp. 80–85.

8. Complete statement inside the front covers of Gramick, Nugent, and Oddo, *Homosexual Catholics;* and Leopold and Orians, *Theological Pastoral Resources*.

9. "Dignity Speaks to Bishops," in Leopold and Orians, p. 55.

10. McNaught, "The Sad Dilemma," in ibid., p. 76. The parenthetical citation following also refers to this article.

11. Zubro, *Only Good Priest*, p. 31.

12. Comstock, *Unrepentant*, p. 98, on the basis of the study by Primiano. Compare the women's testimonies in Curb and Manahan, pp. 91, 106, and so on.

13. For an account of the first service, see Perry, *The Lord Is My Shepherd*, pp. 131–38.

14. Wilson, *Our Tribe*, perhaps especially pp. 7–22.

15. Guy Hocquenghem, *La derive homosexuelle*, p. 57.

WORKS CITED

Lengthy bibliographies serve different purposes. Some are intended to establish an author's credentials. Others testify to an author's bibliomania. This does neither, because is not a systematic bibliography. In it, I mean only to give basic information about the sources cited in the text. I have selected the sources for different chapters using different criteria, but in no case do I pretend to have cited every important work on the topics discussed. There can be no such thing as a complete bibliography for any of those topics. They are too old and too complicated. These days, in any case, comprehensive bibliographies must be stored electronically.

Adam, Barry D. "Accounting for Sex." *GLQ* 3 (1996): 311–16.

Alan of Lille (Alain de Lille). *Liber poenitentialis.* Edited by Jean Longère. Analecta Mediaevalia Namurcensia, vol. 18. Louvain: Éditions Nauwelaerts; and Lille: Librairie Giard, 1965.

Albert, John. "Oscar Wilde and Monasticism Today: The Homosexual Question." *American Benedictine Review* 41 (1990): 113–40.

Andreas Capellanus. *The Art of Courtly Love.* Translated and edited by John Jay Parry. New York: Columbia University Press, 1960.

Anonymous. *Awful Exposure of the Atrocious Plot formed by Certain Individuals against the Clergy and Nuns of Lower Canada, through the Intervention of Maria Monk.* New York: Jones & Co. of Montreal, 1836.

Anonymous. "Sex, Sexuality, and Religious Formation." In *Nurturing the Gift: Gay and Lesbian Persons in Seminary and Religious Formation* (*CMI Journal* 11 [autumn 1988]), pp. 8–13.

Anson, Peter F. *Churches, Their Plan and Furnishing*. Revised and edited by Thomas F. Croft-Fraser and H. A. Reinhold. Milwaukee: Bruce, 1948.

Antoninus of Florence. *Summa theologica = Sancti Antonini Archiepiscopi Florentini Ordinis Praedicatorum Summa Theologica*. Verona: Typographia Seminarii, Augustinus Carattonius, 1740. Reprint, Graz, 1959.

Apuleius. *Opera quae supersunt*. Edited by Rudolf Helm. 2d ed., 2 vols. Leipzig: B. G. Teubner, 1955.

Arenas, Reinaldo. *Antes que anochezca: Autobiografía*. Barcelona: Tusquets, 1992.

Avila, Armand, and Jim Kyger. Letter to author, February 22, 1999, with a draft of reflections on the early history of Dignity compiled in 1998.

Babuscio, Jack. "Camp and the Gay Sensibility." In *Camp Grounds*, edited by Bergman, pp. 19–38.

Baldwin, John W. *The Language of Sex: Five Voices from Northern France around 1200*. Chicago: University of Chicago Press, 1994.

Barry, William A.; Madeline Birmingham; William Connolly; Robert Fahey; Virginia Finn; and James Gill. "The Experience of Phil" (in "Affectivity and Sexuality: Their Relationship to the Spiritual and Apostolic Life of Jesuits. Comments on Three Experiences"). *Studies in the Spirituality of the Jesuits* 10, nos. 2–3 (March–May 1978): 122–41.

Baum, Gregory. "Catholic Homosexuals." *Commonweal* 99, no. 19 (1974): 479–82. Reprinted in *Theological Pastoral Resources*, edited by Leopold and Orians, pp. 7–10.

Beecher, Edward. *The Papal Conspiracy Exposed, and Protestantism Defended, in the Light of Reason, History, and Scripture*. Boston: Stearns, 1855.

Benjamin, Walter. "Das *Passagenwerk*." In *Gesammelte Schriften*, edited by Rolf Teidemann, vol. 5, no. 1. Frankfurt: Suhrkamp, 1982.

Bergman, David, ed. *Camp Grounds: Style and Homosexuality*. Amherst: University of Massachusetts Press, 1993.

Bernanos, Georges. *The Diary of a Country Priest*. Translated by Pamela Morris. New York: Carroll and Graf, 1983.

Bernardino of Siena. *De horrendo peccato contra naturam*. In *Opera omnia*, vol. 3, edited by the Fathers of the Collegio San Bonaventura, pp. 268–84. Quaracchi: Collegio San Bonaventura, 1950–1965.

———. "Della sodomia." In *Le prediche volgari (Firenze 1424)*, edited by Ciro Cannarozzi. Pistoia: Pacinotti, 1934.

———. "Questa è la predica dello vizio della sodomia." In *Le prediche volgari (Siena 1425)*, edited by Ciro Cannarozzi. Florence: Rinaldi, 1958.

Betsky, Aaron. *Queer Space: Architecture and Same-Sex Desire.* New York: William Morrow, 1997.

Bieler, Ludwig, ed. *The Irish Penitentials.* Scriptores Latini Hiberniae, vol. 5. Dublin: Dublin Institute for Advanced Studies, 1963.

Billington, Ray Allen. "Maria Monk and Her Influence." *Catholic Historical Review* 27 (1936–37): 283–96.

Biot, René, and Pierre Galimard. *Guide médical des vocations sacerdotales et religieuses.* New edition. Paris: Spes, 1952.

Bishop, Edmund. "Leaves from the Diary of a Papal Master of Ceremonies." In *Liturgica Historica: Papers on the Liturgy and Religious Life of the Western Church,* pp. 434–43. Oxford: Clarendon Press, 1962.

Blankeney, R. P. *Manual of Romish Controversy: Being a Complete Refutation of the Creed of Pope Pius IV.* Revised edition. Edinburgh: G. M. Gibbon, after 1870.

Boccaccio, Giovanni. *The Decameron.* Translated by Mark Musa and Peter Bondanella. New York: Penguin, Mentor, 1982.

Bolton, Brenda. "*Via ascetica:* A Papal Quandary?" In *Monks, Hermits, and the Ascetic Tradition: Papers Read at the 1984 Summer Meeting and the 1985 Winter Meeting of the Ecclesiastical History Society,* edited by W. J. Sheils, pp. 161–91. Studies in Church History, vol. 22. Oxford: Blackwell, Ecclesiastical History Society, 1985.

Boswell, John. *Christianity, Social Tolerance, and Homosexuality: Gay People in Western Europe from the Beginning of the Christian Era to the Fourteenth Century.* Chicago: University of Chicago Press, 1980.

———. *Same-Sex Unions in Pre-Modern Europe.* New York: Random House, Villard Books, 1994.

Bouldrey, Brian, ed. *Wrestling with the Angel: Faith and Religion in the Lives of Gay Men.* New York: G. P. Putnam's Sons, Riverhead Books, 1995.

Boyd, Malcolm. "The Sexuality of Jesus." *The Witness* 74 (1991): 14–16.

Boyle, Leonard. "An Ambry of 1299 at San Clemente, Rome." *Mediaeval Studies* 26 (1964): 329–50.

Bray, Alan. *Homosexuality in Renaissance England.* Morningside edition, with a new afterword. New York: Columbia University Press, 1995.

Brentano, Robert. *Rome before Avignon: A Social History of Thirteenth-Century Rome.* New York: Basic Books, 1974.

Brett, Philip. "Musicality, Essentialism, and the Closet." In *Queering the Pitch: The New Gay and Lesbian Musicology,* edited by Brett, Elizabeth Wood, and Gary C. Thomas, pp. 9–26. New York: Routledge, 1994.

Brooten, Bernadette. *Love Between Women: Early Christian Responses to Female Homoeroticism.* Chicago: University of Chicago Press, 1996.

Bruguès, Jean-Louis. "Elements of Pastoral Care for Homosexual Persons."

L'osservatore romano: Weekly Edition, June 18, 1997, pp. 14–15. Translation of "Elementi di una pastorale per le persone omosessuali," *L'osservatore romano*, April 23, 1997, p. 6.

Brundage, James A. *Law, Sex, and Christian Society in Medieval Europe*. Chicago: University of Chicago Press, 1987.

———. "Playing by the Rules: Sexual Behaviour and Legal Norms in Medieval Europe." In *Desire and Discipline: Sex and Sexuality in the Premodern West*, edited by Jacqueline Murray and Konrad Eisenbichler, pp. 23–41. Toronto: University of Toronto Press, 1996.

———. "The Politics of Sodomy: Rex. V. Pons Hugh de Ampurias (1311)." In *Sex in the Middle Ages*, edited by Joyce Salisbury, pp. 239–46. New York: Garland, 1991.

Burkett, Elinor, and Frank Bruni. *A Gospel of Shame: Children, Sexual Abuse, and the Catholic Church*. New York: Viking, 1993.

Butler, C. M. *Inner Rome: Political, Religious, and Social*. Philadelphia: Lippincott, 1866.

Cahill, Lisa Sowle. *Between the Sexes: Foundations for a Christian Ethics of Sexuality*. Philadelphia: Fortress Press; New York: Paulist Press, 1985.

Cajetan, Cardinal (Thomas de Vio). "Commentaria" on Thomas Aquinas, *Summa theologiae*. In "Leonine *Opera omnia*" of Thomas Aquinas.

Carrasco, Rafael. *Inquisición y represión sexual en Valencia: Historia de los sodomitas (1565–1785)*. Barcelona: Laertes, 1985.

Carrier, Joseph. "Miguel: Sexual Life History of a Gay Mexican American." In *Gay Culture in America: Essays from the Field*, edited by Gilbert Herdt, pp. 202–24. Boston: Beacon Press, 1992.

Carson, Michael. *Brothers in Arms*. New York: Pantheon, Random House, 1988.

Catechism of the Catholic Church. New York: Doubleday, Image, 1995.

Cavanagh, John. *Counseling the Invert*. Milwaukee: Bruce, 1966.

Chiniquy, Charles Paschal Telesphore. *Fifty Years in the Church of Rome*. New York: Fleming H. Revell, 1886.

Clark, William. "Four Days of Heaven." *Le Petit Seminaire* 16, no. 1 (1930): 34.

Cleaver, Richard. *Know My Name: A Gay Liberation Theology*. Louisville: Westminster John Knox Press, 1995.

Codex iuris canonici [Pentecost, 1917]. Edited by Lorenzo Miguélez Domínguez, Sabino Alonso Morán, and Marcelino Cabrero de Anta. Madrid: Biblioteca de Autores Cristianos, 1951.

Codex iuris canonici, auctoritate Ioannis Pauli PP. II promulgati [January 25, 1983]. Vatican City: Typis Polyglottis Vaticanis, 1983.

Coleman, Gerald D. "The Homosexual Question in the Priesthood and Religious Life." *Priest* 40 (1984): 12–19.

Collins, Harold E. *The Church Edifice and Its Appointments.* Westminster, Md.: Newman Bookshop, 1946.

Comstock, Gary David. *Unrepentant, Self-Affirming, Practicing: Lesbian/Bisexual/Gay People within Organized Religion.* New York: Continuum, 1996.

Congregation for Catholic Education. *Directives on the Formation of Seminarians Concerning Problems Related to Marriage and Family* [June 6, 1995]. English translation in *Origins* 25, no. 10 (August 10, 1995): 161–67.

Congregation for Seminaries and Universities. *I Romani Pontefici* [Circular Letter to the Italian Bishops, July 25, 1928]. In *Enchiridion Clericorum: Documenta Ecclesiae sacrorum alumnis instituendis,* pp. 684–94. Vatican City: Typis Polyglottis Vaticanis, 1938.

Congregation for the Doctrine of the Faith. *Nota doctrinalis* Professionis fidei *formulam extremam enucleans* [June 29, 1998]. *Acta Apostolicae Sedis* 90 (1998): 544–51.

———. *Homosexualitatis problema* [Letter on the Pastoral Care of Homosexual Persons, October 1, 1986]. *Acta Apostolicae Sedis* 79 (1987): 543–54. English translation in Siker, *Homosexuality in the Church,* 39–47.

———. "Notification Regarding Sister Jeannine Gramick, SSND, and Father Robert Nugent, SDS." Dated May 31, 1999; publicly released July 13, 1999.

———. *Persona humana* [Declaration on Certain Questions Pertaining to Sexual Ethics, December 29, 1975]. *Acta Apostolicae Sedis* 68 (1976): 77–96.

———. Profession of Faith and Oath of Fidelity [January 9, 1989]. *Acta Apostolicae Sedis* 81 (1989): 104–6.

Congregation for the Sacraments. *Quam ingens Ecclesiae* [Instruction on the Scrutiny of Seminary Students, December 27, 1930]. *Acta Apostolicae Sedis* 23 (1931): 120–29.

Cooney, John. *The American Pope: The Life and Times of Francis Cardinal Spellman.* New York: Times Books, 1984.

Coste, Jean, ed. *Boniface VIII en procès: Articles d'accusation et dépositions des témoins (1303–1311).* Rome: Fondazione Camillo Caetani, "L'Erma" di Bretschneider, 1995.

Crowley, Mart. *The Boys in the Band.* In *Three Plays by Mart Crowley: The Boys in the Band, A Breeze from the Gulf, For Reasons that Remain Unclear,* pp. 1–131. Los Angeles: Alyson, 1996.

Crowley, Paul. "An Ancient Catholic: An Interview with Richard Rodriguez." In *Catholic Lives,* edited by Ferraro, pp. 259–65.

Curb, Rosemary, and Nancy Manahan. *Lesbian Nuns: Breaking Silence.* New York: Warner Books, 1986.

Curran, Charles E. *Catholic Moral Theology in Dialogue.* Notre Dame: Fides, 1972.

————. "Homosexuality and Moral Theology: Methodological and Substantive Considerations." *The Thomist* 35 (1971): 447–81.

————. "Sexual Orientation and Human Rights in American Religious Discourse: A Roman Catholic Perspective." In *Sexual Orientation and Human Rights,* edited by Olyan and Nussbaum, pp. 85–100.

————. *Transition and Tradition in Moral Theology.* Notre Dame: University of Notre Dame Press, 1979.

D'Agostino, Francesco. "Should the Law Recognize Homosexual Unions?" *L'osservatore romano: Weekly Edition,* May 21, 1997, pp. 9–10. Translation of "Matrimonio tra omosessuali." *L'osservatore romano,* April 9, 1997, p. 4.

d'Alverny, Marie-Thérèse. *Alain de Lille: Textes inédits.* Études de philosophie médiévale, vol. 52. Paris: J. Vrin, 1952.

"Dangerous Bedfellows" [i.e., Ephen Glenn Colter, Wayne Hoffman, Eva Pendleton, Alison Redick, David Serlin], eds. *Policing Public Sex: Queer Politics and the Future of AIDS Activism.* Boston: South End Press, 1996.

Dellamora, Richard. *Masculine Desire: The Sexual Politics of Victorian Aestheticism.* Chapel Hill: University of North Carolina Press, 1990.

De Villiers, Alexandre. "Roger Peyrefitte." In *Homosexuels et bisexuels célèbres,* edited by Larivière, pp. 276–77.

Dinshaw, Carolyn. *Chaucer's Sexual Poetics.* Madison: University of Wisconsin Press, 1989.

Dlugos, Timothy. "A Cruel God: The Gay Challenge to the Catholic Church." *Christopher Street* 4, no. 2 (September 1979): 20–39. Reprinted in *The Christopher Street Reader,* edited by Michael Denneny, Charles Ortleb, and Thomas Steele (New York: Putnam, Perigee, 1983), pp. 300–29.

Dowling, Linda. *Hellenism and Homosexuality in Victorian Oxford.* Ithaca, N.Y.: Cornell University Press, 1994.

Dubay, Thomas. *The Seminary Rule: An Explanation of the Purposes Behind It and How Best to Carry It Out.* Westminster, Md.: The Newman Press, 1954.

Duvernoy, Jean, ed. *Le Régistre d'inquisition de Jacques Fournier, évêque de Parmiers (1318–1325) (Manuscrit no. Vat. Latin 4030 de la Bibliothèque vaticane).* Toulouse: É. Privat, 1965.

Egerton, Brooks. "Therapy Ended Attraction to Teen Boys, Kos Says." *Dallas Morning News,* May 25, 1997, pp. 1A, 17A.

Empereur, James L. *Spiritual Direction and the Gay Person.* New York: Continuum, 1998.

Escobar y Mendoza, Antonio de. *Liber theologiae moralis viginti quatuor Societatis Iesu Doctoribus reseratus in Examen Confessariorum.* Lyons: Prost, Barde, Arnaud, [n.d].

Farley, Margaret. "An Ethic for Same-Sex Relations." In *A Challenge to Love,* edited by Nugent, pp. 93–106.

"Father Aelred." "Without Shame." In *Homosexuality in the Priesthood,* edited by Gramick, pp. 170–77.

"Father Paul." "We Shall Not Cease from Exploration." In *Homosexuality in the Priesthood,* edited by Gramick, pp. 134–44.

Ferraro, Thomas J., ed. *Catholic Lives, Contemporary America.* Durham, N.C.: Duke University Press, 1997.

Foucault, Michel. *Ethics: Subjectivity and Truth,* edited by Paul Rabinow, pp. 121–33. Vol. 1 of *Essential Works of Michael Foucault, 1954–1984.* New York: New Press, 1997.

———. *Histoire de la sexualité,* vol. 1: *La volonté de savoir.* Paris: NRF, Gallimard, 1976.

———. "Sex, Power and the Politics of Identity" [interview with B. Gallagher and A. Wilson]. *The Advocate* no. 400 (7 August 1984), pp. 26–30 and 58. Reprinted in Foucault, *Ethics: Subjectivity and Truth,* edited by Rabinow, pp. 163–73.

———. "Sexual Choice, Sexual Act" [interview with James O'Higgins]. *Salmagundi* 58–59 (fall 1982/winter 1983): 10–24. Reprinted in Foucault, *Ethics: Subjectivity and Truth,* edited by Rabinow, pp. 141–56.

Fox, Thomas C. *Sexuality and Catholicism.* New York: George Braziller, 1995.

Frantzen, Allen J. *Before the Closet: Same-Sex Love from* Beowulf *to* Angels in America. Chicago: University of Chicago Press, 1998.

Füser, Thomas. "Der Leib ist das Grab der Seele: Der institutionelle Umgang mit sexueller Devianz in cluniazensischen Klöstern des 13. und frühen 14. Jahrhunderts." In *De ordine vitae: Zu Normvorstellungen, Organisationsformen und Schriftgebrauch im mittelalterlichen Ordenswesen,* edited by Gert Melville, pp. 187–245. Vita regularis: Ordnungen und Deutungen religiosen Lebens im Mittelalter, vol. 1. Munster: Lit, 1996.

Gilmour-Bryson, Anne. "Sodomy and the Knights Templar." *Journal of the History of Sexuality* 7 (1996): 151–83.

Ginzburg, Carlo. "The Inquisitor as Anthropologist." In *Clues, Myths, and the Historical Method.* Translated by John and Anne C. Tedeschi, pp. 156–64. Baltimore: Johns Hopkins University Press, 1989.

Goergen, Donald. *The Sexual Celibate.* New York: Crossroad/Seabury, 1974.

Goldberg, Jonathan, ed. *Reclaiming Sodom.* New York: Routledge, 1994.

Goodich, Michael. "Sodomy in Ecclesiastical Law and Theory." *Journal of Homosexuality* 1, no. 4 (1976): 427–34.

———. *The Unmentionable Vice: Homosexuality in the Later Medieval Period.* Santa Barbara: Clio Press, American Bibliographical Center, 1979.

Gordon, Mary. Review of *Faith, Sex and Mystery,* by Richard Gilman. *New York Times Book Review,* January 18, 1987.

Gramick, Jeannine, ed. *Homosexuality in the Priesthood and the Religious Life.* New York: Crossroad, 1989.

———. "Rome Speaks, the Church Responds." In *The Vatican and Homosexuality,* edited by Gramick and Furey, pp. 93–104.

Gramick, Jeannine, and Pat Furey, eds. *The Vatican and Homosexuality: Reactions to the "Letter to the Bishops of the Catholic Church on the Pastoral Care of Homosexual Persons."* New York: Crossroad, 1988.

Gramick, Jeannine, and Robert Nugent, eds. *Voices of Hope: A Collection of Positive Catholic Writings on Gay and Lesbian Issues.* New York: Center for Homophobia Education, 1995.

Gramick, Jeannine; Robert Nugent; and Thomas Oddo. *Homosexual Catholics: A Primer for Discussion.* Fourth printing. N.p.: Dignity, 1977.

Greeley, Andrew M. *Priests in the United States: Reflections on a Survey.* Garden City, N.Y.: Doubleday, 1972.

Greenberg, David F. *The Construction of Homosexuality.* Chicago: University of Chicago Press, 1988.

Grelon, Jean. "Homosexualité et pratique judiciaire de l'Église: Vers un nouveau regard des tribunaux ecclésiastiques?" In *L'homosexuel(le) dans les sociétés,* edited by Schlick and Zimmermann, pp. 9–14.

Griffin, Leslie. "American Catholic Sexual Ethics, 1789–1989." Reprinted in *Dialogue about Catholic Sexual Teaching,* edited by Charles E. Curran and Richard A. McCormick, pp. 453–84. Readings in Moral Theology, vol. 8. New York: Paulist Press, 1993.

Gunn, D. W., and J. Murat. "Roger Peyrefitte" [interview published in 1979]. Excerpted in Leyland, ed., *Gay Roots,* p. 412.

Haliczer, Stephen. *Inquisition and Society in the Kingdom of Valencia, 1478–1834.* Berkeley: University of California Press, 1990.

Halperin, David. *One Hundred Years of Homosexuality and Other Essays on Greek Love.* New York: Routledge, 1990.

———. *Saint Foucault: Towards a Gay Hagiography.* New York: Oxford University Press, 1995.

Hampe, Karl. "Eine Schilderung des Sommeraufenthaltes der römischen Kurie unter Innocenz III. in Subiaco 1202." *Historische Vierteljahrschrift* 8 (1905): 509–35.

Hanigan, James P. "Sexual Orientation and Human Rights: A Roman Catholic View." In *Sexual Orientation and Human Rights,* edited by Olyan and Nussbaum, pp. 63–84.

Hanson, Ellis. *Decadence and Catholicism*. Cambridge: Harvard University Press, 1997.

Häring, Bernard. *Free and Faithful: An Autobiography, My Life in the Catholic Church*. Liguori, Mo.: Liguori, Triumph, 1998.

————. *My Witness for the Church*. Edited and translated by Leonard Swidler. New York: Paulist Press, 1992.

Harris, Daniel. *The Rise and Fall of Gay Culture*. New York: Hyperion, 1997.

Harris, Michael. *Unholy Orders: Tragedy at Mount Cashel*. Markham, London: Penguin, Viking, 1990.

Harvey, John F. "Counseling the Invert in Religious Life." *Bulletin of the Guild of Catholic Psychiatrists* (October 1962): 210–21.

————. "Homosexuality and Vocations." *American Ecclesiastical Review* 164 (January 1971): 42–55.

————. "Reflections on a Retreat for Clerics with Homosexual Tendencies." *Linacre Quarterly* 46, no. 2 (May 1979): 136–40.

Hazlitt, William. *Miscellaneous Writings*. Vol. 20 of *Complete Works*. Edited by P. P. Howe, after the edition of A. R. Waller and Arnold Glover. London: J. M. Dent and Sons, 1934.

Helldorfer, Martin. "Homosexual Brothers: Sources of New Life." In *Prejudice*, edited by Timothy McCarthy, pp. 42–45. Romeoville, Ill.: Christian Brothers National Office, 1982.

Helminiak, Daniel A. "A Policy on Gay Seminarians." In *Nurturing the Gift: Gay and Lesbian Persons in Seminary and Religious Formation* (*CMI Journal* 11 [autumn 1988]), pp. 21–28.

Hemrick, Eugene F., and James J. Walsh. *Seminarians in the Nineties: A National Study of Seminarians in Theology*. Washington, D.C.: National Catholic Educational Association, 1993.

Hemrick, Eugene F., and Dean R. Hoge. *Seminarians in Theology: A National Profile*. Washington, D.C.: USCC, 1985.

Hendrickson, Paul. *Seminary: A Search*. New York: Simon and Schuster, Summit Books, 1983.

Henze, Anton, and Theodor Filthaut. *Contemporary Church Art*. Translated by Cecily Hastings, edited by Maurice Lavanoux. New York: Sheed and Ward, 1956.

Herdt, Gilbert H. "Fetish and Fantasy in Sambia Initiation." In *Rituals of Manhood: Male Initiation in Papua New Guinea*, edited by Herdt, pp. 44–98. Berkeley and Los Angeles: University of California Press, 1982.

————. *Guardians of the Flutes: Idioms of Masculinity*. New York: McGraw-Hill, 1981.

———, ed. *Third Sex, Third Gender: Beyond Sexual Dimorphism in Culture and History.* New York: Zone Books, 1994.

Herman, Didi. *The Antigay Agenda: Orthodox Vision and the Christian Right.* Chicago: University of Chicago Press, 1997.

Herr, Vincent V.; Magda B. Arnold; Charles A. Weisgerber; and Paul F. D'Arcy. *Screening Candidates for the Priesthood and Religious Life.* Chicago: Loyola University Press, 1964.

Hilgeman, John P. "The Sycamore Is Not the Only Kind of Tree outside My Window." In *Homosexuality in the Priesthood,* edited by Gramick, pp. 181–93.

Hilliard, David. "Unenglish and Unmanly: Anglo-Catholicism and Homosexuality." *Victorian Studies* 25 (1981–1982): 181–210.

Hocquenghem, Guy. *La derive homosexuelle.* Paris: Jean-Pierre Delarge, 1977.

———. *Le désir homosexuel.* 2d edition. Paris: Jean-Pierre Delarge, 1972. English version: *Homosexual Desire.* Translated by Daniella Dangoor, with a preface by Jeffrey Weeks and an introduction by Michael Moon. Durham, N.C.: Duke University Press, 1993.

Hoge, Dean R. *The Future of Catholic Leadership: Responses to the Priest Shortage.* Kansas City, Mo.: Sheed and Ward, 1987.

Hoge, Dean R.; Raymond H. Potvin; and Kathleen M. Ferry. *Research on Men's Vocations to the Priesthood and the Religious Life.* Washington, D.C.: USCC, 1984.

Holleran, Andrew. "The Sense of Sin." In *Wrestling with the Angel,* edited by Bouldrey, pp. 83–96.

Holtz, Raymond C., ed. *Listen to the Stories: Gay and Lesbian Catholics Talk about Their Lives and the Church.* Garland Gay and Lesbian Studies, vol. 6. New York: Garland Publishing, 1991.

Housewright, Ed. "Kos Trial Judge Warns Monsignor." *Dallas Morning News,* August 8, 1997, pp. 37A, 39A.

———. "Parents of Abused Boys Share Blame in Kos Case, Ex-Diocese Official Says." *Dallas Morning News,* August 8, 1998, pp. 1A, 34A.

———. "Priest Sought Bishop's Help in Kos Case." *Dallas Morning News,* May 28, 1997, pp. 1A, 28A.

Housewright, Ed, and Brooks Egerton. "Diocese, Kos Victims Settle for $23.4 Million." *Dallas Morning News,* July 11, 1998, pp. 1A, 24A.

Housewright, Ed, and Pete Slover. "Kos Arrested in San Diego on 8 Sex-Related Charges." *Dallas Morning News,* October 16, 1997, pp. 1A, 21A.

Huas, Jeanine. *L'homosexualité au temps de Proust.* Dinard: Danclau, 1992.

Hunt, Lynn, ed. *The Invention of Pornography: Obscenity and the Origins of Modernity, 1500–1800.* New York: Zone Books, 1993.

Hurewitz, Daniel. *Stepping Out: Nine Walks through New York City's Gay and Lesbian Past.* New York: Henry Holt, 1997.

Huysmans, J. K. *À rebours.* Edited by Marc Fumaroli. 2nd edition. Paris: Gallimard, 1977.

Ingebretsen, Edward J. "'One of the Guys' or 'One of the Gals'?: Gender Confusion and the Problem of Authority in the Roman Clergy." *Theology and Sexuality* 10 (1999): 71–87.

Jacob, Margaret C. "The Materialist World of Pornography." In *Invention of Pornography,* edited by Hunt, pp. 157–202.

James, Henry. "The After-Season in Rome." In *Italian Hours.* 1909. Reprint, Hopewell, N.J.: Ecco Press, 1987, pp. 190–96.

Jenkins, Philip. *Pedophiles and Priests: Anatomy of a Contemporary Crisis.* New York: Oxford University Press, 1996.

Jerome. *Liber interpretationis hebraicorum nominum.* In *Opera,* vol. 1, no. 1, edited by Paul de Lagarde, pp. 57–161. Corpus Christianorum Series Latina, vol. 72. Turnhout: Brepols, 1959.

Johannes Capreolus. *Defensiones theologiae divi Thomae Aquinatis.* Edited by C. Paban and T. Peguès. Frankfurt/Main: Minerva, 1967.

John Paul II. *Ad tuendam fidem* [Apostolic Letter, May 18, 1998]. *Acta Apostolicae Sedis* 90 (1998): 457–61.

———. *Pastores dabo vobis.* English translation in *Origins* 21:45 (April 16, 1992): 718–59.

———. "Seminarians' Healthy Psychosexual Development" [address to a group of American bishops during their *ad limina* visit]. *Origins* 23:5 (June 17, 1993): 77–78.

Johnson, William R. "The Good News of Gay Liberation." In *Loving Women/ Loving Men,* edited by Sally Gearhart and Johnson, pp. 91–117. San Francisco: Glide Publications, 1974.

Jonsen, Albert R., and Stephen Toulmin. *The Abuse of Casuistry: A History of Moral Reasoning.* Berkeley and Los Angeles: University of California Press, 1988.

Jordan, Mark D. *The Invention of Sodomy in Christian Theology.* Chicago: University of Chicago Press, 1997.

———. "Making the Homophile Manifest." In *Swinging Single: Representing Sexuality in the 1960s,* edited by Hilary Radner and Moya Luckett, pp. 181–205. Minneapolis: University of Minnesota Press, 1999.

Jouhandeau, Marcel. *Journaliers,* vol. 20. Paris: Gallimard, 1974.

Kaiser, Charles. *The Gay Metropolis 1940–1996.* Boston: Houghton Mifflin, 1997.

Katz, Jonathan Ned. *The Invention of Heterosexuality.* New York: Penguin, Dutton, 1995.

Keane, Philip S. *Sexual Morality: A Catholic Perspective.* New York: Paulist Press, 1977.

Keenan, James F. "The Casuistry of John Mair, Nominalist Professor of Paris." In *The Context of Casuistry,* edited by Keenan and Thomas A. Shannon, pp. 85–102. Washington, D.C.: Georgetown University Press, 1995.

Kelty, Matthew. "The Land I Love In." In *Homosexuality in the Priesthood,* edited by Gramick, pp. 145–50.

Kennedy, Eugene C., and Victor J. Heckler. *The Catholic Priest in the United States: Psychological Investigations.* Washington, D.C.: Publications Office of the USCC, 1972.

Kierkegaard, Søren. *Fear and Trembling, Repetition.* Translated by Walter V. Hong and Edna H. Hong. Kierkegaard's Writings, vol. 6. Princeton: Princeton University Press, 1983.

Klossowski, Pierre. *La vocation suspendue.* Paris: Gallimard, 1950.

Koestenbaum, Wayne. *The Queen's Throat: Opera, Homosexuality, and the Mystery of Desire.* New York: Random House, Vintage Books, 1994.

Kosnik, Anthony; William Carroll; Agnes Cunningham; Ronald Modras; and James Schulte. *Human Sexuality: New Directions in American Catholic Thought, A Study Commissioned by the Catholic Theological Society of America.* New York: Paulist Press, 1977.

Krafft-Ebing, Richard von. *Psychopathia Sexualis, mit besonderer Berücksichtigung der konträren Sexualempfindung: Eine medizinisch-gerichtliche Studie für Ärzte und Juristen.* "Dreizehnte, vermehrte Auflage." Edited by Alfred Fuchs. Stuttgart: Ferdinand Enke, 1907.

Kraft, William. "Homosexuality and Religious Life." *Review for Religious* 40 (May/June 1981): 370–81.

Kropinak, Marguerite. "The Wooden Beam in Our Eyes: Heterosexism in Formation Programs." In *Nurturing the Gift: Gay and Lesbian Persons in Seminary and Religious Formation (CMI Journal* 11 [autumn 1988]), pp. 16–20.

Labalme, Patricia H. "Sodomy and Venetian Justice in the Renaissance." *Legal History Review* 52 (1984): 217–53.

Lancaster, James. "Litany for Divine Intervention." In *Equal Rites: Lesbian and Gay Worship, Ceremonies and Celebrations,* edited by Kittredge Cherry and Zalmon Sherwood, pp. 140–44. Louisville: Westminster John Knox Press, 1995.

Larivière, Michel, ed. *Homosexuels et bisexuels célèbres: Le dictionniare.* Paris: Delétraz Éditions, 1997.

Laumann, Edward; John Gagnon; Robert Michael; and Stuart Michaels. *The Social Organization of Sexuality: Sexual Practices in the United States.* Chicago: University of Chicago Press, 1994.

"Lawrence, Chris." "Growth in Community." In *Nurturing the Gift: Gay and Lesbian Persons in Seminary and Religious Formation* (*CMI Journal* 11 [autumn 1988]), pp. 38–40.

Leopold, Kathleen, and Thomas Orians, eds. *Theological Pastoral Resources: A Collection of Articles on Homosexuality from a Pastoral Perspective.* 6th ed. Washington, D.C.: Dignity, 1981.

Leyland, Winston, ed. *Gay Roots, Twenty Years of* Gay Sunshine: *An Anthology of Gay History, Sex, Politics and Culture.* San Francisco: Gay Sunshine Press, 1991.

Liguori, Alphonsus Maria de. *Theologia moralis.* Edited by Michael Haringer. In *Sämmtliche Werke des heiligen Bischofes und Kirchenlehrers Alphons Maria von Liguori.* Abtheilung 3: Moraltheologische Werke. 2nd edition. Regensburg: Georg Joseph Manz, 1879.

Lonsway, Francis A. *Seminarians in Theology: A Study of Backgrounds and Personalities.* Washington, D.C.: Center for Applied Research in the Apostolate, 1968.

Luther, Martin. *De votis monasticis.* As in *Werke: Kritische Gesammtausgabe*, vol. 8. Weimar: Hermann Böhlan, 1889.

Lynch, Bernard J. "A Land Beyond Tears." In *Lesbian and Gay Visions of Ireland: Towards the Twenty-first Century,* edited by Íde O'Carroll and Eoin Collins, pp. 212–20. London: Cassell, 1995.

Maggi, Armando. "The Discourse of Sodom in a Seventeenth-Century Venetian Text." *Journal of Homosexuality* 33, nos. 3–4 (1997): 25–43.

Maguire, Daniel. "The Morality of Homosexual Marriage." In *A Challenge to Love,* edited by Nugent.

Mahony, Roger. "Prayer Brings Men Clamoring to Serve" [Letter to the Editors]. *Commonweal* 114, no. 15 (September 11, 1987): 494–96.

Marcetteau, B. F. *The Major Seminarian.* Paterson, N.J.: St. Anthony Guild Press, 1948.

"Maria Monk." *Awful Disclosures of the Hotel Dieu Nunnery of Montreal.* Revised edition. New York, 1836.

Mauriac, François. *Flesh and Blood.* Translated by Gerard Hopkins. New York: Carroll and Graf, 1989. Translation first published by Farrar, Straus & Giroux, 1954.

Mayerhoffer, Vincent Philip. *Twelve Years a Roman Catholic Priest.* Toronto: Roswell & Ellis, 1861.

McBrien, Richard P. "Homosexuality and the Priesthood." *Commonweal* 114, no. 12 (June 19, 1987): 380–83.

McDannell, Colleen. *Material Christianity: Religion and Popular Culture in America.* New Haven: Yale University Press, 1995.

McLoughlin, Emmett. *Crime and Immorality in the Catholic Church.* New York: Lyle Stuart, 1962.

McNaught, Brian. "The Sad Dilemma of the Gay Catholic." *U.S. Catholic,* August 1975, pp. 6–11. Reprinted in *Theological Pastoral Resources,* edited by Leopold and Orians, pp. 73–77.

McNeill, John J. *Both Feet Firmly Planted in Midair: My Spiritual Journey.* Louisville: Westminster John Knox, 1998.

———. *The Church and the Homosexual.* Kansas City, Mo.: Sheed, Andrews, & McMeel, 1976; 4th rev. ed., Boston: Beacon, 1993.

———. "The Christian Male Homosexual." *Homiletic and Pastoral Review* 70 (1970): 667–77, 747–58, 828–36.

———. *Freedom, Glorious Freedom: The Spiritual Journey to the Fullness of Life for Gays, Lesbians, and Everybody Else.* Boston: Beacon, 1995.

———. *Taking a Chance on God: Liberating Theology for Gays, Lesbians and Their Lovers, Families and Friends.* Boston: Beacon, 1988.

Ménard, Guy. *De Sodome à l'Exode.* Montreal: L'Aurore/Univers, 1980.

Michael, Robert T., et al. *Sex in America: A Definitive Survey.* Boston: Little, Brown, 1994.

Miller, D. A. *The Novel and the Police.* Berkeley and Los Angeles: University of California Press, 1988.

———. "Sontag's Urbanity." *October* 49 (1989): 91–101. Reprinted in *The Lesbian and Gay Studies Reader,* edited by Henry Abelove, Michèle Aina Barale, and David M. Halperin, pp. 212–20 (New York: Routledge, 1993).

Miller, Neil. *In Search of Gay America: Women and Men in a Time of Change.* New York: Atlantic Monthly Press, 1989.

Mitchell, Mark, and David Leavitt, eds. *Pages Passed from Hand to Hand: The Hidden Tradition of Homosexual Literature in English from 1748 to 1914.* Boston: Houghton Mifflin, 1997.

Moers, Ellen. *The Dandy: Brummell to Beerbohm.* New York: Viking Press, 1960.

Monette, Paul. *Last Watch of the Night: Essays Too Personal and Otherwise.* New York: Harcourt Brace, 1994.

Monter, William. *Frontiers of Heresy: The Spanish Inquisition from the Basque Lands to Sicily.* Cambridge: Cambridge University Press, 1990.

Moore, Gareth. *The Body in Context: Sex and Catholicism.* London: SCM Press, 1992.

Moore, Stephen. *God's Gym: Divine Male Bodies of the Bible.* New York: Routledge, 1996.

Moran, Gabriel. "Sexual Forms." In *Sexuality and Brotherhood,* edited by Martin Helldorfer, pp. 43–47. Lockport, Ill.: Christian Brothers' National Office, 1977.

Mormando, Franco. *The Preacher's Demons: Bernardino of Siena and the Social*

Underworld of Early Renaissance Italy. Chicago: University of Chicago Press, 1999.

Morris, Charles R. *American Catholic: The Saints and Sinners Who Built America's Most Powerful Church*. New York: Random House, Vintage, 1998.

Morrison, Douglas A. "Friendships in Religious Life—A Formational Issue." *Journal of Pastoral Counseling* 22 (1987): 77–86.

Muir, Edward. "Observing Trifles." In *Microhistory and the Lost Peoples of Europe*, edited by Muir and Guido Ruggiero, pp. vii–xxviii. Baltimore: Johns Hopkins University Press, 1991.

Muñoz, José Esteban. "Ghosts of Public Sex: Utopian Longings, Queer Memories." In *Policing Public Sex*, edited by "Dangerous Bedfellows," pp. 355–72.

Murdoch, Iris. *The Bell*. London: Penguin Books, with Chatto & Windus, 1962.

Murphy, Sheila. *Delicate Dance: Sexuality, Celibacy, and Relationships among Catholic Clergy and Religious*. New York: Crossroad, 1992.

Musa, Mark, editor and translator. *Dante Alighieri's Divine Comedy*. Bloomington: Indiana University Press, 1996–.

Myers, Rawley. *This Is the Seminary*. Milwaukee: Bruce Publishing Co., 1953.

Nabuco, Joaquim. "The Form of Vestments." *Ecclesiastical Review* 106 (1942): 241–54.

National Conference of Catholic Bishops [U.S.], Committee on Marriage and Family. "Always Our Children: Pastoral Message to Parents of Homosexual Children and Suggestions for Pastoral Ministers." *Origins* 27 (1997): 285, 287–91. (The revision, which is now the official version, appears under the same title in *Origins* 28 [1998]: 97, 99–102.)

National Opinion Research Center. *Catholic Priests in the United States: Sociological Investigations*. Directed by Andrew M. Greeley. Washington, D.C.: Publications Office of the USCC, 1972.

Nietzsche, Friedrich. *Jenseits von Gut und Böse (Beyond Good and Evil)*. In *Sämtliche Werke: Kritische Studienausgabe* vol. 5. 2d ed. Edited by Giorgio Colli and Mazzino Montinari. Munich: DTV; Berlin: de Gruyter, 1988.

Norberg, Kathryn. "The Libertine Whore: Prostitution in French Pornography from Margot to Juliette." In *The Invention of Pornography*, edited by Hunt, pp. 225–52.

Norton, Rictor. *The Myth of the Modern Homosexual: Queer History and the Search for Cultural Unity*. London: Cassell, 1997.

Nugent, Robert. "Homosexuality and Seminary Candidates." In *Homosexuality in the Priesthood*, edited by Gramick, pp. 200–18.

———. "Priest, Celibate and Gay: You Are Not Alone." In *A Challenge to Love*, edited by Nugent, pp. 257–77.

————. "Seminary and Religious Candidates." In *Building Bridges,* edited by Nugent and Gramick, pp. 105–120.

————. "Statement." Released July 14, 1999; revised July 15, 1999.

————, ed. *A Challenge to Love: Gay and Lesbian Catholics in the Church.* New York: Crossroad, 1983.

Nugent, Robert, and Jeannine Gramick, eds. *Building Bridges: Gay and Lesbian Reality and the Catholic Church.* Mystic, Conn.: Twenty-third Publications, 1992.

Nygren, David, and Miriam Ukeritis. "Executive Summary" [of survey released September 16, 1992]. *Origins* 22, no. 15 (September 24, 1992).

O'Connell, J. B. *Church Building and Furnishing: The Church's Way, A Study in Liturgical Law.* Notre Dame: University of Notre Dame Press, 1955.

The Official Catholic Directory for the Year of Our Lord 1998. New Providence, N.J.: P. J. Kenedy, 1998.

Olyan, Saul M. "'And with a Male You Shall Not Lie the Lying Down of a Woman': On the Meaning and Significance of Leviticus 18:22 and 20:13." *Journal of the History of Sexuality* 5 (1994): 179–206.

Olyan, Saul M., and Martha C. Nussbaum, eds. *Sexual Orientation and Human Rights in American Religious Discourse.* New York: Oxford University Press, 1998.

Oraison, Marc. *La question homosexuelle.* Paris: Eds. du Seuil, 1975. Translated as *The Homosexual Question* by Jane Seni Flinn (New York: Harper and Row, 1977).

Orsi, Robert A. "'Mildred, is it fun to be a cripple?': The Culture of Suffering in Mid-Twentieth-Century American Catholicism." In *Catholic Lives, Contemporary America,* edited by Ferraro, pp. 19–64.

Paglia, Camille. *Vamps and Tramps.* New York: Vintage Books, 1994.

"A Papist Seminarian." "The Death of a Catholic Seminary." *Homiletic and Pastoral Review* 95, no. 8 (May 1995): 18–26.

Pascal, Blaise. *Les Provinciales.* Edited by José Lupin. Paris: Le Livre de Poche, 1966.

Pater, Walter. *Marius the Epicurean.* Edited by Michael Levey. New York: Penguin, Viking, 1985.

Payer, Pierre J. *Sex and the Penitentials: The Development of a Sexual Code, 550–1150.* Toronto: University of Toronto Press, 1984.

Pelletier, Pierre. "L'intervenant pastoral et les homosexuels." *Sciences pastorales* [Ottawa] 6 (1987): 7–24.

————. "Morale et pastorale des homosexuels." *Sciences pastorales* [Ottawa] 5 (1986): 151–62.

Pennington, M. Basil. "Vocation Discernment and the Homosexual." In *A Challenge to Love,* edited by Nugent, pp. 235–44.

Perez Escohotado, Javier. *Sexo e Inquisición en España.* Madrid: Temas de Hoy, 1992.

Perry, Mary Elizabeth. "The 'Nefarious Sin' in Early Modern Seville." *Journal of Homosexuality* 16, nos. 1–2 (1988): 67–89.

Perry, Troy D. *The Lord Is My Shepherd and He Knows I'm Gay.* "25th Anniversary Edition." Los Angeles: Universal Fellowship Press, 1994. Originally published 1972.

Perry, Troy D., with Thomas L. Swicegood. *Don't Be Afraid Anymore.* New York: St. Martin's, 1990.

Peter Damian. *Liber Gomorrhianus = Epistola 31.* In *Die Briefe des Petrus Damiani,* vol. 1, edited by Kurt Reindel. Monumenta Germaniae Historica: Die Briefe der deutschen Kaiserszeit, vol. 4. Munich: MGH, 1983.

Peter Lombard. *Sententiae in IV libris distinctae.* Edited by members of the Collegium S. Bonaventurae. Grottaferrata: CSB, 1981.

Peyrefitte, Roger. *Propos secrets.* Paris: Albin Michel, 1977.

Pilant, Craig Wesley. "The Evolution of Pastoral Thought Concerning Homosexuality in Selected Vatican and American Documents from 1975–1986." In *Homophobia and the Judaeo-Christian Tradition,* edited by Stemmeler, pp. 117–45.

Pius XI. *Ad catholici sacerdotii* [Encyclical Letter on the Catholic Priesthood, December 20, 1935]. *Acta Apostolicae Sedis* 28 (1936): 5–53.

Pius XII. *Menti nostrae* [Apostolic Exhortation on the Promotion of the Sanctity of Priestly Life, September 23, 1950]. *Acta Apostolicae Sedis* 42 (1950): 657–702.

Potvin, Raymond H. *Seminarians of the Eighties: A National Survey.* Washington, D.C.: National Catholic Educational Association, 1985.

Potvin, Raymond H., and Antanas Suziedelis. *Seminarians of the Sixties.* Washington, D.C.: Center for Applied Research in the Apostolate, 1969.

Pronk, Pim. *Against Nature? Types of Moral Argumentation Regarding Homosexuality.* Translated by John Vriend. Grand Rapids: William B. Eerdmans, 1993.

Puff, Helmut. "Localizing Sodomy: The 'Priest and Sodomite' in Pre-Reformation Germany and Switzerland." *Journal of the History of Sexuality* 8 (1997): 165–95.

Quigley, E. J. *Church-Making and Church-Keeping, Including the Letter Issued to All Ordinaries and the Rules and Suggestions from the Cardinal Secretary of State, December, 1925.* Dublin: M. H. Gill & Son, 1926.

Rabelais, François. *Oeuvres complètes.* New edition. Edited by Mireille Huchon with François Moreau. Bibliothèque de la Pléiade, vol. 15. Paris: Gallimard, 1994.

Ragan, Bryant T., Jr. "The Enlightenment Confronts Homosexuality." In *Homosexuality in Modern France*, edited by Jeffrey Merrick and Ragan, pp. 8–29. New York: Oxford University Press, 1996.

Rambuss, Richard. *Closet Devotions*. Durham, N.C.: Duke University Press, 1998.

Ratzinger, Joseph, with Vittorio Messori. *The Ratzinger Report: An Exclusive Interview on the State of the Church*. Translated by Salvator Attanasio and Graham Harrison. San Francisco: Ignatius Press, 1985.

Rey, Michel. "Police and Sodomy in Eighteenth-Century Paris: From Sin to Disorder." *Journal of Homosexuality* 16, no. 1–2 (1988): 129–46.

"Ricci, Scipio de." *Female Convents: Secrets of Nunneries Disclosed, Compiled from the Autograph Manuscripts of Scipio de Ricci by Mr. de Potter*. Edited by Thomas Roscoe. New York: Appleton, 1834.

Rice, David. *Shattered Vows: Exodus from the Priesthood*. Belfast: The Blackstaff Press, 1991.

Rico, Francisco, ed. *La novela picaresca española*. Vol. 1. Barcelona: Planeta, 1967.

Roche, Pat, compiler. *Dignity/USA 25: A Chronology, 1969–1994*. Washington, D.C.: Dignity/USA, 1995.

Rocke, Michael. *Forbidden Friendships: Homosexuality and Male Culture in Renaissance Florence*. New York: Oxford University Press, 1996.

Rodriguez, Alphonsus (Alonso). *Practice of Perfection and Christian Virtues*. Translated by Joseph Rickaby. 3 vols. Chicago: Loyola University Press, 1929.

Rodriguez, Richard. *Days of Obligation: An Argument with My Mexican Father*. New York: Penguin, 1992.

Roper, Lyndal. *The Holy Household: Women and Morals in Reformation Augsburg*. Oxford: Clarendon Press; New York: Oxford University Press, 1989.

Rosser, B. R. Simon. *Gay Catholics Down Under: The Journeys in Sexuality and Spirituality of Gay Men in Australia and New Zealand*. Westport, Conn.: Praeger, 1992.

Roulin, Eugène Augustin. *Linges, insignes, et vêtements liturgiques*. Paris: P. Lethielleux, 1930.

Rudnick, Paul. *Jeffrey*. New York: Dramatists Play Service, 1995.

Ruggiero, Guido. *The Boundaries of Eros: Sex Crime and Sexuality in Renaissance Venice*. New York: Oxford University Press, 1985.

Russell, Jeffrey Burton. *Witchcraft in the Middle Ages*. Ithaca, N.Y.: Cornell University Press, 1972.

Sade, Marquis de (Donatien Alphonse François, Comte de Sade). *The 120 Days of Sodom and Other Writings*. Edited and translated by Austryn Wainhouse and Richard Seaver. New York: Grove Press, 1987.

Sadlowski, Erwin L. *Sacred Furnishings of Churches.* Canon Law Studies, vol. 315. Washington, D.C.: Catholic University of America, 1951.

"Salmanticenses." *Collegii Salmanticensis Fratres Discalceatorum Cursus theologiae moralis.* Venice: Nicolaus Pezzana, 1724.

Sanchez, Thomas. *Disputationes de sancto matrimonii sacramento.* 3 vols. Venice: Ioannes Guerilius, 1619.

Scanlon, Larry. "Unmanned Men and Eunuchs of God: Peter Damian's *Liber Gomorrhianus* and the Sexual Politics of Papal Reform." In *New Medieval Literatures,* vol. 2, edited by Wendy Scase, Rita Copeland, and David Lawton, pp. 37–64. New York: Oxford University Press, 1998.

Schleiner, Winfried. "'That Matter Which Ought Not To Be Heard Of': Homophobic Slurs in Renaissance Cultural Politics." *Journal of Homosexuality* 26, no. 4 (1994): 41–75.

Schlick, Jean, and Marie Zimmermann, eds. *L'homosexuel(le) dans les sociétés civiles et religieuses.* Strasbourg: Cerdic Publications, 1985.

Schoenherr, Richard A.; Lawrence A. Young; and Tsan-Yuang Cheng. *Full Pews and Empty Altars: Demographics of the Priest Shortage in United States Catholic Dioceses.* Madison: University of Wisconsin Press, 1993.

Schweickert, Jeanne. "God Calls, Religious Orders Respond." In *Homosexuality in the Priesthood,* edited by Gramick, pp. 237–45.

———. *Who's Entering Religious Life? An NCRVD National Study.* Chicago: National Conference of Religious Vocation Directors, 1987.

Sedgwick, Eve Kosofsky. *Between Men: English Literature and Male Homosocial Desire.* New York: Columbia University Press, 1985.

———. *Epistemology of the Closet.* Berkeley and Los Angeles: University of California Press, 1990.

Seery, Terence. "To the Statue of Youth, Jesus, in St. James Chapel." *Le Petit Seminaire* 9, no. 1 (1923–1924): 36.

Shand-Tucci, Douglass. *Boston Bohemia 1881–1900: Ralph Adams Cram, Life and Architecture,* vol. 1. University of Massachusetts Press, 1995.

Shekleton, John. "Homosexuality and the Priesthood: Vocations Off the Straight and Narrow." *Commonweal* 123, no. 20 (November 22, 1996): 15–18.

Sherr, Richard. "A Canon, A Choirboy, and Homosexuality in Late Sixteenth-Century Italy: A Case Study." *Journal of Homosexuality* 21, no. 3 (1991): 1–22.

Sherwood, Zalmon O. *Kairos: Confessions of a Gay Priest.* Boston: Alyson, 1987.

Siker, Jeffrey S. *Homosexuality in the Church: Both Sides of the Debate.* Louisville: Westminster John Knox Press, 1994.

Sipe, A. W. Richard. *A Secret World: Sexuality and the Search for Celibacy.* New York: Brunner/Mazel, 1990.

Slover, Pete. "Kos to Face Texas Trial in Sex Abuse." *Dallas Morning News,* October 18, 1997, p. 33A.

Slover, Pete, and Ed Housewright. "Kos Faces Possibility of Life Term." *Dallas Morning News,* October 17, 1997, pp. 33A, 37A.

Smith, Bruce. *Homosexual Desire in Shakespeare's England: A Cultural Poetics.* Chicago: University of Chicago Press, 1991.

Smith, Richard L. *AIDS, Gays, and the American Catholic Church.* Cleveland: Pilgrim Press, 1994.

Sontag, Susan. "Notes on 'Camp.'" In *A Susan Sontag Reader,* pp. 105–19. New York: Farrar, Straus, and Giroux, 1982.

Sparry, C. *The Mysteries of Romanism, Exhibiting the Demoralizing Influence of Popery and the Character of Its Priesthood.* New York: C. Sparry, 1847.

Steibel, Warren. *Cardinal Spellman: The Man.* New York: Appleton-Century, 1966.

Steinberg, Leo. *The Sexuality of Christ in Renaissance Art and in Modern Oblivion.* 2nd ed. Chicago: University of Chicago Press, 1996.

Stemmeler, Michael L., and J. Michael Clark, eds. *Homophobia and the Judaeo-Christian Tradition.* Gay Men's Issues in Religious Studies Series, vol. 1. Dallas: Monument Press, 1990.

Strasser, Robert. "Homosexualité et formation au ministère presbytéral." In *L'homosexuel(le) dans les sociétés,* edited by Schlick and Zimmermann, pp. 121–24.

Struzzo, John A. "Intimate Relationships: Heterosexual and Homosexual." In *Relationships: Issues of Emotional Living in an Age of Stress for Clergy and Religious (The Eighth Psychotheological Symposium),* edited by Sean D. Sammon, pp. 91–111. Whitinsville, Mass.: Affirmation Books, 1982.

Stuart, Elizabeth. *Chosen: Gay Catholic Priests Tell Their Stories.* London: Geoffrey Chapman, 1993.

Sullivan, Andrew. *Love Undetectable: Notes on Friendship, Sex, and Survival.* New York: Alfred A. Knopf, 1998.

———. *Virtually Normal: An Argument about Homosexuality.* New York: Random House, Vintage, 1996.

Syme, Ronald. *Tacitus.* 2 vols. Oxford: Clarendon Press, 1958.

Taddeo, Julie Anne. "Plato's Apostles: Edwardian Cambridge and the 'New Style of Love.'" *Journal of the History of Sexuality* 8 (1997): 196–228.

Tager, Djénane Kareh. "Des prêtres 'pas comme les autres.'" *L'actualité religieuse dans le monde,* no. 112 (June 15, 1993): 40–41.

Tettamanzi, Dionigi. "Homosexuality in the Context of Christian Anthropology." *L'osservatore romano: Weekly Edition,* March 12, 1997, pp. 5–6. Translation of "L'omosessualità nel contesto dell'antropologia cristiana," *L'osservatore romano,* March 1, 1997, p. 4.

Thévenot, Xavier. *Homosexualités masculines et morale chrétienne.* Collection "Recherches morales." 2nd ed. Paris: Cerf, 1985.

Thomas Aquinas. *Opera omnia iussu impensaque Leonix XIII. P. M. edita.* Edited by members of the Order of Preachers. Rome, 1882. Imprint varies. Cited here as "Leonine *Opera omnia.*"

———. *Scriptum super libros Sententiarum.* As in *Opera omnia.* Compiled by Roberto Busa. 7 vols. as supplement to the *Index Thomisticus.* Stuttgart: Frommann; Bad Canstatt: Holzboog, 1980.

———. *Summa theologiae.* Edited by the Institutum Studiorum Medievalium Ottaviensis. 4 vols. Ottawa: Studium Generalis Ordinis Praedicatorum, 1941.

Thompson, B. Russell, and John K. Walsh. "The Mercedarian's Shoes (Perambulations on the Fourth *Tratado* of *Laȥarillo de Tormes*)." *MLN* 103, no. 2 (1988): 440–48.

Thurston, Thomas. *Homosexuality and Roman Catholic Ethics.* San Francisco: International Scholars Publications, 1996.

Tillmann, Helene. *Papst Innocenȥ III.* Bonn: L. Röhrscheid; and Göttingen: Vandenhoeck & Ruprecht, 1954. Translated as *Pope Innocent III* by Walter Sax, Europe in the Middle Ages, Selected Studies, vol. 12 (Amsterdam: North-Holland, 1980).

Toledo, Francisco de (Franciscus Toletus). *Instructio sacerdotum.* Annotated by Andrea Victorellus and Martinus Fornarius, edited by Richardus Gibbon. Lyons: Fr. Anissoniorum & Joan. Posvel, 1679.

Tomassini, Dino. "Castità, requisito essenziale nel candidato al sacerdozio: La 'debita prova.'" In *L'esortaȥione "Menti nostrae" e i seminari: Relaȥioni tenute nel III Convegno dei Superiori e Professori dei Seminari Regionali e Maggiori d'Italia.* 2nd ed. Vatican City: Tipografia Poliglotta Vaticana, 1955.

Townsend, Larry. *The Leatherman's Handbook.* Los Angeles: LT Publications, 1972. Reprinted as *The Original Leatherman's Handbook* (Los Angeles: LT Publications, 1993).

Trexler, Richard C. "Gendering Jesus Crucified." In *Iconography at the Crossroads,* edited by Brendan Cassidy, pp. 107–19. Index of Christian Art Occasional Papers, vol. 2. Princeton: Index of Christian Art, Department of Art and Archaeology, Princeton University, 1993.

Tyler, Parker. *Screening the Sexes: Homosexuality in the Movies.* Rev. ed. New York: Holt, Rinehart, and Winston, 1972. New York: Da Capo Press, 1993.

Ulrichs, Karl Heinrich. *The Riddle of 'Man-Manly' Love: The Pioneering Work on Male Homosexuality.* Translated by Michael B. Lombardi-Nash. 2 vols. Buffalo, N.Y.: Prometheus Books, 1994.

Unsworth, Tim. *The Last Priests in America: Conversations with Remarkable Men.* New York: Crossroad, 1993.

Valdrini, Patrick. "Des ministres homosexuels." In *L'homosexuel(le) dans les sociétés*, edited by Schlick and Zimmermann, pp. 41–46.

Van der Meer, Theo. *Sodoms zaad in Nederland: Het ontstaan van homoseksualiteit in de vroegmoderne tijd*. Nijmegen: SUN, 1995.

Veblen, Thorstein. *Theory of the Leisure Class*. Boston: Houghton Mifflin, 1973.

Vernay, Jacques. "L'homosexualité dans la jurisprudence rotale." In *L'homosexuel(le) dans les sociétés*, edited by Schlick and Zimmermann, pp. 25–40.

Vidal, Gore. *Palimpsest: A Memoir*. New York: Penguin, 1996.

Voltaire. *Candide ou L'optimisme*. Edited by André Morize. Paris: Marcel Didier, 1957.

Wagner, Richard. *Gay Catholic Priests: A Study of Cognitive and Affective Dissonance*. Ph.D. diss., San Francisco Institute for Advanced Study of Human Sexuality, 1980.

Waller, James C. "'A Man in a Cassock Is Wearing a Skirt.'" *GLQ* 4 (1998): 1–15.

Walter Map. *De nugis curialium*. Edited and translated by M. R. James, revised by C. N. L. Brooke and R. A. B. Mynors. Oxford: Clarendon Press, 1983.

Wasserschleben, F. W. Hermann, ed. *Die Bußordnungen der abendländischen Kirche*. Halle: Graeger, 1851. Reprint, Graz: Akademische Druck- und Verlagsanstalt, 1958.

Waugh, Evelyn. *Brideshead Revisited*. New York: Everyman's Library, Knopf, 1993.

Weiss, Andreas. "L'homosexualité a l'Officialité de Rottenburg—Stuttgart." In *L'homosexuel(le) dans les sociétés*, edited by Schlick and Zimmermann, pp. 19–23.

White, Edmund. "What Century Is This Anyway?" *The Advocate* no. 762 (June 23, 1998): 55–58.

White, Susan J. *Art, Architecture, and Liturgical Reform: The Liturgical Arts Society (1928–1972)*. New York: Pueblo, 1990.

Whitehead, James D., and Evelyn Eaton Whitehead. "Three Passages of Maturity." In *A Challenge to Love*, edited by Nugent, pp. 174–88.

Wilde, Oscar. *The Complete Works of Oscar Wilde*. New York: Barnes & Noble, 1994.

Wilson, Nancy. *Our Tribe: Queer Folks, God, Jesus, and the Bible*. San Francisco: Harper and Row, 1995.

Wojtyla, Karol. *The Acting Person*. Analecta Husserliana, vol. 10. Dordrecht and Boston: D. Reidel, 1979.

Wolf, James G., ed. *Gay Priests*. San Francisco: Harper and Row, 1989.

Woods, Richard. "Gay Candidates, the Religious Life and the Priesthood." In *Call to Growth and Ministry* 4 (1979): 24–43.

Zubro, Mark Richard. *The Only Good Priest*. New York: St. Martin's, 1991.

INDEX

À rebours, 73
abbot, 120
abduction, 61
abortion, 100
Abraham, 125, 130, 220
abstinence, 45
activism, Catholic, 79; gay, 37–38
Adam, Barry D., 270n29
Adler, Alfred, 185
administration, church, 97, 143
Administrative Committee of the USCC, 47
adoption, 41, 45
adultery, 61, 135
Advocate, 249
Aelred of Rievaulx, 173–74
aestheticism, 154, 181, 186, 193, 200, 205, 208
Ahern, Patrick V., 198
AIDS, 47, 225, 250
Alan of Lille, 132, 260, 272n13
Albert the Great, 260, 274n60
Aloysius Gonzaga, 162
Always Our Children, 25, 43–49
ambition, 130
André the Chaplain (Andreas Capellanus), 131, 274n52
androgyne, 183
anger, 198
Anglicanism, 187, 240, 242

annulments, opinions on, 29
Anson, Peter F., 280n29
anti-Catholicism, 91–92, 134–35
Antichrist, 133
Antoninus, archbishop of Florence, 62–65, 260
Apostles, 55
Apuleius, 6
Aragon, 126
archbishop: of Florence, 130; of Milan, 93; of Los Angeles, 249
Arenas, Reinaldo, 92
Aristotle, 31
Arnauld, Antoine, 267n19
Arnold the Catalan, 126
art/artistry: bad vs. good, 183, 194; gay, 185; liturgical, 183; modern, 202; of Saint Sulpice, 195; religious (Catholic), 201–6
Art of Courtly Love, 131
artifice, 186, 193
asceticism, 76, 81, 219
atavism, 168
Augustine, 34, 109, 260
authority, 25, 49, 52, 55, 65, 69, 73, 78, 80, 220–22, 224, 226; Catholic, 213–15, 225; church, 91, 216, 245; ecclesial, 35; male, 212, 218,234; moral, 53; papal, 215, 222, 228

Avila, Armand, 283n6
Awful Disclosures of the Hotel Dieu Nunnery of Montreal, 91–92, 135

Babuscio, Jack, 181
Baldwin, John W., 274n51
baptism, 91, 233–35, 244
barbarism, 12
Basel, 123, 125
Basil, 172
Baum, Gregory, 268n38, 283n7
Baum, William (cardinal), 155
Beecher, Edward, 275n80
Belgium, 194
Benjamin, Walter, 15
Bernanos, Georges, 56–57
Bernard, 132
Bernardino of Siena, 63, 132, 260
bestiality, 61, 114
Betsky, Aaron, 277n72
Bible, 16, 48, 58, 76, 242
Bieler, Ludwig, 272n13
bigotry, anti-Catholic, 110. *See also* anti-Catholicism
Billington, Ray Allen, 269n14
bio-power. *See* reproduction
Biot, René, 276n16, 277n63
birth control. *See* contraception
bisexuality, 10, 101
Bishop, Edmund, 280n23
bishops, 26, 32, 39, 89, 121, 147, 243–44; American, 7, 25, 40–41, 43–46, 48, 93, 100, 155, 214, 227, 250, 260; college of, 216
Blankeney, R. P., 275n76
Bloxam, John Francis, 279n14
Boccaccio, Giovanni, 130–31
bodily creation, 76
Bohemianism, 12
Boniface VIII, 117–18, 121
Book of Gomorrah (*Liber Gomorrhianus*), 85, 114, 132
Book of Revelation, 67
Boswell, John, 126, 132, 173, 232, 265n19, 272n10, 273n27
Bowers, Margaretta, 281n52, n63

Boy Scouts, 223
Boyle, Leonard, 272n7
Boys in the Band, 217
Bray, Alan, 137–38, 274n66
Brett, Philip, 279n11
Brooten, Bernadette, 265n21
Bruguès, Jean-Louis, 266n31
Brummell, Beau, 221
Brundage, James A., 272n11, n14, n15, 273n26
Bruni, Frank, 275n83
Buckley, William F., Jr., 215
bureaucracy, 1n, 2, 8; church (Catholic), 74, 110, 214, 224, 239–40, 245–46, 254, 256, 261; ecclesiastical vs. secular, 60; papal (Vatican), 6, 53, 213
Burkett, Elinor, 275n83
Bussen, Jim, 278n88
Butler, C. M., 275n79

Cajetan, Cardinal (Thomas de Vio), 64–69, 260
calculus of moral probabilities, 68, 73
Callas, Maria, 191
Called to Compassion and Responsibility: A Response to the HIV/AIDS Crisis, 47
camp, 181–86, 189, 196, 201, 203–5, 207–8; broad or systemic, 184–85; clerical, 182, 201, 206; in relation to Gothic, 279n8; secular, 184
Campbell, Colin, 270n27
Candide, 134
cannibalism, 206
canon law, 48, 53, 121, 201, 213, 215. See also *Code of Canon Law* (1983)
canonists, 192
capitalism, nineteenth-century, 15
Capuchins, 123
Caramuel y Lobkowicz, Juan, 74
cardinal, 93, 118, 130, 135
Carlyle, Thomas, 282n14
Carmelites. *See* Discalcéd Carmelites of Salamanca
Carrasco, Rafael, 273n35, n37, n42
Carrier, Joseph, 275n5
Carson, Michael, 277n56

Castro, 92

casuistry, 59–60, 64, 66–74, 76

Catechism of the Catholic Church (1992), 25, 33, 48, 76

Catholic dandyism, 220–25

Catholic intellectual life, 214

Catholic moral theology. *See* theology, Catholic

Catholic movements, reforming (radical), 240

Catholic parents, 43–46, 48

Catholic Union of the Sick in America, 282n10

Catholic Worker, 250

Catholicism, 4, 6, 8, 10, 42, 50, 51, 53, 80, 82, 111, 144, 181, 183–84, 187, 202, 211, 214, 220, 226, 230, 241–42, 247–48, 252–53, 256–57, 261; gay, 235, 242; modern (contemporary), 7, 13–15, 25, 54, 87, 179, 200, 213, 215, 225, 234, 239; queer, 256–59

Catholics, American, 214, 218, 246; gay (Catholic gayness), 6, 9–13, 16, 56, 96, 212, 216, 218, 227–28, 233–35, 240, 243–45, 250–51, 253, 260; homosexual, 3, 36, 38, 41, 240–42, 247, 256; lesbian, 9, 96, 227–28, 234, 240, 245, 253

Catich, E. M., 281n58

Cavanagh, John, 276n23, n30

celibacy, 3, 8, 90, 105–6, 132–33, 135, 141, 144, 146–47, 149, 151–52, 156–59, 161, 165, 171, 180, 186, 219, 227, 243, 270n31, 271n32

charity, 81, 172, 213, 222, 258; fraternal, 171, 174

chastity, 26, 72, 133, 146–49, 151, 157, 162, 164, 174, 176, 224

chasuble, 191–93, 199. *See also* vestments

Chaucer, 130

Chicago, 147, 150

child-rearing, 7

Chiniquy, Charles Paschal Telesphore, 135

Christ, 2, 63, 202, 204–6, 238, 248; body of, 203–7, 243, 250

Christ's Passion, 219

Christian belief, 256

Christian ecumenism, 254

Christian life, 221; comparable to military service, 216

Christian Right, American, 36, 46–47. *See also* right wing, Catholic

Christian unity, 238–39

Christianity, 6, 8, 14, 187, 197, 202–3, 223, 241–42, 257, 259; Latin-speaking, 53

Christianity, Social Tolerance, Homosexuality, 126, 232

church courts (law), 120–21, 123–25, 129; judgments, classes of, 67; papal, 62; trials, 96, 121

church governance (policy), 2–3, 9

church hierarchy (Catholic hierarchy), 35, 224, 226–27, 249, 253

church history, 3, 15–16, 56, 93, 144, 211, 232, 239, 254, 257

church membership, 13

circumcision, 206

Cistercians, 132, 173

civil courts/civil cases, 122–23, 127

civil disobedience, 250

civil law, 34, 36, 41, 59

civil prosecution, 66

civil rights/protection, for homosexuals, 25, 32, 40, 42, 225, 242

civil trial, of Rudolph Kos, 95–98

Clark, William, 275n7

Clayton, Dan, 96–97

Cleaver, Richard, 269n43, n44

Clemangis, Nicholas, 135

Clement VII, 126

clergy/clergymen, 5, 5n, 8, 60, 66, 72, 85–91, 94, 98, 100–101, 103, 105, 108–12, 113, 114, 116, 120–21, 124, 126, 130, 135, 136, 141, 145, 146, 152, 160, 179–80, 189, 200–204, 217, 219, 224, 228, 247, 249, 254, 279n3; American, 106, 144, 180; closeted, 4, 6, 9, 16–17; diocesan, 5n, 132, 172; homosexual (gay clergy), 6, 104, 106–7, 109, 181

clerical garb. *See* vestments

clerical immunity, 66

clerical life, 181

closet, 4, 13, 89–90, 94, 99, 103, 107, 161, 181, 217, 220, 224–25, 260

Cluniacs, 273n23
Code of Canon Law (1983), 29, 275n10
Cohn, Roy, 110, 220, 281n50
Coleman, Gerald D., 277n42, n46, n48, n50
College of Cardinals, 118
Colli-Montinari, 282n1
Collins, Harold E., 280n37, 281n56
comic stereotype, 130–31, 136
coming out. *See* out/outing
commandments, 69, 71, 148
Commonweal, 106
communion, 206, 243–44, 248; with Rome, 238–39
communism, 92
community: Catholic, alternate forms of, 49; Christian, 12; building, gay, 9
compartmentalization, 89–91, 176
Complaint of Nature, 132
Comstock, Gary David, 283n2, n12
conception, 64–65
condoms, 47
confession (confessional practice), 3, 16, 70–71, 81, 85–86, 116, 135, 152, 217
confessional handbooks, 121
Congregation for Catholic Education, 276n37
Congregation for the Doctrine of the Faith (CDF), 2–3, 24–26, 33, 37, 40, 42, 47–48, 154, 215–16, 264n16, 268n39, 282n12
Congregation for the Sacraments, 277n70
conscience, 213
conservatism, 14, 220–21, 224–25
Considine, Robert, 198
continence, 154
contraception, 27–28, 31, 37, 100, 149, 223
convents, 91
Cooney, John, 281n51
copulation (coupling), 34, 62, 66, 69, 70, 71, 115, 137–38, 174, 177, 246; heterosexual (male-female), 61, 64, 71; homosexual (male-male), 35, 66, 207, 212, 247; irrational, 113; same-sex, 62, 64, 66, 71, 216
Cosimo Gheri, bishop of Favena, 118
Cosmas, 174
Coste, Jean, 272n3
Counter-Reformation, 72–73, 133, 142

crime against nature, 70, 113, 120
Crowley, Mart, 282n8
Crowley, Paul, 283n3
crucifixes, 203–4
crucifixion, 220
cruising, 4–5, 157, 169
Cuba, 92
culture: clerical, 6, 12, 179–83, 185–86, 204, 208; clerical, as an all-male hierarchy, 180; gay, 46, 98, 101, 157, 170, 182, 218; gay, American, 179
Cum primum, 121
Cunningham, Tom, 270n30, 278n87
Curb, Rosemary, 263n4, 278n86, 283n12
curia, 6, 89, 110
Curran, Charles E., 75–76
Cursus theologiae moralis (Salmanticenses), 69, 71
custody of the eyes, 162–63

D'Agostino, Francesco, 42, 266n32
d'Alverny, Marie-Thérèse, 274n59
D'Arcy, John, 155
da Fabriano, Gilio, 281n62
Dallas, diocese of, 95–96, 98
Dallas Morning News, 98
Damian, 174
Dante, 130
De Maistre, Joseph, 215
deacons, 121
Decameron, 130
Declaration regarding Certain Questions of Sexual Ethics (1975), 24–32, 34–35, 250
deflowering, 61
Dellamora, Richard, 279n15
demonologies, 74
denominations, lesbian and gay. *See* ministry, lesbian and gay
Des Esseintes, 188, 193
Desert Fathers, 172
desire: gay, 223; homoerotic, 107, 174, 186, 204, 214; lesbian, 9; sexual, 34. *See also* love
Diary of a Country Priest (Bernanos), 57
Dignity, 31, 39, 48, 96, 240–41, 244, 248–53, 260, 269n43

Dinshaw, Carolyn, 273n45
dioceses, 146, 159
Discalcéd Carmelites of Salamanca (Salmanticenses), 69–71, 260
discipline, clerical, 4–5
discrimination, 48
*Disputations on the Holy Sacrament of Matri-
   mony* (Sanchez), 66
dissent, 225–26, 228, 233, 240, 246
diva/diva worship, 182, 189–91, 193–94,
   198
divine, 7; law, 26–27; revelation, 26; will, 6.
   See also God's will
divorce, 66, 100
Dlugos, Timothy, 89
doctrine, church (Roman Catholic), 1, 4,
   54, 226
dogma, Catholic, 7
dominatrices, 213
Dominican order, 62, 172
Dorian Gray, 187–88, 193
doubts, 64–65
drag, 184–85, 198–99, 203, 207, 261
dreams, 12–13
drunkenness, 130
Dubay, Thomas, 278n81, n83
Durrell, Lawrence, 119
Duvernoy, Jean, 273n30

ecclesiastical courts, 122, 124
Edict of Faith, 126
education, Catholic, 96; moral, 74; religious, 33; seminary, 174, 177; sex, 164
Edwards, Rev. R., 102
effeminacy, 153, 177, 180, 184, 186–87, 194–
   95, 203–4
Egerton, Brooks, 270n28
ejaculation, 62, 70–71, 115, 147, 149
Ellis, Havelock, 234, 265n18
emission, 64 (*see also* ejaculation); nocturnal, 163–64
Empereur, James L., 278n94
employment discrimination, 41
enclosure, 163
ephebophiles, 94
Ephesians, 16

Ephrem, 162, 172
erections, 163–64
Escobar y Mendoza, Antonio de, 67–69
ethical personalism, 27
ethnic background, 41
Eucharist, 207, 227, 261
eunuchs, 199–200, 203
Evangelists, 67
evil, 33–35, 38, 49, 59
excommunication, 237
exempla, 62
experimentum, 148
Ezekiel, 35, 274n64

fabliaux, 131
facism: contemporary, 37; European, 36
fags, 92
faith, 12, 25–26, 33, 35, 49, 54, 137, 205,
   208, 213, 215–16, 220–21, 226–28, 234
Fall, the, 34
family: relationship, 66; reproductive, 36
family planning. *See* contraception
Farinacci, Prospero (Farinacius), 268n25
Farley, Margaret, 268n38
fellatio, 71, 206, 248; ritual, 87
Fellini, Federico, 184
feminine, vs. masculine, 180, 184–85
feminism/feminist theory, 3, 9, 36, 222,
   238
fertility, 223
fetish/fetishism, 187, 199
Filthaut, Theodor, 281n57
Florence, 122–23, 125
formation program, 159–62, 165–67, 170–
   71, 176–77
fornication, 61, 135, 216
foster care, 41
Foucault, Michel, 22, 72, 91, 229–32
Fournier, Jacques, 126
Fox, Thomas C., 271n31, n33
Frantzen, Allen J., 272n13
Freire, Paolo, 22
Freud, Sigmund, 265n18
friendship, 171–74
Fundamentalist sects, 135
funerals, 244

Furey, Pat, 264n16, 265n25
Füser, Thomas, 273n23

Galimard, Pierre, 276n16, 277n63
gay agenda, 36–38, 40, 46, 59, 104, 214
gay bar, 142
gay bashing, 37–38
gay liberation, 100, 195–96, 231, 250, 253, 255
gay lives (gay life), 3, 17, 21–22, 38, 45–46, 56, 59, 111, 231, 252–53, 259
gay marketplaces. *See* culture, gay
gay rights. *See* homosexual rights movement
gay sensibility, 181
gay visibility/invisibility, 185, 197
gays, 1, 10, 32, 38, 40, 44–45, 50, 78–79, 109, 237–38, 241–42, 245, 255
gender, 69, 75, 79, 81, 180, 184, 186, 199, 201–3, 206–7, 246, 279n3; and language, 251, 258; dissembling, 188; inversion, 203; third (or mixed), 199
gender roles, 180, 185, 263n3; stereotyping, 14
Genesis, 66, 125, 265n19
genital activity/contact, 27–28, 38, 174
genitals, 202–5
Gilman, Richard, 215
Gilmour-Bryson, Anne, 272n12
Giovanni della Casa, 133
gluttony, 130
God, 1–2, 6, 8, 26, 38, 45, 57, 62–63, 124–25, 129, 141, 159, 166, 194, 199, 205–8, 220, 226, 237–38, 240–42, 247, 250–51, 258
God's will, 2–3, 58
gods, Greek, 203
Goergen, Donald, 277n42
Golden Ass (Apuleius), 6
Gomorran Book. See *Book of Gomorrah*
Goodich, Michael, 126, 269n2
Gordon, Mary, 215
Gospels, the, 22, 81, 219, 255
gossip, 164
grace, 6, 34, 38, 78, 115
Gramick, Jeannine, 48, 264n2, n16, 265n25, n26, n28, 277n47, 283n8

greed, 14, 130
Greeks, ancient, 63
Greeley, Andrew, 106, 270n31
Greenberg, David F., 269n2
Gregorian chant, 214
Grelon, Jean, 264n8
Griffin, Leslie, 55
guilt, 5
Gumbleton, Thomas, 42
Gunn, D. W., 269n16
Gutierrez, Gustavo, 22

Haliczer, Stephen, 273n32, n34, n39
Halloween surprise of 1986, 40
Halperin, David, 91, 269n11, 271n55, 282n22
Hampe, Karl, 274n55, nn56
Hanigan, James, 264n4, n7
Hanson, Ellis, 279n15
Häring, Bernard, 54
Harris, Daniel, 182, 193, 281n65
Harris, Michael, 270n21, n27
Harvey, John F., 275n6, n11, 276n13, n18, n22, n23, n24
hate speech, 24, 38, 258
Hazlitt, William, 282n15
Heckler, Victor J., 276n21
hedonism, materialistic, 36, 59
Helldorfer, Martin, 276n40
Hellenism, 197
Helm, Rudolph, 263n2
Helminiak, Daniel A., 277n45
Hendrickson, Paul, 176–77, 275n1, 277n62, 278n73
Henry III, of France, 118
Henry VIII, 122, 133
Henze, Anton, 281n57
Herdt, Gilbert H., 87–88, 263n3
heresy (heretic), 112, 128, 228, 239
Herman, Didi, 265n22
Herr, Vincent V., et al., 276n25
heterosexuality, 38, 154, 175; Catholic, 223
Hilgeman, John P., 271n40, 278n90
Hilliard, David, 187, 280n21
historiography, gay, 232

history, 59, 230, 232, 245; sexual, 104, 269n2; theological, 21, 74

History of Sexuality, 229

HIV/AIDS, 44, 101, 104

Hocquenghem, Guy, 73, 185, 233, 260, 269n5, 271n54, 275n84

Holleran, Andrew, 248

Holtz, Raymond C., 264n15, 265n25, 266n40, 270n30, 271n41, 278n78, n79, n87, n97, n98

Holy Orders, 152

Holy Spirit, 2, 4, 35

Holy Trinity Seminary, Dallas, 96

homoerotic, 6, 8, 203; behaviors, 48, 223; ideation, 170; lives, 77; pleasures, 212–13

homoeroticism, 11–12, 184–85, 196, 228, 233, 247; Catholic, 8; clerical, 143

homophobia, 8, 12–13, 16, 23, 101, 110, 138, 158, 166, 182, 189, 220–21, 224–25, 231, 242, 244–45, 247, 256–57, 259

homosexual activity (action), 4–5, 38

homosexual lives (homosexual lifestyle). *See* gay lives (gay life)

homosexual rights movement (gay rights), 31–32, 41, 74, 223, 231–32, 253

Homosexualitatis problema (1986), 31

homosexuality: as a medicolegal term, 59–60, 71, 264n11, 265n18; as a political problem, 32–33; British, 187; Catholic, 7–9, 13–14, 21, 24, 181; clerical, 4, 11–12, 14, 86–88, 90–92, 94, 97–100, 105–6, 111–12, 113, 135; closeted, 110, 168 (*see also* closet); curable vs. incurable, 28–30; legal and scientific notions of, 29; male, 2–15, 17, 227, 229–35; meanings of, 108–9

homosociality, 108, 170

hope, 213

Hopkins, Gerard Manley, 215

horarium, 169

Horrendum illud scelus, 121, 122

house rules, 169

Housewright, Ed, 270n23, n24, n25, n26, n27

Hugh of Grenoble, 162

human person, 27–29, 32, 36, 264n3

human reason, 26, 31, 33

Humanae vitae, 31

humor, 181, 184, 205, 208

Hunt, Mary, 32, 49

Hurewitz, Daniel, 281n51

Huysmans, J. K., 73, 188, 222

hysteria, 90n, 92–94, 98–99, 106, 109–12, 113–14, 116–17, 119–21, 124, 128–29, 137–39, 165, 196, 202

iconography, 184, 199

identity, 9, 13, 242–43, 249, 251, 257–58, 260–61; gay, 107, 154, 166, 180, 200, 229, 252; homosexual/homoerotic, 160–61, 218, 229–33, 235, 258, 263n3; sexual, 109, 157, 170, 212, 246, 261; sexual, and holiness, 7, 257

ideology, 22

Ignatius, 215

Ignoranti, 275n79

imagination, literary, 10–12

Immaculate Heart of Mary, 184

impotence, 129

incest, 61, 135

Ingebretsen, Edward J., 279n3

initiation, 88

Innocent, 118

Innocent III, 131–32

Inquisition, 126–27

insemination, 69

institutions. *See* organizations

Instruction to Priests (Toledo), 66

intercourse, anal, male-female, 69–71; heterosexual, 149, 163. *See also* copulation

Internet, 214

invert, 9

irony, 181, 184, 186, 205, 208

irrumation, 71

isolation, 89, 147

Italian hermitages, 86

Izzo, Joe, 278n79

Jacob, Margaret C., 274n72

James, Henry, 263n1

James I of England, 118

Jenkins, Philip, 270n20, n22, 275n82, 278n99

Jerome, 16, 63
Jerusalem, 207
Jesuits, 66–67, 69, 103, 126, 133–35, 162, 188
Jesus, 174, 195, 201–4, 207–8; Catholic, 8; teenage, 151
Jew, 112, 128, 130
jewelry, antique liturgical, 184
Johannes Teutonicus, 273n26
John, bishop of Orleans, 119
John Capreolus, 267n10
John Cassian, 164
John Paul II, 24, 27, 77, 144, 215, 246, 276n37
John XII, 118
Johnson, William R., 79
Johnson, Toby, 278n78
Jonsen, Albert R., 267n5
Jordan, Mark D., 264n12, 265n17, n19, 267n6, 274n60
Jouhandeau, Marcel, 56, 208, 281n66
journalism: contemporary, 98; hysterical, 92
Julius Caesar, 63
Julius II, 118
Julius III, 118

Kaiser, Charles, 281n50, n51
Katz, Jonathan Ned, 264n10, 271n55
Kaun, Tom, 278n98
Keane, Philip S., 268n38
Keenan, James F., 267n5
Kelty, Matthew, 277n68
Kennedy, Eugene C., 276n21
Kertbeny, Karoly, 234
Kierkegaard, Søren, 220
Kinsey Report, 103–4, 176
kitsch, 183
Klossowski, Pierre, 56, 119, 223, 269n4
Knights Templar, 119, 122
Koestenbaum, Wayne, 182, 280n22, n47, 281n64
Kos, Rudolph, 95–98, 151
Kosnick, Anthony, et al., 268n38
Krafft-Ebing, Richard von, 29, 234, 265n18
Kraft, William, 276n30

Kropinak, Marguerite, 278n94
Kyger, Jim, 283n6

Labalme, Patricia H., 272n17
L'Alcibiade fanciullo a scola (Rocco), 131
Lancaster, James, 237
language: medical, 29; misogynistic, 204
Larivière, Michel, 272n8
Lateran Council III, 121, 273n27
Latin, 55, 67, 137, 161, 251, 264n3
Laumann, Edward, 99
Lavanoux, Maurice, 281n55, n57
laws, 67, 74; Old and New, 30–31; Old Testament, 76
laypeople (laity), 5, 16, 72, 88, 101, 124, 126, 131, 160, 226, 228, 272n15
Lazarillo de Tormes, 131
Leatherman's Handbook, 217
Leavitt, David, 277n55, 279n14
legislation, 8; antisodomy, 122
Leo X, 118
Leopold, Kathleen, 283n8, n9
lesbian lives (lesbian life), 3, 111, 253
lesbians/lesbianism, 1, 9–10, 38, 40, 44–45, 50, 78–79, 109, 225, 237–38, 241–42, 245, 255
lesbigay, 10; activism, 79; Catholics, 45–46, 48, 239, 241, 248–49, 256, 278n94; church, 254–56; culture, 242; theology, 79–80, 258
Letter to all Catholic Bishops on the Pastoral Care of Homosexual Persons (1986), 24–25, 31–42, 48, 55, 57, 248, 250–51
Levitical rules, 35
Leviticus, 121, 265n20
Leyland, Winston, 271n39
LGBT (lesbian, gay, bisexual, transgendered), 10
liberation movements, 79
liberation theology, 3, 22, 36, 78–81, 268n38
Liguori, Alphonsus, 27, 34, 71–73, 260
litigation, contemporary, 98
Liturgical Arts Society, 201
Liturgical Movement, 188, 191, 194–95
liturgical performance, 185, 188–91

liturgical quarrels, 193–97, 203, 222
liturgical rite, Byzantine, 173
liturgists, 190, 192, 194, 197, 201
liturgy, 12, 39, 146, 180, 186, 187–91, 193–94, 213, 237, 240, 244, 247, 249, 251, 252, 254, 259; committees, 189; Episcopal, 254
Liturgy Queen, 189, 191, 193, 195, 207, 222, 251
Long Island/New England District of the Christian Brothers, 156
Lonsway, Francis A., 276n26
Loreto, shrine of, 122
Los Angeles, 146, 155, 248–50, 253; archdiocese of, 249
Los Angeles Free Press, 249
love (desires): female-male, 16; male-male, 9–10, 31, 175, 260; same-sex, 3, 7–8, 10, 16, 52, 59, 78, 81, 88, 111, 139, 229
Lucerne, 122
Luke, 156
Luther, Martin, 118, 133
luxuria, 60–63, 71
luxury, 199
Lynch, Bernard J., 279n1

Maggi, Armando, 273n49
Magisterium (Teaching Authority), of the Catholic Church, 25, 213, 216, 259
Maguire, Daniel, 268n38
Mahony, Roger, 106, 155
Major Seminarian, The, 161
male bonding, 108
Manahan, Nancy, 263n4, 278n86, 283n12
Manning, Timothy, 249
Many Faces of AIDS, The, 47
Marcetteau, B. F., 277n57, 278n82
Maria Monk, 91–92, 135
Maritain, Jacques, 215
marital love, 23
marriage, 7, 23, 27, 29, 37, 42, 153, 166; heterosexual, 77, 271n32; gay (weddings), 106, 222; law, 142; same-sex, 173
Martinucci, 190
Marxism, 36, 222
Mary (Blessed Virgin), 201, 214
masculinity, 114, 206, 212

masochism, 218–19, 245
mass, 183, 186–87, 189, 191–92, 195, 208, 217, 229, 240, 243, 250–52
masturbation, 26, 28, 30, 64–65, 69, 98, 100, 104, 114–15, 148, 163, 168
materialism, 36
matins, 163
Mattachine Society, 250
Mauriac, François, 275n4
Mayerhoffer, Vincent Philip, 275n75
McBrien, Richard, 105–6
McDannell, Colleen, 194, 281n58
McLoughlin, Emmett, 135
McNaught, Brian, 250
McNeill, John J., 250, 268n38, 269n43, n44, 283n7
media, 11, 51
medicine, 30; Victorian, 35
Medusa, 22
memoirs, 115, 117
Ménard, Guy, 269n43, n44
mentoring, 175. *See also* spiritual direction
mercy, 124
Merton, Thomas, 215
Methodist hymns, 254
Metropolitan Community Churches (MCC). *See* Universal Fellowship of Metropolitan Community Churches
Michael, Robert T., et al., 270n29
Middle Ages, 60–61, 72; new, 72
Miller, D. A., 270n18, 279n6
Miller, Neil, 265n24
Milon d'Amiens, 274n51
ministry, 145, 150, 162; Christian, 9; lesbian and gay, 242; lesbigay Catholic, 31; pastoral, 229, 251
Mirabeau, Gabriel Honoré Riqueti de, 134
misogyny, 161
Mitchell, Mark, 277n55, 279n14
mockery, 130
modernity, 74
Moers, Ellen, 282n14, n15
Molina, Luis de, 67
monasteries: Catholic, 146, 258; Tibetan, 145
Monette, Paul, 263n1, 271n39, n52

monk-warriors, 120

monks, 121, 131, 133, 135–36, 143, 145, 163, 184, 190

monogamy, homosexual, 247

montage, literary, 15

Monter, William, 273n31, n33

Montez, Maria, 191

Moore, Gareth, 264n11

moral permissivism, 31

moral principles, 27

moral reasoning, 37, 58, 74, 80

moral rules, 34

moral theology, 3, 9, 15, 21, 52, 55–58, 63–64, 66, 68–69, 74–75, 80, 86, 163, 214–15, 259–60, 264n5

Moral Theology (Liguori), 71

Moral Theology of Twenty-Four Theologians of the Society of Jesus (Escobar y Mendoza), 67

moralists, Jesuit, 66

morality, public, 41, 133; sexual, 7, 11, 55–56, 100, 142; sexual, Catholic, 26, 246

morals, 24, 38, 55, 69, 216; Catholic, 53; Christian, 76

Morize, André, 274n69, n70

Mormando, Franco, 274n62

Morris, Charles R., 270n19, 271n50, n51, 276n32

mortification, 214

Muñoz, José Esteban, 279n10

Murat, J., 269n16

Murdoch, Iris, 277n54

Murphy, Sheila, 101

Musa, Mark, 273n43, n44, n46

Muslim, 128, 134

Myers, Rawley, 276n19

mythology, Catholic, 145

Nabuco, Joaquim, 192

National Conference of Catholic Bishops (NCCB), 93; Committee on Doctrine, 47; Committee on Marriage and Family, 43, 47

National Federation of Priests' Councils, 89

National Opinion Research Center, 270n31

natural law, 26–28, 30–31, 33–36, 75

nature, 30, 34, 37, 55, 76

Neo-Thomism, 214

Netherlands, 133

New Christians, 128

New Jerusalem, 254

New Left, 79

New Ways Ministry, 40, 48

New York, archdiocese of, 199, 280n48

Newman, John Henry, 215

Nicene Creed, 215

Nicole, Pierre, 268n19

Nidorf, Pat, 249

Nietzsche, Friedrich, 22, 215

Norberg, Kathryn, 282n9

Norton, Rictor, 265n18, 271n55, 282n19

Nourry, Charles, 134

novels: modern Catholic, 214; utopian, 259

novitiate, 157–58, 172, 175; Xaverian, 171

nudism, 162

Nugent, Robert, 48–49, 264n2, 265n26, n28, 269n9, 276n33, n35, 277n52, 282n3, 283n8

nuns, 91, 131, 135

Nygren, David, 276n39

O'Brien, Thomas, 47

O'Connell, J. B., 281n56, n57

O'Connor, Flannery, 56

O'Malley, John W., 281n59

obedience, 146, 213–17, 219–20, 223, 225–26, 235, 238

Oblates of Mary Immaculate, 172

obsequium, 216

occult, 184

Octavian, 63

Oddo, Thomas, 283n8

offertory, 243

official documents (texts), 11, 21–24, 45, 51–52, 57, 77, 233; as a form of sexual gratification, 73

Olyan, Saul M., 265n20

On Jesus at the Age of Twelve (Aelred), 173

120 Days of Sodom, The, 134

oppression, 80

oral sex, 71

ordination, 5n, 96, 147–48, 150, 155, 160–61, 222

organizations (associations, institutions):
all-male, 120, 211; Catholic, 25; Christian,
7; church, 5, 81, 227
orgy, 6
Orians, Thomas, 283n8, n9
orientation, homosexual, 3, 154–56; sexual,
41, 47–48, 57, 102, 158, 234, 250, 260,
270n24
Original Sin, 34, 47
Orsi, Robert A., 282n10
orthodoxy, 220–21, 223–24
Osservatore Romano, 25, 42
out/outing, 5, 13, 41, 44–45, 80, 98–99,
102, 110–11, 138, 156–58, 160–61, 166,
175, 230, 234, 243–44, 250
outreach programs, gay and lesbian, 240,
251

Pacheco, Francisco, 281n62
pagan, 35, 63
Paglia, Camille, 229
pain, 218–19
Palm Sunday, 93
papal command, 2
paraculture, 185–86
paranoia, 87, 115
parish, Catholic, 7, 240–41, 243, 250–52,
254
Pascal, Blaise, 67–68, 73, 215
pastors, 43–44; Protestant, married, 133
Pater, Walter, 197
Paul II, 118
Paul III, 118
Paul IV, 70
Paul VI, 24, 92–93, 144
Paul of Hungary, 274n60
Payer, Pierre J., 272n13
pederast/pederasty, 94, 97, 131, 150, 220,
223, 268n36
pedophilia, 97–98, 130–31, 135, 151, 155;
clerical, 106; priestly, 94, 97, 99, 112, 151,
175–76
penance, 45; books of, 121
penetration, 62, 70
penile response test, 155
penitentials, 121, 129

Pennington, M. Basil, 175, 277n43
Pentecost, 2, 5–6
Pentecostal sects, 135, 253–56
people of color, 253–54
Perez Escohotado, Javier, 281n62
Perry, Mary Elizabeth, 273n36, n40
Perry, Troy, 253–54, 256
Perseus, 22
perversions, sexual, 29, 72
Peter Damian, 85–86, 88, 111, 114–15, 119,
121, 132, 260
Peter Lombard, 267n10
Peter the Chanter, 260
Peyrefitte, Roger, 92–93, 110
philanthropy, priestly, 95
Philip I of France (Philip the Fair), 117,
118–19, 122
physical exercise, as therapy against libido,
163
Pierluigi (Pietro Aloisio, son of Paul III),
118
Pilant, Craig Wesley, 264n7
Pius V, 121
Pius XI, 149, 264n7
Pius XII, 199, 201, 276n17
Pizarro, Pedro, 127
Plante, David, 56
plateresco churches, 214
pleasures, 61, 217–19, 221–22, 224–25, 228,
233, 238; venereal, 61
polemic, Protestant, 133
political action (politics), 231–32; committees, American religious, 36
political movements: non-Catholic, 36;
women's, 9
pollution, 61, 71
pope, 2, 6, 24, 33, 77, 89, 93, 117, 120–21,
126, 130, 133–35, 155, 190, 192, 198, 202,
213, 216, 222–23, 226, 228, 243, 258
Popery, 188
pornography, 73, 134–35, 170, 196, 213, 218;
theological, 32
Potvin, Raymond H., 276n27, n29
power, 230, 247; bureaucratic, 73, 220, 245,
256; church (Catholic), 3–4, 9–10, 17, 73,
78, 81–82, 123, 213, 215, 217, 220–22,

power, *(continued)*
224–25, 233; clerical, 103–4, 217; police/state, 88, 224; sexual, 28; spiritual, 219
prayer, 58, 259
preaching/preachers, 12, 16; Baptist, 254
prelates, 92, 120–21, 130
Priapus, 248
priesthood, 5n, 6, 9, 81, 85–86, 93, 98–100, 102, 114, 139, 145, 147–50, 152, 156, 159, 199, 207, 212, 227, 238; American, 106; Catholic, 90, 101, 106, 134, 137, 270n20; diocesan, 126, 142
priests, 5n, 7, 13, 32, 39, 46, 82, 87–89, 91, 95, 102, 103, 105, 108, 110, 116, 121–24, 126–28, 131, 134–36, 139, 141, 145–47, 152, 157, 159, 160, 161, 166, 175–77, 179, 180–81, 182–83, 184, 186, 187, 191, 200, 206, 207, 208, 227, 244, 249, 251–52, 280n29; diocesan, 144, 199; gay, 9, 98, 101–3, 105, 107, 111, 181, 185, 218, 228, 245; married, 132; of Cybele, 6–7; pagan, 7; parish, 120, 122
Primiano, 283n12
procreation, 34, 50, 77, 260
Profession of Faith (1989), 282n3
promiscuity, 130
Pronk, Pim, 264n4
prostitution, 91, 216
Protestant movements (denominations), 54, 240, 242, 255
Provincial Letters, 67, 73
prudence, 5, 149
Psalms/psalm verses, 62, 161
psychoanalytic/psychological theories, 108, 151–52, 269n5
psychological testing, 152–53, 155
psychology, contemporary, 30–31
psychosexual maturity, 155–56
psychotherapy, 45–46, 105
puberty rites, 217
publicity, 50
Puff, Helmut, 272n18, 273n22, n23, n25, n28, 274n63
punishment, 86, 121, 124, 129; capital, 123
purity, 161, 165–66, 174; ritual, 35; sexual, 156, 164, 206

queer space, 159, 168
queer theory, 15
questionnaires. *See* surveys
Quigley, E. J., 280n35

race, 41, 79
Ragan, Bryant T., Jr., 274n71, 275n72
rage, 23
Ralph of Tours, 119
Rambuss, Richard, 281n60
rationality, 24, 215
Ratzinger, Joseph, 24, 31–32, 46–47, 76, 154–55, 216, 219, 248, 260
rectories, 199–200
reform, church, 240, 245–48, 250–51; clerical, 132–133
Reformation, the, 131, 133–34, 215, 226
Rehkemper, Robert, 96–97
Reindel, Kurt, 272n1
religious, 5n, 72, 102, 110, 116, 122, 126, 133, 139, 141, 156–57, 172, 218, 228, 245, 263n4; superiors, 89; vows, 150
religious houses, 144, 218, 222; medieval, 142; of formation, 145
religious orders, 108, 121, 123, 126–27, 133, 145–46, 156, 159, 167, 174, 177, 212, 253, 257; all-male, 8–9; liberalization of, 111; member of, 13
religious submission of will and intellect, 215–17. *See also* submission
repentance, 129, 260–61
representation, religious, 201–6
reproduction, 27–28, 36, 223–24 (*see also* procreation); animal, 34
Rey, Michel, 273n24
Reynolds, Stephen, 281n50
rhetoric, 22, 32, 35, 39, 43, 53, 64, 73–74; antihomosexual, 46; church, 116; homophobic, 7; of hysteria, 90; of liberation, 79
rhetorical analysis, 80, 120
rhetorical devices, 10, 11, 22, 23–24, 25, 38, 47, 50, 52–53, 72, 74–75, 214; certainty, attitude of, 55, 58, 66, 73, 75; flattening, 55–58, 66, 73, 75; repetition, 50, 55–56, 58–59, 72–73, 75

rhetorical programs, 52–57, 59–60, 62, 64–66, 75–78, 80, 86, 120
Ricci, Scipio de, 275n77
Richard II, 118
Richard Lion Heart, 118
Rico, Francisco, 274n54
right wing, Catholic, 111
ritual/ritualism, 6, 186–87, 193; public, 180, 189
Rocco, Antonio, 130
Roche, Pat, 283n6
Rocke, Michael, 269n2, 272n19, 273n21, n29, n47
Rodriquez, Alphonsus, 162, 278n85
Rodriguez, Richard, 184, 243, 278n74
roles: clerical, 185; domestic, 180, 183 (*see also* gender roles)
Roman Catholic church, in America, 135, 137, 151
Roman Catholic church (the Catholic church), 1, 3, 6–9, 11, 25, 32, 45, 50, 74, 104, 107, 109, 111, 116, 137, 159, 184, 186, 189, 205, 212, 215–16, 218, 220, 224–25, 227, 230, 232–33, 235, 238–41, 243, 245, 247–48, 250; modern, 5; institutions, 1n, 211
Roman legions, 216
Romans, ancient, 63
Romans I, 35, 121
Rome, 70, 130, 133, 192, 200, 222, 228, 245, 251, 253–54, 275n78
Roper, Lyndal, 274n63
Rosser, B. R. Simon, 271n43, 278n76, n77, n92
Roulin, Eugène Augustin, 192, 194, 197, 280n24
Rudnick, Paul, 269n3
Ruggiero, Guido, 272n17
Russell, Jeffrey Burton, 273n41
Ryan, John, 280n38

sacrament, 12, 67, 227, 244, 249, 252, 261
Sacred Congregation for Seminaries, 162
Sacred Congregation of Rites, 192
sacrifice, 220
Sade, Marquis de, 134

Sadlowski, Erwin L., 192
safe-sex education programs, 47, 225
St. Peter's, 93, 237
saints, 174, 226; gay (homosexual), 3–4, 109
Salmanticenses. *See* Discalcéd Carmelites of Salamanca
Sambia, 87–89
same-sex unions (relations), 42, 56, 78, 242–44
San Diego, 95, 249
San Francisco, 194
Sanchez, Tomás, 66, 69–70, 73, 260
Saragossa, 126
satire, 73, 131–32, 136–37
Scaliger, Joseph, 131
scandal, 93–95, 97–99, 110, 117, 123–24, 139, 148–49, 151–52, 202–4
Scanlon, Larry, 269n1
schism, 228, 239
Schleiner, Winfried, 272n9, 273n50, 274n65, n68
Schoenherr, Richard, 100, 227
scholarship, biblical, 32, 35
Scholastic philosophy, 96
Scholastic sermon, 62–64
scholasticates, 172
Schweickert, Jeanne, 276n38, 277n66, 278n86
science, 29–31, 70; human, 33; natural, 30, 32–33, 59
Scott-Moncrieff, C. K., 277n55
scriptural exegesis, 36
scriptural readings, 52
Scripture, 16, 33, 35, 55, 58–59, 80, 119, 213, 233
secrecy/secrets, 7, 12, 17, 124, 86–90, 93, 96–97, 100, 107, 110, 129, 137, 169, 176, 230–31, 260
secular culture, 185–86
Sedgwick, Eve, 90–91, 187, 271n53
Seery, Terence, 276n20
self-abasement, 13
self-examination, 13
seminarians, 102, 103–4, 142–43, 154, 161–62, 164–67, 169, 171–73, 175–76; American, 153

seminary/seminaries, 93, 99, 102–3, 105, 141–44, 146, 149–50, 154–58, 159–72, 175, 177, 182, 199, 201, 222; American, 142, 144, 150, 165, 172; candidates, screening of, 3; diocesan, 145, 155, 162; hazing, 164; law, 144; liberalization of, 111; major, 147–48; minor, 147–48, 150–52, 161, 163, 171; theological, 151; rectors, 147, 150

semination, 66, 70

sensuality, 149–50

Šeper, Franz, 24

sermon, 62, 64–65, 133, 206

Servites, 171

Seville, 126–27

sex, 55; extramarital, 26; male-male, 114, 121, 139, 274n64

sexual abuse, 95, 175–76; of seminarians, 175, 177

sexual acts, definitions of, 66

sexual harassment. *See* sexual abuse

sexuality, 23, 26, 30, 42, 105, 164, 166, 168, 222, 228, 231, 247, 250, 258; clerical, 4, 174; human, 34, 58, 77, 224, 229; human, norms for, 23; modern system of, 72; of Christ, in Renaissance art, 202, 204

Shakers, 183–84

shame, 217–18

Shand-Tucci, Douglass, 279n15

Shekleton, John, 277n53, 279n13

Sherr, Richard, 272n16

Siker, Jeffrey S., 264n16

silence, 7, 9, 13, 15–16, 51–52, 68, 85–86, 90–91, 94, 97, 100, 107, 110–11, 116, 125, 129, 162, 165, 171, 177, 181, 186, 200, 203, 241, 261

sin, 16, 37, 55, 61–64, 68, 70, 85, 112, 113–15, 117, 119–21, 124, 126, 128–29, 133, 135, 138–39, 148–49, 174, 176, 237, 244, 246, 258, 261; against nature, 60, 62, 65, 124, 149, 233, 267n10; lists, 35; mortal, 65; of lust, 130; priestly, 16; sexual, 26, 132; types of, 67

Sipe, A. W. Richard, 105, 175, 217, 275n2, 276n14, 278n75

Sixtus IV, 118

slander, 131

Slover, Pete, 270n24

Smith, Bruce, 272n20

Smith, Richard, 264n7, 266n34, n36

social membership, 13

Society of Jesus. *See* Jesuits

sociology, 30–31

Sodom, 16–17, 35, 38, 63, 76, 85, 125, 133, 135, 223, 261; destruction of, 121

Sodomite, 9–10, 16, 188, 223, 233, 260–61

sodomy, 9–10, 16–17, 38, 53, 59–60, 62–64, 66–73, 81–82, 85–86, 111, 113–20, 122–27, 129, 132–35, 196, 261; as a military vice, 118; burning as the ordinary penalty for, 69–70; clerical, 86, 115–24, 126, 128, 130–31, 137–39, 229; imperfect vs. perfect, 67–68, 70–71; lay, 123–24; papal, 117–18; priestly, 136, 139

solitary uncleanness, 61

Some Considerations Concerning the Response to Legislative Proposals on the Non-Discrimination of Homosexual Persons (1992), 25, 40–42, 48, 57

Sontag, Susan, 183

soul, 16–17

Sparry, C., 275n74

speech: bureaucratic, 5, 11, 52; canonical, 53; Catholic, 59–60; church, 39; official, 12, 49–50, 52; prudent, 68; public, 24; theological, 58, 72

Spellman, Francis, 198–200

spiritual direction, 175–77, 223

statistics, 99, 105–7

Steibel, Warren, 281n49

Steinberg, Leo, 202, 204

Stocker, Johannes, 123, 125

Stonewall, 100

Strasser, Robert, 271n44

Struzzo, John A., 277n42

Stuart, Elizabeth, 103, 271n40, 277n67, n69, 278n80

Suarez, Francisco, 67

subdeacons, 121

submission, 216–20, 223–24, 234, 282n3; intellectual, 214–16

Sullivan, Andrew, 42, 51, 264n5, n7, 265n23

Summa of Theology (Thomas Aquinas), 60, 62, 64–65

Summa theologica (Antoninus), 62

Suprema, of the Inquisition, 126
surveillance, 167–69, 174
surveys, 94, 99–104, 107–10, 112, 139, 153–54, 156, 164, 175; large-scale, of American priests, 100
Suspended Vocation, 223
Suziedelis, Antanas, 276n27
Swiss Guards, 93
Syme, Ronald, 282n5

Tacitus, 216
Taddeo, Julie Ann, 280n43
Tager, Djénane Kareh, 271n45
teachings: Catholic, 16–17, 33, 48, 80, 216, 218, 227; Christian, 55, 219, 255, 259; church, 56, 58; on homosexuality, 2–4, 15, 22, 24, 29, 31, 38–39, 54, 76–78, 233, 242, 244, 246, 282n3; moral, 2, 5–6, 8, 10–12, 25–27, 43, 53–54, 56, 58, 64–65, 69, 72, 75, 78, 149; spiritual, 65; Vatican's, 33
tedium, 53–56, 58, 72
temperance, 162
terminology, 10–11
theatricality, 181, 208
theologian, moral, 13; staff, 4–5
theological epistemology, 115
theology, 16, 33, 62, 143, 151, 153, 159, 214, 256; Catholic, 2–4, 10–11, 27, 34, 54, 58–60, 70–72, 78, 82, 85, 226, 258; Christian, 119; feminist, 258; gay, 3; lesbian, 3; negative, 259–60; official, 25, 81; queer, 258, 260
Thévenot, Xavier, 275n11, 276n31, 277n49, 278n71
third sex, 7. *See also* gender, third (mixed)
Thomas Aquinas, 26–27, 30–31, 34, 60–62, 64–71, 260
Thomists/Thomism, 27, 65
Thompson, B. Russell, 274n54
Thurston, Thomas, 268n38
Tillmann, Helene, 274n55
Toledo, Francisco de, 66, 134
Tomassini, Dino, 275n8, n10, n11, 276n12, n17, 277n58, n60, 278n91
torture, 128–29
Toulmin, Stephen, 267n5
Townsend, Larry, 282n7

tradition: Catholic, 65, 74, 226, 256; spiritual, 6
transgendered, 10
translation, of documents from Latin, 264n3
transubstantiation, eucharistic, 206–7
Trent, Council of, 11, 54, 60, 72, 118, 137, 251
Trexler, Richard C., 204
tribe of Midian, 63
Trifles, 132
Tyler, Parker, 195–96
Tynan-Connolly, Derrick A., 271n41, 278n97

Ukeritis, Miriam, 276n39
Ulrichs, Karl Heinrich, 74
United Church of Christ, 242
Universal Fellowship of Metropolitan Community Churches (MCC), 240–41, 249, 253–56
university centers, Catholic, Episcopal (University of Minnesota), 39
Unsworth, Tim, 100–1
Urning, 9
Utrecht, archdiocese of, 103

vagina, as a proper vessel, 64, 69
Valencia, 67, 126–27
values: family, 50; gospel, 42, 245; moral, 41
Van der Meer, Theo, 274n67
vanity, 130
Vasquez, Gabriel, 67
Vatican, 1–2, 4–6, 13, 24–25, 27, 29–30, 33, 36–37, 40, 42, 48–50, 76, 95–96, 155, 159, 192, 215, 218, 228, 250–51; documents, 10–11, 27, 29, 52–56, 72–73, 166, 214
Vatican Council (Vatican II), 74, 100, 107, 143, 195
Veblen, Thorstein, 139
Vernay, Jacques, 264n8
vestments, 167, 184, 187–88, 190, 193–94, 197, 199, 201, 207, 218, 221, 251, 253
vice, 60–63, 65, 68, 124, 135, 150, 255; against nature, 61, 64; sodomitic, 65
Vidal, Gore, 115, 281n51

Vietnam War, 79
violence, 52, 110, 123, 130, 151, 225, 233, 237
Virtually Normal, 42
virtues, 67
vocabulary, associated with homosexuality, 57
vocation, 145–46, 151, 156, 159, 161, 165–66, 205; directors, 152, 154, 175; late (older seminarians), 96, 151
Voltaire, 134
von Rheinfelden, Heinrich, 273n22, n23
voyeurism, 73

Wagner, Richard, 103–4
Waller, James C., 281n52, n63
Walsh, John K., 274n54
Walter Map, 132
warfare, 110; Christian political, 119, 127
Warren, Patricia Nell, 56
Wasserschleben, F. W. Hermann, 272n13
Waters, Florence, 282n10
Waugh, Evelyn, 280n20
Weil, Simone, 215

Weimar, 274n64
Weiss, Andreas, 264n9
White, Edmund, 12
White, Susan J., 281n54, n55
Whitehead, James and Evelyn, 277n42
Wilde, Oscar, 279n17
William Rufus, 118
Wilson, Nancy, 254, 283n14
witch, 112, 128; hunt, 24
Wojtyla, Karol, 264n6
Wolf, James, 101–2
women, 9, 65–66, 68–69, 71–72, 131, 216, 225, 246, 253–54, 283n12; denigration of, 14; sex between, 114; silencing of, 10; religious communities, 9
WomenChurch, 238
Wong, Mary Gilligan, 278n86
Woods, Richard, 277n41, n51, n56
World War II draft, 170
writers/writing, Catholic American, 55, 75; Christian moral, 113

zeal, 90n
Zubro, Mark Richard, 271n35, 283n11